PERSECUTION WITHOUT MARTYRDOM

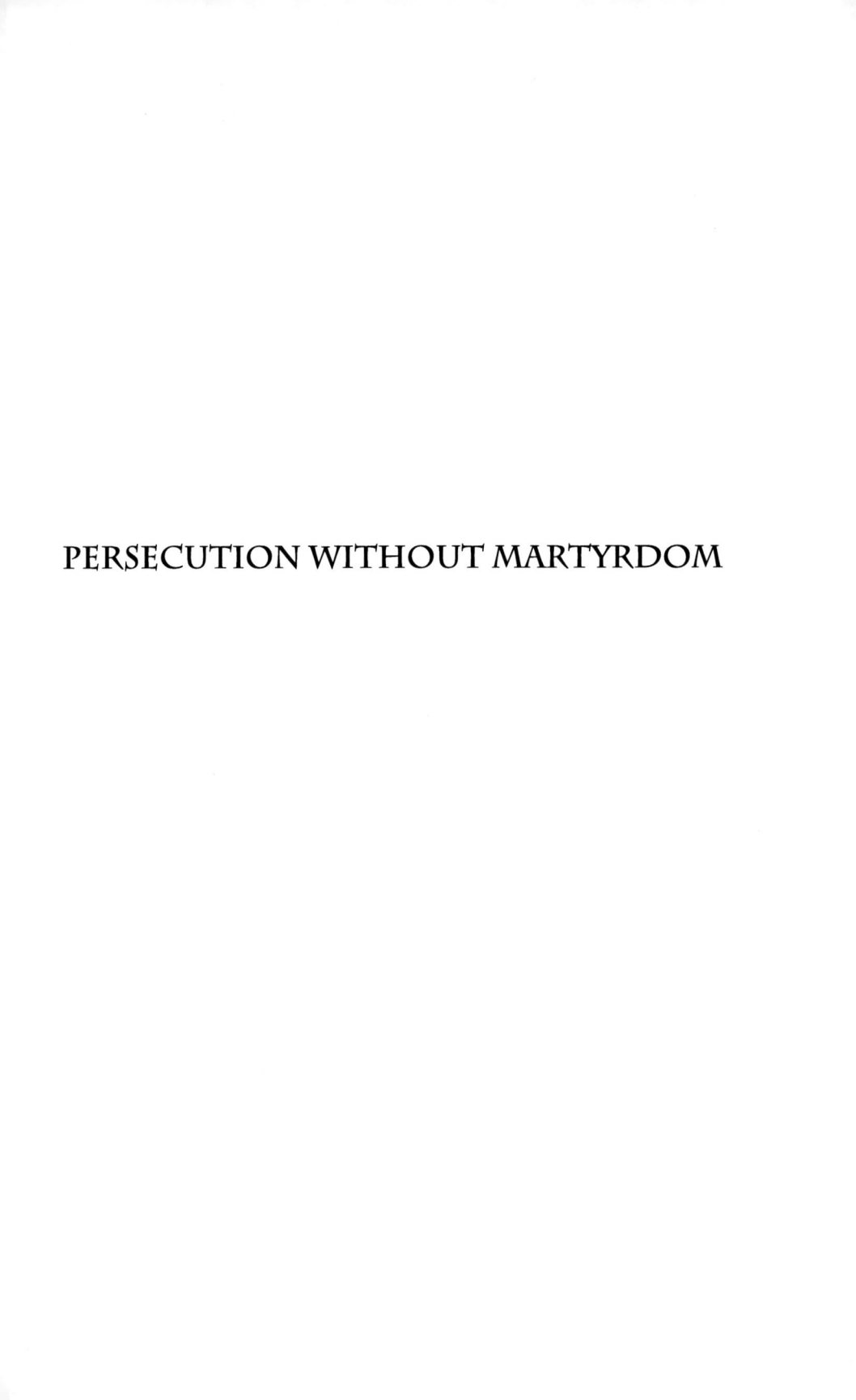

Shall I sit down satisfied because the good humour of a magistrate chooses to indulge me; whilst there are laws of which any miscreant has daily power to enforce the execution? My ease, my property, and my life are at the disposal of every villain, and I am to be pleased because he is not at this time disposed to deprive me of them. Tomorrow his humour may vary, and I shall then be obliged to hide my head in some dark corner or to fly from this land of boasted liberty. It is surely better *not to be* than to live in a state of such anxiety and dreadful uncertainty.

The Revd J. Berington, *The State and Behaviour of English Catholics from the Reformation to 1780* (London: Faulder, 1780).

PERSECUTION WITHOUT MARTYRDOM

THE CATHOLICS OF NORTH-EAST ENGLAND IN THE AGE OF THE VICARS APOSTOLIC 1688–1850

LEO GOOCH

GRACEWING

First published in England in 2013
by
Gracewing
2 Southern Avenue
Leominster
Herefordshire HR6 0QF
United Kingdom
www.gracewing.co.uk

No part of this publication may be reproduced, stored in a retrieval system, or transmitted in any form or by any means, electronic, mechanical, photocopying, recording or otherwise, without the written permission of the publisher.

The right of Leo Gooch to be identified
as the author of this work has been asserted in accordance
with the Copyright, Designs and Patents Act 1988.

© 2013 Leo Gooch

ISBN 978 085244 819 9

Typeset by Gracewing

Cover design by Bernardita Peña Hurtado,
incorporating a view of Capheaton Hall, Northumberland,
the main seat of the Swinburne Family since the thirteenth century.

To
Eustachio Liuzzi
for friendship and hospitality

CONTENTS

Contents..vii

Preface..ix

Abbreviations...xi

Introduction..xiii

Part I: The Laity..1

Chapter 1: The Catholic Community 1688–1851..................3

Chapter 2: The Survival of the Gentry.................................51

Chapter 3: The Catholic Question in North-East Politics....107

Part II: The Mission and Missioners................................175

Chapter 4: The Catholic Mission 1688–1850.....................177

Chapter 5: Mission-Stations in County Durham................263

Chapter 6: Mission-Stations in Northumberland...............327

Conclusion..403

Appendix..411

Bibliography...415

Index of Persons...437

Index of Places and Subjects................................449

PREFACE

In 2000 Leo Gooch and the late Michael Morris co-authored *Down Your Aisles: The Diocese of Hexham & Newcastle 1850–2000*, the companion to this work. The material relating to that more recent history of the diocese was abundant and Dr Gooch had a collaborator who had himself already contributed many articles to *Northern Cross*. Leo Gooch's principal interest, however, has always lain in the earlier period—his work on Jacobitism in the north-east, for instance, has become a key resource—and the depth of research and energetic enthusiasm reflected in this present volume signal that he is more at home there. However, the 1688–1850 period, when the Northern District of the English Catholic Church was under the charge of a Vicar Apostolic, has presented many challenges, mainly the paucity of material on which to bring to life the stories and voices of our Catholic forbears in this part of the country. The fact that he has left no stone unturned or archive untouched (national and local repositories have all been mined) will ensure that this well-written book will become a classic for years to come for its valuable comparison of provincial Catholicism with national trends. His analysis of the wealth of eighteenth-century statistical surveys and of the 1851 Religious Census is particularly revealing, and it is the first time that all the missions in the north-east have been dealt with so extensively.

A major difference between the north-east and Lancashire was the presence of the almighty bishops of Durham, but their relations with local Catholics were generally good, and indeed it is remarkable to see how easily Catholics fitted into local society and prospered throughout the period. There was neither a Catholic ghetto nor much of a Catholic sub-culture. The involvement of many Catholic gentry families in the development of industry is given a prominent place: one example is the enthusiasm of the Salvins of Croxdale for paper-making and railway mania. There is a detailed study of the campaign for Catholic Emancipation in the north-east which saw the emergence of new leaders from the professions rather than from the gentry. Dr Gooch highlights the surprising phenomenon of a rise in the Catholic population at the beginning of the eighteenth century followed by a decline at its end which differs from received opinion. This book shows Catholicism flourishing before Ushaw College existed, which is a comfort. But, how might 'Geordie Catholicism' survive without the college, we might ask today. This book will become, furthermore, a valuable aid in the compilation of an inventory of the Ushaw collections for the future. It will also act as a spur to further research on the earliest mission registers and the origins of native vocations to the religious life and priesthood.

I am pleased that the Diocese of Hexham and Newcastle at last possesses a standard history about its origins which compares favourably with the published histories of post-Reformation Catholicism in the north-west. The author is to be congratulated on making the early history of post-Reformation Catholicism in the north-east so accessible for the first time.

Abbot Geoffrey Scott, OSB, MA, PhD, FSA, FRHist.S
December 2012

ABBREVIATIONS

AA	*Archaeologia Aeliana*
BTHR	British Transport Historical Records
CRS	Catholic Record Society
DCLHSB	*Durham County Local History Society Bulletin*
DCRO	Durham County Record Office
DUL	Durham University Library
GEC	*The Complete Peerage by G. E. C.* [G. E. Cokayne]
GPL	Gateshead Public Library
HMC	Royal Commission on Historical Manuscripts: *Calendars*
JEH	*Journal of Ecclesiastical History*
LDA	Leeds Diocesan Archives
LRO	Lancashire Record Office
NC	*Northern Cross*
NCC	*Northern Catholic Calendar*
NCH	*Northern Catholic History*
NCoH	*Northumberland County History*
NRO	Northumberland Record Office
NYCRO	North Yorkshire County Record Office
ODNB	*Oxford Dictionary of National Biography*
OP	Order of Preachers
OSB	Order of St. Benedict
PD	*Parliamentary Debates*
PSAN	*Proceedings of the Society of Antiquaries of Newcastle upon Tyne*

RH	*Recusant History*
SCH	*Studies in Church History*
SJ	Society of Jesus
SS	*Publications of the Surtees Society*
TRHS	*Transactions of the Royal Historical Society*
UCM	Ushaw College Manuscripts
UM	*Ushaw Magazine*
VCH	*Victoria County History*
YAS	Yorkshire Archaeological Society: *Records Series*

INTRODUCTION

Until comparatively recently, historical studies of English Catholicism have lavished attention on the 'Age of Martyrs' of the sixteenth and seventeenth centuries or on the 'Second Spring' of the nineteenth century, while the eighteenth, a century of 'persecution without martyrdom' as Edwin Burton described the life and times of Richard Challoner, is largely passed over.[1] That neglect is wholly unwarranted. The creation of the four Vicariates Apostolic in 1688 marks the foundation of the modern Roman Catholic Church in England and Wales and a series of significant ecclesiastical developments affecting the disposition and operation of the mission followed over the next century and a half: its emergence from 'seigneurial' rule, its shift from its rural strongholds into the towns, and its metamorphosis into a centrally-managed organization. In the secular field, this was the age when major political crises relating to Catholicism arose, when Catholics threw off discrimination and oppression and by degrees emerged from recusancy to full citizenship; and when their sociological character changed almost completely. These were all important enough singly, but cumulatively they amounted to nothing less than a radical transformation of the structure and outlook of the English Catholics. The later achievements of the Church of Cardinals Manning, Wiseman and Newman could not possibly have been won without the perseverance and vigour of the eighteenth-century recusants.

Indeed, the convert cardinals of the nineteenth century betrayed a startling ignorance of the social history of the Catholic community however much they may have come to know about its political and ecclesiastical past. On his entry into 'the narrow community of the English Catholics', Manning said he felt as if he 'had got into

St. James's Palace in 1687. It was as stately as the House of Lords ...' He dismissed the interval between the Reformation and the Restoration of the Hierarchy in 1850 as a dark age in which the English Catholics languished in a condition, as he put it, 'not of suspended animation only but of organic dissolution'. He viewed the return of the bishops 'as the re-founding of the Church in England after a period of stagnation or even virtual death'. In his sermon 'The Second Spring', given at the first Synod of Westminster in 1852, Newman spoke of the 'resurrection' of the English Catholic church brought about by the Oxford Movement and the Irish migration. He reduced the Fathers to tears with a description of what he supposed English Catholic life had been like in 1800. The community, he said, had dwindled to 'a few adherents of the Old Religion' who, 'though noble of bearing and said to be of good family', went 'silently and sorrowfully about'. They lived in old-fashioned mansions of gloomy appearance behind high walls, iron gates and yew hedges. Others were to be

> found in corners, and alleys, and cellars, and the housetops, or in the recesses of the country; cut off from the populous world around them, and dimly seen, as if through a mist or in twilight, as ghosts flitting to and fro.

Newman's hyperbole was perhaps excusable given that the occasion on which he spoke demanded recognition of the distance the English Catholics had travelled from the darkest days of persecution to those of a newly-restored hierarchy, but he described a literary invention, not an historical reality. His source was more likely to have been Charles Dickens's *Barnaby Rudge* (1841), which deals with the period of the Gordon riots, rather than his own experience or, indeed, that of his audience.[2]

Neither was Thomas B. Macaulay fully in tune with recent Catholic history. In 1834 he called on Nicholas Wiseman at the Venerable English College in Rome and was most surprised to find the rector's room fitted out in the English style and very like the rooms of a senior fellow of Trinity College, Oxford. On the same occasion Macaulay was introduced to Lords Clifford and Shrewsbury and thought them not at all what he imagined Catholics of old family to be: proud and stately and with an air of being men of rank but not of fashion. Evidently, then, Macaulay, Manning and Newman had not come across many English Catholics before and knew little of their eighteenth-century experience. Moreover, as late as 1828, the year before emancipation was enacted, Bishop Thomas Smith was told 'we Catholics still continue to wear the honourable badge of persecution.'[3]

Despite contradictory evidence that has since become available, these portrayals have proved difficult to modify. The primary aim of this work is to use that evidence to revise their interpretations and to restore the period to its proper place in English Catholic history. The evidence for a reappraisal of the sociological and demographic history of the English Catholics in the eighteenth century is now easily accessible. There were around a dozen head-counts of the Catholics in the north-east between the revolution and the end of the Napoleonic Wars – the 'long eighteenth century'. Since no other minority religious group was enumerated as often in the period, the English Catholic body is the one about which we can know most. Much of the data, admittedly, was collected using different criteria and was not gathered by the same authority. Some surveys were made by Anglican officials and others by Catholics; some counted all papists, others communicants only, and yet others were concerned only with heads of households. Eight surveys, however, were conducted by Anglican parochial officials using the same criteria, and hence form a coherent series which can be used to define the social character of the northern Catholics across the whole period. These were the Parliamentary Returns of Papists made in 1705, 1767 and 1780;[4] and the Episcopal Visitation Returns of Durham made in 173[2], 1774, 1792, 1810 and 1814.[5]

Clearly, the civil and Anglican ecclesiastical authorities were required to take pains in keeping records of the English Catholics, for security purposes, if nothing else. It has, however, been doubted whether their surveys were thorough.[6] But it was the plain duty of Anglican clergymen and church-wardens to identify Dissenters and Catholics, and they would be no less efficient in counting them when asked to do so than they would when collecting church revenues. Almost half the parishes in the region contained around one hundred families; with such small populations to monitor, the authorities would indeed have had to be careless not to have known who was who. In 1705 the vicar of Horton reported there were no papists in his parish to his 'great comfort and satisfaction'; the vicar of Ingram clearly had little difficulty in coping, for he wished 'the Dissenters were as soon numbered'.[7] In 1814, the rector of Falstone (with 147 families) observed 'The Idea or Meaning of Popery is, I believe, not in the least comprehended in this Chapelry'. The rector of Kirkhaugh could not recall one Catholic inhabitant in thirty years. The vicar of Ilderton was certain that there had been no Catholic residents in his parish between 1764 and 1810. If anyone had any doubts about the matter, he could have followed the example of a vicar of Ryton who wrote to the Catholic priest at Stella asking for the information, 'tonight if possible'. Then, the number reported from Ryton was imprecise because it was so large: 'I do not know the number of papists but it is considerable, not less, as I suppose, than 400'.[8] A vicar of Lanchester was the only clergyman who declined to count the papists at his bishop's behest because, as he bravely declared, 'to number them would be thought invidious'. The majority of parishes missing from the returns had no history of Roman Catholicism, as was confirmed by a diocesan official in 1767 when he endorsed the bundle of returns sent up to

Introduction xvii

London: 'There are no papists or reputed Papists in such of the parishes within the Diocese of Durham as are not mentioned herein'. Finally, while a number of returns made in 1705 omitted children, women and servants, the overwhelming majority of returns made thereafter included all Catholics whatever their age, gender or social standing.

In short, there is no reason to doubt the reliability of this material nor, except on rare occasions, is there any justification for amending the stated figures. Yet the 1767 figures have been 'corrected' to take account of the poor 'conditions of eighteenth century statistical enquiry', and to add as much as 15 per cent to the stated population. In the case of north-east England this is wholly unjustified. Taken as a whole, the returns provide all the information necessary for a methodical and detailed reconstruction of the demographic, economic and social character of the Catholics of the region in the period. (It may be noted, incidentally, that despite the stress placed on its collection nothing was ever done with the information by the authorities except to keep it on file.)

Because of their deficiencies, a number of surveys made by Catholics themselves will not be relied upon. Indeed, judging by the lamentable results of their efforts, the Catholic clergy knew less about their own people than the Anglican clergy did, and their contributions will be cited, if at all, only very cautiously.[9] On the other hand, despite, indeed because of, its inadequacies, the national Census of Religious Worship of 1851 will be examined (using Catholic sources) since it has been used hitherto in the socio-ecclesiastical history of England without proper interpretation. A fully considered treatment will help to ascertain how far the Catholic population changed in the twenty years between Emancipation and the Restoration of the Hierarchy during which there was an increasing Irish presence in the region.

Another reason for writing this study is that there has been a tendency to write the history of English Catholicism in national terms (with an occasional gesture towards the pre-eminence of Lancashire) without distinguishing major provincial variations. Edward Norman, for one, omitted regional factors from his work on the nineteenth-century Church because, he said, 'its quite different emphases and issues' were best left for separate treatment. Jonathan Clarke remarked that although local history was a fully-fledged academic genre, its practitioners had a distinct school of thought.[10] Both Norman and Clarke refer to the fact that local historical work often lacks a wider perspective. On the other hand, studies taking a panoramic national view often mask important differences between one part of the country and another. The Catholic history of England cannot be written from an unqualified series of aggregates (whether of chapels, clergy or layfolk) which convey an impression of uniform change across the nation. At the same time it is not necessary to restrict the field of vision to such an extent that important and coherent trends are obscured; the regional approach best suits that aim. This study therefore contributes to regional studies while avoiding the merely parochial but without making misleading generalisations. To mark the sesquicentenary of the restoration of the English hierarchy, Michael Morris (R.I.P.) and I published a history of the diocese of Hexham and Newcastle from 1850 to 2000.[11] It seemed to me then that the antecedents of the diocese should not be overlooked because, as has been outlined above, they are of considerable importance and interest, and have not been treated systematically. This work, then, examines the ecclesiastical, political and social life of the Roman Catholics of north-east England in the preceding period, the age of the Vicars Apostolic, 1688–1850.

***

It is perhaps appropriate first to add a note on the hierarchical structure of the English Church following the Reformation.[12] When its ancient hierarchy was extinguished at the death in 1585 of Bishop Thomas Goldwell of St Asaph's, England and Wales was left without episcopal government and under canon law became a missionary state. In such cases the Holy See appoints vicars apostolic as the local ecclesiastical superiors until the Church is free from persecution and is permitted to restore the ordinary hierarchy. Whereas a *bishop in ordinary* has full personal and independent episcopal powers in a territorial see, a *vicar apostolic*, though enjoying episcopal rank with a titular see *in partibus infidelium*, has only those powers delegated to him by the Holy See, to whom he is directly responsible. In practice this means that a bishop can resolve most problems locally but a vicar apostolic has to refer almost all of them to Rome.

Cardinal William Allen exercised informal jurisdiction over the secular clergy after Bishop Goldwell's death but between 1598 and 1621 governance was discharged by archpriests: George Blackwell, George Birkhead and William Harrison successively. In 1623 Pope Gregory XV responded to the repeated requests of the English Catholics for a bishop by conferring episcopal jurisdiction over England, Scotland and Wales on William Bishop. Twenty archdeacons (Cuthbert Trollop for the north) and a Chapter of twenty-four canons was established to advise and assist him. Bishop died within nine months of his arrival in England and he was succeeded by Richard Smith but then Smith resigned in 1631. He was not replaced and jurisdiction was exercised by the Chapter for the next fifty or more years; communications with the Holy See were conducted through a Clergy Agent in Rome.

The Chapter frequently petitioned for a bishop but it was not until the accession of the Catholic king James II that the Holy See agreed; even then, it was decided to maintain normal practice for the time being and appoint a vicar apostolic instead. Accordingly, in September 1685, John Leyburn, of a Westmorland family and a former President of the English College, Douai, was created Vicar Apostolic of England and Wales and consecrated Bishop of Adrumetum *in partibus infidelium*. He divided the country into four Districts, Northern, Midland, Western and London, placing each under a vicar general. (The powers of the Chapter lapsed at this point and henceforth a canonry in what came to be known as the 'Old Chapter' was a wholly honorary distinction.) It quickly became apparent that the task of episcopal government could not be conducted efficiently by one man. For one thing, Leyburn's confirmation tour in 1687 was a marathon (he was catching up on a fifty-year back-log) and could not be a regular event. In 1688, therefore, at the request of Leyburn and the king, the Holy See appointed a vicar apostolic to each District. The Northern District was entrusted to James Smith who was consecrated Bishop of Callipolis *in partibus infidelium* in May 1688. The four Districts remained unchanged until 1840 when the number was doubled. Ten years later the English Church returned to government by bishops in ordinary.

The Northern District in 1688 comprised all England between the Humber and the Tweed but we are here concerned with Northumberland and Durham. Though these counties formed only part of the District, they can be treated as a cohesive region, encompassed as they are on the east and west by substantial physical boundaries. The nearest Catholic mission to the west lay across the Pennines at Corby and Warwick Bridge. To the north, Scotland, except Berwick, was never included in any English Catholic jurisdiction. Only in the south is the border less palpable, for the Catholics of North Yorkshire always maintained close social and ecclesial links with their co-religionists on the north bank of the river Tees. It may be noted that the two counties do not

Introduction

correspond with the Anglican diocese of Durham which included Alston in Cumberland and Craike in Yorkshire but excluded Hexham and its shire which belonged to the archdiocese of York.

The book is a synthesis of my own published and unpublished work. My postgraduate theses have been plundered, and material from a number of conference papers and articles of recent years has been extracted and revised as necessary. I am most grateful to the editors of the journals for permission to use those pieces, especially Professor V. Alan McClelland of *Recusant History*, and the late Robin Gard (and subsequently myself) of *Northern Catholic History*. Three topics will be touched on only briefly. Firstly, Jacobitism: I have nothing to add to my own *The Desperate Faction? The Jacobites of North-east England 1688–1745* (1995) except for a section on the mission at Dilston Castle which has not hitherto been explored in detail. Secondly, the history of seminary education which has been dealt with by David Milburn in *A History of Ushaw College* (Ushaw, 1964), *Ushaw Magazine* (1891–1994) and *Douai's Day: The English College at Douai 1568–1793* (Ushaw, 2008). Thirdly, the Irish migration, which, in any case, came towards the end of this study's time-scale and has been, and continues to be, chronicled extensively elsewhere, especially by Roger Swift and Sheridan Gilley.

Notes

[1] B. Hemphill, *The Early Vicars Apostolic of England 1685–1750* (London: Burns & Oates, 1954), p. 154, quoting a Catholic Truth Society Tract by Burton.

[2] D. Gwynn, *Father Dominic Barberi* (London: Burns Oates, 1947), p. 47; D. Gwynn, *The Second Spring 1818–52* (London: Burns Oates, 1942), pp. 11ff; E. S. Purcell, *Life of Cardinal Manning* (New York & London, MacMillan, 1896, 2 vols), II, p. 631.

[3] J. M. Hagerty, 'Notes on the Northern District under Bishop Thomas Smith

1821–1831' in *Northern Catholic History* [NCH] 27 (1988), p 27.

4 House of Lords Record Office, Main Papers, Returns of Papists 1705/1706 Dioceses of Durham and York; E. S. Worrall (ed.), *Returns of Papists, 1767, Dioceses of England and Wales except Chester* (Catholic Record Society [CRS], Occasional Publication No. 2, 1989); House of Lords Record Office, Main Papers, Returns of Papists, 1780.

5 Durham University Library [DUL]: Archives and Special Collections, Auckland Castle Episcopal Records: Clergy Visitation Returns, 1774 (to Bishop Egerton); 1792, 1810, 1814 (to Bishop Barrington). Odd visitation returns also survive for 1758 and 1801 but have not been used in this survey because of the lack of a series long enough for a sensible interpretation.

6 The chief sceptic is J. Bossy, *The English Catholic Community 1570–1850* (London: Darton, Longman & Todd, 1975), pp. 184ff.

7 Henceforth extracts from the returns are identified in the text by parish and year without further footnotes.

8 Ushaw College Manuscripts [UCM]: 11/147, Mirehouse to Eyre, 20 April 1792.

9 Catholic surveys not examined here, because of their deficiencies include: 'Bishop D. Williams' Visitation and Confirmation, 1728' in CRS 25 (1925), p. 110; UCM: W. V. Smith Papers: 'List of Non-Jurors of County Durham, 1744'; 'Jubilee Returns by Jesuit Missioners, 1750' in H. Foley, *Records of the English Province of the Society of Jesus* (London: Burns and Oates, 1877–1883, 7 vols), 5, Series 12, pp. 666–667; J. H. Whyte, 'The Vicars Apostolics' Returns of 1773' in *Recusant History* 9/4, (1968), pp. 205–214; L. Gooch, 'The Last Recusants of the North-East: the Reports of 1780 and 1787' in NCH 27 (1988), pp. 7–11.

10 E. Norman, *The English Catholic Church in the Nineteenth Century* (Oxford: The Clarendon Press, 1984), Preface; J. C. D. Clarke, *Revolution and Rebellion: State and Society in England in the Seventeenth and Eighteenth Centuries* (Cambridge University Press, 1986), ch. 4.

11 M. Morris & L. Gooch, *Down Your Aisles: The Diocese of Hexham & Newcastle 1850–2000* (Hartlepool: *Northern Cross*, 2000).

12 This note is based on Hemphill, *Early Vicars Apostolic*, passim.

Part I

1 THE CATHOLIC COMMUNITY 1688–1851

THE REVOLUTION OF November 1688 was accomplished no less easily in north-east England than elsewhere in the country. King James had begun to place his men in positions of power from early in his reign. The town charters of Durham, Newcastle and Morpeth were revised and the bench and the lieutenancy were purged. By 1688 the king had controlling majorities on all the institutions of local government. Sir William Creagh, an Irishman and 'zealous Catholic', was imposed as Mayor of Newcastle; a number of Catholics were nominated as aldermen, including Edward Widdrington and Thomas and John Errington. The Widdringtons and other Catholics kept Morpeth loyal; and fifteen Catholics were appointed magistrates in Durham. Despite these extraordinary measures, however, the king's policy did not have the desired effect but gave rise to general dissatisfaction and provoked widespread insubordination instead.[1]

James's supporters in the region included the Earl of Derwentwater who raised six companies of fifty men in each, officered mainly by Catholics, including his younger brothers. William Tempest commanded the garrison in Tynemouth Castle (guarding the entrance to the Tyne and known as 'the key' to Newcastle), and independent companies were raised by other Catholic gentlemen, among whom were Sir Thomas Haggerston, Lieutenant Governor of Berwick ('whose zeal to the Catholic cause was so well known') and Ralph Widdrington his predecessor. In the event, these pitifully small military forces proved unable to put up an effective resistance and nor were James's political placemen able to affect the course of events and were prevented from mobilising the people against

William. The leading Williamite in the region was Richard, Lord Lumley, of Lumley Castle near Chester le Street. He was born a Catholic and was educated abroad. He helped to put down Monmouth's rebellion in 1685 but a growing dissatisfaction with King James's ultra-Catholicising policy led him to apostatise and to resign his offices. Lumley joined the group of plotters who invited William to invade and deliver the country, and he undertook to secure the north-east, which he did without the inconvenience of a military engagement or civil disturbance. For his services Lumley was created Earl of Scarbrough and appointed Lord Lieutenant of Northumberland and Durham. All Catholics were ejected from office.[2]

In the aftermath of the Revolution a number of town-houses in Newcastle belonging to Catholics were plundered and the Catholic chapels in Newcastle and Durham were sacked. The statue of King James II which had been erected by Mayor Creagh was demolished. In Sunderland the industrialist Ambrose Crowley had petitioned the king in 1688 that because 'many of his workmen were foreigners and Catholics, and they did not altogether meet with a friendly reception', they needed protection from molestation. Nathaniel Crewe, Bishop of Durham, was ordered to ensure the safety of the workers but the antagonism continued and in 1691 Crowley was compelled to move his ironworks to Ryton where he leased land from Catholic sympathisers and had no further trouble.[3] In general, however, most people were satisfied with the ousting of the Catholic king and they expected the Catholics to fade once more into the background. That was a fond hope, however, for the chapels were soon discreetly reopened. Moreover, Jacobitism, the counter-revolutionary movement, attracted significant support in the north-east.

Although not all Jacobites were Catholics or vice versa, the authorities kept a close watch for signs of subversion among the deposed king's co-religionists. Because of his great wealth and close relationship with the court in exile, the first Earl of Derwentwater, seated at Dilston, was feared as the most dangerous Jacobite in the north. He and his five adult sons controlled widespread and important landholdings including agricultural properties in the border counties, collieries in Northumberland and Durham, and extensive lead-mining interests on Alston Moor. Edward, the second earl, maintained the family's Jacobite loyalties and the third earl would lose his head in 1716 for his attachment to the cause. The Widdringtons with their long royalist and Catholic history were also influential Jacobites. The third baron died in 1695 leaving three sons, William, Peregrine and Charles, and 'entailed on them a high and chivalrous but unfortunate attachment to the House of Stuart'. Many other Catholic gentlemen maintained their Jacobite loyalties including the Charltons, Erringtons, Salvins, Smythes, Brandlings and Kennets.[4] In 1703 Simon Frazer, Lord Lovat, found Durham 'full of good Catholics of the gentry of the country, who were very faithful to the King his master.'[5] Observing the Jacobite and Catholic sympathies of the magistrates in Newcastle in 1708, James Clavering prompted Lady Cowper, wife of the Lord Chancellor, to enquire of her husband whether it might be feasible to add some gentlemen to the Commission of Peace who would not fine 'the Roman Catholics half crowns a man [but] afterwards returned them'. Scarbrough wished 'the county afforded more choice' to fill the Northumbrian bench.[6] There was, then, compelling evidence of the antipathy of the northern Catholics to the new dynasty. That might not have mattered too much except that they were seen to form an increasingly significant socio-religious body.

The documentary evidence of the size and composition of the northern Catholic population at this time is contained in the returns from the first systematic national post-reformation episcopal visitation which was undertaken by the new vicar apostolic,

John Leyburn. His tour of the north-east began on 7 August 1687 at Cliffe Hall at the northernmost point of the North Riding where he confirmed six hundred and forty people, many of whom would have been from the villages on the Durham side of the river Tees. Two days later he made his first stop in the Bishopric proper where, in the city of Durham

> he was met by the magistrates and received an invitation from the bp of Durham [Crewe] to dine with him at his castle which he did, and he confirmed above 1000 [1,083] roman catholics in his several circuits.[7]

It is a pity that more details of the 'several circuits' in the county were not given. Leyburn then went up into Northumberland: Newcastle (358 confirmands), Netherwitton (243), Cartington (146), Callaly (293), Swinburne (123) and Dilston (481). By the end of the tour on 20 August, Leyburn had confirmed a total of 2,727 individuals in the two counties.[8]

Alarming reports of the significance of the northern Catholic population began to emerge in later years. On a visit to the city of Durham in 1697, Celia Fiennes noted that there were 'many Papists in the town, popishly affected and daily increase'. At the turn of the century the Archdeacon of Durham remarked that the Catholics were 'the most formidable of all the dissenters both for Quality and Great Estates'. The apparent danger to the state from Catholics and Jacobites thoroughly unnerved the government and in March 1705 the House of Lords ordered the Anglican diocesan clergy to conduct a census of the English Catholics.[9]

The census of 1705 is the principal civil source of information on the English Catholics in the late Stuart period. Unfortunately, however, only about half of the parishes in Northumberland in which Catholic groups are known to have existed are represented among the surviving returns. The absence of returns from, for example, Alwinton, Ancroft, Bellingham, Corbridge, Chollerton,

Ellingham and Rothbury partly accounts for the very low reported total of 450 Catholics. And then, the returns from Hexhamshire went to York, not Durham, and those parishes accounted for about 170 Catholics who must be counted as Northumbrians. A more likely number for the whole geographical county would be 1,100. Similarly, not all returns from parishes in County Durham having a Catholic population have survived. The returns listed 960 Catholics but it is likely that there were about 1,300 in the county when omissions are taken into account. The overall total for both counties was down on the total number of *confirmandi* in 1687 but, given the contemporary perception that the number of Catholics was increasing, the estimate of 2,400 may be a conservative one and it is reasonable to suppose that they numbered no less than they had in 1687 and perhaps as many as three thousand. Even taking the larger figure, however, they represented no more than 1 per cent of the whole population of the region.

The power and influence of the Catholics was of greater interest than mere numbers or religious practice for the 1705 survey was entirely concerned with their 'qualities, estates and abodes' rather than with any arrangements for their spiritual care: there is no reference in any Northumberland return to priests or chapels. There was, however, some anxiety that Papists might have had the presentation of Anglican livings in their gift, and information on that point was specifically required. The concern proved to be unjustified because only three parishes in the whole of the diocese of Durham reported Catholic patrons: the vicar of Hurworth said that John Jenison 'pretends to an alternate right of presenting to this parsonage'; and the vicars of Bywell St. Andrew and Slaley (adjacent parishes in Tynedale) reported the same Catholic patron but neither knew his name, only that he was one 'of the family of the Thorntons' (actually it was John Thornton). The Earl of Derwentwater owned the tithes of Hartburn, worth £100 a year.[10]

The wealthiest Northumbrian Catholic was the 16-year-old James Radcliffe, third Earl of Derwentwater, with some £6,200 a year. He was abroad and so was not listed but five others in the family were and they held property in Northumberland worth £3,000 a year. Lord Widdrington of Widdrington Castle had £4,000 a year; he was married to Jane Tempest (a former Maid of Honour to Queen Catharine, consort of Charles II); her father Sir Francis Tempest was a wealthy landowner in Durham who had married a daughter of Sir Thomas Haggerston. Edward Horsley Widdrington of Longhorsley Tower, aged 12, had about £2,000 a year held in trust by his mother. The 17-year-old Sir Carnaby Haggerston was not listed because he was abroad on the Grand Tour but his estate brought £1,350 a year. His uncle Edward Haggerston of Ellingham Hall enjoyed £900 a year. William Selby of Biddlestone Hall and George Collingwood of Eslington Hall each had about £1,000; John Clavering of Callaly Castle, Edward Riddell of Swinburne Castle and William Widdrington of Cheeseburn Grange each had about £800 a year. Sir John Swinburne of Capheaton Hall and John Thornton of Netherwitton Hall received £500 each as did three members of the Errington family: William of Beaufront Castle, Nicholas of Ponteland and Edward of Walwick Grange. About a dozen individuals had yearly incomes of between £10 and £100. The rest had no estates to speak of and most of them earned a living on the land in one way or another. Large numbers of farmers, husbandmen and herdsmen are listed; similarly, cottagers, millers and agricultural day-labourers were to be found in most rural parishes. The professions were represented by one or two attorneys, physicians and a handful of stewards, agents or factors of gentry estates. The Tyneside industrial parishes listed wrights of various kinds and coal-miners. Finally, servants and labourers appear in all parishes; one or two individuals received parish alms and there was one Catholic in Newcastle Gaol.

The Catholics of Durham were sociologically similar to those in Northumberland though the gentry were less wealthy. Sir Edward Smythe of Esh Hall and Thomas Maire of Hardwick Hall had around £1,000 a year. John Forcer of Durham had £600 and Anthony Meaburne of Pontop Hall had £500 a year. John Jenison of Walworth Castle, Ralph Salvin of Tudhoe, James Shaftoe of Tanfield and Marmaduke Witham of Preston-upon-Tees each got around £200 a year. Mrs. Blakiston of Tanfield and John Jenison of Hurworth each had £100 and there were twenty others with yearly incomes of between £10 and £100 each. The rest were poor. The Catholic community included a goldsmith, a tobacconist, a music teacher, a schoolmaster and the wife of a Yorkshire rector. Master mariners and merchants worked out of Sunderland on the Wear, and pitmen, sinkers and staithmen worked in the collieries on the south bank of the Tyne. Large numbers of yeomen, husbandmen and herdsmen are listed; millers, cottagers and agricultural day-labourers were also to be found in most rural parishes. The urban parishes listed wrights of various kinds in addition to numbers of butchers, shoemakers, carpenters and innkeepers. Finally, servants and labourers appear in all parish returns.

In the 1680s the Thorntons of Netherwitton would 'let no land to any unless they revolt to Popery' but the returns of 1705 do not reveal any marked tendency for Catholic landowners to rent only to their co-religionists. Clearly many tenants would be Catholics in the heavily Catholic enclaves such as Callaly, Croxdale, Eslington and Netherwitton. Thus most of the Clavering farms were tenanted by Catholics: at Biddlestone in 1736 '4 parts and half of six parts of the land belonged to Papists'. Salvin farms in the immediate vicinity of Tudhoe Hall were all let to Catholics but those further afield were not.

It is surprising that various incongruities in the returns appear not to have been noticed. Eyebrows might have been raised had it been noticed that the wives of the Governor and the Clerk of Tynemouth Castle were papists and disquiet might have been aroused if complete sets of parochial returns from York and Durham had been collated to reveal the concentration of upwards of three hundred and fifty Catholics in Tynedale (the Derwentwater fiefdom).

The loss of several returns obviously detracts from the overall value of the 1705 survey, but it is clear from the surviving records that the Catholics of the north-east were to be found at all social levels and in all situations; they were well-entrenched, prosperous and confident. They were widely dispersed and did not predominate in any parish, although it was reported from Whittingham that 'most' of the inhabitants of the village of Callaly were papists. Crucially, the Catholics were peaceable: the vicar of Chatton reported the few papists in his parish as behaving 'themselves very civilly, with a mighty reservedness'.

***

When ordering the census in 1705, the House of Lords had been more interested in the secular condition of the Catholics rather than in their ecclesiastical affairs. But James Mickleton, a Durham diocesan official, was determined to draw the attention of the authorities to the inroads made by the Catholic mission which he observed all around him. He compiled the following paper (which may have been intended to be sent to London with the census returns) in terms obviously calculated to raise alarm – in the capital if not in the bishop's palace.[11]

> *Popish Chapells within 7 miles of ye Bpp. of Durham Palace.*
> 1. At Sr Nic. Tempests seat at Stanley
> 2. Richd Smith Esqr at Esh
> 3. Mr Jo Johnson at Brandon
> 4. Mr Mic Johnson at Twizell

5. Mr Ra. Mare in Gillygate Durham. Mr Rivers ye priest there perverted Tho Nicholson, Mr Markingdale & others lately.
6. Mr Rowells in Durham & a School taught there.
7. Mr Pudsey in Durham
8. Jo Forcer Esqr House in Durham
9. Hen. Grey Esqr at Sunderland Bridge
10. Gerrard Salvin Esqr at Croxdale where 20 familys almost all ye inhabitants of that parish are lately perverted
11. Mr Jo Hildridge at B. Midlam–& a public School or Seminary there, in ye Bps manor House. 26 boys taught openly. Several Children lately baptized there publickly
12. At Mr Nich. Kennetts at Coxhoe, where many of ye neighbourhood are perverted, particularly one Jacksons Daughter very lately whom he has taken into his Family, & Mr Thompson ye parish Minister dayly converseth at that house, & with ye popish Clergy. Mr Kennet lately carryed his Niece to a Monastery in France, & was at ye Court of St Germans & returned into England without a License from ye Secretary of State.
13. At Jo Winters or Mr Forcers at Kellow where many are perverted dayly
14. At Mr Ra. Salvins at Tuddo
15. At Mr Suttons at Cowndon
16. At Tho Conyers Esqr house at Layton
17. At Mr Lambs at Hetton on ye Hill & many more, in ye late Scotch plot Capt Murray & others named in ye proclamation concealed by ye papists at & near Durham & great resort of strangers to them.
Their priests appear publickly.
The popish gentlemen have weekly meetings with many of ye Justices of peace at Hallywell & Sedgefield.
Divers popish Children lately sent from this County to ye Seminarys beyond seas as Mr Forcers Daughter Mr Lambs

Daughter & divers others carryed over by Mr Ashman ye priest. There is not the least notice taken at ye Bps late visitation of these matters altho' they are notorious & publick.

These people are more countenanced & favoured publickly than ye protestant Dissenters. And Mr Archdeacon of Durham was publickly slighted and affronted for taking notice of them & endeavouring to Suppress ye Schools & Chappels & Discouraging their perverting of protestants.

There is now a Building at Durham a noble Structure said to be for Madam Ratcliffe but really designed for a Nunnery (as at York) for entertainment of young Ladys of that perswasion.

The Jesuits have a great Fund or Sum of money in that County. There are dayly Considerable Sums collected & gathered by that party & their Agents for what ends are unknown.

It is clear from Mickleton's research that the Catholics of County Durham were extremely well-served pastorally even though he omitted the important mission at Chester le Street and five others further afield in the county. But he did not distinguish between permanent and supply or shared missions, although he might not have appreciated the distinction. In any examination of his survey of the mission, then, it is appropriate to eliminate those about which Mickleton was mistaken, clarify the status of others, and note those few more which did not survive long.

Nothing further is heard of missionary activity at Brandon, Bishop Middleham, Hetton on the Hill or Twizel. It is clear that these were houses in which Mickleton assumed Mass was being said regularly simply because they were owned by Catholics. He also conflated the houses at Croxdale, Sunderland Bridge and Tudhoe, leading his readers to conclude that a priest was resident in each, whereas one served all three. A similar situation obtained in north-west Durham where Stanley Hall, Lintz Hall, Pontop Hall and Hamsterley Hall were all Catholic houses within a short distance of each other served by one, perhaps two priests. Four of the other missions listed did not survive into the long term. Harbourhouse was a residence of the Forcer family and a Jesuit chaplaincy until 1719 when the 80-year-old chaplain, Ralph Jenison died. The chaplaincy then lapsed, either because of a shortage of priests or, more likely, because the property had passed into the possession of Basil Forcer, who lived in London. The Kennets of Coxhoe Hall had a secular chaplain from the 1680s, and John Yaxlee was there for forty years from 1691. Nicholas Kennet, the last in the male line, died in May 1715 (fortuitously only a few months before he would have had to commit to the Jacobite rising) leaving the estate to his daughter Mary who married William, fifth Earl of Seaforth, a Jacobite. They fled the country after the failure of the 'Fifteen and the estate was sold to relatives. The mission-station was discontinued when Yaxlee died in 1731. The house at Layton, near Sedgefield, continued to receive visiting priests until the Conyers family became extinct in 1748. The Suttons, who provided a house-chapel at Coundon, had left the county by mid-century.[12]

Despite its inaccuracies, however, Mickleton's analysis shows that within a mere fifteen years of the revolution not the slightest notice was being taken of the penal laws by either Catholic or Protestant, and that the archdeacon had been reproved (he does not say by whom) for trying to apply the law more stringently even though the laxity in dealing with the Catholics in and about the cathedral city apparently ran counter to Bishop Crewe's recent visitation. There was, however, sufficient ambiguity about the policy of the Jacobite-inclined bishop to embolden the Catholics to bank on his disinclination to insist on a rigorous pursuit of a religious minority with which he had some sympathy. That being so, the Catholics of County Durham were not constrained from practising their religion openly, even brazenly.

In 1692, of ten priests in the county, six had been in place for eight or more years and only two were newly-arrived. As Mickleton indignantly made clear, they appeared publicly and fraternised with their Anglican counterparts; the Catholic gentry travelled freely, they proselytized among their tenants, they collected money to build chapels and schools and were on the best of terms with the magistrates. It comes with little surprise that in 1710 Luigi da Cugna reported to Cardinal Paoluci, that the only penal laws in operation were those on double taxation and the tests. Otherwise

> as regards the exercise of their religion itself, [the Catholics] enjoy complete freedom. There is no person of distinction who wishes and is able to keep a chaplain, either in the city or in their country house who does not have one...[13]

***

Notwithstanding their fervent expressions of devotion to the cause earlier, it is clear that the Jacobite Rising of 1715 cannot be described as a Catholic one. Catholic gentlemen with responsibilities for estates and families had no illusions about the risks involved and few of them went out. Unsuccessful though the rising was, however, the government was determined that 'the Roman Catholic Interest' in the northern counties be 'entirely ruined'. Two acts of parliament were passed which were aimed at impoverishing the Catholic gentry so as to prevent any further insubordination. The first act specified that the estates of all persons convicted of high treason were to be forfeited and vested in the crown for disposal. Entailed and marital estates were exempt and lawful debts protected but estates given over to 'superstitious uses' (that is, to support the mission) were forfeit. The second act ordered all Catholic landowners to register their real estates and all income arising out of landed property so that they could be assessed for a contribution 'to all such extraordinary expenses as are, or shall be brought upon this Kingdom by their treachery'.[14]

Now, the English Catholics had long experience of protecting their property from a predatory government and, as a matter course, each generation made the necessary legal arrangements for the preservation of their inheritances. Estates were entailed or placed in trust, with friendly Protestants if necessary. Property was often put into the possession of female relatives as jointures or committed as dowries for unmarried daughters. It was a relatively simple matter to take additional precautions in a crisis such as mortgaging or making over a property as security on a debt (which may, or may not, have been notional). A legal challenge could be mounted and spun out to an extent that a buyer would lose interest in the property. Sabotage of an industrial property could reduce its productivity and discourage potential investors, leaving the Catholic family to recover it cheaply and surreptitiously later on. By adopting such methods, only nine convicted Catholic Jacobites lost real estate after the 'Fifteen (Derwentwater, Widdrington, Radcliffe, Errington, Collingwood, Thornton, Hodgson, Gibson and Swinburne) and even then only after devious and acrimonious delaying tactics followed by lengthy litigation. In 1721 after five years in existence, the Commission for Forfeited Estates informed parliament that of property worth £47,627 a year, they had only been able to dispose of estates valued at £5,000 a year. Through subterfuge of one kind or another almost every Catholic Jacobite family in the north-east contrived to rescue enough to go on almost as before. Indeed, they salvaged a great more than might have been expected, for, in the long term the overwhelming majority of families regained their estates and survived into the nineteenth century.[15]

The Catholics were no less resourceful in coping with the new Registration Act. At first they did not appreciate how serious the government was; they expected that the act would turn out to be a dead letter or that it would be held over their heads *in terrorem* and indeed it was not until 1717 that the Commissioners got to work. Even then the Catholics took their time about registering because they did not want to reveal their financial affairs to the prying eyes of rival coal- and land-owners. Ralph Salvin considered ignoring the new law and only grudgingly accepted his lawyer's advice to register. It was not until 1725 that all the Catholics of the region were brought to book. Even then, some evaded registration by placing their property in trust with non-Catholics and never did register.

Catholics not only dragged their feet in complying with the new law but they also took great pains to portray their financial condition in as unfavourable a light as possible. Coal-owners took advantage of a recession in the coal trade to describe their mines as 'unwrought' or 'drowned and unlet'; coal-royalties which varied from year to year and could not be calculated accurately were gladly omitted. Proprietors registered all outgoings and encumbrances to which an estate was subject such as mortgages, jointures, portions and reserved annuities; all debts and taxes were listed as were allowances made to tenants. These were all declared to exaggerate the obligations of proprietors in the hope that they would reduce their liability to tax. Therefore any analysis of the registers to produce an assessment of the wealth of the Catholic gentry should be cautious. The cumulative effect of a long process of decline as a result of recusancy was bound to show up in some cases but this should not be exaggerated just because mortgages and debts were emphasised by a proprietor. Again, the lack of comparable data about the wealth of non-Catholics may lead to the wrong conclusions about the relative condition of one or other group. The registers do nonetheless yield useful information.[16]

The national total of all income enjoyed by land-owning Catholics revealed by the act was £375,000; those in the counties of Northumberland and Durham had £32,941 and North Yorkshire had £21,150 and were among the top ten on the list (which was headed by Buckinghamshire with £57,997). About ten per cent of the Catholic population of the north-east were property-owners comprehended by the act and two thirds of them had estates valued at £100 or less. These were mostly minor gentry families farming on their own account or deriving an income from farm-rents. About a quarter were living on their jointures; the priests were all annuitants. Some fifty individuals had a yearly income of between £100 and £500 and twenty others received up to £2,000 a year. Again, about a quarter of this group were ladies living on their jointures including two Radcliffe nuns in Louvain. The wealthiest person listed was their niece, the widowed Countess of Derwentwater who registered her jointure of £2,000 secured on properties at Dilston and Lanchester.

Notwithstanding their position in the national league table, however, the Catholics of the north-east sought to play down the extent of their wealth, though a close reading of their registers reveals a much less precarious financial situation than they would have had the registrars believe. John Clavering of Callaly Castle listed debts of £5,700 which, he made it appear, he was unable to bear on an annual income of £840. But the castle had been improved in 1676 and again in 1707; the park was enclosed and extensive walled gardens and other ornamentations were completed in 1704. It is somewhat suspicious that in 1717, when the registers were being compiled, the estate was in the hands of his creditors who were, as it happens, two local Catholic tenant-farmers, yet it was back with the family five years later. Ralph Clavering began another series of alterations to the castle in 1727; his son Ralph completed a major rebuilding programme in 1748 and a chapel was added in 1750. Edward Riddell of Swinburne Castle listed commitments of £10,000 for annuities, portions, mortgage repayments, interest and debts but he received £1,000 a year excluding coal royalties. Similarly, William Errington, Edward Haggerston and Edward Horsley Widdrington sought to convey the impression of being in dire straits because of heavy outgoings but their annual incomes could easily cope. The Haggerstons managed their affairs with consummate skill. Haggerston Castle was severely damaged by fire in 1687 when £6,000 of damage was done (and a fine library lost) but the restoration was completed without difficulty and in 1719 Sir Carnaby (III) registered an annual income of £2,202 unencumbered by debt. The estates were the principal source of dairy produce for Berwick and their value quintupled during the century. None of these families was even remotely near bankruptcy

It has to be said, however, that there were families in difficulties. Those with small estates were often unable to accumulate enough resources to withstand the financial penalties attendant on recusancy and fecundity. In 1717 John Jenison of Walworth near Darlington registered an estate worth £262 a year but in 1729 he was compelled to lease the estate to raise an income for his son and dowries for his three daughters. His successor died in 1759 leaving four sons and a daughter. The three eldest sons became Jesuit priests (and had to be bought out) and so the estate devolved on the youngest who fathered nine sons and seven daughters. Parts of the estate began to be sold off in 1766 and ten years later the estate was dissolved; Francis Jenison went abroad to enter the service of the Elector of the Rhine Palatinate. Although other families found themselves in a similar predicament and went to the wall during the century, the majority of Catholic gentlemen fell between the extremes of Haggerston and Jenison, and there is no reason to suppose that they were all struggling to make a living.

***

Small as it was, the participation of the Catholic gentry in the 'Fifteen, was bound to have an impact on pastoral arrangements in

Northumberland. The chapel at Dilston Hall, which dated from 1616 and had been served continuously by chaplains, closed and the priest moved into Hexham in 1720. The Catholics gathered for a time in Dilston House, Corbridge, the home of a Derwentwater steward, Mr Busby, but they were reduced to seven by 1730. The mission that had flourished in Eslington Hall since the 1660s was lost and the Jesuit chaplain moved to Ellingham Hall. The Eslington congregation switched to Callaly Castle, a mile or so to the north. Lord Widdrington maintained a Jesuit priest at Widdrington Castle in the early years of the eighteenth century but the forfeiture of the estate led to the removal of the priest in 1720; the Catholic household of forty-six was reduced to four Catholic families by 1736. (The castle was demolished in 1761.) The chaplain at Netherwitton Hall feared for the security of his post when the estate was forfeited by the Thorntons but he was no doubt relieved when the property was saved by the family.

Although three Catholic houses were lost, in missionary terms the 'Fifteen caused no more than a temporary dislocation in Northumberland: only the loss of Widdrington Castle can be said to have had long-term consequences. Priests resumed their work after a brief interval and the mission continued as before, largely in the seclusion of the country houses under the old management. The outlaw Ralph Widdrington returned to England around 1718 as if he had been merely absent on holiday and reopened the chapel at Cheeseburn Grange. The Dominican chaplain at Stonecroft Farm, home of the Gibsons, who 'was forced to be absent for a while', and the Benedictine chaplain at Stella Hall, who was arrested, were soon back at their posts. Three years later two missions were opened in Hexham by ex-chaplains of gentlemen who had been out in the 'Fifteen.

***

It is evident that the northern Catholics quickly recovered their aplomb after the first Jacobite Rising. Daniel Defoe, who once remarked that 'an Englishman hates Popery, not knowing whether it is a man or a horse', must have been disconcerted to find that the city of Durham in 1724 was

> full of Catholicks who live peaceably and disturb no body, and no body them. For we being there on a holiday, saw them going as publicly to Mass as the Dissenters did on other days to their meeting-house.[17]

At about the same time, a French visitor observed that the Catholics lived 'in perfect peace and security, with every facility for celebrating their religion publicly'.[18]

In about 1725 Edward Chandler, Bishop of Durham, compiled 'A list of the principal Roman Catholic gentlemen in Northumberland and of some others' which, while not of major significance, is interesting in that it is virtually a list of chaplaincies. The location of eleven priests is given; 'one Sebourn a busy man' was with John Thornton of Netherwitton; in Longhorsley: 'Caryn is the priest, middle aged, a weak man, belongs to Mr Widdrington'; the Rev. Farmer, chaplain at Capheaton, is also identified but the others are not named. This was by no means a complete survey (no comparable list for County Durham has survived) but it does show that the bishop at least was becoming more interested in the activity of the Catholic clergy than in the wealth of the Catholic gentry as in earlier enquiries.[19]

The number and whereabouts of the northern Catholics were next investigated at Bishop Chandler's episcopal visitation of 173[2].[20] Out of the eighty Anglican parishes in Northumberland only ten are missing from the surviving returns, and six of those are of parishes having no history of Roman Catholicism. The short-fall in the overall count is only about 175 Catholics. In addition, there were 105 Catholics in Hexhamshire but that is a substantial under-estimate because in 1743 the figure was 285. In County Durham, however, twenty of the seventy returns are missing, half of which related to parishes having a significant Catholic presence. The resulting shortfall is around 500 Catholics. Taking those factors into account, the visitation showed that there were some 3,800 Catholics in the region. Even by comparison with the seriously deficient 1705 returns, Catholic numbers had clearly increased; the 'Fifteen had had no perceptible effect on distribution, and the Catholics were to be found generally in the same locations as at the beginning of the century.

Moreover, as Bishop Chandler may have noted, the Catholics were served by an extensively distributed ministry; in fact, he had compiled his list when the mission had reached its widest extent. A number of chapels had been opened in the previous century but the institution of the vicars apostolic in 1688 had so reinvigorated the mission that within a remarkably short time a network of some thirty-four mission-stations was established across the region (with four more house-chapels immediately accessible south of the Tees). Most chapels were housed in the mansions of the gentry but chapels operated more or less openly in some of the towns. A high proportion of Catholics had regular access to the sacraments and they had a reasonable expectation of continuous pastoral care; indeed the vicars apostolic increasingly lamented the shortage of priests. Another sign of easier times could be discerned in the gradual disuse of priest-holes (or hides) which had been constructed routinely in Catholic mansions hitherto. Discretion continued to be necessary, of course, and many years would elapse before Catholics were able to lower their guard. Notwithstanding its geographical and pastoral reach, however, it would be misleading to think of the mission in the region as a centrally controlled clerical operation, for it was largely subject to the gentry and is better described as comprising a group of semi-autonomous mission-stations only loosely linked organisationally.

***

Notwithstanding the almost complete lack of interest shown by the northern Catholics in the Rising of 1745, they were presumed to have supported it, by the mob at any rate. Durham had been unscathed in the aftermath of the 'Fifteen, but not so after the 'Forty-five and a number of public chapels and houses in the county were sacked in 1746. After looting the chapel in Sunderland the mob proceeded to visit Catholic houses in the locality, extorting protection money from one, plundering another and demolishing a third. The Jesuit chapel in Old Elvet, Durham, was attacked, windows were broken and the priest's house was ransacked. The mob also attacked Hardwick Hall precipitating the flight of the chaplain and the death of Francis Maire, the squire, two days later. At about one o'clock in the morning of 26 January, the mob 'set a mission house, with a Popish chapel in it, on fire' in Gateshead and proceeded to Newcastle and attacked the secular chapel in The Nuns later that day. The firing of Catholic chapels was seen by some as unfair: 'There has been too much of it, from the mob thinking the people of that profession encouraged rebellion'. The Duke of Cumberland happened to be passing through the region at the time and he gave instructions to the military commanders in Newcastle to help the magistrates to restore order. A notice signed by the Town Clerk, appeared in the *Newcastle Journal* on 1 February offering a reward of £50 for information leading to the arrest of the 'disorderly persons' who had broken into the Newcastle chapel and 'took away or destroyed several goods and other things'. The culprits, however, were never found. Officially, then, it seems that the Catholics were to be given protection; certainly Mr Salvin and the Revd Maire, the secular missioner in Durham, felt able to ask for the Bishop of Durham's assistance, presumably confident that it would be forthcoming. Although the mission was disrupted by these attacks it recovered fairly quickly, though not entirely. The chapels at Durham and Hardwick reopened immediately, but both Gateshead House and the property in Sunderland were beyond repair. Gateshead's Jesuit took refuge with the Brandlings of Felling Hall before shortly moving into Newcastle to open a new chapel. So, although the Catholics of Gateshead lost their resident priest, they could attend Mass just across the river Tyne where their erstwhile pastor had taken up residence. The congregation of Sunderland was not so fortunate; the priest moved to Witton Shields, and Sunderland became a supply mission for the next twenty years, attended by John Bamber, the Maire's chaplain in Gilesgate, Durham.[21]

The first Jacobite rising had greatest effect on the mission in Northumberland, and the second did most damage in Durham, but neither had disastrous consequences. Indeed, the Catholic mission of the north-east emerged from the Jacobite era largely unscathed. In 1747 it was much regretted that

> notwithstanding those several prohibitions, enforc'd by high penalties, are there not known Mass-houses in many parts of the kingdom? Is not the resort to them open and public?[22]

Nonetheless, the Jacobite episodes showed that the Catholics had to exercise great discretion if they were to be left alone. Public chapels in particular were at risk in times of crisis and would be attacked with impunity. Hence all Catholic mission buildings erected in the latter half of the eighteenth century were located in remote places. New town-chapels were hidden in backyard outbuildings and were devoid of any specifically ecclesiastical architectural features. It is perhaps no coincidence that when, in 1746, Dom Anthony Raffa took over as missioner in Chester le Street, he gladly accepted the offer of a piece of land in the secluded village of Birtley (mid-way between Chester le Street and Gateshead), and quickly moved the mission there.

It might reasonably be supposed that the Revolution of 1688 and the two Jacobite risings of 1715 and 1745, combined with the application of the penal laws, would have had a debilitating if not destructive effect on the Catholic community of north-east England in the late Stuart and early Hanoverian period. Contrary to expectations, however, the census of 1705 showed that the small Catholic population was well-established, confident and possessed of a capacity for growth. Two decades later their estate registers showed that the Catholics were flourishing economically and that the gentry were not without respectable capital resources. Most Catholics survived the Jacobite period almost unscathed financially although it had been intended to subject them to severe penalties for their loyalty to the Stuarts. Bishop Chandler's investigations in 1725 and 173[2] showed that the Catholics of the region were served by an extensively distributed mission and that the Jacobite Risings had had no adverse effect on the demography of the Catholic community. Such a development was greatly encouraging within the Church, but there were many Protestants who feared that these were the very conditions which would engender expansion and an increase in popish influence, and should not be tolerated.

***

From around 1765 newspapers began to criticise the Anglican bishops for neglect of duty by allowing a 'dangerous increase in popery' to take place under their noses.[23] In an attempt to silence the critics by proving that such claims were exaggerated, the Archbishop of York proposed that a national census of the Catholics be taken, and parliament agreed. The census was held in 1767 and it turned out to be a virtually comprehensive survey of the Catholic population in England and Wales and so was by far the most important taken during the period.[24] The Lords seem not to have been too concerned by the results; at any rate the first Catholic Relief Act was passed in 1778. The Gordon Riots which followed were alarming, however, and many parliamentarians sought to alleviate Protestant fears by emphasising that the Act was intended merely to *tolerate* Popery, not to *encourage* it. Nonetheless, some extremists wished to repeal the Act and introduce new legislation to prevent any Catholic from teaching non-Catholic children and thus increase the number of converts. (There were some fifteen Catholic dame schools open in the north-east at the time.) The moderates, on the other hand, were quite certain that there was no need for such action. A compromise was agreed whereby another census of the Catholics would be taken to establish exactly what the growth of Catholicism had been since 1767. Accordingly, in July 1780, the House of Lords agreed to a motion by which the Anglican bishops were to give orders to all their clergy 'to make an exact enumeration of the Roman Catholics within their districts'.[25] To the great satisfaction of the extremists, the national total did show an increase in the Catholic population; but the moderates pointed out that although the *absolute* total had undoubtedly risen, *proportionately* the Catholic population had fallen. The anti-Catholic case therefore collapsed and ten years later the second Catholic Relief Act passed without substantial opposition. There were also four routine Episcopal Visitations of the diocese of Durham between 1774 and 1814, the last head-counts to be taken before Catholic Emancipation.[26]

Analysis of this series of returns shows that, proportionately, the Catholic population of the north-east rose significantly in the first half of the eighteenth century, but then fell back so that at the end of the war in 1814/5 it was about the same as it had been over a century before. The Catholic population of 1705 has been calculated by comparison with later years. That is, the number of Catholics in parishes for which there is a complete series of returns from 1705 to 1814 represents about half the total on each occasion. The figure from those parishes in 1705 was 1,279, which, if it conforms to the pattern, would give a total of around 2,588 Catholics, or 1.2 per cent of the population. The population of the region in 1767 was about 235,000 of which Catholics represented 2 per cent. In 1814 there were 3,772 Catholics, representing 1 per cent of the population of 350,000. The great increase would come in the following decades: In 1839 Bishop Briggs reported 7,000 Catholics in the two counties[27] and by 1851 the Catholics numbered some 27,000, but even then they formed only 3.6 per cent of the whole population.

The rise and fall of the Catholic population over the period is not easy to explain, indeed it is contradictory. The rise occurred in the period of the two Jacobite Risings when Catholic numbers might have been expected to fall as a reflection of their unpopularity and consequent self-effacement. It seems, however, that the relatively newly-established mission, under the enthusiastic patronage of the gentry, imbued the Catholic body with a self-confidence which encouraged cohesion and growth against the odds. The fall in Catholic numbers later in the century took place contrary to their potential for natural growth and when the social characteristics of the northern Catholics were similar to those of the population in general.

The decline undoubtedly took place and it was widely remarked upon. The visitation returns from Lamesley, Whickham, Newcastle St Andrew, Newcastle St Ann, Darlington, Stamfordham and Sunderland all noted the fall. In 1810 the curate of Belford observed that the children of the half-dozen Catholics were beginning to attend the established church, and in 1814 the vicar of Chollerton noticed the same development. One of the two Catholics living in Warkworth often attended the parish church. The vicar of Sockburn rejoiced that he had only one Catholic woman, aged 80, in his parish, while 'at the last visitation holden by Bishop Thurlow there were two Popish families'. In 1792 the curate of Carham said it was 'a rarity' to see a Catholic in the parish; there had been five in 1780.

Disruptions to the Catholic mission were partly responsible for the decline. The chapel at Hesleyside was closed for financial reasons and in 1774 the vicar of Simonburn reported that there was 'no Mass-house, thank God, in the parish'. In 1810 he expressed delight at having 'no Popish school or Seminary in my parish', and went on, 'I hope the number of Papists does not increase with us: and I am happy that I have converted one large family to the Communion of our Church'. In 1814 there were no more than twenty Catholics in the parish; there had been around eighty in 1780. In 1810 the curate of Kyloe and Lowick anticipated gains:

> Mr Clavering of Berrington having sold his Estate lately, they will soon disappear in that quarter, and as the Haggerstone family do not scruple to take a good Tenant from among the Protestants, they are, I think, upon the decrease in both parishes.

Similarly, the curate of Netherwitton remarked in 1774 that

> a Protestant Gentleman having about 2 years ago married one of the coheiresses of the Principal Roman Catholic family [Thornton], the P[opish] Priest had been sent out of the Chapelry and that Interest is now on the decline and some converts have been made.

The Catholic community of one hundred in 1767 declined to seventy in 1792 and a report of 1827 said 'few Catholics are now remaining here'. In 1792 it was noted that Catholic numbers had fallen in Kirkwhelpington each year since the apostasy of Sir John Swinburne to the Church of England, and the Catholic community of Felling was decimated following the secession of Charles Brandling, the Catholic squire.

These examples show that contributory factors to the decline of the Catholic population included isolation, a lack of pastoral care and the temporary insolvency or apostasy of a Catholic land-owner bringing about the closure of a chapel and the dismissal of the chaplain. Areas which maintained their Catholic populations were those sizeable rural enclaves with a relatively settled community. In Ryton and Lanchester, where the Church was visible and strong, and where the Catholic population was long-established, numbers held up. In those, usually urban, areas where the Catholic population was less settled, or where there was a small Catholic presence in a rural parish, or where the church was inconspicuous, numbers fell. In Darlington there was a small and apparently well-established Catholic community, but it was served by a monthly supply mission until 1824; the Catholic population fell by 70 per cent yet over half the Catholics were aged 30 under thirty in 1767 and could have been expected to reproduce themselves. Similarly, a large rural Catholic community could fall markedly if the Catholic landowner, and hence principal employer, left the Church. There were exceptions to the general pattern; a small urban group of Catholics could flourish, given an active missioner, which was the case at Berwick towards the end of the century and at North Shields some years later.

To some extent, war and the demographic change associated with industrial development also served to hinder the growth of the small Catholic body. Moreover, though there were only 1,873 Methodists in County Durham in 1767 (concentrated on Tyneside and in the western dales), the rapid proliferation of Methodism later in the century suggests that the legal disabilities and political uncertainties associated with Catholicism were also important influences.[28] It was certainly not a time for zealous evangelism, living as Catholics did in a state of informal toleration. Such a policy would have been seen by many Protestants as provocative, just as many Catholic lay gentlemen would have considered it inexpedient for their chaplains to be seen casting about for converts in their localities. It is clear, at any rate, that there were few conversions except through marriage. In 1792 the vicar of Esh said that Catholic 'numbers have not increased except by the ordinary methods of population rise'.

The few and ageing priests had to be content to minister to existing Catholics but, despite their best efforts, they were fighting a losing battle in the towns and remoter areas. They were unable to visit regularly those Catholics living in the widely scattered farmsteads and hamlets of the region. Yet the maintenance of the faith depended on such support because religious practice is very difficult to sustain in isolation. A solitary, remotely-located family would almost inevitably leave the Church in one or two generations without regular encouragement to persevere. In Bothal in 1792 the Catholics were 'an old man and his wife and their son and his wife but the children of the latter have been baptised in the Church [of England]'. Missionary discretion had to be kept up even after the first stage of Relief had been achieved; the Gordon Riots reminded Catholics not to over-reach themselves, and the ill-tempered debate on the Catholic Question would continue for a further fifty years. Protestant England would prove very reluctant to grant formal and civil political liberty to Catholics in 1829 despite having welcomed numbers of exiled French priests and accepted the repatriation of the English colleges and convents from Europe after the French Revolution.

In general, the small Catholic population was widely dispersed throughout the region. Almost 90 per cent of Anglican parishes reported Catholic inhabitancy at one time or another. There were, however, some populous parishes, mostly in the remote western uplands, which had no Catholic residents at all, and the best example is Stanhope in Weardale (population of five thousand), which was, in any case, assiduously evangelised by John Wesley. Conversely, one third of all Catholics in County Durham lived within five miles of Durham City, and 10 per cent of families in the city were Catholic. None of the other towns had more than 1½ per cent Catholic inhabitants.

The principal, and unsurprising, feature of the distribution of the Catholics in the region was that the largest groups were to be found in the vicinity of the Catholic missions. A mission-station was generally established by a country gentleman on his estate and the nucleus of the congregation was formed from members of the household and estate workers. The geographical range of the mission quickly expanded so that some were attended from considerable distances by people unconnected with the patron. Before a resident missioner was appointed at Berwick, for example, the Catholics travelled to Haggerston Castle for Sunday Mass, a tiring round trip of over twelve miles. Alternatively, of course, the missioner could do the travelling; in 1805 the Berwick missioner said he had 'walked no less than 1,000 miles' on missionary duty in the previous year.[29] That was exceptional, for most Catholics lived within range of a chapel. Nonetheless, the widespread distribution of the Catholic population necessarily involved substantial amounts of walking or riding if those in the remoter areas were to practise their faith regularly.

Normally, the Episcopal Visitation questionnaire enquired about the number of individual Catholics in the parishes, but in 1774 it asked for the number of families, thus revealing the average size of a family to be four persons. Since it also asked for the total number of families in the parish, a direct measurement of residential density can be calculated for the Catholic population. The average size of the Anglican parish in the north at this time, however, was over ten thousand acres, and so the parish is not always the most useful geographical unit by which to illustrate this feature of the population, although that is how the information was collected.[30] In 1750 the Catholic chaplains at Haggerston Castle and Berrington Hall reported that a total of some 230 people of all ages attended one or other of the two chapels. That figure was corroborated in 1767, allowing for growth, when the four parishes of Ancroft, Belford, Holy Island and Lowick returned 256 Catholics (56 families in 1774). The two principal returns came from Lowick and the chapelry of Kyloe in Ancroft. The villages of Kyloe and nearby Fenwick (where there was a Catholic school) belonged to the Haggerstons, as did Lowick, two and a half miles to the west. Haggerston and Berrington (which belonged to the Claverings) lay about three miles to the north. Virtually all the Catholics of the area lived in those five villages, and so the geographical spread and residential density of the Catholic population is distorted when taking the parish as the base unit of measurement. In Hartburn parish, 6 per cent of the families were Catholic, but if the village and chapelry of Netherwitton are taken separately (as was usual) then the distribution of Catholic families is seen to be concentrated, for it amounts to 22 per cent of the chapelry's population. In the same way, most of the Catholic families in the parish of Whittingham lived in settlements close to Callaly Castle. Such concentrations are to be attributed to the presence of Catholic gentry houses and chapels: the Thorntons at Netherwitton, Salvins at Croxdale, Smythes in Esh (Lanchester), Silvertops in Stella (Ryton), and so on. Although in no parish did the Catholics form a majority of inhabitants, a few villages associated with Catholic gentry estates did have relatively large Catholic communities. Apart from those enclaves, the remainder of the Catholic population was distributed thinly. None of the towns of the region, except Durham, had a large Catholic community. The Catholic body, then, was not a conspicuous component of the region's population.

In 1767 parish officials were asked to state how long the Catholics had been resident in their present domiciles. Clearly, the overwhelming majority of children under 15 years of age were living where they had been born, or had moved with their parents, and that group, which is about a third of the whole, can be excluded from any analysis of free geographical mobility. Just under half of the Catholic adults in each county were living in their native parishes, and about a third had moved into their present localities within the previous ten years. Although the rural Catholics were considerably more settled than those in the urban areas, that was not invariably the case; the Catholics of Ellingham and Lanchester were as likely to be newcomers as long-term residents. Close analysis indicates that the geographical mobility of the northern Catholics was governed largely by economic circumstances rather than by religious considerations. Agriculture had long been, and would remain for some time, the staple industry in such places as Croxdale, Kyloe and Whittingham, just as coal-mining had a long history in Ryton. The populations of those parishes were therefore unlikely to change markedly. The towns, on the other hand, were fast-growing industrial and commercial centres which had a relatively mobile and young population (half the Catholics of Newcastle and two thirds of those in Alnwick were under 30 years of age).

Not surprisingly, the young were the most mobile and the old were the most settled groups in society. On reaching working (or marriageable) age, individuals moved away from their native parishes if suitable opportunities did not occur locally. A readiness to move about was maintained throughout a working life, but as people got older they became less likely to move. Commonplace as this conclusion is, it does at least indicate that the pattern of geographical mobility exhibited by the Catholics of the region was similar to that which might be expected of any economically active population. There is nothing to indicate that there was any largescale movement into the Catholic strongholds, nor were the Catholics constrained or inhibited from moving into new localities to seek work or a spouse.

Religious practice is at greater risk, however, when a population is mobile or when social change is taking place.[31] A family moving from a rural area into an urban centre has to be able to reconnect with the Church after moving. If the Church's organisation is weak or inconspicuous, or if regular religious services are not maintained, the chances are that the family will be lost. Obviously a number of migrants did reconnect, but there was no overall increase in the urban Catholic population until the 1820s at the earliest, yet it was into the towns that the population had been moving since late in the previous century. Hence, leakage as the result of migration was another factor contributing to the decline in overall Catholic numbers.[32]

The age and gender of 90 per cent of the north-eastern Catholics in 1767 is known. The structure of the Catholic population of the north-east was remarkably similar to that of the nation as a whole, as computed in 1750 and 1815.[33] Their age pattern was pyramidal and the genders were in rough balance. About 40 per cent were aged between 20 and 40, and it is from this group that natural increase was to be expected. Since the composition of the Catholic population was clearly suited to growth, the decline in numbers over the next half-century cannot be attributed to a lack of fecundity or a shortage of suitable Catholic mates in the same age group.

The 1767 returns give the marital status of 94 per cent of the Catholics of the region. Children up to the age of 15 years (the age at which the majority seem to have become economically active) represent a third of the whole. Single men and women comprised 30 per cent; 5 per cent were widows or widowers; and 30 per cent were married. The large numbers of single people indicates that Catholics followed the national practice for a first marriage to take place in the middle to late twenties. Of major significance for present purposes, however, is the extent to which Catholics married within their own church, or sought a spouse without regard to ecclesiastical affiliation.

Just over half of all marriages were between Catholics and hence the rest were apparently denominationally 'mixed'. Mixed marriages are difficult to identify with certainty, since the returning officer may not have intended to imply one, whereas one may be inferred from the way the entry is written. In Durham there was 'the wife and daughter of a Mr Hanby, a Plumber'. The presumption is that Mr Hanby was not a Catholic. Also in Durham there was 'Mr Walton, a teacher of the French language, and his infant son'. Is it justified to assume this to be a mixed marriage because the wife is not mentioned? Mr Walton may have been a widower, or perhaps the vicar did not think to mention the wife, assuming it to be obvious. There are some difficulties, then, but these are mostly to do with a minority of cases in which the husband is Catholic but the wife (apparently) is not.

Mixed marriages were almost as common as those between two Roman Catholics. As perhaps was to be expected, the highest incidence of mixed marriages occurred in the towns, but no other correlation can be established. The number of mixed marriages was relatively high in such Catholic strongholds as Ellingham and Croxdale. In the parish of Netherwitton where the large Catholic population was well established, only 17 per cent of marriages were mixed, but in Longhorsley which also had a relatively large settled Catholic community, only 16 per cent of marriages were between two Catholics. In the small and less settled Catholic population of Newcastle over half of marriages were between two Catholics. This pattern was not uncommon. The Catholic priest Joseph Berington noted that mixed marriages were 'now very usual' in the south, and in 1803 the Vicar Apostolic of the Western District reported an increase in mixed marriages as well as a decline in attendance at the sacraments and a general relaxation of the barriers between Catholics and Protestants.[34] In 1737 a Mrs. Shirley, known to be a 'good Catholic', visited Spencer Cowper, Dean of Durham:

> She was offered to be conducted to Mass, but she very politely declined it, and contented herself with going to our cathedral twice o'day, and seemed a good deal pleased with our choir service.

Thomas Davison, vicar of Norton, had seventeen children, two of whom became Catholics, and one of those married an Anglican clergyman. Late in the century the Catholics of Ryton flocked to hear Wesley preach.[35]

The implications of a generally high incidence of denominationally mixed marriages are twofold. Firstly, it suggests that since the choice of marriage partner was not restricted to their co-religionists, Catholics were securely based in society, and were neither insular or ostracised. Secondly, the outcome of a mixed marriage varied and affected the growth in the Catholic population. In 1792 the vicar of Lanchester said:

> During a residence of 13 years in the parish there have been four instances of Protestants marrying Papists and turning to their Communion, whilst I have only got one from them in a similar instance.

In Norton that year one wife was 'perverted to Popery on her marriage. The two sisters of the husband came over to the Communion of our Church on their marriages'. In 1801 there was a large family in Wolsingham in which the father and sons were Catholic while the wife and daughters were Anglican; in Longhoughton the opposite was the case. In Ellingham in 1810 it was reported that

> The wives and daughters of two other farmers are Papists: but the fathers and sons of the established church. Several

instances of the same kind occur among the Cottagers and married servants of Mr Haggerston, and one or two where the husband is a Roman Catholic and the wife of the established church. I am not aware of any persons having lately been perverted to Popery in this parish. Where however the parents of any new born child, dependent on the Haggerston family are of different persuasions as above mentioned, the children are mostly baptized by the Roman Catholic priest.

In Warkworth in 1792 a farmer, Thomas Wilson, 'being the son of Protestant parents' married a Catholic and afterwards he appeared 'to be a Papist, as he had had his son baptized by a popish priest'. This was a constant theme in the reports on the northern Catholics. In 1732 the vicar of Gainford expressed great irritation with the Catholics in his parish who, among other things, were 'wont to be marryed by a Popish Priest without Banns or License'. He sought his bishop's advice on another mattter:

> When a Papist [of Piercebridge] chances to marry a Protestant, the Papist for the most part causes the children to be baptized by a Popish Priest and to be brought up in his own religion. The vicar of Gainford, to prevent the mischief last mentioned, has several times required the parties to observe this Rule, viz: That the boys should follow the Religion of the father and the girls that of the mother. But the Papists will not keep to the Rule.

He went on to complain about another stratagem:

> Francis Jakes, a poor man of the said town, was lately seduced to the Roman Catholic Religion, probably by some of the family at Cliff, the seat of a Roman Catholic gentleman near Piercebridge in Yorkshire. That the said Jakes sends two of his children to be brought up Papists on

consideration (as the report is) of their being taught to read and write gratis.

He concluded with a plea for advice on how to 'restrain the aforesaid practices tending to increase the Popish party' in his parish. It is not known whether the bishop came to the vicar's assistance; probably not, because Mr Witham and his chaplain at Cliffe Hall continued as before. These examples show that a mixed marriage could result in apostasy, recruitment, or have no effect on ecclesiastical affiliation, but since Catholic numbers fell in the period it seems as if losses through denominationally mixed marriages outnumbered gains.

The English social pyramid, though steep in terms of income, was almost flat above the base and the number of individuals holding a social rank was very small. The 1705 returns taken in conjunction with the estate registers showed that there were three, more or less distinct, groupings. There was a tiny group (3 per cent) of wealthy land-owners and annuitants (mostly widows), with incomes of between £100 and £4,000 a year. Then there was a small group (7 per cent) of tradesmen, lesser gentry and farmers, in possession of property such as houses, shops and small-holdings which yielded incomes of under £100 a year. Over half the properties had a value of £25 or less and three-quarters were valued at under £10, like Thomas Kirby's dwelling worth six shillings. The professions were represented by one or two attorneys, physicians and a handful of stewards, agents or factors of gentry estates. The majority (90 per cent) were ordinary folk without any capital resources to speak of, and most of them earned a living on the land in one way or another.

At the beginning of the eighteenth century the socio-economic structure of the northern Catholic community was similar to that of the population as a whole: Catholics were to be found at all social levels and in all situations.[36] That structure was unaltered at the time of the Relief Acts. In 1767 there were farmers and merchants, doctors and teachers, labourers, publicans and shopkeepers. Industry was represented by managers, wheelwrights, enginewrights, millwrights, and so on. Unskilled, semi-skilled and skilled jobs were listed together with gardeners, seafarers, miners and servants. The breeches-maker, mantua-maker, cheese-seller, petticoat-quilter, lint-heckler, tallow-chandler and flax-dresser appeared with the goldsmith, clerk, milliner, clockmaker, midwife, apothecary, nurse, barber, fiddler and fortune-teller. Catholics were therefore to be found in most, if not all, occupations available in the region; they were certainly not languishing in the gaols or the workhouses but were gainfully employed. But whether they were under-or over-represented in any particular occupation can be ascertained in a general way only because of the absence of directly comparable material.[37]

Catholics were under-represented in agriculture, public service and in the professional and commercial classes. Since the professions and public service were closed to them under the penal laws, it is somewhat surprising that as many as 4 per cent of Catholics managed to take up a professional career at all. Durham City, however, was wellknown for the high number of Catholic doctors in practice there at this time.[38] The reduced number in agriculture and trade was doubtless because those were capital-intensive occupations. For the most part, the region's Catholics were predominantly of what has since come to be known as the working-class and hence were over-represented in the manufacturing and service sectors. The Durham Catholics in 1792 included some who were 'the Remains of Gentry' but more generally it is striking how often the Anglican clergy referred to the Catholics as 'chiefly of low rank', 'none of them of any Note', 'not persons of much condition in life', 'mostly servants, mechanics and labourers', 'plebeians' or 'common people'. Joseph Berington, who gave an account of the English Catholics in 1780, held a similar view:

> The inferior orders are little distinguishable from the corresponding classes of their Protestant neighbours. Here the broad features of distinction almost disappear industry, association, necessity, obliterate the characteristic traits. Generally speaking, they are farmers [i.e., farm-workers], shop-keepers, artisans and labourers.[39]

Several inter-related conclusions can be drawn from this analysis. The notion that by the eighteenth century the English Catholic body was reduced to an insignificant group of decaying gentry is wide of the mark; for much of the period there were more Catholics than Methodists in the north-east. In every respect the Catholics of the region possessed social characteristics virtually indistinguishable from those of their neighbours. They were represented at every social level and in almost all localities; their ages and gender were typical; their employment, residential and marital patterns indicate that they were securely integrated into local society. They lived openly and they had achieved a large degree of economic autonomy and social acceptance long before their political emancipation in 1829. Total exclusion was maintained only in the professions and political life but they were otherwise free to engage in productive work appropriate to their social and financial condition. This was by no means peculiar to the north-east, for a similar situation obtained in North Yorkshire, York, Birmingham, Lancashire and Staffordshire. There was no Catholic ghetto, nor was there a Catholic sub-culture, except perhaps among the lay gentry, who for the most part married within their own small circle and took their leisure in the same kind of company.[40]

In short, English Catholics of this time were well-assimilated into local life and theirs was 'the healthy religion of a normally structured society'.[41] They were not, however, particularly conspicuous in their religious practice, the one thing that set them apart from their contemporaries – most people would never know a Catholic in their lives. To a large extent that was their surety; they found it possible to live in peace because they practised their religion discreetly while at the same time avoiding any tendency to social insularity. In 1701 and 1715 the vicars apostolic asked Rome for a reduction in the number of holydays because they could not be observed by Catholics working in a predominantly Protestant world. It was not until 1777 that the Holy See (Pope Pius VI) agreed. For similar reasons, in 1814 a group of laymen appealed for a relaxation of the abstinence laws for the various vigils and ember and rogation days:

> Living as we daily do in intercourse with our Protestant citizens, employed as the great bulk of the Catholic Manufacturers are by Protestant Capitalists, engaged as many Catholics are in the pursuits of Agriculture, mining and Commerce, where they are daily and hourly intermixed with their Protestant neighbours and from which their presence cannot without the greatest difficulties to their families and their masters be dispensed with, difficulties so great and so multiplying from the high price of labour, the increased application of machinery and the constant and daily intercourse between persons of different religions, as to render some of these regulations ... so difficult of observance particularly the Saturdays and Wednesdays, arising from the circumstances of their being the general market days thro'out Great Britain ... [42]

The appeal was successful and, in the subsequent political campaigns for their relief and emancipation, Catholic leaders could justifiably emphasise their social congruity with their fellow-citizens and that accordingly they should be granted full political and religious rights.

***

In theory at least, the surveys treated above were meant to produce the total number of Catholics in the region. The *Census of Religious Worship, 1851* (taken in conjunction with the decennial Census of Population) is not therefore strictly comparable because it sought only to establish the extent of religious *practice*. In any case, the published Report misunderstood or ignored the attendance requirements of the Catholic Church and it also omitted quantities of important data submitted by the priests. For both these reasons the census needs reassessment.[43]

In order to ensure that no churchgoer was left out, the census took care to obtain the attendance figures for all services held on Easter Sunday, 30 March 1851. A formula was then applied to take account of those present at more than one service. It was assumed that half of those attending in the afternoon and two-thirds of those present in the evening were likely to have been at church in the morning. But that methodology ignores the Catholic discipline of the Sunday Mass obligation. Attendance at Sunday school or Vespers is laudable, of course, but it is not an acceptable substitute for attendance at Mass and cannot therefore be taken as a proper measure of the number of practising Catholics.[44] This was helpfully pointed out by Frederick Betham at the Gateshead mission: 'Mass or Morning Service is the only obligatory service in the Cath. Church'. Since Mass was not celebrated in any church or chapel in the region in the afternoon or evening, the application of the formula devised in this census could not result in any useful figure. Conscious, moreover, of the danger of obtaining inflated figures by taking the census on Easter Day, the authorities asked an additional question about the average number in the congregation during the preceding year but then failed either to analyse or publish that information. Michael Ellis, priest at Lartington, reported that on Easter Sunday 'The persons enumerated in the afternoon are the same as attended in the morning' (131) but his regular congregation over the previous year was 86.

Furthermore, the report did not print the contents of the Remarks column of the census form, notwithstanding its obvious explanatory value. Thomas Wilkinson, the priest in Wolsingham, recorded an attendance of 150 in the morning and 40 in the afternoon. His average congregation was 150 but, he added under Remarks,

> The numbers attending Divine Service in this congregation cannot be fairly represented in a return of this kind because very many, 1/5th of the men, are at work every second Sunday at Mr. Francis Attwood's Iron Works [in Tow Law] and thus are only able to attend alternate Sundays.

William Fletcher of Durham had a congregation of 470 adults and 110 scholars at Mass and 550 at his evening service but, he added under Remarks,

> According to a census lately taken of Roman Catholics belonging to the congregation of Durham, the number is 1,200. The chapel being too small to contain them many do not come to the chapel on Sundays.

On Easter Sunday in Newcastle there were almost 1,700 people at Mass at St Mary's and a similar number at St Andrews. Joseph Cullen, priest at the latter, remarked:

> There are 10,000 Roman Catholics in Newcastle, 6,000 of whom are served by one priest attached to the chapel. About 1,000 labourers having families in Ireland attend the chapel. 2 services in the morning.

John Smith, missioner in Bishop Auckland, reported an average attendance of 240 during the previous year but

> If it be desired to know how many persons are able and do attend from time to time during the year the stating of the

average number of persons attending on a Sunday will not be satisfactory as many persons from distant residence or other causes are impeded and only come to church on the Sunday occasionally. The number of persons so able will not be less than 900.

James Burchall at Cowpen reported that he had 220 people at Mass on Easter Sunday but

> There are in this congregation about 400 Catholics including children. About 100 are from 4 to 6 miles from Cowpen; the rest are within 3 miles.

Thus the returns are more complex than indicated in the formal Report and it is more fruitful to leave it aside and examine the individual census returns to arrive at more accurate figures about Catholic religious practice.

Attendance at Mass on Easter Sunday totalled 13,639, but the key figure is the extent of *regular* massgoing. Some of the returns give the attendance figure for Easter Sunday but omit the average attendance over the year. It seems, however, that unless a remark was added, the priest intended the figure to be the same. The congregations in the rural areas were smaller, more easily enumerated and substantially more observant. In most of the major towns and cities, where populations were much less identifiable, the priests added a general assessment of numbers. In total, the census returns (See Appendix) show that there were 9,868 regularly practising Catholics in the region, including the missions close by on the south bank of the Tees and Ushaw College.

The natural tendency is to go on to estimate the total *nominal* Catholic population. The regularly observant rural Catholics numbered 4,979 and it is safe to say that they represented almost the full Catholic populations in their localities. The priests reported 15,820 Catholics living in the major towns. But that does not include Sunderland; in 1840 the priest had reported 320 Easter communicants; in 1844 there were said to be 600 Catholics in the town. The return of 1851 states only that the average attendance was '950. Copied from letter sent by Registrar'. If that followed the pattern of other industrial towns then there would have been a nominal Catholic population of some three thousand on Wearside. Other sources say that there were some four thousand Irishfolk living in the town, an implausible quadrupling of the population in five years. Similarly, the returns from Brooms in north-west Durham and Birtley, Chester le Street, have not been found but there were around two thousand Irish-born adults in those areas, though not all of them will have been Catholics.[45] Although the raw returns must be given due attention, then, caution is still required. A certain amount of rounding-up of the figures is evident, though that would not alter the totals substantially. Taking all these factors into account, in 1851 the Catholic population of the region probably numbered some 27,000 of which 50 per cent were at Mass on Easter Sunday and 35 per cent practised regularly throughout the year. Without identifying the sources, however, the diocesan *Status Animarum 1830–1930* gives the 'approximate' population for 1850 as 46,000. That far exceeds any reasonable approximation based on known figures submitted by the parochial clergy in 1851 and, objectively, that discrepancy is inexplicable.[46]

At any rate, whichever way the census is read, the Catholic population of the region rose from about 3,700 in 1814/5 to some 7,000 in 1839 and to almost four times that number by 1851. Even then, Catholics formed a tiny proportion (no more than 3.6 per cent) of the whole. The growth occurred almost entirely in the urban and newly-industrialising centres. Self-evidently that rise cannot have been achieved by natural growth alone over two generations, therefore migration must have accounted for most of the increase. And, indeed, famine in Ireland, coupled with an industrial boom in north-east England, drew large numbers of Irish people into the region during the late 1840s, many, if not all, of them claimed as Catholics by some priests in their returns of 1851.[47]

***

The many statistical surveys of the recusants of the north-east in the period show that they were sturdy and self-assured: their discretion should not be understood as submission. Indeed, it was their tenacity which ensured the survival of English Catholicism and the achievement first of Relief and then of Emancipation. The idea that the history of Catholicism in England in the nineteenth century is largely a study of the Irish is therefore inaccurate; it was not until towards mid-century that the indigenous Catholics became a minority and the old sociological homogeneity of the English Catholic community was all but obliterated. No longer would Catholics be indistinguishable from the rest of the population and be represented at every social and economic level in rough proportion to their overall numbers. They would instead be a highly conspicuous ethnic group, distrusted politically and disliked culturally.

Notes

[1] The most detailed accounts of the revolution in the north are given in M. S. Child, 'Prelude to Revolution: the Structure of Politics in County Durham 1678–88', (University of Durham PhD thesis, 1972); B. D. Henning, *The History of Parliament: The House of Commons, 1660–1690* (London: Secker & Warburg, 1983, 3 vols); D. H. Hosford, *Nottingham, Nobles and the North: Aspects of the Revolution of 1688* (Hamden, Conn: Archon Books, 1976).

[2] Child, 'Prelude', p. 427; C. J. Bates, *History of Northumberland* (London: Eliot Stock, 1895); A. M. C. Forster, *Selections from the Disbursements Book (1691–1709) of Sir Thomas Haggerston Bart.* (Surtees Society [SS] 180, 1969).

[3] M. W. Flinn, *Men of Iron: The Crowleys in the Early Iron Industry* (Edinburgh University Press, 1962), pp. 40–1; W. Mitchell, *History of Sunderland*

(Sunderland: The Hills Press, 1919), p. 68.
4. R. Arnold, *Northern Lights: The Story of Lord Derwentwater* (London: Constable, 1959), pp. 41–45.
5. C. S. Terry, *The Chevalier de St George* (London: David Nutt, 1901), pp. 31, 40.
6. L. Gooch, *The Desperate Faction: The Jacobites of North-East England 1688–1745* (The University of Hull Press, 1995), pp. 18–22.
7. J. M. Tweedy *Popish Elvet* (Durham: St Cuthbert's Church, 1981, 2 parts), 1, p. 62.
8. J. A. Hilton (et al. eds), *Bishop Leyburn's Confirmation Register of 1687* (Wigan: North West Catholic History Society, 1997), pp. 38–83; F. J. Vaughan, 'Bishop Leyburn and his Confirmation Register of 1687' in *Northern Catholic History* [NCH] 12 (1980), pp. 14–18.
9. C. Fiennes, *Through England on a Side-Saddle in the Time of William and Mary* (London, Field & Truer, 1888), pp. 173–182; *Journals of the House of Lords 1705–1709* (London: s. n. 1774), XVII, pp. 685/686, 720/721.
10. Citations from the 1705 returns are identified by reference to the parish without further end-noting.
11. Durham University Library [DUL]: Mickleton and Spearman Manuscripts, No. 91, fol. 135, 141.
12. The Forcers moved from Kelloe to Harbourhouse late in the 17th century, cf. W. Fordyce, *The History and Antiquities of the County Palatine of Durham* (Newcastle: T. Fordyce, 1857, 2 vols), I, pp. 386, 404; II, pp. 342, 376. Basil Forcer died in 1774 and the estate was sold to John Tempest of Old Durham, cf. Durham County Record Office [DCRO]: D/Ph115/4, but Fordyce dates Forcer's death to 1782; Tweedy, *Popish Elvet*, I, pp. 99–102; G. Anstruther, *The Seminary Priests: A Dictionary of the Secular Clergy of England and Wales, 1558–1850* (Ware: St Edmund's College; Durham: Ushaw College, c.1968–1977, 4 vols), 4, sub Yaxlee; Ushaw College Manuscripts [UCM]: DIO 58; J. Burke, *A Genealogical and Heraldic History of the Commoners of Great Britain and Ireland* (London: H. Colburn, 1836–1838, 4 vols), IV, pp. 300–303.
13. E. N. Williams, *The Eighteenth Century Constitution, 1688–1815* (Cambridge University Press, 1960), p. 340
14. The two acts were Geo. I c.50 and c.55.
15. L. Gooch, '"Incarnate Rogues and Vile Jacobites": Silvertop v. Cotesworth,

1718-1723' in *Recusant History* [RH] 18/3 (1987), pp. 277-288.

[16] The following analysis is based on the published registers: J. C. Hodgson (ed.), *Northumbrian Documents of the 17th and 18th Centuries, comprising the Register of the Estates of Roman Catholics in Northumberland* (SS 131, 1918); C. R. Hudleston (ed.), *Registrations of Durham Recusant Estates, 1717-1778* (SS vols 173 & 175, 1962 & 1965). See also *Report to the Commons of the Commissioners to Enquire into the Estates of Certain Traitors and Popish Recusants, 1719*, Appendix 2, pp. 6, 14-15. For the general political and social background see, C. Haydon, *Anti-Catholicism in Eighteenth Century England c. 1714-1780: A Political and Social Study* (Manchester University Press, 1993).

[17] D. Defoe, *Tour thro' the Whole Island of Great Britain* (London: Parker 1734), p. 9.

[18] M. V. Muyden, *A Foreign View of England in 1725-1729* (Hampstead: Caliban Books, 1995), p. 203, quoting a letter of M. de Saussure.

[19] A tabular summary, 'Roman Catholics in Northumberland', is at *Proceedings of the Society of Antiquaries of Newcastle upon Tyne* [PSAN] (3), 8 (1917-1918), p. 69.

[20] DUL: 'Bishop Edward Chandler's Parochial Returns & Remarks on his Visitation 173[2]'. From internal evidence this can be dated to c.1732 and hence would have been his primary Visitation.

[21] L. P. Crangle, 'The Roman Catholic Community in Sunderland from the 16th Century' in *Antiquities of Sunderland* (Sunderland Antiquarian Society, 1969) 24, p. 66; W. Speck, *The Butcher: The Duke of Cumberland and the Suppression of the '45* (Oxford: Blackwell, 1981), p. 111; DRO: Londonderry Papers D/Lo/F 752; W. V. Smith, *Catholic Tyneside* (Newcastle: C. T. S., 1930), pp. 52/53; A. M. C. Forster, 'The Maire Family of County Durham' in RH 10/6, (1970), pp. 335/336.

[22] J. Sterne, *The Danger Arising to our Civil and Religious Liberty from the great increase of Papists* (York and London: s.n., 1747), p. 12.

[23] For critical press comment see, *inter alia*, *The Monthly Review* 32 (1765), pp. 370, 472, 479-480; 35; (ibid, 1766), pp. 246-247, 487; 37 (ibid, 1767), pp. 317-318. Thomas Hollis, a zealous Low-Church Whig, published a 'Plan for Preventing the Growth of Popery in England' in *The London Chronicle* on 22-24 September, 1768, in which he advocated the introduction of new penal laws.

[24] The returns from the north-east have been published in full: E. S. Worrall

(ed.), *Returns of Papists 1767: Dioceses of England and Wales except Chester* (Catholic Record Society [CRS], Occasional Publication No. 2, 1989). A full study of the returns is at L. Gooch, '"Chiefly of Low Rank": The Catholics of North-East England 1705-1814' in M. B. Rowlands, *Catholics of Parish and Town 1558-1778* (CRS Monograph No. 5, 1999), pp. 237-257.

25 *Parliamentary History* (London: Hansard, 1780), XXI, passim. House of Lords Record Office: Main Papers (presented 5 March 1781). The 1780 returns from the diocese of Durham were endorsed: 'making in the whole 4,677. R. 31st Octr. 1780.' The 1767 returns had shown there to have been 4,888 Catholics in the diocese.

26 The visitation returns of 1810 and 1814 are almost identical, and are treated as one here. The question asked at the visitation of 1792, and with minor variations in other years, was: 'Are there any reputed papists in your parish or chapelry? How many, and of what rank? Have any persons lately perverted to popery; by whom; and by what means? Is there any place in your parish or chapelry in which they assemble for divine worship, and where is it? Doth any popish priest reside in your parish, or resort to it? And by what name doth he go? Is there any popish school in your parish to which the children of Protestant parents are admitted? Hath any Visitation or confirmation been holden in your parish lately by any popish bishop?'

27 Actually he included Westmoreland. W. M. Brady, *The Episcopal Succession in England, Scotland and Ireland, A. D. 1400-1875* ([Rome: 1877-1878], Farnborough: Gregg Reprints, 1971, 3 vols), III p. 280.

28 S. Ayling, *John Wesley* (London: Collins, 1979), pp. 242, 310.

29 UCM: Eyre Mss., No. 88, Philip Besnier to Thomas Eyre.

30 A. D. Gilbert, *Religion and Society in Industrial England, 1740-1914* (London: Longman, 1976), p. 101.

31 R. Currie et al, *Churches and Churchgoers: Patterns of Church Growth in the British Isles since 1700* (Oxford: The Clarendon Press, 1977), pp. 7, 103.

32 J. Bossy, *The English Catholic Community, 1570-1850* (London: Darton, Longman & Todd, 1975), pp. 300-301 gives comparable mobility patterns in Staffordshire.

33 M. Rose, *The Economic History of Britain since 1700, Vol. 1, 1700-1860* (Cambridge University Press, 1972), pp. 22/23.

34 J. Berington, *The State and Behaviour of English Catholics from the Reformation to the Year 1780* (London: Faulder, 1780), p. 118; J. P. Chinnici, *The*

[35] *English Catholic Enlightenment: John Lingard and the Cisalpine Movement 1780-1850* (Shepherdstown, USA, The Patmos Press, 1980), p. 70.

[35] E. Hughes (ed.) *Letters of Spencer Cowper, Dean of Durham, 1746-74* (SS 165, 1950), pp. 186-187; Hudleston, *Durham Recusant Estates* p. 43; W. Bourn, *History of the Parish of Ryton* (Carlisle: Coward, 1896), p. 5.

[36] W. R. Ward, *Religion and Society in England 1790-1850* (London: Batsford, 1972), p. 25.

[37] R. Porter, *English Society in the Eighteenth Century* (London: Allen Lane, 1982), p. 388; P. Deane & W. Cole, *British Economic Growth 1688-1959* (Cambridge University Press, 1964), Tables 30 & 31.

[38] W. V. Smith, 'Recusant Doctors in Northumberland and Durham, 1650-1790' in NCH 23 (1986), pp. 15-26.

[39] Berington, *State and Behaviour*, p. 118. Berington also noted the fall in the overall number of Catholics, cf. ibid. pp. 111-124.

[40] J. C. H. Aveling, *Northern Catholics: The Catholics of the North Riding of Yorkshire 1558-1790* (London: Chapman, 1966), pp. 400-403; idem, 'Some Aspects of Yorkshire Catholic Recusant History' in *Studies in Church History* 4, (1967), pp. 118-121; idem, *Catholic Recusancy in the City of York 1558-1791* (CRS Monograph 2, 1970), chapters 4 & 5; Bossy, *English Catholic Community*, ch. 13; D. Holmes, *More Roman than Rome: English Catholicism in the Nineteenth Century* (London: Burns and Oates, 1978), pp. 21-23; J. F. Champ, 'St. Martin's Parish, Birmingham, in 1767: A Study of Urban Catholicism' in RH 15/5, (1981), pp. 342-269.

[41] A. Hastings, *A History of English Christianity, 1920-1985* (London: Collins, 1986), p. 134.

[42] B. Hemphill, *The Early Vicars Apostolic of England 1685-1750* (London: Burns & Oates, 1954), App. VII; UCM: DIO II; Chinnici, *Catholic Enlightenment*, pp. 68-70.

[43] *British Parliamentary Papers* (London, 1853), 86, p. cxlvii and Tables D, F & H.

[44] This point has not been made by Catholic historians of the period, e.g., W. V. Smith, 'The 1851 Census of Worship and the Irish Immigration into County Durham' in NCH 7 (1978), pp. 20ff. See also G. Milburn, 'The Census of Worship of 1851' in *Durham County Local History Society Bulletin* (1974), 17, p. 3 (for Durham) and 'Catholicism in Mid-Nineteenth Century Northumberland' in *Tyne n Tweed* 32 (1978), pp. 16ff.

45 F. Neal, 'Irish Settlement in the North-East and North-West of England in the Mid-Nineteenth Century' in R. Swift and S. Gilley (eds), *The Irish in Victorian Britain* (Dublin: Four Courts Press, 1999), pp. 88–90; V. Fetherston, 'Irish Catholicism in Sunderland in the Nineteenth Century' in NCH 43 (2002), pp. 47ff. Since this text went to proof, it has been discovered that the Return from St Cuthbert's, Brooms, was submitted on the incorrect form and consequently was included among the Anglican returns. The return, however, does not affect the argument advanced here that some 2,000 Catholics should be added to the county total to compensate for the omission, as indeed the Revd Francis Kearney reported: 'The total number of sittings in this chapel is 240 while that of the congregation amounts to 2,000 souls'. His further remark that the *average* weekly attendance at the chapel was 2,000 is clearly implausible. Cf. A. Munden (ed.), *The Religious Census of 1851: Northumberland and Durham* (SS vol. 216, 2012) pp. 311/312.

46 J. Lenders, 'Statistics of the Diocese of Hexham and Newcastle 1830–1930' at NRO: RCD 2/1, (reprinted in *Northern Catholic Calendar,* 1932 between pp. 80/81. Lenders was careful to exclude Cumberland and Westmorland which then formed part of the diocese); UCM: 287; In October 1829 the *Catholic Magazine* reported that there were 8,000 Catholics in Northumberland and in 1832 around 2,000 communicants in Co. Durham. These are illustrations of the difficulty in finding consistent figures from Catholic sources.

47 Brady, *Episcopal Succession,* III p. 280. No reference is made to the north-east in the Parliamentary Report on *The State of the Irish Poor in Great Britain* (London, 1836). The total Irish-born population of the north-east in 1851 was 31,167, 4.4 per cent of the whole (cf. Neal, 'Irish settlement', p. 77); R. Cooter, 'On Calculating the Nineteenth Century Irish Catholic Population of Durham and Newcastle' in NCH 2 (1975), pp. 16ff. Rev. Cullen of Newcastle got his estimate of the Irish in Newcastle and Gateshead right, cf. T. P. MacDermott, 'The Irish Workers on Tyneside' in N. McCord (ed.), *Essays in Tyneside Labour History* (Newcastle Polytechnic, 1977), p.159. See also P. Hughes, 'The English Catholics in 1850', in G. Beck (ed.), *The English Catholics 1850–1950* (London: Burns Oates, 1950), p. 50, for Irish totals in both counties.

2 THE SURVIVAL OF THE GENTRY

INHERENT IN THE Elizabethan anti-Catholic penal laws was the belief that if its leadership could be destroyed then the Church would die out. The secular provisions of this legislation were therefore largely designed to deprive the Catholic gentry of the economic means of survival and thus prevent them supporting and financing the mission. Means to this end included: fines, double taxes, sequestration of property; the denial of official and court places; disfranchisement, and exclusion from the armed services and the universities. Self-evidently, the eradication of English Catholicism was not realised; as has been shown in the previous chapter many gentry families were doing quite well financially. Moreover, by the eighteenth century Catholics had come to enjoy a substantial degree of informal toleration. They were able to worship in their own houses without interference, they were accorded the respect and deference due to their social rank, they enjoyed friendly relations with their neighbours and inter-marriage with Anglicans was not infrequent. They went to law confident of a fair hearing and a just decision; private legislation was passed on several occasions; grants of arms were obtained without difficulty; and they were occasionally entrusted with diplomatic missions. They were normally buried with their ancestors in the aisles, chancels and choirs of their parish churches, in which many of them have large memorials; and many a public house carried the name and arms of the local Catholic gentry family.[1] That was, of course, a more tolerant age. In 1733 Archbishop Blackburne of York told Lord Carlisle that Catholics who 'are quiet and peaceable will find the Penal Act, for my part, as harmless as they can wish'. In 1745 Lord Hardwicke remarked, wistfully perhaps, that 'the laws against papists as they stand in the statute book are so severe that they are the cause of their own non-execution'.[2] Clearly, then, the quiescence of the Catholics and the inhumanity of the law goes some way to explaining their survival. But there was more to it than that.

Two kinds of evasive legal action were commonly adopted to ensure the uninterrupted transmission of an estate to successive generations. In a large number of cases Catholic land-owners executed deeds putting their property into the hands of friendly Protestants, in trust, thereby safeguarding it from sequestration in the event of an anti-Catholic scare. This practice fell into disuse after the second Jacobite rising. The other device was the strict settlement or tail male which restricted an owner's interest in the family estate to his lifetime only; it had to be passed on to the heir unimpaired, hence no government could seize more than a recusant's life-interest in the estate. A strict settlement could specify the line of succession up to three generations; and it could make provision for a lack of male heirs. It also forestalled any tendency to dissolution or mismanagement by preventing a landowner from disinheriting lawful heirs or disposing of property which he only held in trust for future generations.

Although the necessity for Catholics to adopt such stratagems was clear enough, it could give rise to practical problems. Catholic capital was far from fluid to begin with, for any spare cash was needed to live; only the wealthiest had investments on the stock exchange. Annuities, for example, were usually paid by settling the rent-income of one or more properties on the person concerned, or by raising a mortgage. The former fragmented an estate and inhibited its development as a cohesive and profitable whole, which added to the risks of its long-term future; the latter meant that the landowner became more indebted. The raising of mortgages was generally practised in the eighteenth century, however, it was not peculiar to Catholics in straits, as has often been suggested.[3] Difficulties arose when several dowries had to be found in one generation and when revenue from the property was low, or a supplementary source of income could not be secured. General life-expectancy probabilities applied to Catholics no less than to anybody else, of course, and simple biology led to dynastic problems. The last Lord Widdrington and his brothers all died childless. In a large number of cases an estate was bequeathed to an indirect descendant on condition that he adopt the name of the testator to avoid its extinction. Hence, the Catholic gentry brooded over the continuity of their ancient names, and few families were 'unspoilt by the ambiguities of female line and deed poll' as Nancy Mitford observed (of the English gentry in general).[4]

The survival of English Catholicism must therefore be attributed to the tenacity with which the gentry held on to their ancestral estates and their capacity for estate-management. Whereas Anglicans might enjoy pensions, lucrative perquisites, and be able to place their younger sons in the professions, and in those ways reduce the financial demands on their estates, such supplementary sources of income were not available to Catholics. Because of their perilous legal status as buyers and sellers of land, by and large, the Catholic gentry tended to remain in one locality for many generations and it became essential for a family's survival that improvements to the productivity of the estate were continually effected, because it was the sole capital asset and source of income. So it was just as well that Catholic land-owners had a large degree of economic autonomy in that they were able to engage in commercial and industrial enterprise privately. Many land-owners became enthusiastic experimental agriculturalists in the eighteenth century; Sir Marmaduke Constable, Sir Edward Gascoigne and Philip Howard were keen students of Flemish root-crops and rotation systems. Howard introduced artificial grasses into Cumberland and he was also the first in the county to use turnips as cattle-feed. Most land-owners built lime-kilns on their properties when the significance of lime as a means of improving yields became known at the beginning of the century and gave generous discounts on farm-rents to tenants who used it as a fertiliser.[5]

They also sought to increase revenue by fostering industry, lead-mining and coal-mining. Survival was assured if an estate had exploitable resources and was well managed. In the north-east, active involvement in the coal industry was always socially acceptable and that source of recruitment brought new blood and new money into older gentry circles. Fortunate marriages bringing new capital into a family and windfall acquisitions of property on the extinction of cadet branches were also important in the maintenance of Catholic fortunes. Gentry decline could be associated with large numbers of daughters requiring dowries and long-lived dependent relatives, especially widows living on their jointures. Debt, incompetence, extravagance and a lack of business acumen would have greatest effect on small, marginally productive estates.[6]

The fortunes of the Catholic gentry, then, depended on several factors, some common to all gentry, but others arising out of their recusancy. The size and profitability of an estate, its protection from the depredations of the penal laws and from mismanagement, and the arrangement of suitable marriage alliances were all more or less the permanent preoccupations of a Catholic gentleman, circumscribed as he was by strict settlements, a lack of financial liquidity and the relatively small socio-religious circle within which advantageous marriages could be arranged. In 1724 Nicholas Blundell complained about the difficulty of finding an acceptable suitor for his daughter, nevertheless, he would not marry her off, even to a baronet's son with £1,500 a year, unless he was satisfied that she could live comfortably with the man's person, parts and humours. In 1741 Stephen Tempest warned his son:

> Let no consideration whatever induce you to marry into a mad family. The house of Broughton is perfectly clear of

that taint by which Providence has thought fit utterly to destroy many an ancient and opulent family.

The Tempests were indeed fortunate because, as Graham Greene remarked, Roman Catholicism in England has always been a great breeder of eccentrics.[7]

For all these reasons, then, it might be expected that the Catholic gentry would decline since the choice seemed to be one of remaining Catholic but poor or of becoming Protestant and prosperous, and some did apostatise. Others solved the problem by spending long periods abroad where they could live more cheaply: Viscount Fauconberg (III) of Newburgh lived mostly at Brussels; Sir Marmaduke Constable of Everingham, a lifelong bachelor, left his estates in the care of his chaplain and spent many years wandering in France and Italy; Sir Edward Gascoigne (VI) of Parlington moved his entire household to the continent and travelled widely indulging his cultural tastes.

Of those who stayed, a number of minor gentry families went to the wall because of the cumulative effect of the penal laws over several generations; their estates were liquidated because they had been reduced to an unprofitable size or because the lineage failed or because of irresponsibility. The Withams of Preston on Tees, Jenisons of Walworth, Jenisons of Hurworth, Maires of Hartbushes and the Forcers of Kelloe and Harberhouse, all found increasing difficulty in maintaining small and marginally productive estates, and sold up. Those with larger estates were much better able to cope with the peculiar nature of Catholic ownership. The Smythes owned extensive property at Ushaw, Esh, and Brancepeth and were never financially embarrassed. Similarly, the Salvins possessed large estates around Croxdale and they too prospered and their daughters made good marriages. Some of the richest coalmines on Tyneside were in Catholic ownership and several Catholic families possessed substantial estates in Northumberland and were never in any danger. Moreover, these families lived in some style and large staffs were kept. 'In excellence of workmanship, good proportions and withal, "liveableness", such houses as Eslington and Callaly have never been surpassed'. Berrington Hall, Callaly Castle, Capheaton Hall, Dilston Hall, Eslington Hall, Haggerston Castle, Hesleyside, Widdrington Castle and many other houses in the north were substantially rebuilt between the Revolution and the second Jacobite rising. Furthermore, Catholic land-owners felt secure enough to put their estates into Protestant trusteeship when occasion demanded and they found little difficulty in raising loans when necessary.[8]

It should not be thought that the Catholic gentry lay 'amouldering at home piously waiting for extinction or emancipation to catch up with them. They lived much the same kind of lives as other gentlemen: they were not refused the deference due to men of property, nor were they ostracised from county society; their births, marriages and deaths, as well as their accidents, financial affairs and travels were reported in the papers. The northern Catholic gentry were particularly keen on field-sports. The Riddells of Felton Park became well known as racehorse breeders and did well at most northern meetings; Thomas Riddell's horse Doctor Syntax was known as 'the Catholic horse' and won twenty Gold Cup Races — at least two Northumbrian public houses are named after it. The Meynells started the Quorn Hunt and the Vavasours the Bramham.[9] Like everyone else, the Catholic gentry went to York, Scarborough, Buxton, or even Bath, in season, and attended the Assembly Rooms, Assize Weeks and Races; they had their portraits painted and kept up with the fashions. Indeed, some were anxious not to overdo things: Stephen Tempest cautioned his son against cutting too expensive a dash in society. While spending the winter in York and the summer at Broughton was rightly 'accounted the most elegant way of living', both households should not be kept going at the same time; in any event the London season was to be avoided at all costs.[10]

Such was the high degree of social integration that it can be said, without undue exaggeration, that the proscribed religion was professed by one half of society and treated with exceptional toleration by the other. It is certainly clear that in general the Catholic gentleman of the eighteenth century followed a life-style similar to that of any gentleman of the day. Indeed, he deliberately cultivated the demeanour of a squire, which of course he was. But, other than that he attended his own chapel not his parish church, and took religious counsel from his domestic chaplain not the Anglican rector or vicar, there were three important identifiable secular differences between the Anglican and Catholic gentleman of that time.

***

Firstly, education. Standards at the English public schools and universities were not impressive in this period and as many as a quarter of the peerage and forty per cent of the Anglican gentry were educated privately at home by tutors. Edward Gibbon described his time at Oxford in mid-century as the most idle and unprofitable of his life. In any case, a university career was by no means the socially correct thing for a gentleman; the universities were in effect seminaries for the Anglican clergy; even at the end of the century only ten per cent of undergraduates entered for medicine or law.[11] At the same time, however, almost all English Catholic gentlemen, even those of relatively modest means, were given a rigorous education at the expatriate colleges on the continent (principally at the English College, Douai). Their sisters, too, were often sent as parlour-boarders in the convents of the exiled religious communities or to the Bar Convent in York.

In May 1766, at the height of agitation about the growth of English Catholicism, the *Gentleman's Magazine* carried a Protestant's report of his investigation into the number of Catholic children at all known colleges in Boulogne, Bruges, Brussels, Calais, Douai, Dunkirk, Ghent, Gravelines, Lierre and St Omer. He found three hundred and seventy-five boys and three hundred girls aged between 8 and 15 (excluding some Irish and about fifty Protestant girls he had been horror-stricken to discover in one convent in Calais)[12]. Had his search extended further afield, to Dieulouard, Lisbon, Rome or Valladolid, or even in Paris where he lived, he would have counted perhaps as many as seven hundred and fifty children and that would have been the case each year until the outbreak of the French Revolution. The total is close to nine hundred when the Bar Convent is included. Fees were £20 - £25 a year and were 'much dearer than many Schools about London', and when the cost of travel was added, those arrangements became expensive and inconvenient but they were willingly borne, for these institutions were vital to the education of the Catholic laity. The colleges did not just train future priests and nuns; on average only twenty priests a year were ordained for the English mission in the third quarter of the century and three-quarters of students at Douai College did not proceed to ordination. Only one in ten of boarders at the Bar Convent became a nun.[13]

The majority of English Catholic gentlefolk therefore received a well-ordered general education. The curriculum at the Bar Convent was 'more intellectually challenging than the education then provided generally for girls'. The Philosophy course at Douai 'was well-abreast of contemporary thought' in astronomy and physics and served to introduce the more scholarly-minded to the various scientific controversies which then enlivened the intellectual life of France, Italy and the Low Countries. They were put in touch with the European Catholic tradition, they had an opportunity to gain a fluency in foreign languages at first hand, to enjoy a cosmopolitan cultural experience during school holidays, and to develop tastes which they might share with the aristocracy but which were not common among the rural gentry of England who 'seldom went farther from home than their county town, from the squire with his thousand acres to the yeoman who cultivated his hereditary property of one or two hundred'.[14] And an education of that quality was particularly appropriate for the large number of young gentlemen who went on to the Grand Tour before returning home.

The golden age of the Tour coincided with the thirty-year period of peace in Europe after 1764, and the ancient cities of Italy were the most esteemed destinations, Rome above all.[15] Apart from Catholic pilgrims, Protestant sceptics and Jacobite devotees, the Eternal City attracted British scholars in passionate pursuit of the arts of Antiquity and the Renaissance. It would be idle to suggest, of course, that all Grand Tourists had high-minded cultural aims. The Revd Alban Butler who travelled with James and Thomas Talbot, and later with Edward Howard, remarked:

> Most young gentlemen seem to travel merely to dine and sup, or at least to visit their countrymen in every town they pass through ... Some travel as if they only designed to be painters, &c., and the greater number merely to spend the most precious time of life in wandering throughout Europe, acquiring no useful knowledge, but squandering a great deal of money.[16]

He spoke from experience, no doubt, but it is clear that many Catholics acquired an appetite for more scholarly tourism as they matured and many of them did the Tour two or three times. Grand Tours were not rushed; an itinerary which included Italy usually lasted two years although the less wealthy might only manage short spells in Paris and Brussels.[17] The principal attractions on the Tour were the galleries, museums and churches in the major cities where famous art-objects were to be seen and in the process many tourists became discerning collectors. The wealthier of them bought Old Master and contemporary pictures, antique sculpture, medals, gems, porcelain, furniture and other luxury goods to grace their English homes, but few Catholics from the north-east could afford to do so. Nonetheless, they engaged guides and took courses in art history from a local cicerone and many had their portraits painted by prominent artists. Most Italian itineraries included visits to the main sites of the ancient classical world: in and around Rome, of course, but also Pompeii, Herculaneum, Selinunte, Paestum and elsewhere in the south. As well as this lofty intellectual self-improvement, younger tourists were expected to acquire social polish by keeping respectable company in expatriate English Catholic circles.

Catholic tourists usually chose (or had chosen for them) a scholarly priest as travelling-tutor, such as Alban Butler, one-time Professor of Philosophy at Douai and lecturer on 'the Newtonian system then gaining ground in the foreign universities'; or John Turberville Needham, a scientist who became a Fellow of the Royal Society (1747), the Society of Antiquaries (1761), the French Royal Academy of Sciences (1768), and the Society of Antiquaries of Scotland (1781); he was also the founding Rector of the Imperial Academy in Brussels (1768–80) and he guided important English visitors around the city. He supervised Philip Howard of Corby; William Constable wanted him to tutor his half-brother Marmaduke Tunstall. In 1776 Joseph Berington, 'an accomplished gentleman [and] a distinguished scholar', went as chaplain to Miles Stapleton of Carlton Hall 'to allow himself more leisure for his literary pursuits', but he was quite happy to lay his books aside to accompany the son on a two-year tour of France and Germany.[18] Priest-tutors were also required to make the tour partly a pilgrimage. Hence, while attendance at Carnival was permitted, reluctantly, it was almost obligatory to be in Rome for Holy Week and Easter and in Venice for Ascension Day. Excursions to Loreto and

Assisi were also undertaken. Tutors were under strict orders to prevent their charges from a headlong pursuit of wine, women and gambling. This was not invariably successful and coded references to improper liaisons appear in some diaries.

The most-travelled northern Catholics were the Swinburnes of Capheaton.[19] Sir John Swinburne (III) was at Douai from 1712 and he toured France from 1716 to 1719. His contemporary, Sir Carnaby Haggerston, set out in 1711, aged 13 and under the supervision of a priest-tutor, to visit Germany, France and Italy, and did not return until 1719. The absence abroad of Swinburne and Haggerston during the Jacobite 'Fifteen protected their families' fortunes, just as the return of the Radcliffes in 1710 destroyed theirs. The three brothers in the next Swinburne generation were also enthusiastic tourists. In 1749 Sir John Swinburne (IV) left to spend three years roaming around France during which he visited his brother Edward, a wine merchant in Bordeaux. In 1763 Edward succeeded his brother in the baronetcy and he instantly gave up work and began to travel, firstly in Spain, then in Hungary and Moravia and finally in Italy. He took up residence at Capheaton in 1772 but he did not stay long for off he went again in 1774, this time spending three years in France and Austria.

Undoubtedly, Henry Swinburne (1743–1803), the youngest of the three brothers, was the most dedicated and discriminating Grand Tourist. He was educated, firstly, at Scorton Hall in Yorkshire, then in the monastic seminary of La Celle near Paris, and in Bordeaux (probably under the guardianship of his brother Edward), and finally at the Academy of Turin devoting most attention to art and literature and where he learned Italian and studied *virtù*; he also visited Genoa and Florence. In 1763, Sir John Swinburne (III) had given him Hamsterley Hall with lands at Medomsley and an annuity, presumably at the time of Henry's coming of age. Now that he had come into independent means he made his Grand Tour. On his way home he stopped in Paris where he met Martha Baker (daughter of John Baker of Chichester, solicitor to the Leeward Islands) a fellow-Catholic who was studying at the Ursuline convent: a linguist, a musician and interested in the fine arts. Four years later they were married at Aix-la-Chapelle: he was 24 and she was 20 years of age. They spent the first six or seven years of their marriage at Hamsterley and Henry rebuilt the mansion in the Strawberry Gothick style around 1770, incorporating doors, fireplaces and so on from other disused mansions; the gardens were landscaped 'with a painter's eye.' Finding, however, that their neighbours thought of little else than 'corn or turnips, unless indeed it were the pursuit of foxes', they decamped early in 1774 for Europe and spent much of their time on what was almost a continuous Grand Tour.

Swinburne did most of his travelling with Sir Thomas Gascoigne, (VIII) (1745–1810) of Parlington in Yorkshire – described by a contemporary as 'a sensible, genteel, well-bred man'. Gascoigne financed these journeys and Swinburne provided the cultural expertise. The Swinburnes started a family but, presumably thinking that they would be an encumbrance, Henry left his wife and children behind when he went on long tours.[20] Mrs Swinburne was left at Tarbes while the two men toured Spain in 1775/6 'with two coaches, two sets of horses, two saddle mules and ... protected by a train of servants'. Swinburne's *Travels in Spain* was his most popular publication; it was the first major travel book on the country by a British author and was reissued several times in England and was translated into French and German.[21]

The reunited family (and Gascoigne) sailed from Marseilles for Italy. The party reached Rome at Easter 1778 and were given audience by Pope Pius VI – Swinburne was uninhibitedly critical of the pontiff's appearance and manner. They fitted easily into expatriate Benedictine and artistic society, and both men undertook a course on art with the Scot James Byres, an antique- and art-dealer. As was customary, they had their likenesses taken: busts were made by Christopher Hewetson, and they sat for Pompeo Batoni, as did Gascoigne.[22] Swinburne and Gascoigne travelled widely in southern Italy and Henry's description of their ventures in *Travels in the Two Sicilies in the years 1777, 1778, 1789 and 1780*, illustrated with his own drawings, also became highly influential.[23] It was very well-received in the press and became the century's most important guidebook to the kingdom. While giving a comprehensive history and guide of southern Italy it was written with wit and humour though highly erudite and prolix. 'A little genteel young man' is how he struck Hannah More: 'He is modest and agreeable; not wise and heavy like his books.' After a brief interlude in England, a visit to Naples, capital of the Kingdom of the Two Sicilies brought this extraordinary six-year long tour to an end and the party returned home in July 1781. But by 1783 the Swinburnes were again in Paris and they spent much of the eighties there, making forays into Germany and Hungary. Swinburne would later conduct negotiations between the British and French governments for the exchange of prisoners of war.

Seemingly effortlessly, Henry and Martha Swinburne gained access to royal and aristocratic circles wherever they went. They were received at Versailles; young Henry Swinburne became a page to Marie Antoinette and Martha would later suggest that the queen disguise herself as her maid and so escape from France.[24] The Spanish King Charles III welcomed them to his palace at Aranjuez. In Vienna, Emperor Joseph II stood as godfather to Henry's son, and Empress Maria Theresa made gifts to Martha. Queen Carolina of Naples stood as godmother to young Caroline Swinburne and lavished gifts on her and her mother. Commenting on the Italian proverb, '*Vedi Napoli e poi mori,*' Swinburne said, 'on the contrary, that after living in Naples it is impossible not to wish to *live* that one may return to it'. In Rome they encountered the Stuart princes Charles and Henry; Martha was a devoted Jacobite but Henry was not much taken with them. His socialising was recorded in his diaries and letters which were published in two volumes as *The Courts of Europe at the Close of the Last Century, By the Late Henry Swinburne* (1841).[25]

Martha Swinburne inherited a substantial trading fortune in the West Indies from her father in 1779 but it declined and was substantially gone by the late 1780s. Henry was sent by the English government as Commissioner to treat with the French for the exchange of prisoners. He was later appointed to the lucrative post of vendue-master for Trinidad in 1801 but he died there from sunstroke two years later. The extent of his scholarship then became fully evident at the sale (over seven days) of his library; it featured numerous volumes in Latin, Greek, French, German, Italian, Spanish and Arabic as well as English. There were volumes of classics, English literature, philosophy, theology, economics, history, natural history, mathematics and art and architecture. Hamsterley Hall was sold in 1806. Martha died in 1809.

Sir Edward Swinburne had three sons: John Edward, Robert and Edward. Sir Edward accompanied the two older boys to school in Lille and in 1781 he joined them in Paris and took them on a tour of Flanders, Switzerland and Vienna to finish off their education. John Edward would make an independent tour in 1786 but it was cut short by his father's death. Edward Swinburne (who established himself as a leading amateur artist) also travelled: to Italy in 1792 and again in 1797, and he visited France and Germany, making his last journey in 1814. Other Catholic northerners to be seen in European cities in the late eighteenth century included Thomas, William and Edward Haggerston, Henry Errington of Beaufront (whose travelling companion was Laurence Sterne), Thomas Horsley Riddell of Swinburne Castle and his brother Edward, and

Edward Smythe of Esh and his son Edward. The Salvins of Croxdale are known to have spent much time abroad but no written accounts of their tours survive.

In 1797 Henry Joseph Swinburne abruptly left Naples because the approach of the French armies made it prudent for Englishmen to quit Italy. (Emma Hamilton was captivated by his good looks and lamented that the Neapolitan ladies all ran after him.) When the French entered Rome in 1798, tourists and British residents were forced to flee and the golden age of the Grand Tour came to an end. There was, however, a curious postscript: George Silvertop of Minsteracres toured France and Italy at the end of the war in 1814; he secured an interview with Napoleon on Elba, and it is said that Lord Liverpool sent him on a secret embassy to the Holy See.[26]

***

The second key difference between the Catholic and Anglican gentleman was the former's exclusion from the political life of the nation. Sir Edward Gascoigne (VI) of Parlington succinctly expressed the general Catholic view at the time of the 'Forty-five when he told his friend Lord Irwin that he had been taught since infancy to have nothing to do with politics; he felt it incumbent on Catholics to behave as true and faithful subjects.[27] Although the English Catholics kept out of the political arena, they were always very interested spectators, and they could be electorally useful. In 1748 during a parliamentary by-election campaign in Northumberland, the Whigs complained that the Catholics were doing all they could to persuade their tenants to support Lancelot Allgood, the Tory candidate. When Sir George Savile, a proponent of Catholic Relief, stood for re-election as member for the county of York in 1780, he solicited William Constable's support and Constable offered his small Interest in the county to you, which from every tie of gratitude and respect I must ever devote to your service and beg you will direct as your superior judgement may suggest.[28]

Exclusion from political life was not altogether a bad thing, for although Catholics were denied the patronage, titles and other perquisites that went with political office, they avoided the inevitable unpleasantnesses of party strife and were spared the ruinous costs of electioneering as well as extended and expensive visits to London for each parliamentary session and Season which consumed the wealth of many land-owners. For similar reasons the penal laws were seen as a boon at the local level by Marmaduke Tunstall:

> I think no small benefit accrues to us at present from some of our disabling acts, as among others being exempted by them from being sheriffs and serving on juries, offices both troublesome and expensive.[29]

Their exclusion from parliament did not prevent Catholics campaigning for their own relief, however, and many of them became seasoned political lobbyists. After the turn of the century when Catholic Emancipation became a hotly contested issue they felt obliged to electioneer in support of the Whigs, and it was then financially downhill all the way.

One exclusion in particular irked the English Catholics, highly sensitive as they were to the charge of disloyalty. Although they were willing to risk their lives and to shed their blood in defence of their Protestant King, they were precluded from holding a military commission in his service. Thomas Sheldon, who was prevented from joining the army at the outbreak of the Napoleonic Wars, told his mother that being a Catholic was something he would not wish on his worst enemy. In 1789 Cuthbert Tunstall heard that

> A young man, one Dormer, a civil behaved person, a nephew of Lord Dormer, has just set up as wine-merchant at *our* Richmond [in Yorkshire] by the assistance of his Aunt Lady Shrewsbury. He served for four years aboard the royal navy, in which he saw a good deal of service and ever behaved well; was with Howe at the relief of Gibraltar and notwithstanding this could not even obtain a lieutenancy without taking the oaths of Supremacy &c. What a disgrace to this country at this time of day...[30]

John Silvertop offered his services at the outbreak of the war with France only to be rebuffed. His son George described what happened when General Musgrave, in command of the northern district, called at Minsteracres:

> to state to him his wish, that he would raise two troops of volunteer cavalry. My father willingly complied, and sent me up to London with the proposal. I had the honour of submitting to Mr Secretary Dundas, afterwards Lord Melville, the proposal, which was, that the clothing and equipment should be at my father's own expense, and the arms to be supplied by government. The proposal was accepted in terms most flattering towards my father. One troop was raised, cloth was bought, and other expenses incurred, when an official letter arrived stating that my father's commission could not be signed, he being a Roman Catholic!! I can most positively assert, that until the day of his death, this circumstance wounded and preyed upon his truly loyal and honourable mind.[31]

Significantly, if the decision in these matters had been left to the local commander there would have been no difficulty, but the formal reference to London was fatal.

Thomas Haggerston and George Silvertop were outraged at being denied commissions in the Northumbrian militias. It was only after the turn of the century that commissions were granted.

In 1803 when there were several invasion scares, George Silvertop was appointed Captain Commandant of the Derwent Rangers; he later occupied a similar position at the head of the Bywell Troop of Volunteer Yeomanry Cavalry. Two members of the Salvin family joined the Durham Volunteer Association, Sir Carnaby Haggerston raised the North Durham Troop of Volunteer Cavalry of some fifty men, and Thomas Selby of Biddleston commanded the Coquetdale Rangers. These were not highly important military appointments, but they did have symbolic value in that they allowed the Catholic gentry to make the same kind of contribution to the defence of their country against the French as their Protestant friends and neighbours. Such demonstrations of loyalty paved the way for the Relief Act of 1817 which indemnified Catholic naval and military officers from the consequences of not taking the Oath of Supremacy.[32]

The struggle for emancipation was so prolonged and hard-fought that many Catholics became extremely frustrated at the slow rate of progress. Apostasy therefore became a great temptation for any Catholic hankering after a service or parliamentary career, and some did give in. In 1756 Charles Brandling of Felling married a Protestant lady and they moved into a new mansion in Gosforth, north of Newcastle. He did not take a chaplain although he and six daughters were included in the 1767 return from Gosforth. But then: 'About the year 1771 Charles Brandling of Gosforth-hall renounced the Roman Catholic religion and became a Protestant of the Church of England.' He later became High Sheriff of Northumberland and Tory Member of Parliament for Newcastle upon Tyne without, it has been remarked, 'greatly affecting the course of history'.[33] Sir Thomas Gascoigne (VIII), the last of his line, was born and educated in France. He returned to Yorkshire in 1779 aged 34 and he apostatised the following year to enter parliament. He was so fervent a radical that, using stone he had ear-marked for a new mansion, he erected a triumphal arch at

Parlington to celebrate the French Revolution. (The Prince Regent refused to take lunch with him.)

Sir John Swinburne (VI) was also born in France and became a friend of Mirabeau and Wilkes. He returned to England on succeeding to the baronetcy in 1786 at the age of 25 and immediately renounced Catholicism. He wrote:

> It is absurd to sacrifice my consideration in my own country, my prospects in life, to condemn myself to eternal insignificance and oblivion for Tenets I did not believe and Ceremonies I never practised.

In December that year his uncle Henry Swinburne remarked:

> I have half persuaded the curate [chaplain] that the masses he has said on the altar of which you laid the first stone are not worth a farthing since you made the perilous leap.[34]

Henry Rutter, chaplain at Minsteracres, who thought the Swinburnes were 'all of a piece', was not in the least surprised when Sir John renounced 'the errors of Popery with a view, as it is believed, of sitting in parliament for this county; for there is a vacancy by the death of the Duke of Northumberland'. Swinburne had married Emilia Bennet, a niece of the duke and he hoped to succeed his kinsman Lord Percy as member for Northumberland when the latter was elevated to the dukedom. In the event Charles (afterwards Earl) Grey took the seat and Swinburne had to wait until 1788 before the duke could get him into the Commons as a member for Launceston, Cornwall. He also became Grand Master of his masonic lodge. Swinburne turned out to be a radical; he was described by his grandson Algernon, the poet, as 'one of the most extreme politicians' of his day. Barbara Charlton remarked that Swinburne and a Dr Fenwick rode about the county calling each other Citizen at the time of the French Revolution. Lady Swinburne also went about lisping 'all for equality' from the windows of her carriage and four, attended by two powdered footmen who were doubtless gritting their teeth. In general, however, the majority of Catholics held to their ancestral faith despite the secular disabilities it entailed.[35]

***

The third major difference between the Catholic and Anglican gentleman of the eighteenth century arose from the combined effects of the former's education and civil disabilities. The careful attention which had been given to his schooling and continental travel as well as his exclusion from public life meant that he had both learning and leisure, and, in not a few cases where prudent management of property and matrimonial strategy had paid off, money. These circumstances created a particular kind of gentleman: the scholar, the dilettante, the connoisseur. Obviously, not all English Catholic gentlemen were intellectuals or were the only people to pursue academic studies or that they were the best, but, relative to their number in the population as a whole, a disproportionately high number did achieve distinction in the arts and natural sciences and become celebrated members of the learned bodies which dominated the intellectual life of the nation. Around 11 per cent of the members of the Royal Society in the 1660s were Catholics, yet the Catholic population numbered no more than 2 per cent Scholarship had been pursued in recusant mansions around the country for over a century. The 'Towneley Group', founded by the Catholic Lancastrian Richard Towneley, became a flourishing scientific circle at his home near Burnley around the time of the Civil War, in parallel with similar research cooperatives emerging at Oxford and Cambridge and London. Towneley inherited from his father's generation a tradition of humanistic learning, strongly in favour of experimental, systematic natural philosophy. Among other things, he is regarded as a founding father of meteorology. Towneley and his colleagues were not obscure gentlemen-amateurs but associates and correspondents of Flamsteed, Gascoigne, Thoresby, Lister and many other men of science at home and abroad who were in almost constant touch on the scientific problems of the day. Robert Boyle cheerfully admitted that his Law originated as 'Mr Towneley's Hypothesis'.[36]

That scholarly outlook was emulated in many Catholic gentry families into the eighteenth century As a glance at the *Biographical Dictionaries* of John Kirk and Joseph Gillow and the *Oxford Dictionary of National Biography* shows, there were many like-minded Catholics at this time occupied with scientific or cultural research and amassing expert knowledge at home and abroad. There were also those trying to follow a professional career despite their formal exclusion. Those attracted to the law included: Mannock Strickland, Francis Plowden, John Maire, Edward Jerningham, Henry and Vincent Eyre, Charles Butler and Henry Clifford. Most of them became expert conveyancers but others practised as chamber-counsel until they were allowed to appear publicly at the bar after 1791. A number of Catholic gentlemen took to medicine and created private practices: Francis and James Eyre, Richard Worswick, John Maire, Sir Walter Blount and Charles Jerningham. There were authors, naturalists, travellers and artists such as Sir John Throckmorton, Henry Jerningham, Henry Swinburne, Giles Hussey and Charles Waterton. Many were elected Fellows of the Royal Society and the Society of Antiquaries, including a number of clerics.[37]

***

The foregoing general discussion of the factors governing the economy, public life and culture of the English Catholic gentry in the eighteenth century can be illustrated with particular examples. In the following pages it will be seen that families could adopt different strategies as they sought to survive as Catholic and economically viable dynasties given their peculiar standing in society and local circumstances.[38]

Silvertops appear in the parish registers of Ryton as yeomen from the late sixteenth century and were convicted recusants in the 1670s. In 1687 members of the family were confirmed by Bishop Leyburn in Newcastle. William Silvertop was viewer and steward of the collieries belonging to the Tempests of Stella, and his son Albert succeeded him in that occupation. The estate passed out of the family at the marriage of Jane Tempest to William, fourth baron Widdrington in 1700, but Albert Silvertop was retained in his employment. He was known as a hard-nosed businessman and agent, a characteristic which proved invaluable to his employer. He did all in his power to frustrate the exploitation of the estates in Ryton when they were held by William Cotesworth and Joseph Banks during a thirty-year sequestration consequent on Widdrington's participation in the 'Fifteen. Albert Silvertop also became a coal-owner on his own account, leasing property from Widdrington which he farmed and mined. He died in 1738 aged 71 having become a power in the coal trade, carving out for himself an enviable business in the face of considerable opposition from the Tyneside coaling magnates. He was an example of the hard-headed professional businessman who was taking over from the old gentry, rising from employee to employer. He laid the foundations of his family's fortune and his son George would consolidate that achievement and raise the Silvertops from trade to landed gentry.[39]

George Silvertop was a married man aged 33 when his father died. He had been involved in the coal industry all his adult life as steward of Anthony Meaburne's small coal estate at Pontop and he had assisted his father at Stella. He was thus well-qualified to take over as Widdrington's coal agent. George pursued his father's policy of aggressive independence and totally ignored the monopolistic pressures of the Newcastle coal-owners – the Company of

Hostmen and the Grand Allies. In 1742 they tried to isolate him by agreeing 'to consider of some proper method to find how and by whom Mr Silvertop vends his coals' but they were evidently powerless to keep him in check for seven years later they were still trying to 'restrain the said Mr Silvertop from exercising the said trade'. It is unlikely that anything could have been done because the vital infrastructure of wagonways, staiths and keelrooms at Stella were firmly under Widdrington-Silvertop control and no obstacles could be put in their way.[40]

By 1750 Silvertop had the second largest shareholding in the Stella Grand Lease and his business continued to expand. He bought a colliery in 1757, and in 1761 he bought another at Kyo from 'the heirs of Mrs Meaburne'. In 1767 there were twenty-one collieries on the Tyne producing a total vend of some 950,000 tons, of which the Silvertop collieries produced 10 per cent. His output was worth some £25,000 which was very similar to those of other coal-owners, and illustrates the parity that Silvertop had achieved with the magnates of the coal trade. He made further acquisitions of coaling property. Henry Francis Widdrington died childless in 1774 and the Ryton estates passed to his nephew Thomas Eyre of Hassop (who had married Mary Theresa, youngest daughter of the fourth Viscount Widdrington). Eyre was disinclined to take an active role in the business and therefore leased the whole of the Stella operation to Silvertop. Eyre received some £1,506 a year in rents and royalties from the collieries.[41]

Although we have no precise record of Silvertop's personal financial situation in these years he was clearly very successful, and the profitability of his coal business can be assessed by examining the growth of his personal landed estate. His father Albert had started the Minsteracres estate in 1721 and George bought up contiguous farms in the 1740s; in 1751 he converted the ninety-nine-year lease to one of a thousand years. In 1747 he bought the

Hartbushes estate from the Maires; in 1753 he bought a large farm at Common Crook for £1,100; in 1773 he bought another at Unthank for £3,000; in 1779 he bought land at Kyo for £2,500; and in 1781 he acquired five hundred and forty-three acres at Bolbec for £1,508. His major acquisition, however, was the Ponteland estate of Thomas Stapleton which he bought in 1776 for £22,200. He also bought a house in Cavendish Square, London.

Silvertop married Bridget Whittingham, of an old Lancashire recusant family, by whom he had six sons but all died young except John. He felt sufficiently secure by 1758 to describe himself as George Silvertop Esquire of Minsteracres and to apply for a grant of arms. Now that he was possessed of an extensive industrial and agricultural estate, and had achieved armigerous status, he took the predictable step of creating a country seat. In 1775 he moved into Hall Farm on the Minsteracres estate (where he had established a mission in 1765 with William Gibson as missioner and tutor to his son John). He concentrated on improving the grounds at Minsteracres and the park he devised was notable for its extent and its wealth of diverse foliage, including probably more variations of conifers than were to be found in any other part of the country. Silvertop was indulging the new enthusiasm for landscape gardening promoted by the Northumbrian Lancelot 'Capability' Brown. (A number of local gardens were redesigned at this time. On inheriting Hamsterley Hall in 1763, Henry Swinburne began to lay out the estate 'with a painter's eye'. In 1776, William Charlton had a plan drawn up for the re-design of his Hesleyside estate for which, family tradition has it, 'Capability' Brown was responsible.)[42]

Silvertop seems to have retired at about this time, handing over the coal business to his son John who re-negotiated the Stella Grand Lease, incidentally securing terms identical to those obtained by his father forty years earlier. George Silvertop died in 1769 aged 84 having achieved a great deal both socially and industrially. As an obituarist rightly remarked

> He was one of the leading coal-owners in his day, of extensive knowledge and of strict honour and integrity, he had travelled and had been introduced to all the foreign courts of Europe, and was so much respected that his famous Whitefield coals had the preference of all other collieries on the Continent. By his industry he had accumulated an ample fortune honourably got.[43]

In 1772 John Silvertop married Catherine Lawson of Brough, heiress to the estate of the Lartington Maires, and the couple lived in Benwell House, Newcastle, where they had a chaplain, John Taylor. They moved to Stella House in 1779 when John took over the family business. In contrast to his father, who had devoted his energies to the acquisition of wealth, John preferred to enjoy it, and he was the first of the family to adopt fully the lifestyle of an English sporting country gentleman. Although he maintained a close interest in his coal enterprises, his attention seems to have been concentrated on the completion of the mansion at Minsteracres, planned by his father. It was built between 1798 and 1800, incorporating such innovations as water-closets and bathrooms. He died suddenly in 1801 aged 51. His yearly income had been about £8,000, but his capital expenditure on the house had been, heavy, no doubt based on future coal profits and on his wife's expectations. He left debts amounting to some £59,000 which could not be paid out of his personal estate and his heir, George, had to obtain a private act of parliament permitting him to sell parts of the entailed real estate. In a complicated settlement George actually came out with a profit. The Minsteracres estate of some two thousand acres (worth £50,000) and the coal business were left intact so that the family was by no means embarrassed.[44]

The bachelor George Silvertop became head of the family at the age of 27. He was born at Benwell House and educated at Douai. At the outbreak of the French Revolution he returned to England and completed his education at Old Hall. He inherited the estate in the middle of the war when he was preoccupied with military matters. His immediate concern was to resolve the financial mess left by his father, but when that was sorted out he made it clear that his interests did not lie with industry and, from 1803, he began to lease his collieries to (Catholic) entrepreneurs. The Silvertops, who had been in the forefront of industrial capitalism for over a century, dropped out of the coal trade. This was not altogether unexpected, or inappropriate, for that matter. Unlike his father and grandfather, George had no experience of the business before succeeding to the family estate. In any case, the collieries on the upper Tyne had had their day; mining had moved eastward along the Tyne and to new pits on the east Durham plateau. The Silvertop interests were left on the periphery and were becoming progressively less important.

George Silvertop was to some extent compelled to withdraw from an active industrial life, but he was inclined to take such a course for he was less a business-man than an intellectual. He was a founder member of the Catholic Board and from 1808 he was prominent in the campaign for Catholic Emancipation. His 'liberal' Catholic views were not always approved by the vicars apostolic and he, like many other leading Catholics, rallied to the Whigs and was often to be seen on the hustings. In the general election of 1826, he spent a great deal of time electioneering for Lord Howick, and his last public appearance was in 1847 soliciting support for Lord Harry Vane at Darlington. In 1831 he was pricked for High Sheriff of Northumberland and it seems he was offered a parliamentary seat on several occasions. George died in 1849, bringing the direct line of Silvertops to an end.[45]

The upward social mobility achieved by the Silvertops was exceptional, though not unique; the Dunns and Humbles were other plebeian Catholic families to enjoy successful industrial and social careers at about the same time and for similar reasons: entrepreneurial ambition and efficiency. In one sense, however, upwardly mobile families had an advantage in that they were free from any concerns about the preservation of an ancient name and landed inheritance. Their outlook might have been more cautious if they had had a family history of sequestrations and feared further losses. To ascertain the effect of that kind of constraint on industrial or commercial entrepreneurship, we can compare the behaviour of two families of long-standing gentry status.

***

The Brandlings rose to prominence in the political and economic life of north-east England in the sixteenth century. Members of the family sat in parliament for Newcastle and others became mayors, sheriffs and aldermen of Newcastle and of Northumberland. As successful businessmen, there were always Brandlings in the Company of Merchant Adventurers and in the Company of Hostmen. The family owned property in Newcastle, Gosforth, Jesmond and Broxfield in Northumberland, and Felling in Durham. In Elizabethan times the Brandlings were to be found on the fringes of recusancy, but they all conformed in the Jacobean period. They gravitated back into Catholicism in the middle of the seventeenth century when Charles Brandling (c.1620-1666), an Anglican and royalist colonel, married the Catholic Ann Widdrington in 1651; all five of their children were raised as Catholics.[46]

The estates passed to Ralph Brandling who was born at Alnwick Abbey, the family seat. He entered Gray's Inn in 1685. On his return to the north Ralph sold Alnwick Abbey and settled at Felling Hall, taking a chaplain. He was chosen by James II as one of the new corporation of Newcastle. Although dismissed in 1689, he remained conspicuous in the region both as a Tyneside coalmaster and a papist. Ralph began the development of coal-mining at Felling and he attempted to exploit the coal deposits at Plessey and Newsham near Blyth, estates which he bought in 1690, mortgaging Felling to do so. But he seems to have over-reached himself for he sold Plessey and Newsham to his fellow-Catholics Lord Widdrington and Thomas Riddell shortly afterwards and was unable to redeem the Felling mortgage. When he registered his estates in 1717 he stated that the yearly rent of £140 on the Felling colliery and the coal-royalties of ten shillings a ton were being paid to the trustees of Thomas Owen 'who was entitled to a forfeited mortgage for the sum of £3,400'. This meant that Brandling received no income from his principal property, but he was by no means a poor man; he owned coaling properties at Gosforth, Jesmond and Bensham which, together with other wayleave, wagonway, staith and keelroom rents, provided him with a respectable income of some £1,500 a year. Furthermore he had removed to live at Middleton in the West Riding of Yorkshire, where, in 1697, he married Ann Leigh, the Catholic heiress of Middleton Hall. The Middleton estate which Ralph acquired on his marriage included 'A Wrought Colliery or Coal Mine with a Water Engine and Smithy' which enjoyed the monopoly of the large and profitable Leeds coal market. Unsurprisingly, the Middleton colliery became his main concern; indeed, when in 1716 he recovered the Felling colliery he immediately re-let it at £300 a year. Negotiations over that lease had begun in 1715 but were delayed because of his imprisonment in York Castle 'on account of Religion'.[47]

Brandling died childless in 1749 and the estates passed to his nephew Ralph who lived at Felling, but he died within a month of his uncle, and the estates passed to his younger brother Charles Brandling, then aged 18. He, no doubt highly gratified at coming into a large fortune so unexpectedly, built a new mansion at

Gosforth, leaving his widowed mother in residence at Felling Hall, and the Middleton estate under the superintendence of (the Northumbrian Catholic) Richard Humble. In 1756 Charles married a Protestant lady, Elizabeth Thompson of Shotton, County Durham. Charles Brandling devoted himself to the substantial and flourishing coal business at Middleton, Felling and Gosforth, and he introduced new technology into the mines.[48]

The perennial problem of all colliery owners in the eighteenth century was that of getting the coal to the consumer. Compared with the actual mining operation, transport was always more difficult and expensive, and any means of reducing costs was always welcomed. The three-mile journey between Middleton and Leeds was undertaken by pack horse and river barge; not only was this costly, it was slow and was a restraint on coal output. Brandling, no doubt advised by Humble, decided to introduce a modern transport system. In 1758 he sought parliamentary approval for a railway 'such as is used for and about the coal works and coal mines in the Counties of Durham and Northumberland', and secured an act 'for laying down a Waggon-way, in order for the better supplying the Town and neighbourhood of Leeds, in the county of York, with coals.' This was the first act of parliament to authorise the construction of a railway, and it marked the birth of a new era in the English coal trade. The act stipulated that Brandling was to supply not less than 24,000 tons of coal a year, a 'contract' worth about £5,000 a year. Brandling obtained a second act in 1779 empowering him to double his output and to increase the price of coal, making the colliery worth £12,000 a year. John Smeaton designed and installed a Newcomen steam engine at Middleton in the following year. A third act, of 1793, permitted a further price rise and brought Brandling almost £14,080 a year. By the end of the century the average annual output of the colliery was 76,500 tons of coal worth £27,000. Brandling was equally enterprising at Felling; a steam engine was installed in 1776 and a deep pit was won there three years later.[49]

As a successful coal-owner in three counties, Brandling had amassed a considerable fortune by the time he was 35 years old, and he doubtless commanded respect and consideration from his fellow coal-owners. He was, however, a Catholic and, as such, was excluded from the honours and offices normally associated with men of his standing; he could not even be appointed a Justice of the Peace, the least he might have expected. These affronts must have seemed particularly absurd given that he had been permitted to sponsor three important acts of parliament. Such deprivations were borne by other Catholic gentlemen, more or less with equanimity, but not by Brandling, and he apostatized. His defection may have been based on religious doubts, of course, but his parents were converts, his wife was not a Catholic and, although the first eight of his seventeen children were girls and were brought up as Catholics, his son and heir was raised an Anglican. It is difficult to avoid the conclusion that Brandling's Catholicism was lightly borne and that he found it impossible to live as a gentleman outside the established church: he was not prepared to have his ambitions thwarted for refusing Anglican Communion. At any rate, in 1781 he was pricked for High Sheriff of Northumberland and in 1784 he was elected to parliament as member for Newcastle (offices which, he no doubt recalled, had been held by many of his forbears). Gosforth Hall became the centre of Tory political life in south Northumberland. Brandling's lapse, therefore, seems to have been motivated by social and political ambition which over-rode his ecclesiastical allegiance.[50]

***

For some six centuries an uninterrupted succession of Salvins has been in possession of Croxdale Hall in the parish of St. Oswald south of Durham.[51] Their post-reformation history is not one of solid recusancy but by the end of the seventeenth century they had settled firmly for Catholicism and had begun to keep a chaplain at Croxdale. Nonetheless, although many Salvin boys were educated at Douai, none became priests.[52] Throughout the eighteenth century they avoided the more public manifestations of their religion. No Salvin took part in the rising of 1715 and hence no property was sequestrated or confiscated. They did little to further the cause of Catholic relief or emancipation. That policy kept the family estates intact and allowed the Salvins to maintain their position as major land-owners in the county and to enter the nineteenth century on a firm economic footing.

A list of Catholic 'Persons of Quality' of 1704 placed the Salvins (and Maires of Esh) in the category of 'Gentlemen of considerable Estates', that is, with property having a value of more than £1,000. Gerard (V) registered his estates in 1717. He received a yearly income of £760 in rents from farms in Croxdale, Sunderland Bridge, Shotton, Wolviston, Burntoft, Butterwick and Owton. His son Bryan (II) registered an estate worth £400 a year from farms at Butterwick and Elwick. His cousin Ralph (II) registered property at Tudhoe, parts of which he had inherited from his uncle Ralph (I) in 1705, and parts of which he bought between 1717 and 1724; this estate was worth £419 a year. By the 1750s all the Salvin estates in Durham had devolved into the possession of William (II) and he received an income of £2,156 yearly in rents.[53]

The Salvin estates consisted predominantly of farms but attempts at raising non-agricultural revenue were made in the seventeenth and eighteenth centuries. A brief venture into lead-mining came to nothing, but paper-making was more successful: Croxdale Paper Mill was the first to be established in the county. Gerard (V) registered it in 1717 (worth £9) and its rental value steadily increased. William Salvin rebuilt the mill in 1771 and leased it out for twenty-one years (at £72 a year). An additional drying house was built in 1792 and the mill was again rebuilt in 1816 by William Thomas Salvin, and leased at a yearly rent of £154. An account between Salvin and the lessee shows that the mill had a turnover of £6,000 in 1812. In 1820 Salvin bought an estate and paper mill at Butterby. He modernised the plant with steam engines, and replaced the waterwheel with a rotary engine (a recent invention). The mills at Butterby and Croxdale mill were leased at an overall yearly rent of £250, not including royalties. Papermaking at Croxdale, then, was a continuous and expanding enterprise from its inception, and the Salvins kept pace with technological change. If the turnover of £6,000 achieved in 1812 was typical, and if a return of five per cent was made (as it was in the coal industry), then Salvin would have got about £500 a year from the operation and that kind of return would certainly justify his investment in new machinery. Forestry, a related activity, was another major source of income. Around 1725 Bryan Salvin (II) undertook a large-scale tree-planting programme. In 1768 W. T. Salvin could say,

> I have made many thousands of pounds by the industry of my G—father Bryan Salvin without doing any injury to the picturesque Beauty of Croxdale. But I have done much to improve the place and such I hope that those that come after me will find it with a treasure of timber.

Throughout the eighteenth century the Salvins obtained a very substantial living from agricultural rents and papermaking revenue and they could reasonably be described as affluent. Croxdale Hall was rebuilt in 1758 (a chapel was added in 1807); and towards the end of the century William (II) had £60,000 invested in government stocks. In 1806 his successor W. T. Salvin bought the Burn Hall estate nearby for his 27-year-old bachelor brother Bryan. The latter bought the neighbouring Farewell Hall estate in 1834 with an eye to colliery development which, together with the railways, was about to transform rural Durham.[54]

Thomas Meynell, squire of Yarm and a wealthy Catholic merchant, was a leading promoter of a railway to link the coalfield around Auckland with the port of Stockton near the mouth of the Tees which would afford 'a flattering prospect of indemnifying the proprietors'. He organised a technical survey, the results of which swung opinion behind the railway in 1818. Although the enterprise came to be dominated by Quaker interests, Meynell was elected first chairman of the Stockton and Darlington Railway Company in 1821 and he remained in office until 1829. (He engaged Ignatius Bonomi as the company's architect.) The inauguration of the Stockton and Darlington railway took place on 23 May 1822 when, accompanied by the Quaker Benjamin Flounders and two Catholic priests (Thomas Storey of Stockton and John Bradley of Yarm), Meynell arrived in Stockton to lay the first rails. The line was completed three years later and officially opened with a ceremonial journey from Witton Park colliery to Stockton. Meynell took the chair at the celebration dinner flanked by William Wright of Kelvedon, the Catholic banker, and by W. T. Salvin. Salvin presumably owed his place at the top table to his friendship with Meynell rather than to any involvement with the railway in which he had no financial interest. The occasion, however, was his introduction to the newly emergent industry and he was sufficiently impressed with its potential that he became deeply involved both paternally and financially.[55]

Edward John Salvin (third son of W. T. Salvin) became 17 years of age in 1827 and it was proposed that he be apprenticed to George Stephenson, the leading railway engineer. Stephenson had refused to take other lads, so W. T. Salvin made an approach through Meynell. Stephenson agreed to take Edward for five, six or seven years for two hundred guineas. Edward took up the apprenticeship at Liverpool but in April 1830 he died. At the same time as arranging his son's apprenticeship, W. T. Salvin became interested in the railways as an investment. Some of his landholdings lay over the central Durham coalfield and a line to Hartlepool had been under consideration for some time. Salvin took forty £100 shares in the Clarence Railway (1828) initially and subscribed a further £550 a year or so later. He did not limit his investments to local railways. He was in regular correspondence with Stephenson who continually pressed him to take shares in his railway concerns and he did so. He invested some £3,000 in the Leicester and Swannington Railway of 1830, becoming one of the largest shareholders. Salvin also invested £1,250 in the London and Birmingham Railway. Stephenson therefore acted as investment adviser to Salvin in the critical early years of the railway age. This association between the leading railway engineer of the day and the rather shrewd Catholic country gentleman began with the apprenticeship of the latter's son, but it developed into a mutually beneficial commercial relationship. Stephenson sought private finance for the railways with which he was concerned, and Salvin required sound projects for capital investment.

In 1832 Salvin invested in and was elected to the board of the newly formed Hartlepool Dock and Railway Company which was intended to open the port to the mid-Durham coalfield, a project which Stephenson disdained: 'I think very few of the North country Railways will be good investments'. He listed those Railways which he considered 'safe concerns', and except for the Stockton and Darlington railway all were in the midlands and south and mostly his own ventures. Whereas Salvin was a purely passive investor in the midlands railways, however, his interest in the Durham lines arose from an active concern for marketing coal from mines close to his estates and from a colliery he hoped would be established on his own land. Thus, although he normally took Stephenson's investment advice, and was probably despondent at his lack of confidence in the northern lines, Salvin was committed to them for reasons of industrial development rather than capital gain and he could not easily withdraw his backing. Robert Stephenson's assessment that the Hartlepool line would be of greater value to coal-owners than to railway shareholders was not altogether unwelcome, for Salvin hoped soon to be both.[56]

All Durham land-owners assumed that coal was present and winnable under their lands, and at one time or another they attempted to get it out themselves or through agents. W. T. Salvin was receiving an increasing income (£800 in 1834) in coal royalties from Lord Londonderry, to whom he had leased his south-west Durham properties in the neighbourhood of Wynyard (Burntoft, Tofts, Butterwick and Owton). The county was in a ferment of industrial development and in 1837 the Salvins decided to try for coal. W. T. Salvin was then aged 70 and his brother Bryan John, of Burn Hall, was 58. Borings were made at Croxdale, Farewell Hall and Tudhoe. At the same time, the Durham and Sunderland Railway Company began to lay a branch line from Sherburn to serve Shincliffe, Houghall and Croxdale collieries. Doubtless the family anticipated a lasting and profitable exploitation of their mineral assets as a complement to their railway interests. Their optimism would, however, be short-lived. A geological fault intruded into the locality and a catastrophic explosion at Croxdale rendered the pit wholly unworkable. Moreover, the quality of coal mined at Farewell was inferior and unprofitable to mine. Tudhoe to the south, however, was well clear of the fault and coal-mining was notably successful there for many years. [57]

The role of W. T. Salvin in the formative years of the railway industry was to contribute to the capital requirements of new lines in Durham and to provide 'outside' rentier finance for distant projects. In the absence of an organised national capital market, the private investor was a key source of finance and, until experience and confidence grew, those investors in the railways ran considerable risks. It is not surprising, therefore, that Salvin did not speculate in railway shares but took care to obtain the best advice and to invest only in schemes which were either safe or of immediate relevance to his own estate development.

W. T. Salvin and his brother died in 1842. The opening of the Croxdale and Tudhoe estates to coal-mining was the last commercial decision they made, although some of those plans came to nought. The Croxdale estate passed to Gerard (VII), and the Burn Hall and Farewell Hall estates were bequeathed by Bryan John to his nephew Marmaduke, younger brother of Gerard. Despite the collapse of coal-mining at Croxdale, Gerard maintained his father's involvement in the railways and Marmaduke had the colliery at Tudhoe. The evidence given here shows that from an early date the Salvins were as committed to industrial capitalism as any other Durham land-owning family. Marmaduke Salvin summarised this approach in a remark he made to his brother Gerard in 1845, 'I am all for making money and encouraging industry'.[58] Religion had nothing to do with it.

***

The pursuit of the arts and sciences among the Catholic higher classes during the period has been remarked upon earlier, and one family exemplifies particularly well how those interests flourished in the north-east. The Tunstalls of Thurland Castle in Lancashire migrated to Wycliffe in the North Riding in the first half of the seventeenth century. Francis Tunstall (1637–1713) married Cecily, sister of William Constable (1654–1718) of Burton Constable in the East Riding. Tunstall had four daughters, who all became nuns at St. Monica's in Louvain, and two sons who survived into adulthood. Marmaduke Tunstall was over 40 when he inherited the patrimonial estate of Wycliffe in 1713. Little is known of him but he seems to have followed the traditional way of life of a country gentleman: managing the family estate with his father and then as squire in his own right; around 1719 he had £1,287 a year, making him the wealthiest Catholic commoner in the county. The family kept a chaplain from the reign of James II and the first four vicars apostolic lived at Wycliffe at various times; a chapel was added to the house in 1748.[59]

More is known of his younger brother Cuthbert Tunstall who was born about 1680. He was educated at Douai and went on to graduate as Master of Arts and Doctor of Medicine in 1707 at Montpellier, where a number of English Catholics qualified as physicians. In 1719 he registered an income of £427 a year, his share of the Wycliffe estate, but, in August 1718, and conditional on his assuming the name of Constable, he inherited Burton Constable from his maternal uncle who had died without issue aged about 64. In addition to his medical interests, Cuthbert was a bibliophile, an antiquarian and an experimental scientist; he was well versed in ancient and modern languages and he corresponded with many of the literati of the day. He began the remodelling of the redbrick Elizabethan and Jacobean mansion at Burton Constable, a project which his son would complete; between them they transformed it into an impressive Georgian house. A small domestic chapel on the top floor of the south tower of the mansion was served by a resident chaplain until the end of the seventeenth century, but he then moved out to the village of Marton nearby, though still under the family's patronage.[60]

Cuthbert Constable was twice married; firstly in 1719 to Amey Clifford, the 14-year-old daughter of Lord Clifford of Chudleigh, by whom he had two daughters, and a son William who was born on 31 December 1721. William was tutored privately at home until he was 15, partly perhaps by the priest at Marton. William was sent to Douai in July 1737 but in January 1739 he left for an unnamed college at Rouen 'by order of his father'. The reason is not given but it seems that he, or his father, found the syllabus at Douai did not meet his more detailed scientific interests. At any rate, Constable completed his education in 1742 with a period in the environs of Paris engaged in scientific study under the supervision of a Dr Molyneux. He probably returned home fairly soon, however, it being increasingly unwise for a young Catholic gentleman to be dawdling around the French capital when it was clear that the Jacobites at St. Germain were planning a second rising, even if the Constables were not known to be supporters of the Stuarts. William remained single until he was 54 when, in December 1775, he married Catherine, the youngest sister of Philip Langdale, the Catholic squire of Houghton Hall in the parish of Sancton, some sixteen miles to the west of Burton Constable.[61]

Amey Constable, aged 26 and six months pregnant, died in July 1731 of small-pox and in 1735 Cuthbert took as his second wife, Elizabeth, daughter of George Heneage of Hainton, Lincolnshire, by whom Marmaduke Cuthbert Constable was born in July 1743. His father died four years later and William, 26 years old, adopted a paternal interest in his young half-brother. Marmaduke ('Dukey') went to Douai College at the age of 14 and had progressed to Logic by 1760 but at that point William intervened to recommend that he do his Philosophy under a tutor at Paris. The study

> is chiefly experimental, and the experiments are infinitely better performed at Paris than at Douai. He might during the progress of the year see all the best Cabinets relating to the study of Natural Philosophy.[62]

William's desire to get Marmaduke out of Douai was not only because of the shortcomings of the syllabus as with the fact that Marmaduke had just become very wealthy, having inherited the Wycliffe estates from his uncle Marmaduke Tunstall who had died in 1760, and he was, of course, William's heir-presumptive as well. William's real fear, as he told the young man's mother, was that

Douai and the Gentlemen [secular priests] thereunto belonging would not only endeavour to persuade Dukey to stay his Philosophy out, but his Divinity too if it lay in their power[. S]taff would try to persuade Marmaduke to stay on to study for the priesthood. You, dear Madam, are too good and too generous to suspect good people of interested views, but most of the individuals are so, and all Communitys [the Regulars]. The first low born, poor and indigent, are always crying at first for much drink and clothes and then for what they can get. And Communitys have always the excuse that they act for the body but was it for themselves, they assure you, if you will believe them, that they desire not a farthing ... What immense sums have the priests got from Lady [illeg.]. Mr Mitchell paid the Clergy £22,000 which ou[gh]t to have been ours and many a family have they thus ruined. Their business is Spirituals but as to Temporals, whenever they meddle they act out of character and not therefore to be trusted.[63]

Marmaduke was a highly eligible 18-year-old and destined for marriage not the priesthood. 'Miss Petre[64] with £12,000 a year' was already being talked of for him, and William was thinking about the social possibilities of the Parisian scene. Marmaduke could

have without inconveniencing his studies, or interrupting them, the best Dancing Master and a Fencing Master ... as our friend seems chiefly to want a genteel carriage and perhaps confidence ... for young men are naturally so fond of riding horses that they seldom pay much attention to other exercises, and the dress and graces belonging to excellence in horsemanship are not very compatible with the delicacy of the dance.

William suggested that after a year or so in Paris Marmaduke might go to the Academy in Angers and enter the company of young people, company which he must come into some time or other. He might accustom himself to the company of ladies, gentlemen, fiddles, dance with young women, and have some little vanity as to person and gentility, without which, Madam, we men, no more than ladies, neither hold up our heads nor turn out our toes.

So, Marmaduke left Douai without undertaking the Philosophy course and he was in Paris during 1762, but the date of his return to England is not known. In accordance with the terms of his uncle's will he had adopted the name of Tunstall and he was thenceforth known as Marmaduke Tunstall. He spent much of his time researching in natural history, living partly in Yorkshire but mostly at his London town-house in Welbeck Street. Despite his mother's expectations, Marmaduke remained a bachelor until 1776 when, aged 33, he married Mary, heiress of George Markham of Hoxley, Nottinghamshire and he began to spend more of his time in the north.

William Constable and his half-brother Marmaduke Tunstall were twenty-two years apart in age. Tunstall married in his early thirties but Constable remained a bachelor until he was well into middle-age. Marmaduke enjoyed good health but William was something of a valetudinarian, yet the former died at the age of 47 while the latter lived until he was 71; they died within six months of each other and neither left issue. Although they came from the same background and shared many interests, their outlook differed in some ways and whereas William did the Grand Tour (1769–1771)[65] Marmaduke was content with Yorkshire and London. His intellectual outlook and pursuits are of particular interest here and can be illustrated from his papers.

Though unambiguously Catholic, Tunstall was very much an ecclesiastical liberal. He willingly stood as godfather to a Quaker child; he quite admired Wesley, 'the old Patriarch of the Methodists', and he cherished a close friendship with Thomas Zouch, the Anglican incumbent at Wycliffe. He applauded the toleration of Protestants in France and he hoped that the 'liberty nobly extensive in religious matters in the United States, Virginia particularly, should prove a model to the Mother-Country'. And when it came to negotiating the second Catholic Relief Bill, Tunstall, like Constable, thought that toleration would prevail in the long run ('even in *Scotland* and *Portugal*' and 'in spite of Scotch Synods and Spanish Inquisition') and it was not worth arguing about now, else 'the hackneyed cry of popery, that dreadful bugbear, may be again renewed'. Anyway, as he said in 1786, the first Relief Act of 1780 had done enough to satisfy him:

> We are at present tolerably easy in our situation, the tumults &c [the Gordon Riots] have pretty well subsided [and] our embarrassments in regard to property seem nearly done away by the late repeals

and it would be prudent therefore to let sleeping dogs lie. In any case, he deplored the divisions within the Catholic Committee and he disapproved of Charles Butler's tactics, and he would have nothing to do with it or him:

> I am no Tory and think the mad conduct of James [II] could scarce at any time have failed to hurl him from his throne [but] perhaps the churlish easterly wind in November [1688], which wafted over our great deliverer, did much less mischief than many since.

In 1790 he proposed that the current negotiations be adjourned *sine die,* or until the Catholics were united.[66]

Tunstall was perfectly happy with his lot as a country landowner, collector and naturalist, and did not want the way of life he had enjoyed for so many years threatened. He had been elected Fellow of the Society of Antiquaries in 1764, at the age of 21, and Fellow of the Royal Society six years later in recognition of his ornithological research (His *Ornithologia Brittanica* came out in 1771). He carried on a correspondence with many distinguished scholars and formed an extensive cabinet of natural history. It was in connection with the societies and his collections that he spent most of the month in London, travelling by sea from Stockton or Yarm. From about 1773, however, he began to devote his efforts to the refurbishment of the 'long-neglected house and grounds' at Wycliffe. The mansion was ready for re-occupation by 1780 and the Tunstalls closed their London house. For the last ten years of his life, when he was not occupied in managing his estate, Tunstall immersed himself in his extensive library, gallery, museum of antiquities and collection of stuffed birds (on which he spent some £5,000), enjoying a way of life much like that of Constable in Holderness.[67]

Tunstall aired many of his preoccupations in his letters to Constable and to his uncle W. T. Salvin. As may be imagined, he expatiated on his antiquarian and ornithological studies. He bought most books on travel and natural history as they came out and he reviewed them uninhibitedly. Gilbert White of Selborne was a 'pedantic little parson' whose book contained many insignificant minutiae and curious observations. William Hutchinson's *Durham* was interesting enough but he hoped that succeeding volumes would be more entertaining. Tunstall followed international affairs, about which, however, he was not always percipient: the French, he said, would not be able to cope with liberty and 'the King and royal party will be at last called back to resume their royal power'. Closer to home he thought the nation would 'bear much more with the errors of a Prince of Wales' than with a king's, but he hoped nonetheless that there would be no issue from the Prince's marriage with Maria Fitzherbert. He was especially scathing about slavery and he execrated the West Indian slave-owners.[68]

Catholic affairs were of consuming interest, of course: the campaign for Relief, the land tax, the Gordon riots, and the births, marriages and deaths of the great national Catholic cousinage. But he also had, perforce, to note the less salubrious goings-on of the brethren. Gaming, he said, had been 'carried to a great height in the Capital and by none more than by *our people*'; Lord Stourton had lost over £30,000 at one sitting and Thomas Giffard, the wealthy young Staffordshire squire, having lost at the tables, hoped to get out of trouble by marrying the non-Catholic Lord Courtney's daughter, but, Tunstall gloated, 'her fortune will not repair his finances much, being, as I am told, only £5,000'. Giffard had to live at Rouen on an allowance for six or seven years until his fortunes were restored. The current apostasies were also remarked upon: 'Hear the poet [Edward] Jerningham has renounced the errors &c. no great loss [to us] nor gain to his new friends'. Tunstall discussed various genealogical questions on his own pedigree and those of others. On one occasion he solicited Constable's assistance with the Customs on behalf of Francis Eyre who had consigned his luggage from Leghorn to Hull. Eyre was entirely willing to pay the duty but he wanted to prevent his books, prints, and marbles being damaged and 'some books of the Gregorian notes &c being seized on as *popish* books'. Tunstall had very little to say about the clergy – he never mentioned his chaplains.[69]

Tunstall wrote a great deal on personal legal and financial matters, his mortgages, trusteeships, annuities, and so on. He held the presentation to the Anglican living of Wycliffe and, despite objections from Oxford University, he sold it for £400 to George Allan of Darlington who wanted it for one of his sons. The weather fills many a page, especially when it affects the harvest or the bag of partridge and moor-game. His house-guests; the price of cattle; his need for fawns to balance the number of buck; the quality of Salvin's home-grown grapes and pineapples; the capacity of his tenants to pay their rents; and the difficulty of finding sober and reliable out-door staff who knew a bit about horticulture, all feature in the letters. Like many others he found particular pleasure in writing about his colds and his gout; he gained some benefit by taking the waters at Bath, though his enthusiasm for the better Burgundies seems not to have improved matters. He died in 1790, in his forty-eighth year.[70]

***

In 1790 there were some two hundred and fifty English Catholic gentry families. As in any social group there were gains and losses. Upward and downward social mobility, extravagance and the extinction of ancient names through natural causes are not exclusive to any one element in society, religious or secular, but are common to all. The number of Catholic gentry families had halved during the century, but they had become richer. Indeed, Catholics did rather better for themselves in the wake of the Jacobite risings and as members of a proscribed body than they might have had reason to expect. This was partly because of the amalgamation of estates through marriage, as cadet branches died out and as main lines allied with each other; and it was because of a general rise in prosperity.[71] It can, however, also be attributed to certain unintended consequences of the penal laws which had been intended to impoverish the Catholic gentry but, by forcing them to concentrate on the maintenance of their houses and the productivity of their estates, had the opposite effect. Survival had become more of an economic than a legal problem. Families in possession of large landed estates which were prudently managed survived without difficulty; just as those having property in developing areas prospered. The role of the Catholic gentry of County Durham in coal-mining and in the early stages of railway development has been examined here, and Catholics in Northumberland, Lancashire and Yorkshire were similarly entrepreneurial.

The Silvertops flaunted their Catholicism and yet can be numbered among the principal coal-mining capitalists in the region. The Brandlings lapsed from Catholicism to gain political preferment but that does not detract from the enterprising spirit of their Catholic period. The Salvins kept their religion in the background while prospering on a rising income from agriculture, forestry and paper-making and by investing in the latest transport technology. The Haggerston estates were the main source of dairy produce for the markets of Berwick and they steadily increased in value from £2,200 in 1720 to £5,450 fifty years later. This is almost exactly the same increase achieved by the Everingham estates which brought £2,500 in 1700 and £5,000 in 1800. Both Marmaduke Tunstall and William Constable died without issue and left their estates to Edward Sheldon, a nephew; he is said to have come into an income of £16,000 a year and could afford to give £2,000 a year to charity. Throughout the north Catholics could be found wherever industrial potential seemed promising. Sir Henry Lawson (1750–1834) of Brough was 'a very shrewd man of affairs with an eye to every possible source of profit', and Lancashire Catholics have been described as being 'as adroit as any at seizing the opportunities offered to the sharp *entrepreneur*'. Their religion was irrelevant; what really mattered was having the right kind of property and the right frame of mind to develop it.[72]

In the same way, the penal laws which excluded Catholics from the universities and the professions drove the Catholic gentry abroad for an education; the result was that most of them, girls as well as boys, and those of relatively minor rank, obtained a higher level of education and an access to European culture that they might not otherwise have had and which was not common among their non-Catholic social peers. Many of them acquired a solidly-based intellectual reputation and made significant contributions to science; others were responsible for bringing important collections of paintings, antiquities and *objets d'art* into England; they have been described as a cousinhood of Catholic antiquarians and bibliophiles.[73]

On the whole, then, the English Catholic gentry of the eighteenth century practised their religion discreetly but that did not prevent them making the best of their economic opportunities and enjoying an outgoing social and sporting country life, enhanced by a variety of cultural pursuits, artistic and scientific, which kept them in the social and intellectual mainstream. Crucially, they were untroubled by the sordid business of party-political strife. It may be thought superficial that in the later decades of the eighteenth century the Catholic gentry came to have a certain social prestige and were regarded as the untitled nobility of England so that it even became highly fashionable to be a Catholic, but that achievement would serve them well in the political arena when the question of Catholic Relief and Emancipation came to the forefront of public affairs.[74]

Notes

[1] Examples are given in L. Gooch, *From Jacobite to Radical: The Catholics of North-East England 1688–1850* (PhD thesis, University of Durham, 1989), ch. 1.

[2] F. Colman, 'A History of Barwick in Elmet' in *Thoresby Society* 17 (1908), p. 154 n. 2.

[3] E. Hughes, *North Country Life in the Eighteenth Century: The North-East 1700–1750* (Oxford University Press, 1952), p. xvii. See L. Gooch, *The Desperate Faction?: The Jacobites of North-East England, 1688–1745* (The University of Hull Press, 1995), Preface, p. xii for other culprits.

[4] N. Mitford, *Love in a Cold Climate* (London: Hamish Hamilton, 1949), ch. 1.

[5] P. Roebuck, (ed.) *Constable of Everingham Estate Correspondence 1726–1743* (Yorkshire Archaeological Society, 136, 1976), passim.

[6] L. Gooch, 'The Religion for a Gentleman: The Northern Catholic Gentry

in the Eighteenth Century' in *Recusant History* [RH] 23/4 (1997), n. 4.

7 M. Blundell (ed.), *Blundell's Diary and Letter Book 1702-28* (Liverpool University Press, 1952), pp. 216-218; M. Lancaster, *The Tempests of Broughton* (Broughton, H. Tempest, 1987), p. 95; G. Greene, *Collected Essays* (London: Bodley Head, 1969), p. 260.

8 G. Smith, *In Well Beware* (Kineton: The Roundwood Press, 1978), p. 95; Gooch, *Desperate Faction?* pp. 38-41, 63-68.

9 J. C. H. Aveling, *The Handle and the Axe* (London: Blond & Briggs, 1976), p. 277.

10 J. C. H. Aveling, *Catholic Recusancy in the City of York 1558-1791* (Catholic Record Society [CRS] Monograph 2, 1970), pp. 125/126.

11 *The Memoirs of the Life of Edward Gibbon with Various Observations and Excursions, by Himself* ([1737-1794]; London: Methuen, 1900), pp. 50-67; I. Collins, *Jane Austen and the Clergy* (London: Hambledon Press, 1993), p. 37; N. Hans, *New Trends in Education in the Eighteenth Century* (Routledge & K. Paul, 1951), pp. 23, 184; J. Lawson & H. Silver, *A Social History of Education* (London: Methuen, 1973), p. 203 and ch. VI passim; M. Bence-Jones *The Catholic Families* (London: Constable, 1992), p. 42.

12 *Gentleman's Magazine*, May 1766, p. 226. The letter is dated Paris, 21 March 1766.

13 P. R. Harris (ed.), *Douai College Documents 1639-1794* (CRS vol. 63, 1972), p. 146; D. A. Bellenger, *English and Welsh Priests, 1558-1800* (Bath: Downside Abbey, 1984), p. 246; S. O'Brien, 'Women of the "English Catholic Community": Nuns and Pupils at the Bar Convent, York, 1680-1790' in J. Loades (ed.), *Monastic Studies* (Bangor: Headstart History, 1990), pp. 270-272. O'Brien notes that the school run by the Blue Nuns in Paris took 'only 155 girls—many of them French—between 1732 and its closure in 1792'.

14 M. Sharratt, 'Copernicanism at Douai' in *Durham University Journal* 67 (1974), p. 48; O'Brien, *Monastic Studies* p. 273; J. E. Austen-Leigh, *A Memoir of Jane Austen* (1867; Oxford: The Clarendon Press, 1926), ch. 1. He also relates that his grandfather, the Revd George Austen, was once asked by a squire 'of many acres' for an answer to the perfectly serious question, was Paris in France or France in Paris?

15 J. Black, *The British Abroad: The Grand Tour in the Eighteenth Century* (Stroud: Sutton, 1992), esp. pp. 248-250.

16 A. Butler (posth.), *Travels Through France & Italy & Part of Austrian, French*

[17] Lancaster, *Tempests of Broughton*, p. 94.

[18] J. Gillow, *A Literary and Biographical History, or Bibliographical Dictionary, of the English Catholics: From the Breach with Rome, in 1534, to the Present Time* (London: Burns & Oates, c.1885–1895, 5 vols), sub nomen for Butler, Needham and the Beringtons.

[19] Accounts of the Swinburnes include: A. French, *Art Treasures in the North: Northern Families on the Grand Tour* (Norwich: Unicorn Press, 2009), pp. 37–58; *Oxford Dictionary of National Biography* [ODNB]; J. Ingamells, *A Dictionary of British and Irish Travellers in Italy 1701–1800* (New Haven & London: Yale University Press, 1997).

[20] Their daughter Martha, about five and a half years old, was left with the Blue Nuns in Paris while they toured France in 1774–1775. She died three years later in Rome and a monument to her stands in the chapel of the Venerabile.

[21] *Travels Through Spain* (London: Elmsley, 1787).

[22] The latter's full-length portrait, now at Lotherton Hall, depicts the busts on a table in the background.

[23] *Travels in the Two Sicilies in the years 1777, 1778, 1789 and 1780* (London: Elmsley, 1783).

[24] It seems that when Martha was trying to leave France, her carriage was stopped at Boulogne by the mob which took her for the mistress of the Duc d'Orléans. She only got away by putting her head out of the window and declaring that she was neither young nor beautiful. Cf. H. E. G. Rope, 'Notes on Some Members of the Swinburne Family', *Biographical Studies* 2/1, (1968), p 89.

[25] Swinburne wrote candidly of all those he came across. Queen Carolina of Naples had a disagreeable manner of speech, she gesticulated wildly and her eyes goggled. '[W]hen the Emperor was here and standing at a balcony with his brother-in-law [King Ferdinand], the latter made a very unwarrantable noise and by way of apology said *"E necessario per la salute, fratello mio."* ' Cf. *The Courts of Europe at the Close of the Last Century, By the Late Henry Swinburne* (London: Colburn, 1841, 2 vols) I, pp. 132, 144.

[26] F. Dobson, *The Life and Times of George Silvertop of Minsteracres* (Newcas-

tle: Minsteracres, 2004), p. 121.

[27] J. C. H. Aveling, *Northern Catholics: The Catholics of the North Riding of Yorkshire 1558–1790* (London: Chapman, 1966), pp. 368/369.

[28] Gooch, *Desperate Faction?*, p. 175; Gooch, *Jacobite to Radical*, p. 250; Bodleian Library, English Letters [BLEL] C.229: W. Constable to Sir G. Savile (n. d., c. Sep. 1780); also to Mr Duncombe 11 Sep. 1780. Savile introduced the Catholic Relief Bill enacted as 18 Geo. II c. 60. His house was fired and plundered in June during the Gordon riots. Although the Catholic gentry kept out of politics, the Catholic nobility did not. The Duke of Norfolk spent a great deal of money trying to get Henry Howard into the Commons, cf. Durham County Record Office [DCRO]: D/Sa/C 78.107, 7 Feb. 1789.

[29] BLEL C.229, draft of a letter c. 1780, Tunstall to Charles Butler, Secretary of the Catholic Committee.

[30] Roman Catholics were debarred from military service by the act 2 Geo.III c.20. Bence-Jones, *Catholic Families*, p. 45; BLEL C.229, Tunstall to Constable, 1 Aug. 1789. Silvertop's offer was strongly supported by Lord Darlington cf. DCRO: NCB I/JB/1297, Silvertop to J. Buddle, 29 May 1798, in which Silvertop quotes Darlington. DCRO: NCB I/JB/1297, G. Silvertop to J. Buddle, 29 May 1798.

[31] Dobson, *Silvertop*, p. 56

[32] J. Lenders, *Minsteracres* (Rochdale, Orphans Press, 1932), p. 31; *Proceedings of the Society of Antiquaries of Newcastle on Tyne* [PSAN] (3), VII, No. 8 (1915), p. 98.

[33] E. Walsh & A. Forster, 'The Recusancy of the Brandlings', RH 10/1, (1969), p. 55.

[34] G. Scott, 'The Benedictines in the North East in the Eighteenth Century' in *Northern Catholic History* [NCH] 32 (1991), p 39; *Gothic Rage Undone: English Monks in the Age of Enlightenment* (Bath: Downside Abbey, 1992), p. 100.

[35] Bence-Jones, *Catholic Families*, pp.45, 78; C. Y. Lang (ed.), *The Swinburne Letters* (New Haven: Yale University Press, 1959–1962, 4 vols), I, p. 11; P. Henderson, *Swinburne* (London: Routledge & Kegan Paul, 1974), pp. 6/7; J. C. Hodgson (ed.), *Six North Country Diaries* (Surtees Society [SS] 118, 1910), p. 306. By 1809, the Petre family had given some £15,000 towards the Whigs' election expenses, cf. R.W. Linker, 'The English Roman Catholics: The Politics of Persuasion in *Journal of Ecclesiastical History* 27/2

(1976), p. 160. Linker pursues a similar theme in 'English Catholics in the Eighteenth Century' in *Church History* 35 (1966), pp. 288–310.

36 H Stubbe, *Legends no Histories* (London, n. p., 1670), pp. 19/20; E. Andrade, A Brief History of the Royal Society (London: Royal Society, 1960), p. 25; H. Hartley, *The Royal Society: Its Origins and Founders* (London: Royal Society, 1960), p. 204; M. Purver, *The Royal Society: Concept and Creation* (London: Routledge & Kegan Paul, 1967), ch. 6; L. Mulligan, 'Civil War Politics, Religion and the Royal Society' in *Past & Present*, (1973), p. 108; C. Webster, 'Richard Towneley (1629–1707), The Towneley Group in Seventeenth Century Science' in *Transactions of the Lancashire & Cheshire Historic Society* 118 (1967), p. 68. (Half of the members of the group were Catholics.)

37 Bishop Charles Walmesley, D. D., O. S. B., a mathematician of European standing; Bishop John Milner a distinguished architectural historian; the Revv. Alban Butler, John Needham and the convert Yorkshireman Theodore Augustus ('Abbe') Mann). The latter was elected F. R. S. in 1788 and an honorary member of the Society of Antiquaries in 1792.

38 The following discussion has been taken from L. Gooch, 'The Durham Catholics and Industrial Development 1560–1850' (University of York MA thesis, 1984).

39 Public Record Office E 377/68 (Recusant Roll 32 & 36 Charles II); J. A. Hilton (et al. eds), *Bishop Leyburn's Confirmation Register of 1687* (Wigan: North West Catholic History Society, 1997); Lenders, *Minsteracres*, passim; G. Ornsby (ed.), *The Remains of Denis Granville, D. D.* (SS 47, 1866), p. 239; Anon., *History of Blaydon*, (n.p., n.d.), pp. 23ff.

40 Hudleston, *Durham Recusant Estates*, pp. 168/169; Gateshead Public Library [GPL]: CN/II/157; DCRO: D/Lo/F 775(18); F. V. Dendy (ed.), *Extracts from the Records of the Company of Hostmen of Newcastle upon Tyne* (SS 105, 1901), p. 203; P. Cromar, 'The Coal Industry on Tyneside 1771–1800' in *Economic Geography* 53 (1997), p. 285.

41 DCRO: D/Lo/F 766; NRO: ZCO viii/2–4; DCRO: NCB/I/JB/2377(v); 1767 Papist Return; North East Institute of Mining Engineering, Newcastle [NEIME], shelf 46, No.15. Brandling's Felling Colliery produced 4 per cent, cf. DCRO: NCB/I/X/145(i); GPL: ZCO i/23(c) lease of 1768; Hudleston, *Durham Recusant Estates*, Nos. 40, 88, 89, 180, 181. See also *Catholic Magazine* I (1838), no.12, pp. 773ff; *Northern Catholic Calendar* (1914), pp. 114ff; G. Nicholson, 'Stephen's Hall and its Occupants' in

Durham County Local History Society Bulletin 19 (1976), p. 47; R. Meredith, 'The Eyres of Hassop, and some of their Connections from the Test Act to Emancipation' in RH 9/1 & 9/6 (1968), passim.

42   GPL: ZCO viii/2–4 shows that the Winlaton colliery yielded a profit of £3,503 over the years 1761–1768 which was shared equally among Silvertop, his mother and four sisters; Hodgson, *Estates of Roman Catholics in Northumberland*, p. 25n; DCRO: NCB/I/JB/1298; GPL: ZCO viii/3; ZCO i/1, 2. 7, 11, 12d, 14, 16, 20, 24. Ponteland was placed in trust with Sir Bellingham Graham of Norton Conyers. Hartbushes was entrusted to David Mordue. Silvertop's estate amounted to 3,653 acres: Lenders, *Minsteracres*, pp. 28/29; unidentified newspaper cutting 1789 in GPL; *ODNB*; L. E. O. Charlton, *Memoirs of a Northumbrian Lady 1815–1866* (London: Cape, 1949), p. 143.

43   DCRO: D/Lo/F 162/3, 724/5; W. Bourn, *History of the Parish of Ryton* (Carlisle: Coward, 1896), p. 12, quoting R. Edington, *Treaty on the Coal Trade* (1813).

44   UCM: DIO 11; DCRO: D/Lo/F 851(3); Cromar, 'Coal Industry on Tyneside', p. 85; GPL: ZCO v/5. The running costs of Minsteracres were £2,500 in 1800 (GPL: ZCO viii/2/5). John Silvertop acquired the barony of Bolbec from George Baker of Crook in 1800 under 42 Geo. III c 68, see especially 2nd and 5th schedules. In the long term the estate grew again. In 1876 the Silvertops held 4,222 acres in Northumberland and Durham with a gross annual value of £3,475. At the same time, the Salvin estates of Durham extended to 2,080 acres with a yearly value of £15,224. Revd G. Witham of Cliffe had 7,510 acres in the North Riding valued at £3,848 yearly, cf. J. Bateman, *The Great Land-owners of Great Britain and Ireland* ([1876], Leicester University Press, 1971), pp. 394, 407, 486.

45   NEIME: Safe, vol.14, no.1; vol.33, no.99; Bundle 58, no. 4, passim. R. Welford, *Men of Mark 'Twixt Tyne and Tweed* (London and Newcastle: Scott, 1895), pp. 111, 395; Lenders, *Minsteracres*, pp. 31–35.

46   On the Brandlings generally see E. Walsh & A. Forster, 'The Recusancy of the Brandlings' in RH 10/1 (1969), pp. 35–64; Welford, *Men of Mark*; R. Surtees, *The History and Antiquities of the County Palatine of Durham* (London and Durham, Andrews, 1816–1840, 4 vols), II, p. 91.

47   Hudleston, *Durham Recusant Estates* (SS 173), No. 12; Hodgson, *Estates of Roman Catholics in Northumberland* (SS 131), Nos. 15, 127, 133; Walsh & Forster, 'Brandlings', p. 45; their statement (p. 47) 'after 1690 Ralph was

never troubled for his religion', is therefore incorrect. The literature on Middleton is considerable, see esp. M. Lewis, *Early Wooden Railways* (London: Routledge & Kegan Paul, 1970); J. Bushell & M. D. Crew. *The Middleton Colliery Railway, Leeds* (Middleton Railway Trust, 1968); G. Rimmer, 'Middleton Colliery' in *Yorkshire Bulletin of Economic & Social Studies*, 7/1; GPL: CK/4/15–19.

48   R. Welford, *A History of the Parish of Gosforth* ([1879], Newcastle: Graham, 1975), pp.16–17; Welford *Men of Mark*, passim. Felling Hall became an inn.

49   31 Geo. II c.22 (1758). Although railways or wagonways had been built in the north-east without parliamentary approval, this act was necessary because Brandling's line passed over lands he did not own or rent. Of course, he obtained the necessary way leaves, but the act secured his railway against their revocation. 19 Geo. III c.11 (1779); R. Galloway, *Annals of Coal Mining and the Coal Trade*, ([1898], Newton Abbot: David & Charles, 1971, 2 vols), I, pp. 271, 294, 321, 391; Geo III c.66 (1793); Bushell & Crew, *Middleton Railway*, p. 6.

50   C. Hodgson (ed.), *Six North Country Diaries* (SS 118, 1910), p. 306; Welford, *Gosforth*, p. 17; Welford, *Men of Mark*, passim.

51   The Salvins have not been treated at length by any historian. Two short pamphlets give the basic information: Anon., *The Salvins* (France, c.1870) and Anon., *Croxdale Hall* (Croxdale, 2004).

52   The Benedictine Peter Salvin (c.1605–1675) served on the English mission in the earlier part of the 17th century. Cf. A. Allanson, *Biography of the English Benedictines* ([1842], Ampleforth Abbey: Saint Laurence Papers IV, 1999), p. 89.

53   DCRO: D/Sa/C 18; D/Sa/C 20–22. J. A. Williams, 'The Distribution of Catholic Chaplaincies in the Early Eighteenth Century' in RH 12/1, (1973), p. 42. Hudleston, *Durham Recusant Estates*, Nos. 133–139. The estates were all entailed and subject to jointures and so on. Tudhoe seems to have been earmarked both as a residence and to provide income for the younger adult brothers. It went in turn to Gerard (VI), Bryan (III) and Edward; all died unmarried and Tudhoe reverted to William (II) and remained the eldest son's property thereafter.

54   The detailed financial development of the Salvin businesses can be followed in DCRO: Salvin Papers; A.H. Shorter, *Papermaking in the British Isles* (Newton Abbot, David & Charles, 1971), passim; C. F. Maidwell, *Paper-*

making in County Durham (Newcastle: History of the Book Trade, 1959), under Croxdale; V. Chapman, *Rural Durham* (Durham County Council, 1977), p. 58.

55 T. Meynell, *A Report Relative to the Opening of a Communication by a Canal or a Rail or Tramway from Stockton by Darlington to the Collieries* (Stockton, Meynell, 1818). See also, D. A. & L. T. D. Heppel, 'The Meynell family at Yarm 1770–1813' in *Cleveland & Teeside Local History Society Bulletin* 13 (1971), pp. 20ff and *Bulletin* 18 (1972), pp. 11ff; J. W. Wardell, 'The Recusants of the Friarage, Yarm' in RH 8/3, pp. 158ff.; W. V. Tomlinson, *The North Eastern Railway* (Newcastle: Reid, 1914), pp. 45–47, 63/64, 87, 93, 114.

56 DCRO: D/Sa/C 139.5/7/8/15

57 Tomlinson, *North Eastern Railway*, pp. 236–240, 476/477, 518, 778; C.R. Clinker, 'The Leicester and Swannington Railway' in *Transactions of the Leicestershire Archaeological Society* 38 (1954), p. 105; *Parliamentary Papers* (1846), XIV, p. 527; DCRO: D/Sa/C 139.17; W. T. Salvin transferred his Clarence shares to Gerard in 1840 (BTHR CLA 2/5). The Stephenson/Salvin correspondence has been worked by M. Reed in 'George Stephenson and W. T. Salvin: the early railway capital market at work' in *Transport History* I/1 (1968). My reading of the letters coincides with his, although I am more specific in locating Salvin's initial interest in railways to the proposals of 1818 and 1823 to route lines through or near to Croxdale. (References to BTHR above are taken from Reed's article.)

58 DCRO: D/Sa/C 205.14

59 *Report of the Commissioners to Enquire into the Estates of Certain Traitors and Popish Recusants* (London: House of Commons, 1719), App. 2, pp. 20–22; B. Hemphill, *The Early Vicars Apostolic of England 1685–1750* (London: Burns & Oates, 1954), p. 127 n1. The basic genealogical information on the family is at, J. Burke, *Genealogical and Heraldic History of the Landed Gentry* ([1849 et seq.] London: Harrison, 1952); I. & E. Hall, *Burton Constable Hall* (Hull City Museum, 1991); and Anon., *Burton Constable Hall* (East Yorkshire Local History Society, 1998).

60 East Yorkshire County Record Office [EYCRO]: Burton Constable Archive *DDCC* 135, 154/155 (29 June & 2 Oct. 1716); Hall, *Burton Constable*, p. 11. Marton and Burton Constable are often conflated in mission history but no resident chaplain can be placed in the mansion whereas an uninterrupted succession of priests at Marton can be identified,

cf. L. Gooch, *Paid at Sundry Times: Yorkshire Clergy Finances in the Eighteenth Century* (Ampleforth Abbey: St Laurence Papers X, 1997), passim.

[61] E. S. Worrall (ed.), *Returns of Papists 1767* (CRS Occasional Publication No. 2, 1989), p. 54; E. H. Burton & E. Nolan (eds), *Douay College Diaries. The Seventh Diary 1715-1778* (CRS 28, 1928), pp. 213, 221; Hall, *Burton Constable*, p. 25; J. C. H. Aveling, *Post Reformation Catholicism in East Yorkshire 1558-1790* (East Yorkshire Local History Society, 1960), pp. 43-45.

[62] Harris, *Douai College Documents*, sub nomen. William Constable to Elizabeth Constable his stepmother (n. d. but endorsed '1761' by her), cf. EYCRO: Constable Burton Archive, DDCC 144/149, from which the following is taken.

[63] The lady and Mitchel are unidentified; but the latter may be the York solicitor Thomas Mitchell who acted for the mission on occasion (cf. Gooch, *Sundry Times*, No. 65).

[64] One or other of Catharine, Barbara or Julia, daughters of Robert, Lord Petre (VIII).

[65] A summary of William's interests and a detailed itinerary of the Tour is given at Leo Gooch, 'The Religion for a Gentleman: The Northern Catholic Gentry in the Eighteenth Century' in RH 23/4 (1997), pp. 556-561.

[66] BLEL, C.229: Tunstall to Constable, 13 Jan. 1788; 10 June 1789; 20 June 1789; 18 Feb. 1790; 23 Mar. 1790. DCRO: D/Sa/C 78 to W. T. Salvin, 14 June 1789; D/Sa/C 277 to same, 19 Feb. 1782; Jan. 1790; 12 Mar. 1790; 21 Apr. 1790.

[67] BLEL, C.229: Tunstall to Thomas Pennant n. d. [1782]. His collections were bought for £700 by the Natural History Society of Northumberland, Durham and Newcastle on Tyne and are now in the Hancock Museum in Newcastle.

[68] BLEL, C.229: Tunstall to Constable 12 Feb. 1788; 10 Dec. 1788, 17 Aug.? 1789; 18 Feb. 1790. DCRO: D/Sa/C 277 to W. T. Salvin 26 Apr. 1786.

[69] BLEL, C.229, Tunstall to Constable 10 June 1789; 20 June 1789; 18 Aug. 1787; 8 June 1789. DCRO: D/Sa/C 277 to W. T. Salvin 26 Apr. 1786; 14 June 1788. The chaplains were: Revv. J. Holden (1735-43); J. Dixon (1745-59); J. Wilson (1760-3); T. Penswick (1763-91), cf. Gooch, *Sundry Times*, sub nomen.

[70] DCRO: D/Sa/C 277 to Salvin, 14 Oct. 1783; 14 June 1788; and passim.

71 Bossy, *English Catholic Community*, pp. 325–327; G. E. Mingay, *English Landed Society in the Eighteenth Century* (London: Routledge & Kegan Paul, 1982), p. 26.
72 J. Nichols, *Illustrations of the Literary History of the Eighteenth Century* (London, for the author, 1825), p. 510; Aveling, *East Yorkshire*, p. 52; Gooch, *Durham Catholics*, p. 120 n4; Gooch, *Jacobite to Radical*, p. 58.
73 Bence Jones, *Catholic Families*, ch. 5; Linker, *Roman Catholics and Emancipation*, p. 154.
74 D. Gwynn, *The Second Spring 1818–1852* (London: Burns Oates, 1942), p. 12; Aveling, *Handle and Axe*, p. 265.

3 THE CATHOLIC QUESTION IN NORTH-EAST POLITICS, 1800–1850

ONLY TEN SESSIONS of parliament passed between 1800 and 1829 without the Catholic Question being raised. Ten bills for full or partial relief were introduced before emancipation was finally enacted, and the matter played a prominent part in six of the eight changes of Cabinet in the period. The eventual success of the Catholic campaign inspired the Reform movement, the Chartists and the Anti-Corn Law League and was thus 'of fundamental importance in British and Irish History. It marks the transformation of the politics of the old order into the politics of the new'.[1] It is therefore appropriate to examine the Catholic Question in the politics of the region.

The long debate on the Catholic Question had a particular resonance in north-east England because leading members of the pro- and anti-emancipation groups had their bases in Northumberland and Durham. The See of Durham was occupied between 1791 and 1826 by Shute Barrington who had kept alive, almost single-handedly, the spirit of No-Popery since the imprisonment (and conversion to Judaism) of Lord George Gordon in 1788. Barrington placed a number of anti-Catholic divines in the more lucrative livings of his diocese, and continually exhorted them to write and preach against the abominations of Rome, and they did so enthusiastically. Barrington's protégés (as well as his own successor and his clergy) can be counted among the more distinguished anti-Catholic campaigners in the land. The most vociferous and persistent of these was the Revd Henry Phillpotts, whose sixty-year career in political and theological controversy began in Durham in 1805 over the Catholic Question.

At the same time, the diocese of Durham was home-base for some of the most determined secular pro-Catholics in the country, chief among them Charles Grey, later Lord Howick and Earl Grey, leader of the Whig Party, M. P. for Northumberland, and champion of Catholic Emancipation, parliamentary reform and the abolition of slavery. In County Durham, Grey's son-in-law John ('Radical Jack') George Lambton, afterwards Earl of Durham, was equally committed to Catholic relief and other liberal causes. He helped to found the *Durham Chronicle* in 1820 as a counterblast to the *Durham County Advertiser* (published until 1814 as the *Newcastle Advertiser*) which was the mouthpiece of the Tory and Anglican establishment in the north. Many of the principal landed magnates of the region were Whiggish on the Catholic Question, as were many of the lesser gentry, though the Tories had powerful advocates, such as the Duke of Northumberland. (He would become pragmatic over Catholic Emancipation, but never pro-Catholic.) John Lingard, the Catholic priest later to be celebrated for his *History of England,* was a professor at the newly-established seminary at Crook Hall and Ushaw until 1810, and he was the principal Catholic clerical voice in the debate. The proximity of strongly pro- and anti-Catholic national figures in the region was bound to give a keen edge to any local discussion of Catholic Emancipation, particularly during election campaigns.

Anti-Catholicism comprised two main elements. Firstly, to a greater or lesser extent, Protestants held that Catholic beliefs and practices were idolatrous, blasphemous and sacrilegious. Secondly, religious conformity was required by English law. Since the crown claimed spiritual as well as temporal authority, it was treasonable to adhere to a religion which owed spiritual allegiance to any other authority such as the Pope (who was himself, in any case, a temporal ruler). Dissent from the religion of the state was equivalent to opposition to the state; religious deviance was regarded as politically subversive and hence a matter of national security. There were other elements in the anti-Catholic case. From 1688 to 1788 the Catholic exiled House of Stuart maintained a claim to the English throne. It did not help that the Jacobite court in exile was on papal territory after 1715. In 1817, Grey argued that John Locke's objection to relieving the Catholics had rested on their attachment to the Stuarts; and now that that reason could no longer be advanced, there was no justification for their political exclusion. The extinction of the Stuarts made little difference, however, for the Pope remained as an alternative and supposedly more dangerous focus of Catholic allegiance. Catholics were held to support the Pope's deposing power by which he could relieve them of their civil allegiance, and to believe that it was sinful to keep faith with heretics, and that they could entertain mental reservations on any oaths tendered to them which conflicted with their Catholic tenets. Catholics could not, therefore, be entrusted with English citizenship. This line was developed by the Bishop of Durham in a debate in the House of Lords in 1805. It was sufficient, he said, to show charity and kindness to people holding a different faith, but that did not mean they should be given political power. England had received and protected French émigré priests with all the warm charity of Christians, and the liberality of Englishmen, undeterred by the lack of 'security against the introduction of spies and enemies'. He wished to treat the Irish with the same kindness, and to improve their social and economic condition, but without granting them political power: 'Let us keep inviolate the barriers of our religious and political constitution'.[2]

John Wesley believed that 'No government not Roman Catholic ought to tolerate men of the Roman Catholic persuasion'. In the nineteenth century, Wesleyan Methodism was politically, ecclesiastically and socially conservative, a position necessarily opposed to Catholic Emancipation. Wesleyan opposition to the Catholic claims was part of a wider fear of radicalism, popular discontent and infidelity. The development of a highly authoritarian central bureaucracy among the Wesleyans, alienated many in the movement and, in 1810, a group of working-class radicals, calling themselves Primitive Methodists, broke away to recover their more revivalist origins. The Primitive Methodists were no less opposed to Catholic Emancipation than the Wesleyans, because of the perceived illiberalism of Popery. Nonetheless, official Methodism did not wish to become involved in a question 'so decidedly political', and the leadership made attempts 'to discourage anti-Catholic sentiment from becoming anti-Catholic political activity'. For the majority of Methodists out in the country, however, the issue was primarily a religious one, and they disregarded the advice from London and vigorously opposed Catholic Emancipation in their own localities.[3]

Similarly, within the Dissenting bodies, the leadership and the rank and file went their own ways. The Dissenters were chiefly concerned with the repeal of the Test Act, and the Committee of the Three Denominations expressed support for the Catholics in what was seen as an analogous case to their own. No such similarity was acknowledged in the country, however, and individual Dissenters campaigned alongside Methodists against Catholic Emancipation. Consistency was also lacking among the Radicals with no religious affiliation. Officially, Catholic Emancipation was a simple matter of religious toleration and equality. After Emancipation, however, it became clear that the support of the Radicals had not been based on any principle of religious toleration, but was merely an adjunct to their main aim of political reform. From 1832 Radicals were seen to be as anti-Catholic as most other Englishmen by conflating Catholicism with reactionary politics and illiberal Popery.[4]

Roman Catholicism, then, aroused a powerful dual antagonism—religious bigotry and xenophobia; those disinclined to religious persecution could join the crusade to keep out the foreigner, and vice versa. Anti-Catholicism served as a national cum religious identity; Papists were not just non-Protestant but un-English. Idolaters, blasphemers, and those owing any kind of loyalty to a foreign power could not be tolerated. Quite simply, it would be a constitutional outrage to admit Roman Catholics to places of trust and authority under the crown.

The Catholic laity fully appreciated the deep-rooted fears of the Protestants, and they were prepared to go to considerable lengths to remove the stigma of popery. They would accept the appellation 'Protesting Catholic Dissenters' and agree to a crown veto on episcopal appointments. They would also allow official censorship of correspondence between English ecclesiastics and the Roman Curia. In fact, so far as the vicars apostolic were concerned, the latter would have little effect, for Rome might as well not have existed for all practical purposes. In 1773 Propaganda told Bishop Petre to send an account of his vicariate since it was so long since they had heard from him. Propaganda complained in 1821 that they would have to publish its *Status Missionem* from reports sent in seven years before. In any case, that from the Northern District was missing, and it was urgently required. Robert Gradwell, Roman Agent of the vicars apostolic, wrote to Bishop Smith

> Propaganda complains not one report of the state of the district has ever been sent them from the North. ... [and] naturally supposes that it is in a very bad state, that abuses prevail which the bishop is ashamed to describe, that the clergy are disorderly ... that no chapels are built, no schools instituted, nothing worth describing in the northern Counties ... [5]

Gradwell noted that Propaganda said it knew more about China and America than northern England and entreated Smith to respond immediately. Bishop Poynter also urged Smith to submit a report. On another occasion Bishop Hay advised Bishop Gibson to show a little more deference to Rome. The Pope observed in 1839 that he had to learn what he could about the state of the Church in England from the newspapers.[6]

At any rate, the proofs of loyalty to the British Constitution and detachment from Rome proposed by some representatives of the English Catholics illustrate their anxiety to allay Protestant fears, as well as their passionate desire for political emancipation, almost to the exclusion of other factors, even the danger of schism. More generally, they entertained the hope that their evident peaceable behaviour would lead to their relief. Grey told the House of Lords in 1810 that there were in Northumberland, Catholics

> of ancient and respectable families, who, as friends and neighbours, as parents of families, and in all the relations of society, conducted themselves with the greatest propriety, and this he believed to be the general character of that body.

Grey again told the Lords that 'he enjoyed the honour of an acquaintance' with many Catholics in Northumberland and that in the

> exemplary discharge of the duties of life they could not be excelled, and if religion was to be appreciated by the conduct of those who professed it, he must at least say that the religion which produced such fruits could not be a bad one.[7]

Another pro-Catholic argument advanced in parliament was that the English Catholics were 'as a body of men, however respectable, small in number and forming only an exception to the general mass of the population'. The converse was advanced in relation to Ireland where, it was pointed out, three-quarters or more of the people were Roman Catholics. Indeed, by far the most important advantage held by the Catholics was the risk posed to national security in Ireland. The Irish had to be kept loyal in a time of war, and they were, therefore, in a powerful bargaining position. After 1798 the Catholic Question became an Irish political question; and throughout the campaign for emancipation the English Catholics and pro-Catholic Protestants took care to remind parliament of the danger represented by an aggrieved Ireland.[8]

The French Revolution benefited the British Catholics in two ways. Firstly, the severity of French anti-Catholic persecution served to mitigate English intolerance, and the Relief Act of 1791 was passed without substantial opposition. Ideologically, the act was justified under a principle of toleration which could countenance different kinds of non-Anglican worship, but exclude non-Anglicans from political power. In any case, an oath of loyalty was required under the act. Secondly, patriotic feelings against France allowed the British to welcome some five thousand exiled French priests, and to accept the repatriation of English Catholic schools and religious communities from the continent. The presence of large numbers of Catholics in various parts of England transcended, at least superficially, the mistrust of papists.[9]

All these factors, the extinction of the Stuarts, the willingness of lay Catholics to demonstrate their detachment from Rome, their small number and social integration, the Irish problem and the effects of the French Revolution, went towards creating a climate favourable to emancipation, and were exploited by the English Catholics throughout the campaign. They certainly did not cringe in the face of intolerance or meekly accept their political disabilities. On the contrary, they became energetic and confident campaigners. Tracts, letters, speeches and petitions poured forth, most of which were couched in persuasive and responsible terms, intended to soften, if not eradicate Protestant suspicions of Roman Catholicism.[10] Probably the most extensive and detailed examination of the Catholic case in the north-east occurred in a lengthy controversy between Shute Barrington and John Lingard which began in 1807.

The Ministry of All the Talents proposed a bill relieving Catholics in the Army and the Royal Navy. King George III forced its withdrawal and demanded a promise that ministers would never raise the Catholic Question again. Unable to accept such a constraint, the ministry resigned in March and brought about a general election. The Tories under Spencer Perceval made it a 'No-Popery' election by going to the country on one issue: 'Support the King and the British Constitution'. During the parliamentary crisis, Barrington published his diocesan visitation address of 1806 as a pamphlet: *A Charge Delivered to the Clergy of the Diocese of Durham*. Lingard was somewhat disturbed by the offensive tone and inaccuracy of this work and he published, anonymously, a response to it entitled *Remarks on A Charge...* Lingard's tone was conciliatory; the line he took was that he was responding to the bishop more in sorrow than in anger that Roman Catholicism had been so wrongly represented. No sooner had Lingard's pamphlet appeared than the bishop reissued his but under a new title: *The Grounds on which the Church of England Separated from the Church of Rome*.[11] Lingard immediately reissued his *Remarks* but with a new and less conciliatory preface, in which he accused the bishop of having taken advantage of 'the ferment of a general election' to whip up the anti-Catholic prejudices of the electorate: 'From one extremity of his diocese to the other he preached a holy crusade against the opinions, I had almost said the persons of Catholics'. After such provocation, Lingard said, 'we certainly may be allowed to speak in our own defence', and that was precisely what he intended to do.[12]

Lingard was 35 years of age at this time and he had been a priest for ten years; he was Vice President of the seminary at Crook Hall. He had spent much of his life in an academic environment, the first fruits of which was the publication in 1806 of his *Antiquities of the Anglo-Saxon Church*. It is unnecessary to comment on this work save to note his historical method, for it was also the approach he adopted in his polemical writings. He believed that if the misunderstandings which the English Protestants had of the Roman Catholic faith were corrected, not only would the penal laws be repealed, but the way would be clear for Christian unity. This was a fond hope, but it was nonetheless the sense in which he has to be read. Lingard knew, moreover, that his only chance of reaching the audience he desired lay in a sober and unimpassioned exposition of the facts. He wished to be a man of reason rather than a bigot, and to use irony and humour to make his case rather than sarcasm and ridicule.[13]

Barrington was twice Lingard's age. He was the son of a peer, his brothers included an admiral, a general, a judge and a Chancellor of the Exchequer; he married the daughter of a duke and he became Chaplain in Ordinary to kings George II and III. He has been described as 'a fine example of the harmless and even meritorious clergyman who owed great preferment to family interest'. Barrington had been made a bishop in 1769, that is, two years before Lingard's birth. He was firstly Bishop of Llandaff, then of Salisbury (1782) and he was translated to Durham in 1791. He spoke in a parliamentary debate on only ten occasions in an episcopate of fifty-seven years, and all those utterances were in fervent support of the establishment. He was a staunch opponent of Catholic Emancipation, in accordance with the Tory doctrine of the indivisibility of Church and State. He preached to the House of Lords in 1799 on the need to preserve the English Protestant establishment from popery on the grounds that the French Revolution could be traced to the corruptions of the Church of Rome—a similar fate would befall England if Catholics were granted political emancipation. He said much the same thing in his *Charges* in 1797, 1801 and 1806. Indeed, the topic was something of a fixed idea for which he became notorious. In 1802 the Revd Joseph Berington asked Hannah More to drop the 'insulting words' Papist, Popery and Romanist which, he said, were 'fit only for the Bishop of Durham'. Now, in 1807, much to Lingard's disgust, he presented his latest *Charge* to the general public for purely political purposes.[14]

Barrington inveighed against Roman excesses which, he said, complicated the plain message of the gospel by 'ostentatious pageantry'. The clergy of Durham were therefore urged to be vigilant in the defence of authentic, that is, Anglican Christianity: the 'zeal of the Romanist especially should operate as a strong caution against indifference to the corruptions of their church'. The French Revolution had driven numerous societies of the Romish Church to settle in England, 'this land of charity and freedom'. Furthermore,

> The education which the English Catholics used to seek in foreign countries, they now have it in their power to obtain at home in ample seminaries of their own communion. Various other civil privileges and indulgences have within these few years been granted them by the Legislature.

The danger from this apparent encouragement was clear.[15]

Barrington went on to outline the ecclesiastical reasons for the Anglican separation from Roman obedience. The material was familiar, and consisted of all those beliefs and practices with which the reformers had been concerned. His real concern, however, was with Anglican supremacy, which was not actually threatened, by the Catholics, at any rate, as Lingard was to observe, albeit somewhat equivocally:

> The Protestant is the established church. This should satisfy her ambition. In the present temper of mankind, while she remains in possession of wealth and honour, she may deem herself secure.[16]

Lingard's essential point was that the bishop had wilfully misunderstood Catholic beliefs but he also addressed the civic aspects of the argument. Insofar as the French Revolution being the culmination of the degeneracy of the Church of Rome, Lingard said that 'far from thinking, with the Bishop of Durham, that catholicity was favourable to their projects', the revolutionaries actually 'treated it as their natural and most formidable enemy'. That was, after all, why thousands of French priests had sought refuge in England, and why the expatriate English Catholics had returned to their native shores to open the schools which so worried the bishop. He sought to allay Barrington's anxiety particularly about Ushaw College just outside the city of Durham, which was then almost ready for occupation:

> The toleration which has been granted us by a gracious Sovereign and an enlightened ministry has encouraged us to open schools in England. The country will not lose by it. A domestic education will strengthen our attachment to our native land, and will retain at home the sums which formerly were of necessity expended abroad. The present ruler of France has made us the most tempting offers to resume our former plan of education in that country. His offers have been refused by our Prelates. The Bishop of Durham will, I trust, applaud their patriotism, and wish success to their endeavours.

But he did not.[17]

On the other hand, Charles Butler, a Catholic and Barrington's almoner, remarked favourably on the bishop's charity. Barrington had been generous to the repatriated community of Poor Clares who lived in St. Helen's Auckland Hall for ten years. He was their close neighbour at Auckland Castle and he gave the nuns annual alms. This reflected the bishop's approach which he had outlined in his *Charge*, 'Charity is certainly not incompatible with the most active zeal against erroneous and defective institutions'. He did not, however, contribute to Crook Hall or subscribe to the building costs of Ushaw College. Nonetheless, he employed Ignatius Bonomi to work on Auckland Castle in 1817.[18]

Lingard hardly used the political arguments for Catholic Emancipation in his dispute with Barrington; clearly, he was more concerned, as a priest, to debate points of theology. Only occasionally did he refer explicitly to the bishop's avowed purpose of denying some five million British subjects the common rights of citizenship on what were irrelevant and fraudulent grounds. Religion was irrelevant: together with 'Jews, deists and atheists', Catholics

> might aspire to places of trust, emolument and rank, and obtain the privileges for which our fathers fought and which are the birth-right of every Englishman.[19]

He did, however, join a correspondence which appeared in the *Newcastle Courant* in May 1807 initiated by 'A Liege Subject' who contended that there was a Catholic doctrine of papal infallibility which superseded all national political obligations. The significant remark made by Lingard in his contribution was that Catholics 'would not be obliged to conform to any dispensation from their allegiance and would defend the country, even against the Pope himself, in case he should invade the nation'. It was remarked that this 'caused some sensation', as well it might, for though Lingard had only said precisely what most lay Catholics would have said, not many priests would have put it so bluntly.[20]

The controversy between Lingard and Barrington was joined by a number of (mostly anonymous or pseudonymous) Anglican clergymen who issued *Replies, Answers, Letters* and *Defences* in support of their diocesan. These tracts elaborated, at inordinate length, the arguments already raised and answered by the main protagonists. It was clear that little could be added to the arguments; positions had been stated, reiterated, and nothing new could be said. Lingard ignored most of them but he did become exasperated at one particular feature of the controversy:

> I have often considered it as an extraordinary phenomenon in the history of the human mind that in England the Catholics are not allowed the faculty of understanding their own belief ... Objections which have been a thousand times refuted are confidently brought forward as demonstrations of our folly and impiety; and the misrepresentations of prejudice are eagerly received with the veneration due to simple unvarnished truth.[21]

There were, in any case, more immediate problems engaging Lingard's attention around this time. The new college at Ushaw was hardly finished when the staff and students moved into it in 1808. An outbreak of typhus laid low some fifty residents and eventually carried off five students. Then, in May 1810, the President, Thomas Eyre, died and Lingard acted in his place for thirteen months. By his own admission he was neither an administrator nor a disciplinarian, and that year was for him

> a time of anxiety and misery. Bishop Smith and Mr Gillow employed every inducement to prevail on me to stay with the latter. Though it hurt me to refuse, I did so, because I was convinced that my health, my comfort, and even more than that was at stake. I resolved never more if possible to involve myself in a situation to which I was so ill adapted.

Bishop Gibson had proved extremely difficult to deal with; he was autocratic, would accept no advice and he was regarded as unsound in financial matters. These pressures, then, prevented Lingard taking notice of every anti-Catholic pamphlet that appeared. Those same pressures led him to resign when John Gillow was appointed President of the college in 1811, and Lingard left Ushaw to become incumbent at Hornby, a small country mission near Lancaster, having 'a house well furnished, with a garden and croft and a good salary'.[22]

In 1813 Lingard's part in this long controversy was acknowledged by the Board of Catholics of Great Britain when he was thanked formally 'for his zealous and successful defence of the Catholic Church in his many literary productions…' The Barrington-Lingard dispute, then, was important in that it came at the beginning of the long battle over the political rights of the British Catholics. It was followed throughout the country, and the pamphlets all ran into several editions. It is unnecessary to rehearse these arguments in discussing parliamentary elections in the northeast, but it should be assumed that the pro- and anti-Catholic cases as propounded by Barrington and Lingard were reiterated up to the very moment of Catholic Emancipation in 1829.[23]

***

Until 1834 there were six parliamentary constituencies in the region, each returning two members: Northumberland, County Durham, Berwick, Morpeth, Newcastle upon Tyne and the City of Durham. Of these, Morpeth was a pocket-borough, the remainder were more or less open, though usually managed on the principle of divided representation with one Whig and one Tory member. None of the elections in Berwick or Morpeth during the period had any significance from the Catholic point of view. The Howards (earls of Carlisle) and Ordes who held Morpeth throughout, were committed pro-Catholics and voted accordingly. George, Viscount Morpeth launched his political career in 1826 with a strongly-worded maiden speech in favour of Emancipation. Attention here, then, is concentrated on contests for seats in which Catholic Emancipation was a major issue.

The fall of the Talents and the succeeding general election in 1807 showed that support for the Catholics was not a popular vote-winning issue and nowhere was this more apparent than in the north-east. The purpose of Barrington's *Charge* and *Grounds* was to influence the electorate in the election as Lingard had said, by raising the 'war-hoop of no popery'. Yet in a letter of 20 May, at the height of the campaign, Lingard wrote,

> We are in a great ferment here about the elections. Notwithstanding all the influence of the Bp of Durham and the chapter, the old members have been returned for the city [of Durham]. Every attempt is making to throw out one of the old members for the county, but I think it will be in vain. At Newcastle the old members are also returned. In Northumberland I expect that Lord Percy will turn out Col. Beaumont, Lord Howick will come in. Is it not surprising that all the members in the North (two counties) with the exception of one should vote for the catholics: and of all these I think only one is in danger of losing his seat.[24]

Lingard was not well informed. Although Durham City, Morpeth and Newcastle all returned an unopposed Tory/Whig combination of members, the two counties went to a poll and the Catholic Question was an important issue the hustings.

At a Durham County meeting on 1 June, a Loyal Address declaring approval of Tory policy on the Catholic Question was proposed. The tenth Earl of Strathmore (Bowes) said that the Catholics he knew had always behaved with the 'most gentlemanly conduct' and that they ranked high in loyalty; he nonetheless opposed the policy of the Talents. He was seconded by Matthew Russell of Brancepeth Castle. The ultra-Tory Richard Wharton (unopposed candidate for Durham City) also spoke against any concessions and, as Lingard suggested, the Durham clergy and college may reasonably be suspected of being influential on, if not the instigators of, the address. The policy of the Talents was defended by Dr. J. R. Fenwick who proposed a counter-address. This was seconded by Ralph Milbanke (a Whig candidate) and supported by Sir H. T. Liddell, the retiring county member, and R. J. ('Radical Jack') Lambton, elected for the city. The Tory address was, however, 'carried by a very great majority'. Cuthbert Ellison, the second Whig candidate, was defeated at the polls by Sir H. V. Tempest, a staunch Tory.[25]

The election in Northumberland produced the most significant result in 1807. The Duke of Northumberland decided to run his son, Lord Percy, in tandem with the sitting Tory, Colonel Beaumont, against Lord Howick, the great champion of Catholic Emancipation. Indeed, it was Howick who had introduced the measure which had brought about the general election. Howick could not afford to fight an election against the wealthy duke (polling would take place at Alnwick, under the castle walls, so to speak) and so he withdrew on the eve of the poll; Howick had been the member for twenty-one years. In his election address he had argued for freedom of conscience and he had singled out the Catholics Walter Selby of Biddleston and Mr Haggerston of Ellingham as ornaments of society. Percy did not refer to the matter; Beaumont would not be heard by the mob. Howick had been humiliated in his home constituency over a fundamental Whig policy. He was accommodated in other seats before his elevation to the House of Lords as Earl Grey in November that year, but this defeat was particularly disappointing, and he never forgave the duke. He could not have held the Bishop of Durham in any high regard either.[26]

Of the two electoral contests in the north-east in 1807, then, the anti-Catholics gained a seat in each. The Whigs fell from power as a direct consequence of their championship of the Catholic cause. Nonetheless, under the leadership of Grey, they maintained their pro-Catholic principles as firmly as ever, though in practice they preferred to leave the question in abeyance until circumstances improved. Moreover, they were not prepared to support those Irish Catholics who attacked the Union. The English Catholics, however, would not let matters rest. In November 1807 Grey acknowledged the inevitability of another petition to parliament and he said he would support it, however inopportune, since the Catholics could now do little except petition and hope that the military situation would serve to secure their aims:

> The truth is that the Catholics have now been taught to consider the whole English nation as so hostile to them that they feel comparatively very little interest in the different changes of administration that may take place; and believing that those who have the inclination will never have the power to grant them redress; and being convinced that their only chance of justice is in the wars and in the distresses of England, they are naturally led to press the question without reference to the state of politics as it affects the different parties in Parliament.[27]

Grey might well have been in conversation with George Silvertop, so precise was his analysis. Silvertop held that the only way to remedy existing injustices was to launch an extra-parliamentary 'systematic campaign, unilaterally organised'. In February 1808 he wrote about Catholic opinion in the north:

> One point above all others seems primarily felt which is the non-enjoyment of ... the Elective Franchise; a right enjoyed by the Catholics in Ireland ... which every freeholder in the United Kingdom enjoys except the English Catholics.[28]

The Catholic Board began to issue pamphlets explaining the Catholic case and to take advertising space in the pro-Catholic press, and Catholics around the country began to appear more frequently on the hustings in support of Whig candidates. Indeed, some wished to ally themselves with the Radicals; Bishop Thomas Smith feared the consequences of Catholics appearing at meetings of the Friends of Religious Liberty, which they had joined 'to make themselves conspicuous'. The Catholic gentry did not, however, forego the more moderate tactics of pressure-group politics.[29]

The Catholic Question came up, more or less routinely, at all of the contested parliamentary elections in the region between 1807 and 1829. Most candidates preferred to make a simple statement of their view of the matter and move on to more interesting local topics such as the coal industry, shipping and trade. Neither the Catholics nor the ultra-Tories were prepared to let it pass just like that, however, and they made sure that Catholic Emancipation was given full attention whenever possible. A notable example was the by-election for a Durham City seat in December 1813 caused by the resignation of Ralph Lambton. The contest was between the Tory, George Allan of Darlington, and the Whig, George Baker of Elemore Hall. Allan declared himself as 'friendly to a liberal, extended toleration of the exercise of religious duties of every denomination', but he was, nonetheless, of the opinion that the present claims of the Catholics were 'dangerous and unconstitutional to a high degree'. If he won, then, the city of Durham would be represented in parliament by two anti-Catholic Tories, for the second sitting member was Richard Wharton. Mr Shippersden, proposing Mr Baker, said that Baker would 'rejoice at the arrival of that day which shall give equal privileges to the Catholics with the rest of countrymen of different persuasions'. Baker himself expressed a firm attachment to 'religious liberty and Parliamentary reform'. Baker's pro-Catholic stand and his Catholic connections were seized on immediately by the Tories; indeed, it was the only issue on which he was challenged during the nine-day poll.[30] A hand-bill, for example, referred to Baker's Catholic backing:

> Papist Plot
> See Baker Comes at Papist W—'s call,
> Let Allan stand, then Popery shall fall.
> No W-T-M
> No BAKER
> NO POPERY

W-T-M was the prominent Catholic Henry Thomas Witham of Lartington Hall. Another hand-bill alluded to the impertinence of the Catholics in adopting and working for Baker who, it was said, had been

> avowedly brought forward at the instance of a popish party, Mr W-t-m at the head using every exertion possible, to bring him in member for this city, instead of a firm friend to the protestant establishment... Popery now shews more of its daring front, and, so encouraged, its votaries are become the avowed and active agents of a candidate to be arrayed against our country's establishment; and the watch word is, doubtless, gone forth, for the exertion of all the popish energies on every succeeding parliamentary vacancy.

The Pope was ridiculed at every opportunity and sham papal bulls were circulated. Baker was caricatured as a lover of the pope, of kissing the pope's toe and of having obtained the 'Pontifical Chair' on which he was to be carried in triumph around the streets of Durham. The pope was also said to have supplied money to bribe the electorate into voting for Baker (or Baccari as he was unimaginatively dubbed). Baker ignored it all. Since this was the only policy for which Baker was reproached, it can be assumed that his opponents assessed it as his most vulnerable point, and that the cathedral clergy would be campaigning strongly on the issue. This was, no doubt, the occasion on which the young Nicholas Wiseman was hissed for being a Catholic when he visited his mother in Durham while he was at Ushaw College.[31]

The result of the by-election justified Tory strategy, for Allan won with a majority of eighty. In his victory address, he expressed his satisfaction at having conquered 'every effort which Roman Catholic ingenuity or prejudice could invent' to avert his election. The remark, though exaggerated, does illustrate that Catholics were now openly campaigning for, and even taking a leading role in the selection of pro-Catholic Whig candidates. Catholics were now also prepared to hold public meetings and dinners to press their case, and one meeting in the north-east may be taken as an example.

In 1815, reports of anti-Protestant riots in France gave rise to a wave of anti-Catholicism in England. On 27 December, therefore, 'a most numerous and highly respectable meeting' of Catholics took place in Newcastle under the chairmanship of George Silvertop and the vice chairmanship of W. T. Salvin, to protest the persecution of the French Huguenots. The meeting was, however, as much a contribution to the domestic debate on Catholic Emancipation, for the northern Catholics used it to affirm their attachment to religious freedom for all, including themselves. In the course of the debate it was noted that the British government had said that it was 'its invariable object ... to support and on every occasion to assert the principles of religious toleration and liberty'; a similar commitment had been made at the Congress of Vienna. Silvertop found it impossible, therefore, to avoid mentioning the disabilities suffered by British Catholics for conscience sake; they were deprived of all political privileges, taxed without the power of choosing their representatives; and denied every civil and military office.[32]

In addition to resolutions passed in support of the Huguenots, the meeting in Newcastle also decided to petition parliament and the Prince Regent on their own behalf. In January 1816 the Board of British Catholics sent a vote of thanks to Silvertop and his supporters for their 'Newcastle Declaration'. Others, led by Bishop

Milner (who dubbed Silvertop 'Copperbottom') condemned some expressions in the resolutions in support of freedom of conscience. The *Orthodox Journal* censured what it called the 'Northern Lights' for their views which it thought 'almost if not actually anti-Catholic'. The meeting nonetheless achieved its main aim of gaining publicity for the Catholic case.[33]

Political controversy over Catholic Emancipation rose to new heights in the 1820s and it was a dominant issue in the general elections of 1820 and 1826. The Whigs continued to espouse emancipation as a fundamental party policy; in the run-up to the election of 1820, Grey told Holland, 'To Catholic Emancipation I consider myself so pledged that I could not come in without it'. There was little doubt, however, that that was a minority view, and the Tories were determined to oust the more advanced Whig reformers in the general election of that year. The Tories decided to force a poll in Northumberland with the aim of installing the orthodox C. J. Brandling in place of T. W. Beaumont, who had succeeded his father as Tory member for the county in 1818, but who had turned out to hold some very radical views, such as support for Catholic Emancipation. The plan back-fired, however, when Sir Charles Monck, the second sitting member and a Whig, decided not to run. Brandling and Beaumont were therefore returned unopposed. In Newcastle, the sitting Whig/Tory combination of M. W. Ridley and C. Ellison was challenged by William Scott, Lord Chancellor Eldon's nephew, but he resigned before the polls closed. Richard Wharton, Tory Chief Whip and member for Durham City since 1802, decided to transfer his candidature to the county and run against Lambton, who had represented the county since 1813. His successor as member for the city was General Sir Henry Hardinge, a moderate Tory whose patron and kinsman was the Marquess of Londonderry. He and M. A. Taylor were returned unopposed.[34]

The only real contest in the region, then, was in the constituency of County Durham. The candidates Lambton and Wharton were joined by the second sitting member, the Hon. W. J. F. Vane Powlett, afterwards third duke of Cleveland; as a Whig, he was as much a target for the Tories as Lambton. The election campaign was both expensive and virulent. Ranged against the Whigs in support of Wharton were the parochial and cathedral clergy—it was suggested that there ought to have been a 'Bishop Rampant' on Wharton's coat of arms, and he was variously called the 'College Candidate' and the 'Hireling of the Church'. One of Wharton's principal supporters was Canon Henry Phillpotts, Rector of Gateshead, who took part by correspondence, speech and pamphlet. Indeed, the Whigs made him a target, lampooning him mercilessly

> Harry Phillpotts, Harry Phillpotts,
> Your preferment was ill-got
> By flattering and cringing and fawning
> For thy libellous slander
> Thou base salamander ...
> Shall Priestcraft her triumphant banner unroll
> And bind in her shackles each free British soul.[35]

The election cost Lambton £30,000, but he doubtless considered the money well spent since he topped the poll with 1,731 votes; Powlett was elected with 1,137; Wharton trailed with 874 votes. None of the Tory targets the north was unseated in this election. The only ultra (Wharton) lost, but there was a gain of one Tory (Brandling) who was expected to oppose the Catholic claims. Phillpotts, for one, long remembered the election in Durham. In 1821 he addressed an open letter to Earl Grey in which he deplored the Catholic role in the campaign but was pleased to say that

Popery and Mr Lambton, combined with Lord Grey, and all that he can say or do, will not put down the Reformed Church of England in this Diocese, or elsewhere.

The Whigs had been duped and were actually working for 'the restoration of Popery under the name of Catholic Emancipation'. The disposition of 'that sect of men (foolishly allowed to be called Catholic)' had not changed from that of their ancestors, and the way they would use power if they had it, 'they shewed at the last General Election for this County':

> Must we not remember the ostentation with which your son-in-law went about this County, preceded by the band of a Papist, surrounded by a Popish Gentry, in one instance a Popish priest at his elbow, while he was haranguing a mob in a speech made up of invectives and slanders against one of our Body; these Popish Gentlemen riding all over the County to solicit votes till one of them actually fell sick from over-fatigue; at your last Meetings these Gentlemen, though disabled from voting at County Elections, yet moving or seconding your inflammatory resolutions against the Government of their country.[36]

The band was Meynell's of Yarm. Lambton dined at Lartington Hall with Witham while canvassing Barnard Castle, and it is possible that Witham was the gentleman who wore himself out in the Whig cause, though George Silvertop was also a highly active campaigner. Bishop Poynter was moved to comment in a report to Rome in 1821: 'It is inconceivable how eager our Catholic noblemen and gentlemen are to possess their seats in parliament. It is impossible to stop them.' They had been of that mind for fifteen years at least, though the pace had clearly quickened.[37]

***

Although the general election of 1826 was not a No-Popery election to the same extent as that of 1807, there was worried talk of 'no-popery phrenzy' at the time, and the vicars apostolic felt obliged to put out a declaration that Catholics held no principles incompatible with their civil allegiance. There were no contests in Newcastle or in the City and County of Durham. Only minor differences emerged between the Durham city candidates. Michaelangelo Taylor would not agree to the payment of Catholic priests and their institutions out of English taxes, and General Hardinge wanted securities for the Church of England should Catholics be admitted to parliament. These reservations were doubtless appropriate in a constituency of which 58 per cent of electors were Dissenters. The candidates for Durham County were at one. Powlett deplored the fact that Catholics who had fought for their country should be deprived of the privileges which other Englishmen enjoyed. Lambton's long-held commitment to emancipation had taken a curious turn in the parliament of 1820. He opposed Sir Francis Burdett's Relief Bill of 1825 on the basis that it was a shabby compromise aimed at pacifying the country without granting substantial relief; Grey and Taylor concurred. Now, in his adoption speech, Lambton said he would never be one to keep millions of his fellow-countrymen in slavery and degradation, who firmly adhered to the faith of their ancestors, and who refused to take oaths incompatible with the beliefs. He also observed that 'In this part of the country, at least, he was happy that no cry of intolerance had been raised'. The *Durham Advertiser* disagreed, estimating that three-quarters of Sunderland's electorate was against emancipation. Lambton was elected by acclamation, however, and he was free to go up into Northumberland to help his brother-in-law Henry George Grey, Lord Howick, in his first parliamentary campaign.[38]

The general election of 1826 was known long afterwards in Northumberland as 'the great election'. For four months in the hottest summer on record, the county was 'rent by factions and thrown into a state of the utmost excitement'. The electors, liberally entertained in an acrimonious by-election in February that year, had every reason to anticipate another robust campaign in which no expense would be spared to secure their votes. It was said that 'the hospitalities of the four rivals were dispensed with a ruinous liberality', and that the election cost the candidates a quarter of a million pounds. It would emerge that the rivalries between the four candidates were greatest between those supposedly closest in ideology. Thus, the contempt of the ultra-Tory for the Canningite-Tory was as great as that of the Whig for the Radical, and vice versa. Moreover, the Catholic Question was of primary importance, for the county was a constituency in which sectarians in the electorate were preponderant by four to three. All candidates had to say something about emancipation, but even the most pro-Catholic of them could not declare his support without some caveat or to conflate it with other reform policies. Clarification of every ambiguous statement was demanded by opposing candidates, no other issue was given such detailed attention.[39]

This election is also significant in that not only did the northern Catholics take their by now usual prominent role at political meetings during the campaign, and seize every opportunity to press their case, but they went so far as to anticipate their emancipation by actually voting, and that without the least objection, even from the ultra-Tories. Before tracing the course of the campaigns of 1826, then, it is necessary to explain the apparent *fait accompli* of Catholic enfranchisement, when the question of emancipation was a major issue in the election. Before 1817, the Northumbrian Catholics used their 'interest' to influence the votes of their tenants. The pro-Catholic Whig candidate in the general elections of 1812 and 1815, Sir Charles Monck, received the written support of a number of Catholic gentlemen including George Gibson of Stagshaw, who told him

> I have to regret that the Elective Franchise (the birthright of every Englishman) is not yet conceded to the Catholics of this realm: I have therefore no vote, but the Interest and Influence that I possess shall be most cordially dedicated to your Service; and I am happy to say that this sentiment pervades my neighbourhood.[40]

The Relief Act of 1817 indemnified Catholic candidate naval and military officers from the consequences of omitting the Oath of Supremacy, and it seems a similar approach began to be adopted informally in other circumstances. The Irish Catholics had, moreover, enjoyed the franchise since 1793, and if they could be trusted with a vote, then why not respectable English Catholics? This inconsistency became the subject of the British Roman Catholic Tests Regulation Bill, introduced into the House of Commons in May 1823. The bill proposed to extend the franchise to the English and Scottish Catholics, primarily to place them on the same footing as the Irish, but also because it was ridiculous that Roman Catholic gentlemen could nominate parliamentary candidates but not have an individual vote themselves. In practice Catholic votes were taken with no questions asked; why not, then, formalise the existing system by removing the obligation to take the oaths before voting? No opposition to this measure was expressed, even Peel, the Tory leader, agreed with it. The bill also proposed to open the magistracy to English Catholics on similar grounds, but that section was hived off to form a separate bill. The section on the franchise was renamed the Roman Catholic Elective Franchise Bill and it was passed by the Commons with a majority of fifty-nine. Despite the support of Lord Liverpool, the Prime Minister, however, the bills were lost in the House of Lords. The matter did not rest there, for in 1825 Sir Francis Burdett's Catholic Relief Bill embodied a modified Oath of Supremacy which could be taken by Catholics at the polls, or when taking up office. That bill also passed the Commons but was rejected by the Lords. Notwithstanding these defeats, it seems clear that the principle was established in the last year of the 1820 parliament that English Catholics ought to be treated in the same way at the polls as the Irish. Since Liverpool and Peel had supported a measure which had passed the Commons twice, the Tories in the shires no doubt felt it inappropriate to demand the oaths from their Catholic friends and neighbours in 1826. That, at any rate, certainly was the case in Northumberland. The question had become one of allowing the Catholics into parliament rather than one of their enfranchisement.[41]

On 1 February 1826, four months before the dissolution of parliament, Charles John Brandling, the Tory member for Northumberland, died and a by-election was called. Brandling had succeeded his father, the apostate Catholic, as member for Newcastle in 1798, and he became the recognised Tory leader in south Northumberland; Gosforth House, his residence, was party headquarters. Brandling was defeated in the election of 1812 by the liberal-Tory Cuthbert Ellison, but he was returned to a county seat in 1820 with T. W. Beaumont.

Two young scions of local political families began their public careers in this by-election. On the day of Brandling's death, the Hon. Henry Thomas Liddell, the 29-year-old son of Lord Ravensworth, declared his intention of contesting the seat in the liberal-Tory interest. Henry, Viscount Howick, aged 24, followed suit for the Whigs. The expectation of a straight fight between them was dashed when Matthew Bell, ultra-Tory, shortly declared his candidature. Bell had taken umbrage at Liddell's indecent haste in declaring his intentions before Brandling, Bell's uncle, had been buried. Bell's intervention led Howick to withdraw, with the intimation that he preferred to wait and fight the forthcoming general election. He might have exploited the split in Tory ranks, but he calculated, or was told, that the county would probably vote to retain its political balance and return one or other of the Tories to join the Whig Beaumont in the Commons. Not only would Howick husband his resources, but he could assess how progressive the county's electorate was on the great issues of the day which, he expected, would be discussed on the hustings. The by-election was not particularly illuminating in that respect, however, for although the two Tories had few political differences, they fought each other 'with a vigour and contempt for cost which pointed to the personal matter at issue in the contest', and Bell largely confined himself to abusing Liddell as a foreigner, that is, from Durham.[42]

There was, however, one difference between the two candidates and that was Catholic Emancipation. Indeed, the by-election turned on it, although the candidates obscured their position at first. Bell announced that he would act in accordance with the principles that had been followed by his deceased uncle. Brandling had supported Burdett's bill of 1825, and the Northumbrian Catholics therefore assumed that Bell would support a future Catholic Relief Bill, and they therefore promised him their votes. When Bell later said that he would not concede any political rights to the Catholics, they withdrew their support. Bell was not in the least distressed and he even undertook that

> no impediment should be thrown in the way of their voting by having the oaths of supremacy and abjuration offered to them: thus affording them an opportunity, for the first time since the Revolution, of voting for members of parliament.[43]

Liddell, on the other hand, refused to give any public pledge about emancipation and, as Brandling later recalled, he had railed against the Catholic Church as 'the most dangerous state-engine that could be introduced into a country'. Brandling also alleged that Liddell had let it be known privately that he would support the Catholic claims. He had thereby 'secured the interest' of the Catholics 'and by their assistance would have gained his election' had it not been for the extraordinary efforts of Bell's supporters. Brandling was right; Bell won the by-election by only thirteen votes. A dozen Catholics can identified in the poll-book, all of whom voted for Liddell, as the lesser of two evils. Had more Catholics turned out, then, Bell's slender majority might have been overturned. Bell might then have been less gracious about allowing the Catholics to vote in the impending general election.[44]

The general election campaign began immediately after the by-election polls had closed, the date of the dissolution being so close. The widest range of political ideology was represented by the four candidates for the two seats, and each had a different approach to the Catholic Question. Matthew Bell, the 33-year-old ultra-Tory and newly-elected member, held views directly opposite to those of the other sitting member, Thomas Wentworth Beaumont, ten years older and, with his extensive lead-mining interests in Allendale and Weardale, one of the richest commoners in England. Beaumont had sat for the county since 1818 in succession to his father. Nominally a Tory, Beaumont had developed radical reforming ideas and, when he bothered to attend the Commons at all, he generally voted with the Whigs. An attempt by the Tories to unseat him in 1820 was unsuccessful, and the ultras were determined to oust him in 1826. So were the Whigs, but not only for political reasons. In 1823 Beaumont accused Earl Grey of an adulterous affair with Lady Swinburne which had led to her terminating an engagement between her daughter and Beaumont. The feud came to public notice in 1826 and added further spice to an already acrimonious contest.[45]

The two sitting members were challenged firstly by the Hon. H. T. Liddell, the 29-year-old Canningite-Tory who had been defeated in the by-election. Liddell was not personally popular; he was regarded as bookish, he lived in County Durham, and he did not share in the convivialities enjoyed by the county squirearchy, with whom he did not care to mix too freely. He was unenthusiastic about parliamentary reform and he made both pro- and anti-Catholic declarations during the campaign. Lord Howick, 24 years old, and son of the Whig leader, could be expected to espouse the opposition's reform programme, but his father felt it necessary to stiffen the lad's resolve. Liddell had prevaricated on the Catholic Question during the by-election, and Grey warned Howick that nothing was ever gained by ambiguity and concealment, Howick was not so sure, and he evaded the issue whenever possible. Grey was no doubt relieved that Lambton was available to manage Howick's campaign. Certainly, Lambton accompanied Howick for much of the time, and it was Lambton who would make all the significant pronouncements for the Whigs, much to Beaumont's fury.

Beaumont, standing as an 'Independent Reformer', was less concerned about electoral tactics than with establishing his radical credentials. He was first to declare his policy, which he summarised as

> obtaining a reform in the House of Commons, the total extinction of slavery, and for placing our Roman Catholic fellow-subjects on the same footing with ourselves.

He rebuked the critics of his early and candid support for emancipation by observing that Northumbrians had more sense and were more secure in their own creed than 'to dread innovation from a religion so abundant in errors as that of the Roman Catholics'. He later issued another statement in which he regretted that some Radicals among his supporters still harboured 'groundless fears of popish ascendancy'. He felt proud to belong to a county of which the freeholders 'exceeded all others in Christian tolerance'; at their request he would send them pamphlets and papers on the subject, for

> the better this question is understood, the less apprehension will be entertained of admitting the Roman Catholics into

a fair competition for power and an equal enjoyment of civil rights with Protestants.

Notwithstanding his support, which he evidently considered to outweigh his slur on Catholicism *per se*, Beaumont complained that he had '*not*, as yet, received the assistance of *one great family,* either Whig or Tory, Catholic or Protestant'. He had met with several refusals from gentlemen who considered him to be too warmly attached to Catholic Emancipation at the same time that 'many Catholics had been *splitting* upon two of my opponents'.[46]

Liddell, meanwhile was trying to find out how the land lay among the sectarians. He called on James Losh, the Tyneside Whig barrister, Unitarian and Catholic sympathiser, ostensibly to discuss the Catholic Question, but also, Losh suspected, to find out what Losh was advising his friend Beaumont. Losh reported Liddell as having admitted that he was a Canningite and that he had 'declared strongly his wish for Catholic Emancipation and professed that he was friendly to civil and religious liberty in general'. Losh suspected that that was not a fervently-held principle.[47]

The candidates travelled the county to canvass support and each held a rally in the form of a subscription dinner to celebrate the successful conclusion of the tour. The first was Howick's in Newcastle on 11 April, and Catholics were conspicuous in the places of honour. George Silvertop, James Kirsopp and William Charlton, all members of Howick's election committee, were seated at the top table, and in the body of the hall sat Nicholas Leadbitter and George Gibson with the Revd James Worswick and Dom George Turner missioners at Newcastle and Hesleyside respectively. Howick's speech, long and punctuated frequently by applause, concentrated on parliamentary reform as the prerequisite of progress. A reformed Commons would, for example, abolish the oaths and tests necessary to enter public service. Dr John Fenwick was more explicit about Catholic Emancipation. He thought that a government should not concern itself with the religion of any man unless it interfered with his civil duties or with national security; that did 'not apply to the Catholics of the British islands' who supported the constitution and law and order at home, and had died in the service of their country abroad. They acknowledged the spiritual authority of the Bishop of Rome in the discipline of their church, but, as good British subjects, they were scrupulous in rejecting all his attempts at temporal interference. Silvertop then addressed the meeting as 'one of those old-fashioned persons who still remain attached to the pure principles of the ancient faith', having 'in more instances than one felt the chilling powers of laws of exclusion, and having witnessed their withering effects on others'. No doubt assuming that it fell to him as the leading Catholic present, he dealt in turn with the principal charges levelled at his co-religionists. Firstly, with reference to the Catholic claim to exclusive salvation he, somewhat embarrassingly, outlined the religious history of Dr Fenwick sitting on his right, who

> was born of Catholic parents, baptized and educated a Catholic, and when of mature age, in the sincerity of his heart, renounced the church of Rome. I am descended, like him, from Catholic parents, was baptized and educated a Catholic, and I most firmly believe in the pure principles of the Catholic church, though I do also most sincerely wish for a thorough radical reform in the discipline of that church ... My learned friend has employed his great talents and acquirements in an impartial search into the doctrines of the Catholic church, and has rejected them. I, with equal impartiality, have applied my very Inferior powers to the same inquiry, but with a different result. Though we have so done, I entertain not a particle of doubt, but that with good works the gates of heaven will be equally open to us both.

Fenwick's reaction is not recorded.

Silvertop then dealt with the supposed aversion of Catholics to the 'spread of the Holy Scriptures'. He pointed out that fourteen Catholic editions of the Bible in English had been published since the Reformation and that Pope Pius VII had addressed a letter to the bishops of Great Britain enjoining them to encourage Catholics to read the Bible. Silvertop also told his audience that he was an officer of the British and Foreign Bible Society (founded in 1804). The early nineteenth century was a period in which Bible societies became popular—a development which Bishop Milner dismissed as 'Bibliomania'. There appeared to the vicars apostolic a danger that Protestant versions of the Bible might be foisted upon the Catholics. In 1812, Bishop Smith 'was not a little surprised' to see that at a meeting of which Mr Silvertop was chairman, it was resolved that the propriety of forming a society in Hexham be considered; 'surely', Smith enquired, 'Catholics ought to have nothing to do with it...?' Silvertop had asked Lingard to recommend the edition of the Bible best suited for general circulation. The Catholic Board formed the Roman Catholic Bible Society the following year in an attempt to keep the distribution of the Bible to their people in Catholic rather in Protestant hands. This did not get very far, however, because Rome took fright at the dangers involved. In 1818 Marlow Sidney (a convert) edited and published a cheap edition of the New Testament, revised by the priest Richard Horrabin to omit 'the notes distasteful to Protestants'. Naturally, that infuriated Bishop Milner who denounced the project. Silvertop did not allude to these difficulties in his speech.[48]

Liddell's final stops on his canvass of the county were at Whittingham, Wooler and Alnwick. He was received by John Clavering at Callaly Castle. He addressed the estate-workers and expressed the hope that the day would shortly arrive when, by his individual exertions, he might assist in the furtherance of those measures which would not only confer a well-merited boon on our Catholic fellow-subjects, but ultimately be of benefit to the whole realm.

On the following day, at his public dinner in Wooler, Liddell referred to the great pleasure it had been for him to 'publicly avow before the door of his excellent friend Mr Clavering', his sentiments in favour of the Catholic claims, though he was 'still hostile to the haughty and domineering spirit of their *church*'. He firmly believed that if the Catholics were emancipated, 'the exclusive character of their situation would gradually be lost'. He did not really believe that the granting of those claims would be dangerous.

Bell dined at Elsdon and he reiterated his long-held opinions on the Catholic Question:

> However I may respect individuals of that persuasion, and there are many most deserving of respect, I cannot convince myself of the expediency of granting to them as a body any further political power.

The Anglican clergyman Charles Bird was the principal speaker at Beaumont's dinner in Newcastle, and he made a long, and rather academic, speech about freedom of conscience, and he deplored any law which compelled an individual to choose between his religious faith and the exercise of civil rights.

The candidates all campaigned in North Shields. Beaumont said nothing about emancipation on his visit to the port. Liddell had presumably been advised that his remarks at Wooler had been too liberal, because he now made it clear that just as he had declined to give any pledge of his future conduct at the by-election, he would refrain from committing himself even now because he entertained some doubts as to the limits of the Catholic claims. He 'candidly' confessed that it did not appear 'desirable that Roman Catholics should be eligible to some of our highest offices of state'. Bell reiterated that he wished it to be 'distinctly understood' that he was 'averse to making further concessions of political power to the Roman Catholics'. In a pointed reference to Liddell, he said that this was not an opinion he had recently adopted, nor was it intended to serve present electioneering purposes. He was aware that by his open declaration of principle, he would have arrayed against him the whole body of Catholics. He feared not, for his Protestant brethren would never allow him to be beaten down by the Catholics, however formidable. Brandling warned the same audience not to be taken in by Liddell's equivocations. Liddell was pledged to support the Catholic claims, including their admission into parliament. It was clear from his speeches at Callaly and Wooler and 'from the conduct of the Catholics themselves, who are united in his support, no doubt can be entertained of the fact'. Furthermore, the reservations which Liddell had placed on the higher offices of state should not be taken seriously because if Catholics were admitted to parliament they would gain the key to everything else. Howick seemed to think that he had no need to refer explicitly to the Catholic Question since he was the official Whig candidate, and everyone knew what the party's policy was. Silvertop had spoken at one of his dinners and that seemed to have been sufficient for him, but there were some who wished he would go further.

Early in June Howick held a dinner at Morpeth which passed without reference to the Catholics, and another in Alnwick, when the question was again avoided. On the latter occasion, however, Thomas Haggerston was seated at the top table, and he rose to ask whether anyone had any objection, on account of his religion, to hear him say a few words. In case anyone did, he quickly went on to complain of the restraints under which Catholics laboured while their lives and their blood had answered for their loyalty. He concluded his brief intervention by eulogising Earl Grey for his services to the Catholic cause. Lambton, Howick's manager, jumped to his feet to lament that the venerable gentleman had feared that as a Catholic he might be prevented from speaking. Little did Haggerston know of him or of the assembled company if he thought that any such attempt would have been permitted. Yet, Lambton was not surprised that such an idea could have been entertained since many attempts were being made all over the country to revive religious persecution and to prolong political disqualification on religious grounds. Lambton went on to tell Haggerston and, through him, the Catholics of Northumberland, that they would disgrace themselves if they did not make Howick's election the sole object of their attention. Who were they to support if not the son of him who had sacrificed political power for them and their cause? He cared nothing for private pledges but looked for public declarations. Having heard what Haggerston had to say in praise of Grey, and knowing that those views were prevalent among the Catholics, Lambton therefore expected 'to meet them on the day of election, tendering their single undivided votes in favour of Lord Howick'. Well, now Haggerston knew where Howick stood, or at least where Howick's manager said Howick stood. That left only Liddell to clarify his position, unless, of course, his speech at North Shields represented his last word on the matter.

The adoption meeting for the election was held at Alnwick on 20 June. The candidates appeared in alphabetical order to present their manifestoes. On the Catholic Question, Beaumont repeated his support for emancipation, despite the unpopularity of that view. To cheers, he told the Catholics that they could expect nothing from the present perfidious government and that there was a conspiracy against them. His advice was to 'combine and associate—get your rights and privileges'. 'An extreme tumult arose' when Bell advanced his opinion that while he did not wish to 'interfere with the exercise of the religious duties of the Roman Catholics', he believed nonetheless that it would be unwise and unsafe to grant them any further political concessions.[49] Howick, with extreme brevity, declared his agreement with the more liberal elements of the Liverpool ministry 'in wishing to restore to the Roman Catholics their rights. (Cheers)'. Liddell dwelt longest on the topic because, he said, he had been reproached with disingenuousness. He wished to go into parliament entirely unfettered by any commitment and to act in the best interests of all as he would then understand them to be. From being for emancipation, then against, he was now ambivalent. At any rate, the mob cheered his remarks as they had those of his opponents.

The poll lasted fifteen days but the voting pattern was established early. At the count taken at the end of each day, Liddell topped the poll and Bell was second. Howick was in third place until the fourth day when Beaumont overtook him. As soon as the trend became clear, Grey wrote to his son in commiseration and to suggest a line of argument that might retrieve the situation. He thought that no-one could pretend to understand what Liddell's opinion was on any of the subjects concerning 'the Publick Interests at this Moment'. He had got votes from the Catholics by private promises to support their cause, but his most active and powerful supporters were the

> most uncompromising opposers of the Catholick Claims—Has he given them any assurances which may relieve their minds from the pious apprehensions which they entertain of the power of the Pope? His public statements defied all understanding; just when one thought one had understood him, he immediately expressed some qualification so that one had no assurance of what his conduct would be on this important question.[50]

Liddell's equivocations about Catholic Emancipation became the major issue on the hustings. After the seventh day's count, John Grey of Milfield criticised Liddell for this reason and murmured about Catholics who were content to accept a half yes and a half no from Liddell rather than a firm commitment from another. Brandling, speaking in Bell's support two days later, accused Liddell of duplicity 'in giving a pledge in private to support the Catholics, by which he secured their support, whilst in public he said his mind was not made up on the subject'. Liddell interrupted Brandling to say categorically that he 'wished to admit the Catholics into parliament'. There was no longer any need to hedge for Liddell now knew he was bound to be elected.

Lambton and Howick also realised that Liddell could not be overhauled and that Howick could not possibly win the other seat. The greater danger was that Beaumont might hold on to his seat. At the end of the first week, therefore, Howick invited his remaining supporters to split their votes between himself and Bell. On political grounds it was quite extraordinary for a reforming Whig to favour a reactionary Tory in this way, but orthodox Whigs considered Beaumont to be wholly unsuited to parliament and they wanted him dislodged at any cost. It had also emerged that Liddell and Beaumont had formed a coalition to attract the progressive Tory/Whig splitter. That could gain Beaumont the second seat, so the Whigs saw Bell's election as infinitely more preferable.

Beaumont challenged Howick to explain how he could have taken the votes of Catholics and then have dashed their hopes by helping to return a candidate wholly opposed to their relief. Howick turned on Liddell for see-sawing between support for and denunciation of the Catholics. Liddell had said different things in the by-election, and in his speeches at North Shields Callaly and Wooler. His intention had been to gain the support of both sides, 'the Catholics by the hope that he would vote for them—the

Protestants by the hope that he would vote against the Catholics'. Howick said he still had no idea how Liddell would vote in parliament, and demanded that he tell the electors of Northumberland precisely what he meant to do. Liddell replied that he was astonished that anyone could be in any doubt about his opinion. No stone had been left unturned to raise the cry of No-Popery in the county, but he had not wanted to be held responsible for adding to the clamour, and so he had refrained from making any commitment. Nonetheless, he would now say that he was of the opinion that it would be the greatest security to the Protestant Church to afford equal rights and justice to the Catholics, and while he would vote for their admittance to parliament, he would vote for their exclusion from the highest offices of state, many of which had ecclesiastical patronage.

Liddell topped the poll with 1,562 votes, two hundred ahead of Bell (1,380), who beat Beaumont by only forty-five votes. Howick trailed in with 977 votes. Northumberland was one of only eight constituencies to lose a pro-Catholic member in this election.[51] Furthermore, although Bell had predicted that the Protestants would never have allowed him to be beaten by the Catholics, it was a close-run thing. For if the Catholics had been united and if Howick had endorsed Beaumont, Bell might have been unseated, and an avowedly pro-Catholic member returned in his place. The Catholic voting pattern is therefore worth examining. The *Morning Herald* of 24 June said that Northumberland was 'a Catholic county' with one hundred Catholic voters but it is possible only to identify eight Catholic priests and twenty-four Catholic laymen in the poll-book.[52] Since the franchise was based on the ownership of property, no chaplain voted, but all the public missioners in the county did. All the Northumbrian Catholic gentry families are represented in the poll. The table below shows how they voted. (Matthew Bell received no Catholic votes and is omitted.)

Catholic Votes in the General Election of 1826 in the Northumberland Constituency

		Plumpers for			Splitters for		
	Liddell (Tory)	Howick (Whig)	Beaumont (Radical)		Liddell/ Beaumont	Liddell/ Howick	Beaumont /Howick
Laity (24)	1	7	2		5	5	4
Clergy (8)			4		3	1	

Note: Counting two for a plumped vote and one for a split vote, the candidates received the following total number of Catholic votes:

Beaumont 24

Howick 24

Liddell 16

The lay plumpers preferred the Whig, but the Radical was the clear favourite of the clerical plumpers. All but one of the clerical splitters supported Beaumont so that, overall, the priests were decidedly more radical than the laity. The Whig received almost no support from the clerical splitters who preferred the Tory, probably because Howick refused to support the Catholic cause openly, whereas Liddell, although with reservations and only when pressed, did. The lay splitters divided more evenly; as many of them included the Radical in their choice as the Tory or Whig. Nonetheless, about half of Liddell's Catholic supporters at the by-election shifted to the Whig or the Radical at the general election, which shows perhaps that they resented his equivocations more than the Catholic clergy. The Catholic electorate, then, supported candidates of the left by a clear majority, and they gave the Radical as many votes as the Whig. To that extent, the election appears to have been, for them, a single issue contest, and it certainly was for the priests. Since, however, a substantial number of laymen lent support to candidates who equivocated over, or were silent on, the Catholic Question, other considerations must have been at issue for them.

This was the first general election in which Catholics voted although, strictly speaking, they were ineligible until 1829. The lay voters were all landed proprietors of some wealth, or professional men of standing, but they were in a difficult position. They wanted to support the Radical for his avowedly pro-Catholic stand, but they also regarded the election as an opportunity to demonstrate their political moderation and their acceptance of the existing order. The only way to do that was to split their support between the Radical and either a moderate Tory or Whig candidate. Thus while they were well-disposed to the Radical, the Catholics could also be seen to occupy the middle ground. The essence of their campaign for emancipation was, after all, to show that the country would be safe with an enfranchised English Catholic gentry.[53] In any case, Howick was the son of the pro-Catholic champion, Earl Grey, and while he had not supported the cause during the campaign, it could be assumed he would do so in parliament. Liddell had finally said he would vote to open parliament to Catholics, with sureties, and that was enough for the minority of Tory-inclined Catholics. At any rate, the Catholics of Northumberland came close to unseating an ultra-Tory and retaining the seat of a Radical.

***

No further electioneering took place in the north-east during the parliament of 1826. Apart from the hustings, however, the disfranchised could always express a view on matters of immediate concern at public meetings and by means of petitions. Large numbers of petitions were got up whenever the Catholic Question appeared to be making progress, as in 1812 and 1813. Grey had presented a number in favour of relief signed by 'many thousand persons' in the north (Yorkshire, Hull, County Durham and Berwick), 'not all of whom were Roman Catholics, but included Dissenters and members of the established Church'. Viscount Sidmouth presented a petition against the Catholic claims from the Mayor and Corporation of Berwick; three weeks later Grey presented a pro-Catholic petition from the inhabitants of Berwick which had been signed by eighty burgesses who, he said, formed a majority of the Corporation, and he insisted that the previous petition represented a minority view. Anti-Catholic petitions from the Archdeacons of Durham and Northumberland were also tabled in the Commons at this time. Northern members of both houses occasionally presented petitions with which they did not agree. The Marquis of Londonderry had to present an anti-Catholic petition from Darlington in May 1825 although it was 'contrary to his own opinions'. In general, however, petitions were submitted through individuals sympathetic to the petitioners.[54]

Petitions poured into parliament in the immediate run-up to Emancipation. Of the sixty-two sent up from the north-east between 1825 and 1829, twenty-nine were pro-Catholic and were subscribed by groups of inhabitants of various towns and villages; by barristers and attorneys, magistrates, merchants and bankers; by Dissenters and Unitarians; by the Corporation of Newcastle; and by the Catholics themselves. Almost half (fourteen out of thirty-three) of the anti-Catholic petitions were either signed by groups of Anglican clergymen or sponsored individually by them in their vestries. The Earl of Darlington presented a pro-Catholic petition in May 1827, and remarked that only the influence of the clergy had prevented a greater number from signing it.[55] Liddell thought it would do no good to overwhelm the Commons in this way. Although he was inclined to defer to the feelings of his own electorate, he had to say that there had been 'a great deal of clamour mixed up with their petitions', and when he saw so many clergymen active in getting up anti-Catholic petitions, he doubted that they understood their religion. Much mischief was done by inflammatory speeches: some

> members talked as if they thought we were about to have a Romish parliament and a Papist government. It was idle to apprehend any danger to the constitution from the admission into parliament of 5 or 6 Catholic peers and 30 or 40 Catholic commoners.[56]

He was not afraid to meet his electors, the next day if necessary, to justify his support for the Catholics, and he had no fear of the consequences.

The Bishop of Durham presented petitions against further concessions to the Catholics from Bishopwearmouth and Sunderland. Lord Durham (Lambton) said he was instructed to state that the latter petition did not represent the real sentiments of the townsfolk. It was not the result of any public meeting; on the contrary, it was got up by the curate (George Stephenson) having been drafted by the Rector, G. V. Wellesley (brother of the Duke of Wellington). The petition did not reflect the opinions of the gentry, the merchants or the ship-owners, or even a majority of the lower class of persons, despite the great pains that had been taken to circulate it among the poor. He understood from a magistrate that it had been signed by a number of women and two hundred boys. He did not wish to say that the opinions of boys and women were unfit to be heard, but he did wish to point out that the petition was unrepresentative; he knew that sentiment in Sunderland was decidedly in favour of the removal of all civil disabilities on religious grounds. The Bishop merely replied that so far as he knew the petition had been 'respectably signed'.[57]

A similar exchange between Eldon and Grey occurred when the former presented four petitions from parishes in Newcastle. Grey said that the population of Newcastle was not disposed to stir up a question which had been debated for almost thirty years during which time both of their members of parliament had constantly voted for relief. On no occasion had their conduct been censured by their constituents, despite there having been several elections during the period, and no questions on the matter had been put to candidates on the hustings or elsewhere. The electors of Newcastle had always pursued a moderate course, and preferred to leave a decision to parliament. Indeed, while the people were disinclined to meddle with the subject in 1826, the clergy of the town were not.[58] Then, Grey continued, in 1829 a Methodist minister applied to the Mayor to call a public meeting, but the latter declined because there was insufficient demand. The clergy, therefore, got up petitions instead and they were hawked about the town to be signed 'by those who should not' (women and boys, presumably). One petition originated with the vestry of the parish church, where it was proposed to two or three Wesleyans, well known to be hostile to the Catholic claims; when they objected to an expression of attachment to the establishment, the petition was rewritten to accommodate them. Thus, Grey taunted, Eldon would not really like the petition he was sponsoring, for, in trying to guard against the terrors of popery, it would let in something more dangerous. As a result of those petitions, a large number of people, including every considerable person in the legal and medical professions, the principal merchants and several magistrates, requested a public meeting which was allowed by the Mayor.

Grey then described how the clergy had distributed inflammatory addresses inciting anti-Catholics to disrupt the meeting. The Mayor, Robert Bell, who was neutral, took the chair. The pro-Catholics were led by Dr Headlam, James Losh (Grey's informant about the proceedings) and W. H. Ord, (son of W. Ord, M. P. for Morpeth), all leading Whigs. Against the Catholics were J. Clark, a Methodist preacher and publisher, W. Chapman and the Revd F. A. West, a Wesleyan minister. Local Tories were embarrassed by the meeting, since emancipation was now government policy, yet churchmen were still campaigning against it. The Methodists were also out of step with their leadership in London which had decided that, as a body, they would keep out of the political argument.[59] Losh wrote in his diary on 10 March 1829 that at the meeting, the

> Clergy and the Methodists had formed a junction and by bringing up a number of colliers etc., they outnumbered us; in all other respects they made a miserable figure. They had not on their side one magistrate, one barrister, one physician and only one attorney and one surgeon. Their *genteel partizans* consisted of Methodists, a great many of the clergy and a considerable number of old women. Even their majority amongst the mob might easily have been prevented by a very little exertion.

As it was, every liberal proposal was shouted down, and, after some difficulty, a vote was taken. John Brandling had moved a contrary amendment but he was not seconded and he took no further part in the debate. The pro-Catholic motion was lost by a proportion of five to four. Vestry petitions signed by 7,724 persons were immediately sent to London. (Losh said that many of the signatories were children.) The Corporation then met and unanimously decided to forward a petition in favour of Emancipation. Grey added that he would shortly present a pro-Catholic petition signed by a large proportion of the Newcastle townsfolk and added the observation that the Anglican clergy would be better employed combating the proliferation of those sects unfriendly to the establishment. Eldon merely observed that the clergy had always done their duty.

The main opposition to Catholic Emancipation in the northeast, then, came from the Anglican clergy and the lower middle-class and artisan Methodists, rallying to the old cry of No-Popery in a final attempt to 'preserve themselves, their families and their religion from destruction'. As to the feeling of the gentry of Newcastle, Losh told Grey, 'I can only say that I have not met above one or two Anti-Catholics in society since this measure was brought forward'.[60]

The Duke of Wellington, Prime Minister, became convinced by the summer of 1828 that Catholic Emancipation was essential if Ireland was to be kept at peace. The King was told on 1 August but, not unexpectedly, he proved unreceptive and it was not until January 1829 that he (and Robert Peel) would accept the measure, but only on the grounds urged upon them by Wellington—the prevention of an Irish insurrection. In any case, it was clear by this time that all bills relieving the Catholics were and would be passed by the House of Commons, and even in the House of Lords opinion was beginning to change.

There were four important northern peers in the upper house in addition to the Bishop of Durham: the Marquesses of Cleveland and Londonderry, the Duke of Northumberland and Earl Grey. The latter's long-standing commitment to the Catholic cause has already been treated. William Henry Vane, Marquess of Cleveland was of a similar outlook. He had six parliamentary boroughs in his pocket and he was regarded by the *Dublin Morning Post* as one of the most zealous and useful friends of the Catholics: 'He makes it a positive condition with those to whom he gives his influence that they should vote for Catholic Emancipation'. His kinsman William Powlett was a member for County Durham. Lord Charles Stewart succeeded as third Marquess of Londonderry at the death of his half-brother Lord Castlereagh, the Foreign Secretary, in 1822. His sister was married to General Sir Henry Hardinge, M. P. for

Durham City since 1820. Londonderry was an ultra-Tory who came round to the view that peace in Ireland was worth a few Catholics in parliament. Provided emancipation became government policy, he said, 'his exertions would never be wanting in support of the Catholics'.[61]

Hugh Percy, third Duke of Northumberland, was also an ultra-Tory. He had defeated Grey in the No-Popery election of 1807 as a young man of 22, and he had spent five years in the Commons until his elevation to the Lords in 1817 at the death of his father. He withheld his proxy from the opponents of the Catholic Relief Bill of 1825, but he would agree with emancipation only as a government measure and he refused to join the Brunswick Club in 1828. Wellington offered him the Lord Lieutenancy of Ireland in January 1829 because he was 'the most moderate of men: and most particularly so upon the Roman Catholic question'. Northumberland saw no objection to the removal of all points of spiritual doctrine and discipline from the oaths. The government should impose a 'simple but strong' oath of allegiance as the qualification for all civil offices, except some of the higher offices of state which should remain closed to Catholics; no other securities would be necessary. This clear and robust common sense satisfied Wellington, and the appointment was confirmed. Northumberland allowed his proxy vote to be cast in favour of Emancipation.[62]

Of the north-eastern members of the House of Lords, then, only the Bishop of Durham was anti-Catholic. Bishop Barrington died in 1826 to be succeeded by the very junior Bishop of Llandaff, William van Mildert. He was an ultra-High Church bishop of whom it was said, 'orthodoxy oozed out of his pores', and that he 'stood as firmly as any churchman against the nineteenth century'. He made an effective speech against the Catholic Relief Bill in 1825 in which he said that Catholics were excluded from political life not for their religious errors, but because they were Papists, and he advanced the same view in 1829. He was another who used the age-old cliche that some of his good friends were Catholics but he would nonetheless vote against their emancipation. His views were simple enough, he said, 'Only keep the Papists out of Parliament, and I care little what else is done for them'.[63]

The voting record of the north-eastern peers and commoners after 1807 on the Catholic Question was overwhelmingly pro-Catholic; only the Bishop of Durham, Matthew Bell, Richard Wharton and Sir Henry Vane Tempest consistently voted against. The Duke of Northumberland and Lord Ravensworth (Liddell) voted against until it became a government measure. Lord Auckland (Eden) was pro-Catholic. The Bishops of Chester and St. David's, both Durham prebendaries, voted for Emancipation. The *Durham County Advertiser* smouldered with rage against the act, the *Durham Chronicle* exulted.[64]

Catholic Emancipation was enacted in April 1829 with hardly a backward look at the interminable debates of the previous twenty years. The only security contained in the act was the disfranchisement of the forty-shilling Irish freeholders; there were no substantive ecclesiastical restrictions.[65] The conclusion that the best security of all was emancipation without strings, reached by the Whigs long before, was at last, and more painfully, accepted by the Tories. Peace in Ireland was not only worth a Mass, it was worth an unfettered bench of bishops. Furthermore, Wellington had not just achieved a surprise parliamentary majority for his bill, but he had avoided the public unrest that had followed upon the much more modest first Catholic Relief Act. That was partly due to a general acceptance of emancipation as a disagreeable but necessary measure; but it was also because the bill had been introduced by the victor of Waterloo. It was sufficient for ordinary people that their military hero was prepared to emancipate the Catholics, for if he could not be trusted, then who could? He would see to it that the Catholics did not over-reach themselves. He was no party ideologue, but a disinterested and objective national leader; it is doubtful if any other politician could have carried Catholic Emancipation with so little adverse reaction from the common people.[66]

In his *Charge* of 1831, Bishop van Mildert lamented the passage of Catholic Emancipation, and encouraged his clergy to put it out of their minds:

> Far better is it, for the peace of the community, and for its future welfare, that such things should be left to the historian hereafter to dilate upon, with a cooler judgement and a more impartial spirit than can be expected from contemporary observers.

In fact, the peace of the community had not been noticeably affected by the act. James Losh noted in his diary in May 1829 that 'the country is tranquil, and Catholic Emancipation is, I have no doubt, gradually producing the happiest effects'.[67]

***

In 1831, the Earl of Durham (Lambton) said that events had proved Catholic Emancipation to be essentially beneficial; parliament had been opened to 'as loyal, as honest, and as respectable men is are to be found in the country', and it had erased that 'foul blot of religious and political intolerance which had so long disgraced our constitution'.[68] His approbation stemmed partly from the fact that most of the northern Catholics were liberal in their politics. Parliamentary seats were offered by the Whigs to W. T. Salvin, George Silvertop and Henry Witham. It was thought that Salvin's Catholicism might lose him two hundred votes in an electorate of two thousand, and that was acceptable to the Whig party managers. Durham's agent regretted Witham's decision (for financial reasons) not to stand in 1837, because he would have been an excellent candidate whose election could be easily managed.

Charles Towneley of Stella was stopped by his father from standing in the same election, which was probably just as well because John Smith of Brooms thought he would not have received much support, for central Durham was 'supposed to be the most Tory neighbourhood' in the county.[69]

Catholics began to appear in public office in the thirties. Witham was High Sheriff in Durham, and Silvertop, followed by Charlton, in Northumberland. Thompson of Durham and Dunn of Newcastle were elected Mayor of their towns. In July 1831 it was reported from Durham that there were

> three Catholic sheriffs and an alderman at chapel!! [The Vicar Apostolic] Mr Riddell behaved very well for he stayed in town on purpose to come to chapel which he did in his carriage and six!! Consequently we had a full & gay chapel. What will the Reformation Society say to this?[70]

T. Gibson was pricked for Sheriff of Newcastle in 1836 and elected Mayor six years later. He had the Revd W. Riddell of St. Andrew's to say grace at his inaugural dinner, much to the fury of the anti-Catholic *Newcastle Journal*. The hunger for civic responsibility is demonstrated by W. Charlton of Hesleyside, an indefatigable do-gooder after emancipation. In the thirties he built the workhouse at Bellingham, became a magistrate, Poor Law Guardian and Honorary Road Surveyor for the area. His wife remarked that he found his native locality 'without either roads or railways and left it with both'. There was, then, no lack of encouragement or willingness for Catholics to enter public life. Immediately after emancipation the Corporation of Berwick rescinded its prohibition on the appointment of Catholics as Freemen, and unanimously voted the honour on Sir Carnaby Haggerston.[71]

There were, however, some northern Catholics who held to the radicalism inculcated in them during the long struggle for emancipation. That campaign was conducted largely in libertarian terms, and concepts of freedom and justice dominated Catholic political thinking. Catholics always vigorously repudiated any association of their religion with autocracy, reaction and superstition. While the attachment of the Radicals to their cause was a source of embarrassment to most Catholic gentlemen, (but not George Silvertop, Beaumont's proposer at the general election of 1832[72]) who sought to achieve emancipation within the existing political order and who deprecated the excesses of the Irish leaders, a large number of plebeian English Catholics adopted a contrary ideology. Fully imbued with the reforming values of a recently liberated minority, they joined the campaigns for parliamentary reform and other egalitarian causes in the 1830s. That stance was also bound up with another change within the Catholic body. Missions in the towns were now autonomous; most were staffed by priests from the lower middle-class, and were free of gentry control; the urban lay leadership became increasingly self-confident, independently-minded and sympathetic to emergent working-class politics. The most notable exemplar of this radical Catholicism was Charles Larkin a second-generation Irish Tyneside surgeon.

Larkin was born in County Durham in 1800, the eldest son of a gardener turned innkeeper, who kept the *Black Boy* in the Groat Market in Newcastle. He was intended for the Church, and he was sent to Ushaw College but he proved to have no vocation for the priesthood and he left the seminary to enter the medical profession under the tutelage of a Newcastle surgeon. Larkin was not the only one to leave Ushaw College for that reason. The Darlington-born John Wilson Ewbank, R.S.A. (1799-1847) left to follow an artistic career but,

> as prosperity met him, moral fortitude retreated, and he fell, day by day, into habits of dissipation from which no efforts of his friends were ever able to extricate him.[73]

Larkin had a quite different nature. Having qualified as a doctor, he went into practice in Pilgrim Street. He made a name for himself for his joint efforts with the Revd James Worswick in the care of the victims of an epidemic of cholera in the poor Westgate district of the city in 1831. He had also become well known by then as one of the most effective political agitators and orators in the north-east. He was a leading member of the Northern Political Union, formed by the Radicals in June 1831 to fight for political reform and other democratic causes, on which Larkin spoke eloquently and forcefully at an increasing number of public meetings.[74]

The Church was hostile to the development of trade unionism at this time, not because it was a working-class movement, but because of the mystery that surrounded its proceedings. The use of secret oaths and initiation rites was, in the Church's view, synonymous with free-masonry, and in any case could only have been necessary if the real purpose of the union was subversive.[75] And, in fact, a number of working-class insurance schemes did specifically debar Catholics from membership. The Church got round that by establishing its own Friendly Societies in the 1820s, though keeping them under partial clerical control. The Newcastle upon Tyne Catholic Friendly Society was founded in 1823 under the patronage of the Revd James Worswick, the presidency of Anthony Hodgson and the trusteeship of Charles Larkin. The aim of the Society was 'the maintenance and assistance of each other in sickness, advanced age, etc., and for the widows and children of deceased members'. There were one hundred and thirty members at the Annual General Meeting and Dinner in 1826, which was held at Larkin's public house. The convening notice reminded the members of the twenty-third rule of the Society which made any member who neglected his Easter duty for two successive years liable to expulsion. A strong Catholic ethos was apparent in other rules. Members who missed memorial and anniversary Masses for deceased members were fined sixpence, and members who were irregular in their attendance at Sunday Mass were to be reprimanded by the president.[76]

The *Catholic Directory* (1827) said that the Society was the only one in Newcastle to have registered under the regulatory act of 1819. The notice went on

> This institution, which was very much wanted in this town, in consequence of the Catholics being ineligible as members of most of the friendly societies in it, although it has existed only three years, has completely answered the expectations of its promoters.

Ten years later, however, it was reported that the funds of the Society had been decreasing over the previous few years as a result of the cholera epidemic of the winter of 1831–1832, in which some four hundred and fifty lives were lost, eighty of which were Catholic. The Society may have been wound up at this point, for nothing more is heard of it. It may have been absorbed into or succeeded by the Newcastle Hibernian Benevolent Society, which was established in 1835 with similar aims, although wholly Irish in composition, and intended to provide insurance for a cheaper premium which poor immigrants could afford.[77]

Larkin's involvement in the Friendly Society was the least controversial of his activities, for he was an avowed revolutionary; 'revolution is the alternative of reform', he said. In one particularly outspoken speech made in May 1832 about resistance to reform, he warned the king to remember the fate of Louis XVI, and the queen to meditate on what had happened to Marie Antoinette, 'whose fairer head than ever graced the shoulders of Adelaide, Queen of England, rolled upon the scaffold'. Those remarks were debated in the House of Lords and a warrant was issued for Larkin's arrest on a charge of high treason. The Reform Act was passed three weeks later, however, and the charge was dropped. Larkin did not become a Chartist, and he resigned from the Northern Political Union when some members attacked the 'superstitious and savage tyrants of Catholic Spain and Portugal'. He did, however, pursue an independent campaign for further parliamentary reform. In 1836 he even started a newspaper, the *Newcastle Standard,* to promulgate his views, but it lasted only six months.[78]

Larkin was also outspoken and theologically literate in the public defence of the Church. His refutation of *The Awful Disclosures of Maria Monk* (1836) was thought especially effective, and local Catholics presented him with £100 and a silver tea and coffee service. In speech, pamphlet and letters to the newspapers, Larkin also attacked the anti-Catholic fulminations of the Reformation Society on Tyneside, which continued with its No-Popery crusade after Emancipation. Joseph Curr, chaplain at Callaly Castle, became heavily embroiled in a controversy with the Society and the clergy of Coquetdale in 1835. The subject-matter was much the same as that which had been discussed by Lingard and Barrington at the beginning of the century, and showed that anti-Catholicism was alive and well. Catholic Defence Societies were formed in almost every town of the region at this time.[79]

In 1836 Larkin delivered a series of lectures on the evils of the Anglican establishment, which, no doubt, served to confirm the worst fears of the local High Church party that Catholic Emancipation would lead ultimately to dis-establishment. Indeed, Bishop van Mildert held that Larkin's ideas, as well as the prevailing anti-clericalism and the 'spread of free enquiry', were deliberately aimed at the overthrow of the National Church. It was with that consideration in mind that the bishop and one of his canons, Charles Thorp, established the University of Durham. They hoped that, by using ecclesiastical revenues for educational purposes, criticisms of Church wealth would be deflected and that Church endowments could be retained for the use of the diocese. Larkin's views on establishment gained him the admiration of the Nonconformists of Newcastle, and he endeared himself to the Radicals and self-improving artisans in 1842 when he denounced Sabbatarians for proposing to close the Central News Room on Sundays.[80]

Larkin's greatest popularity, however, lay within the growing Irish Catholic community of Newcastle for consistently espousing the Irish nationalist cause. He led the welcome for Daniel O'Connell when the Irish leader visited Newcastle in 1835; O'Connell knew Larkin's writings and praised them. The vicars apostolic, however, treated the Irish with extreme suspicion. In 1835 Bishop Briggs excluded members of the nationalist secret society the Knights of St. Patrick, from the sacraments, and the bishops were most reluctant to place Irish priests on the mission. Philip Kearney, missioner in Sunderland, was the only Irish-born priest practising in the north-east in 1829. Bishop Riddell declined the offer of a priest from Waterford in 1845 because he was 'rather afraid of introducing an Irishman at present so near to Newcastle' where the greatest concentration of immigrants lived. A year later, however, he appointed the Irish ex-Dominican Antony McDermott to Felling. Although McDermott was there only four months, he impressed the bishop because he 'kept very much by himself and always professed a disinclination to mix with the low Irish and take part in their squabbles'.[81] The bishop doubtless had in mind incidents like that which occurred in January 1843:

> As Robert Owen, the wellknown Socialist, was lecturing in the Lecture Room, Newcastle, an Irishman attempted to get on to the platform to reply to the statements of the lecturer. He was, however, ejected, upon which he obtained a reinforcement of his countrymen, and commenced an attack on the doors of the building with sticks, broken bed-posts, chair legs, etc. In a few minutes they forced an entrance and soon compelled the audience to retreat

through the doors and windows. The Irishmen were fortunately satisfied with this victory and did not commit any serious injury.

On another occasion, in 1845, Bernard McAnulty 'with a battalion of Irish navvies', then laying the Newcastle and Carlisle Railway line (for William Charlton of Hesleyside), broke up a meeting of the North of England Protestant Alliance. McAnulty had gone to Newcastle in 1838 from Ireland and made his fortune as a linen-merchant. He became highly active in local Irish politics in the late 1840s as President of the Repeal Association of Newcastle and also as President of the newly-founded Confederate Club, a militant branch of the Young Ireland Movement.[82]

Politically excitable laymen were one thing, but no bishop could allow a priest to become involved, however remotely, in such unseemly behaviour or the Church would suffer. The fear of rabble-rousing priests faded slowly; in 1847 and 1848 two Ushaw-trained Irish priests were appointed to the mission in the region (John Kelly at Felling and Francis Kearney at Brooms), but it was not until the 1850s that Irish-trained and Gaelic-speaking priests were accepted. Ralph Platt was the missioner at Stella where the Catholic population increased from 660 in 1847 to 1,100 in 1855. Many of these were Irish immigrants whose first language was Gaelic. Platt was one of the very few English priests to take the trouble to learn that tongue in order to communicate freely with those for whom he was pastor.[83]

Larkin's devotion to his church did not extend to what he considered to be inegalitarian practices within it. He particularly abhorred pew-rents and door-pence, no doubt having in mind the large numbers of poor Irish people who could not afford either. In 1844, when James Worswick introduced the charges at St. Mary's, Newcastle, Larkin issued *A Letter* addressed to Bishop Riddell on the sin of simony of selling seats in churches. Ambrose Lisle

Phillipps supported him in a private letter but Larkin sent it to a local newspaper with a covering note applauding Phillipps' criticism of the 'vile abuses' of the clergy. Phillipps repudiated Larkin's terminology, but a full-scale row followed. Riddell pointed out that St. Mary's had a debt of £3,000, and there was no income except from the contributions of the congregation. Privately, he deprecated Phillipps' support for someone whom he considered 'one of the bitterest enemies to Catholicity in this town', which was rather unfair in view of Larkin's record of championing the Catholic cause. The bishop, however, went on to doubt if Larkin had 'been to Mass on a Sunday for half a dozen years', that he never went to Mass on holydays, and that he had 'not approached the sacraments for (I daresay) twenty years'. Whatever the truth about Larkin's personal religious practice, he was, nonetheless, tireless in defence of the faith against the anti-Catholicism which was a continuing element in the political and ecclesiastical life of the region, quite apart from the excesses of the Reformation Society.[84]

The general election of 1841 was largely about the establishment of the Church, and several calls were made for the repeal of Catholic Emancipation. It was the restoration of the English Catholic hierarchy in 1850, however, that occasioned the most severe bout of anti-Catholicism in England since the Gordon Riots. Edward Maltby, Bishop of Durham, wrote to the Prime Minister, Lord John Russell, protesting at what he called this 'Papal Aggression'. Russell's reply, published in *The Times,* also condemned the Pope's action, and he deplored Cardinal Nicholas Wiseman's grandiose proclamation of it in the letter *Ex Porta Flaminia.*[85] The restoration represented unacceptable papal interference in the internal affairs of the United Kingdom and a usurpation of the royal prerogative. An outraged parliament passed the Ecclesiastical Titles Act in 1851. It was said that the Catholics caused Sir George Grey, M. P. for North Northumberland, to be unseated by the Liberal Wentworth

Beaumont in the general election of 1852 in reprisal for his role in the affair as Home Secretary. During the agitation, Larkin delivered lectures on 'The Pope and Cardinal Wiseman', on Russell's 'Durham Letter', and on the 'Re-establishment of the Catholic Hierarchy'. These were in influential in calming Anglican sensitivities in the north but they were almost his last contributions to religious controversy, though he wrote an occasional column on political and other current affairs for the local press until 1868. He died a few days after a visit from Bishop Henry Chadwick in February 1879.[86]

It is most unfortunate that none of Larkin's private papers have survived, for he was the dominant lay Catholic figure in the north-east for over twenty years after 1830. He was well to the left in his politics, but he was not untypical or unrepresentative of the newly-enfranchised urban Catholics, both indigenous and immigrant, who clearly gave him considerable support. It has been said that the Catholic Church in Newcastle, though weak in numbers, was strong in enthusiasm and radical in its politics. By national origin and politics, Larkin was its natural lay spokesman. But, while James Worswick, the principal Tyneside priest for almost fifty years, was a close friend and colleague, despite their differences over Church finance, the local Catholic hierarchy did not welcome Larkin as a champion of the Church. His outspokenness on all social, theological and political topics of the day, his enthusiastic radicalism and his Irish nationalism did not incline the bishops to him, at least in the thirties and forties. Nevertheless, Larkin became an unofficial spokesman by default. In 1840 he published, anonymously, an open letter in the *Durham Chronicle* to Bishop Briggs 'on the apathy of the Catholic clergy in the Northern District' in the face of anti-Catholic propaganda. Larkin, then, did fill a gap in the public life of the northern Church in the propagation of the faith, quite apart from his purely political contribution to the advancement of the working-class, of which the Catholic Church on Tyneside was then largely comprised.[87]

The Earl of Derwentwater led the rural Northumbrian Catholics in the Jacobite cause at the beginning of the eighteenth century. A little over one hundred years later, the lay leadership of the northern Catholics had passed to Charles Larkin, a middle-class urban Radical. Thus was exemplified the transformation which the Catholic community had passed through during the period.

Notes

[1] J. C. D. Clarke, *English Society 1660–1832: Religion, Ideology and Politics during the Ancien Regime* (Cambridge University Press, 1985), p. 354.

[2] T. C. Hansard, *The Parliamentary Debates from the Year 1803* (London: Hansard, 1803–1829), (1), XXXVI, col. 667. (Henceforth PD with vol. and col.) U. Henriques, *Religious Toleration in England 1787–1833* (London: Routledge & Kegan Paul, 1961), p. 26; PD (1), IV, 708–711. Bishop W. Gibson was told in 1790 that the government was very willing to relieve the Catholics if it could secure their allegiance: 'The difficulty is not about ye Stuarts, but ye interference of papal authority', cf. Leeds Diocesan Archives [LDA]: Gibson Papers, Pilling to Gibson, 26 Nov. 1790.

[3] J. Todd, *John Wesley and the Catholic Church* (London: Catholic Book Club, 1958), p.100. Wesley does not seem to have come across many Catholics. He did meet one 'cursing, swearing, drunken papist' in Newcastle in 1743 who insisted that Wesley read Richard Challoner's *The Grounds of the Old Religion*, cf. J. Wesley, *The Journal 1703–1791* (London, New Chapel, 1916, 8 vols), III, p. 75. He believed that Catholics could be regarded as sincere though deluded Christians. When his nephew became a Catholic, Wesley remarked, 'better a Catholic than a pagan'. (Todd, *Wesley*, pp. 29/30, 86/87). D. Hempton, *Methodism and Politics in British Society, 1750–1850* (London: Hutchinson, 1984), ch. 5; J. H. Hexter, 'The Protestant Revival and the Catholic Question in England, 1778–1829' in *Journal of Modern History*, 8 (1936), p. 300.

[4] Hexter, *Protestant Revival*, pp. 304–306; Hempton, *Methodism*, p. 141; P. Cadogan, *Early Radical Newcastle* (Consett: Sagittarius Press, 1975), p. 37.

[5] LDA: Smith Papers, 114, 26 May 1821.

6   Ushaw College Manuscripts [UCM]: III/189, Propaganda to Petre, 11 Aug. 1773. Northumberland Record Office [NRO]: RCD 4/89, Hay to Gibson, 4 Oct. 1794. LDA: Gibson Papers, IV, Propaganda to Gibson, 6 Apr. 1821 (in fact, William Gibson had submitted a report in December 1818); B. Ward, *The Sequel to Catholic Emancipation, 1830–1850* (London: Longmans, 1915, 2 vols), I, pp.125, 150.

7   M. Roberts, *The Whig Party 1807–1812* (London: Cass, 1965), p. 39; E. Norman, *The English Catholic Church in the Nineteenth Century* (Oxford, The Clarendon Press, 1984), p. 45; PD(1), XV, 504; PD(1), XVII, 430.

8   PD(1), IV, 654.

9   Clarke, *English Society*, pp. 350–353.

10 The vigour of the Catholics in the political arena is well brought out by R. W. Linker in: 'English Catholics in the Eighteenth Century: An Interpretation' in *Church History* 35 (1966), pp. 288ff. and 'The English Catholics and Emancipation: The Politics of Persuasion' in *Journal of Ecclesiastical History* [JEH] 27/2 (1976), pp. 151ff.

11 The precise chronology of this dispute in its early stages is difficult to establish; the sequence given here is based on internal evidence. Barrington's *Charge* was delivered in Durham cathedral in the summer of 1806 but it was not published until February or March 1807. It went into three editions but Lingard issued his *Remarks* after the first. This must have been in April, for Lingard notes that 'within two months' of publication, Elijah Index and A Clergyman responded. The former dates his contribution to 5 June 1807. Barrington issued his *Grounds* in May 1807 and Lingard reissued his *Remarks* with a new preface. He reviewed the Protestant's *Reply* in June and Elijah Index replied in July. Subsequent interventions came after the election (parliament met on 22 June).

12 Preface to the second edition of *Remarks*.

13 Bishop Milner condemned the *Antiquities* for its reticence and good manners; he suspected Lingard of heresy: M. Haile & E. Bonney, *Life and Letters of John Lingard 1771–1851* (London: Herbert & Daniel, n. d. [1911]), p. 97. G. M. Trevelyan, *Lord Grey of the Reform Bill* (London: Longman, 1929), p. 170.

14 *Oxford Dictionary of National Biography* [ODNB]. Some of Barrington's anti-Catholic 'tracts became standard treatises in the religious world', W. Page (ed.) *The Victoria History of the County of Durham* (London: Constable, 1905, 3 vols), II, p. 68; F. K. Brown, *Fathers of the Victorians* (Cam-

bridge University Press, 1961), pp. 31/32; R. Solway, *Prelates and People; Ecclesiastical Social Thought in England 1783-1852* (Cambridge University Press:1969), p. 72 n3; W. Fordyce, *The History and Antiquities of the County Palatine of Durham* (Newcastle: Fordyce, 1857, 2 vols), I, p. 86f; G. G. Armstrong, 'The Life and Influence of Shute Barrington, Bishop of Durham, 1791-1826' (Durham, King's College, M.Litt., 1936), p. 616.

[15] *Charge*, p. 4.

[16] *Charge*, p. 9; *Remarks*, Preface

[17] *Remarks*, pp. 6, 79, 83, 95.

[18] C. Butler, *Reminiscences* (London: Murray, 1824), pp. 94n, 126-129. Barrington opposed the nomination of Sir Charles Englefield as President of the Society of Antiquaries.

[19] *Remarks*, p. 77; J. Lingard, *Remarks on a Late Pamphlet Entitled "The Grounds..."* (London: Booker, 1809), p. 4.

[20] 'Liege Subject' was the Revd Henry Cotes. Two Catholic gentlemen appealed for peace and fairness in the *Courant*: George Gibson, under the pseudonym of 'A Friend to Peace and Union', and Thomas Selby, as 'A Loyal Freeholder' identified in *Orthodox Journal* vol. 3, no. 99 (1857), p. 62. See also J. Latimer, *Local Records 1832-1857* (Newcastle: The Chronicle, 1857), p. 310. The chaplain at Callaly Castle, Thomas Gillow (a contemporary of Lingard at Douai and at Crook Hall), published a short treatise, *Catholic Principles of Allegiance Asserted* (Newcastle: Walker, 1807) in which he explained that the Pope's supremacy was confined to spiritual matters and that English Catholics would never suffer any foreign power whatsoever to divide their affections or estrange their allegiance. The book does not appear to have been noticed.

[21] Haile & Bonney, *Lingard*, p.122; J. Lingard, *A Vindication of The "Remarks"....* (Newcastle: Hodgson, 1807), p. 4.

[22] Haile & Bonney, *Lingard*, p. 111; Bishop Douglas had considered recalling Lingard from the Northern District in 1797 (cf. LDA: Gibson Papers, Douglas to Gibson 14 June 1797). Lingard would have preferred to accept the mission at Stella (offered to him by the 60-year-old William Hull), but Gibson would not agree, cf. D. Milburn, *A History of Ushaw College* (Durham: Ushaw College, 1964), p. 117; L. Gooch (ed.), *The Revival of English Catholicism: The Banister-Rutter Correspondence, 1777-1807* (Wigan: North West Catholic History Society, 1995), Banister to Rutter 31 Jan. 1796. [Cited henceforth by the name of the correspondent and date.]

23. Haile & Bonney, *Lingard*, pp. 109, 384. Bishop Poynter suggested to Bishop Smith that Lingard be kept ready to respond to any further anti-Catholic publications, cf. LDA: Smith Papers, 4 Apr. 1821.

24. N. Smith (ed.), *Letters of Sydney Smith* (Oxford: The Clarendon Press, 1953, 2 vols), I, p. 414; UCM: Lingard Letters, Add. No. 25, Lingard to Orrell, 20 May, 1807.

25. *Proceedings of the Durham County Meeting on Monday June 1st, 1807, &c*, (Durham: Walker, n. d.); Fordyce, *Durham* I, pp. 152, 348/349; C. Daykin, 'The Parliamentary Representation of Durham, 1675–1832' (Durham University, M. Litt., 1961), p. 308.

26. W. Garnet, *A Collection of Papers, Speeches etc., Relating to the Northumberland Election of 1807* (Newcastle, 1807), passim.

27. Roberts, *Whig Party*, p. 37; C. Grey, *The Life and Opinions of Charles, Second Earl Grey* (London: Bentley, 1861), pp. 158–160: Grey to Tierney, 8 Nov. 1807.

28. Linker, *Catholics and Emancipation*, p. 164.

29. D. Holmes, *More Roman than Rome: English Catholicism in the Nineteenth Century* (London: Burns & Oates, 1978), p. 24, quoting Smith to Poynter, 26 Jan. 1812.

30. Sir Henry Vane Tempest, Tory member for County Durham died on 1 August. John Lambton won the nomination to succeed him on the understanding that his uncle Ralph 'should resign his seat for the city', it being generally regarded that two of the four Durham (county and city) seats should not be occupied by the same family. Cf. the by-election *Poll-Book* (Durham, 1813).

31. E. Reynolds, *Three Cardinals* (London: Burns & Oates, 1958), p. 22; B. Fothergill, *Nicholas Wiseman* (London: Faber & Faber, 1963), p. 20. Wiseman was at Ushaw College from 1810 to 1818.

32. The meeting was extensively reported in the *Durham County Advertiser* [DCA] on 30 Dec. 1815 and 13 Jan. 1816, from which the following is taken.

33. J. Chinnici, *The English Catholic Enlightenment: John Lingard and the Cisalpine Movement 1780–1850* (Shepherdstown, USA, The Patmos Press, 1980), p. 41; B. Ward, *The Eve of Catholic Emancipation* (London: Longmans Green & Co., 1911–1912, 3 vols), II, p. 178.

34. Durham University Library [DUL]: Grey Manuscripts, 18 Feb. 1820; C.

New, *Lord Durham* (Oxford: The Clarendon Press, 1929), p. 59; Cadogan, *Radical Newcastle*, pp. 22, 43.

35 New, *Durham*, p. 60; E. Hughes (ed.), *The Diaries and Correspondence of James Losh* (Surtees Society [SS]) 1956/1959, 2 vols), 1, Diary, Mar. 1820.

36 Anon., *A Letter to Earl Grey from one of the Clergy*, (n. p., n. d.), 22 Jan. 1821. On 15 April Losh referred to the pamphlet as 'an Anon.'s one by Mr. Phillpotts'.

37 *The Durham Election 1820* (in a collection of broadsides, etc., in the City of Durham Library). According to a handbill of 22 March, Mesurier said that Meynell's band was accompanied by a mob of the lowest rabble of Darlington. See Norman, *Catholic Church*, p. 44 for the Poynter remark.

38 UCM: Wiseman Papers, No. 29, Brown to Wiseman, 7 Apr. 1826; Norman, *Catholic Church*, p. 31; Hexter, 'Protestant Revival', pp. 311–312; Daykin, 'Parliamentary Representation', p. 311; New, *Durham*, pp. 80, 87, 91; DCA, 15 Jan. 1826, 17 June 1826.

39 R. Welford, *Men of Mark 'Twixt Tyne and Tweed* (London & Newcastle: Walter Scott, 1895, 3 vols), gives a general narrative of this election under the names of the candidates. He says Beaumont spent £40,634. Trevelyan, *Grey*, p. 293, says that the Greys spent £14,000. L. Cooper, *Radical Jack* (London: Cresset, 1959), p. 93, reckons that Lambton spent £30,000. The by-election cost each candidate £30,000, and presumably those figures would be included in the quarter million.

40 E. M. Halcrow, 'The Election Campaigns of Sir Charles Miles Lambert Monck' in *Archaeologia Aeliana* [AA] (4) 36 (1958), p. 105, quoting Gibson's letter of 24 Mar. 1812.

41 PD(2), IX, 574/1476, ff.; XI, 842; XIII, 766; Linker, 'Catholics and Emancipation', pp. 161/162.

42 *Northumberland By-Election Poll-Book (1826), Including a Complete Collection of Papers, Speeches, etc.* (Alnwick, 1826).

43 *The Truthteller*, III, No. 26 (April 1826), p. 16. W. E. Andrewes, the editor, supported Beaumont and Howick in a leading article and wrote against Liddell.

44 *By-Election Poll-Book.*

45 DUL: Grey Mss GP/H 3 & 5 Sep. 1823; Losh, Diary, I, p. 186.

46 The following is derived from the *Northumberland Poll-Book* (1826) (Alnwick, 1826). DUL: Grey MSS, 16 Feb. 1826.

47 Losh, Diary, 16 Mar. 1826
48 Ward, *Eve*, II, ch. 27; J. Milner, *Supplementary Memoirs of the English Catholics* (London: Keating & Brown, 1820), pp. 239, 240, 244; J. Gillow, *A Literary and Biographical History, or Bibliographical Dictionary, of the English Catholics: From the Breach with Rome, in 1534, to the Present Time* (London: Burns & Oates, c.1885–1895, 5 vols), III, p. 403.
49 DCA, 26 June 1826.
50 G. Machin, *The Catholic Question in English Politics 1820 to 1830* (Oxford: The Clarendon Press, 1964), pp. 72/73.
51 Hexter, 'Protestant Revival', pp. 312/313. Howick was given a Winchelsea seat by the Marquess of Cleveland, cf. Trevelyan, *Grey*, pp. 199, 293. Beaumont was returned for Stafford in 1827. Liddell declined to stand in 1830, so that Bell and Beaumont were returned. Howick and Beaumont won in 1831.
52 The laity: E. Charlton, W. J. Charlton, J. Clavering, G. Dunn, G. T. Dunn, W. Errington, G. Gibson, J. Gibson, Sir C. Haggerston, T. Haggerston, G. Humble, J. Kirsopp, J. Kirsopp, C. Larkin, H. Leadbitter, T. Leadbitter, W. Mather, R. Riddell, R. Riddell, P. J. Selby, W. Selby, G. Silvertop, J. Snowden, E. Storey. The clergy: T. Beaumont, SJ, (Alnwick), W. Birdsall (Berwick), J. Gillow (Wooler), T. Gillow (Tynemouth), H. Lawson, OSB (Morpeth), J. Leadbitter, OP, (Hexham), T. Stout (Thropton), J. Yates (Esh).
53 Norman, *Catholic Church*, p. 41.
54 PD(1), V, 217; XXII, 460; XXIV, 559, 726, 1104; Ward, *Eve*, II, pp. 23ff.
55 *Journals of the Lords and Commons, 1825–1829*, vol. 86, passim; PD(2), XIII, 652; Losh, Diary, 18 Feb. 1825, where he congratulates himself in getting forty lawyers of Newcastle to sign a pro-Catholic petition.
56 PD(2), XX, 833.
57 Daykin, 'Parliamentary Representation' p. 391; PD(2), XX, 705, 720, 968.
58 PD(2), XX, 1304–1313. There were 6,184 signatories.
59 An account of the meeting is given In J. Sykes, *Local Records* (Newcastle: Sykes, 1833, 2 vols), II, 10 Mar. 1829; Cadogan, *Radical Newcastle*, p. 51; Hempton, *Methodism and Politics*, p. 136.
60 Losh, Correspondence: to Grey, 28 Mar. 1826.
61 Vane (1766–1842) was the son of Henry Vane, 2nd Earl of Darlington. As Viscount Barnard he had sat in the Commons for Winchelsea (1790–1792)

and County Durham (1812-1814). He was created Marquess of Cleveland in 1827 and Duke of Cleveland in 1833. He abandoned the Whigs in 1830 over parliamentary reform (ODNB). Seat: Raby Castle. DCA, 11 Nov. 1826, quoting a Dublin newspaper; his six boroughs were two each at Ilchester, Camelford and Winchelsea: he accommodated Howick there in 1826, cf. V. Gibbs (ed.), *The Complete Peerage* [GEC] (London: St Catherine Press, 1910-1959), III, p. 284 note (b); Daykin, 'Parliamenary Representation', p. 391. He offered George Silvertop one of his boroughs, cf. *Gateshead Observer*, 24 Feb. 1849. Powlett changed his name from Vane; he was afterwards 3rd Duke of Cleveland, cf. GEC, III, p. 285 note (d). Castlereagh had been pro-Catholic. Londonderry was not given office by Wellington, while Hardinge was given the War Office; relations between the two kinsmen cooled. The latter declined to stand for the City of Durham seat in 1830 and it was taken by the Marchioness's ultra-Tory nephew Arthur Hill Trevor. Londonderry's daughter Alexandrina became a Catholic. PD (2) XIX, 1198; Edith, Marchioness of Londonderry, *The Life and Times of Frances Anne, Marchioness of Londonderry and her Husband Charles, Third Marquess of Londonderry* (London: MacMillan, 1958), pp. 141, 159, 169; M. Hyde, *The Londonderrys* (London: Hamish Hamilton, 1979), p. xv; DCA, 4 and 26 June 1828. The other northern peers, Lords Morpeth and Howick in the Commons; were pro-Catholic: PD(2), XIX, 1294, 1330; XX, 878.

62   His grandfather Sir Hugh Smithson of Stanwick, (in the North Riding) was a Catholic until he succeeded as 3rd baronet in 1733, aged 19, cf. P. Roebuck (ed.) *Constable of Everingham Estate Correspondence, 1726-1743* (YAS vol. 136, 1976), p. 159, n 63. In 1740 he married Elizabeth Seymour (daughter of the 7th Duke of Somerset), heiress to the Percy estates. He was created Earl of Northumberland in 1750 and the dukedom (of the third creation) was revived for him in 1766 when he was appointed Lord Lieutenant of Ireland (ODNB): Duke of Wellington (ed.), *Despatches, Correspondence and Memoranda of Field Marshal Arthur, Duke of Wellington* (London: Murray, 8 vols), V, pp. 453ff.; A. S. Turberville, *The House of Lords in the Age of Reform, 1784-1837* (London: Faber & Faber, 1958), p. 223

63   O. Chadwick, *The Victorian Church* (London: Clack, 1966, 2 vols), I, pp. 11-13; R. Solway, *Prelates and People* pp. 41, 90; G. F. A. Best, 'The Protestant Constitution and Its Supporters, 1800-1829' in *Transactions of the Royal Historical Society* [TRHS] (5), VIII, (1958), p. 113; C. Ives,

Sermons on Several Occasions and Charges by William van Mildert, D. D. (Oxford: Collingwood for the University, 1838), p. 99; PD(2) XIX, 1174.

[64] DCA, 16 Feb. 1828; Daykin, 'Parliamentary Representation', pp. 395, 407. W. Russell, Tory, who succeeded Lambton in the Commons on the latter's elevation to the Lords, declared himself in favour of Catholic Emancipation, but he was absent from the House during its enactment.

[65] Catholics were allowed to sit and vote in parliament and made eligible for all military, civil and corporate offices except those of Regent, Lord Chancellor of England and Lord Lieutenant of Ireland; they were to take an oath recognising the Protestant succession and denying that the pope had power to interfere in domestic affairs.

[66] Turberville, *House of Lords*, p. 227; Clarke, *English Society*, p. 359.

[67] Ives, *Sermons*, p. 542; Losh, Diary, May 1829

[68] *The Speeches of the Right Honourable the Earl of Durham*, (Durham, 1836) n.62

[69] T. J. Nossiter, *Influence, Opinion and Political Idioms in Reformed England* (Brighton, Harvester Press, 1975), p. 20; A. J. Heesom, 'Lord Durham's Bowlby Letter: National Politics in their Local Context' in *Durham County Local History Society Bulletin* [DCLHSB] 34 (1985), pp. 29, 32, 35; UCM: Smith of Brooms, OS/D201, 9 June and 31 July, 1837; Sykes, *Local Records*, 1831/1832 passim; *Speeches of the Earl of Durham* p. 225.

[70] NRO: 1954/40, R. Simmons to D. Forster, 1 Aug. 1836.

[71] *Newcastle Journal*, 31 Dec. 1842; L. Charlton, *The Recollections of a Northumbrian Lady 1815–1866* (London: Cape, 1949), ch XI, passim.

[72] Latimer, *Local Records*, Dec. 1832. See also 11 Sep. 1832 for the attendance by several prominent Catholics at a major Whig dinner.

[73] Latimer, *Local Records*, 28 Nov. 1847.

[74] Cadogan, *Radical Newcastle*, pp. 37, 77ff; Gillow, *Dictionary* and Welford, *Men of Mark*, have biographies. T. P. MacDermott, 'Charles Larkin, Radical Reformer, 1800–1879' in *Northern Catholic History* [NCH] 28 (1988), p. 13, does not emphasise his leading role in the Catholic life of Newcastle to the same extent as is done here.

[75] J. H. Treble, 'The Attitude of the Roman Catholic Church towards Trade Unionism in the North of England, 1833–42' in *Northern History* 5 (1970), p. 97. See also G. Gonnolly, 'The Transubstantiation of Myth: Towards a New Popular History of Nineteenth Century Catholicism in England' in

JEH 35/1, (1984), pp. 102/103; NRO: ROT 3/73, 25 Mar. 1825: Bishop Briggs admitting members of trade unions (but not Knights of St. Patrick) to the sacraments.

76 *Catholic Directory*, 1825 et seq; W. V Smith, *Catholic Tyneside* (Newcastle: for the C. T. S., 1930), p. 55. S. Meggison, Vicar of Bolam, wrote to Larkin on 26 Mar. 1831 about a dispute with the Reformation Society, in which he abused Larkin as 'a surgeon, not unskilful in your business, clever with the pen, but not very respectable'. He described Larkin's public house as very disorderly, and where the lower sort of Irish and others used to sit and drink and revel on Sunday afternoons, cf. C. Larkin, *A Vindication of the Catholic Religion* (Newcastle, Mackenzie, 1831), Introduction.

77 R. J. Cooter, 'The Irish in County Durham and Newcastle, 1840–1880' (University of Durham, MA, 1973), p. 103.

78 PD(3) XIII, 98. See also col. 728 for Londonderry's attack on Larkin's contribution to a meeting on Reform in Sunderland; Cadogan, *Radical Newcastle*, p. 97.

79 Gillow, *Dictionary*, IV, p. 137, item 6; Latimer, *Local Records*, 6 Mar. 1836.

80 A. Heesom, 'The Founding of the University of Durham' (Durham Cathedral Lecture, 1982), pp. 11ff; E.A. Varley, 'The Last of the Prince Bishops: The Episcopate of William van Mildert (1826–36)' (Durham Cathedral Lecture, 1986), p. 15.

81 NRO: RCD 3/73, 25 Mar. 1835; Riddell Letter Book, Nos. 28, 49, 71; Riddell to Mostyn, Hogarth and Brown, Jan.–June 1845; See also J. D. Gay, *The Geography of Religion in England* (London: Duckworth, 1971), p. 91.

82 Latimer, *Local Records*, 31 Jan. 1843. T. P. MacDermott, 'The Irish Workers on Tyneside' in N. McCord, (ed.), *Essays in Tyneside Labour History* (Newcastle Polytechnic, 1977), pp. 165ff. McAnulty was especially prominent in the latter half of the century.

83 J. Galletly & T. Yellowley, *Ss. Mary & Thomas Aquinas. Stella, 1831–1981* (Stella, 1981), p. 26.

84 NRO: Riddell Letter Book, no. 16, Riddell to Phillipps, 4 Dec. 1844; Gillow, *Dictionary*, IV, pp. 135–139; *Gateshead Observer*, Dec. 1844; *The Tablet*, VI, No. 5, p. 37.

85 The Flaminian Gate held particular importance in recusant history since this was the point of departure from Rome for missionaries northward bound for England through the Channel ports.

[86] G. Machin, *Politics and the Churches in Great Britain 1832–68* (Oxford: The Clarendon Press, 1977), p. 71; Ward, *Sequel*, II, pp. 34–37; E. Norman, *Anti-Catholicism in Victorian England* (London: Allen & Unwin, 1968), pp. 52, 159ff; Chadwick, *Victorian Church*, I, pp.296/297; Charlton, *Recollections*, p. 210.

[87] Cadogan, *Radical Newcastle*, p. 52; Gillow, *Dictionary*, IV, p. 139.

Part II

4 THE CATHOLIC MISSION 1688–1850

THE HISTORY OF each mission-station in the region will be outlined in the next two chapters. Many of those histories have unique features but they also have several things in common. This chapter is therefore intended to serve as an introduction and overview of life on the northern mission. The first section will outline brief biographies of the early vicars apostolic of the Northern District. Attention then turns to the evolution of the Catholic missionary structure in the north-east as well as the question of mission and personal finance which were permanent preoccupations. The later years of the eighteenth century were turbulent times for English Catholics. The census of papists in 1767 seemed to presage a more rigorous application of the penal laws; that fear was allayed by the Catholic Relief Act of 1778 but the Gordon Riots, and a second census in 1780, gave rise to further anxiety. Quite apart from the external political situation, Catholics in the north had internal clerical disruptions to worry about. The suppression of the Jesuit Order between 1773 and 1814 threatened to deprive the mission of priests. The nationalization of the Church in France in 1790 also had major repercussions in England. A large number of French priests were driven into exile and some came to the north-east. The main supply of newly-ordained English priests coming into the country stopped when the expatriate seminaries on French territory were forcibly closed. A long wrangle ensued about the location and management of a replacement for Douai College. The deaths of three Vicars Apostolic of the Northern District and a coadjutor bishop between 1769 and 1790 caused discontinuities in leadership in a critical period. The cisalpine tendencies of the Catholic Committee negotiating the Catholic Relief Act of 1791 became a matter of public controversy, as did their attempts to influence the succession to the Northern and London vicariates which both fell vacant in 1790. Clearly, each of these events alone would have a marked effect on the mission, together they were alarming. Domestic difficulties in the chaplaincies were endemic and, indeed, seem to have been inherent. Since over half of the missions in the region were chaplaincies for much of the century, an explanation of this important feature of missionary life is required and will be found in the private thirty-year long correspondence between the priests Robert Banister and Henry Rutter who expressed their views with unsparing candour. The chapter will close with brief biographies of the later vicars apostolic.

***

During the reign of James II, diplomatic relations with the Holy See were conducted by a papal representative in London but that, of course, ceased at the Revolution. The exiled Stuarts, however, had no intention of allowing their influence on the Holy See to lapse and they brought it to bear whenever possible, particularly over episcopal appointments. Evidently, the Roman authorities did not resist these approaches, for the early vicars apostolic were all appointed with Stuart patronage, though that may also have been because representations were always made through a clerical Agent of the English vicars apostolic who was resident in Rome. The Revd George Witham of Cliffe was Agent until he was appointed Vicar Apostolic of the Midland District in 1703, nominated by Mary of Modena. His successor was Lawrence Mayes of Yarm, another North Yorkshireman. Mayes was ordained at Douai in 1697 and was appointed professor of philosophy, and subsequently second professor of divinity. On his appointment as Agent in 1706, he left for Paris where Dr John Betham, late preceptor to Prince James Stuart, accompanied him to the Court at St. Germain. During the audience James, now 'king', insisted that he should be informed whenever a priest was proposed for a mitre. He did not pretend to the nomination of the vicars apostolic in England although he was well aware that George Witham had passed on a recommendation from his father James II to the Pope and he intended to do the same. Mayes became highly respected by all who knew him in England and Italy. In 1721 he was made *protonotarius apostolicus*. By 1720 Mayes was employed as Latin Secretary to James III. From 1726 to 1729 the Stuart court was in Bologna where the king occupied the Palazzo Fantuzzi. Mayes was appointed chaplain (but not confessor) to the king, a post he held until his death. He said Mass daily in a specially decorated Chapel Royal in the palazzo and wrote that he 'had the honour to say Mass twice and to Communicate his Majesty both times'. Mayes officiated chiefly as preceptor of Prince Charles, 6 years old, who lived next door in the Palazzo Ranuzzi-Cospi, and Mayes went in 'twice a day to teach him his Christian doctrine.' Mayes held the post until Charles reached the age of 18 in 1738. He then repeated the role with Prince Henry from 1729 to 1739. His royal duties do not seem to have interfered with his agency which he held until his death.[1] The Revd Christopher Stonor became his assistant, in 1748; he died at Rome on 23 August, 1749, aged 77, and was buried in the church of the English College.[2]

James Smith was well-born in Hampshire and educated at Douai and in Paris and was made president of his *alma mater*. He was nominated bishop by James II and consecrated in May 1688 for the Northern District when he was 43 years old. He was received at York at the beginning of August with a military guard of honour but at the Revolution six months later he was forced to go into hiding and he laid low at Wycliffe Hall in the North Riding, home of Francis Tunstall. (The other vicars apostolic were all imprisoned.) Smith was highly thought of and in 1694 on the recommendation of the exiled King James (and the Duke of Berwick) he was put up for a red hat to succeed Cardinal Howard as Protector of England, and he was considered for the London District in 1702. He declined these dignities and kept to his District, in which he travelled extensively carrying out his episcopal duties, though secretly and under various aliases: 'Doeing everything with as much caution and circumspection as was possible; goeing only with one companion and a servant.' He died in 1711 on the twenty-third anniversary of his consecration as a bishop and was buried at Wycliffe. He left rent-income for the support of his successors provided they were seculars.[3]

King James II, on progress from Bath to Chester, attended Mass in Worcester on the feast of St Bartholomew in 1687. So impressed was the king with the sermon that he appointed Silvester Jenks, 31 years old and a priest for only three years, a preacher royal. Jenks fled the country at the Revolution but he returned late in the century. He was clearly *episcopabile* and he was nominated to the northern vicariate at the death of James Smith. Two years passed before the formalities in Rome were concluded and the mishandling of his Briefs by Propaganda was rectified. It was then decided to delay his consecration until after the dissolution of parliament. By that time Jenks was seriously ill and he died in December 1714. The Northern District, therefore, was *sede vacante* for five years after 1711, the period of maximum Jacobite activity in the north culminating in the Rising of 1715.[4]

George Witham was born at Cliffe Hall a few miles west of Wycliffe, in 1655 and was educated at Douai and Paris. He was missioner in Newcastle and vicar general to Smith before going to Rome as Agent for the vicars apostolic. He was recommended for a mitre by Mary of Modena and appointed Vicar Apostolic of the Midland District in 1703. He was translated to the Northern District in 1716, aged 61 and becoming infirm, but he was presumably pleased to be returning to live in his family home. He survived for almost ten years although he frequently considered resignation and he asked for a coadjutor every year. He died suddenly in 1725 aged 70 and was buried in Manfield church near Cliffe.[5]

For one reason or another none of Witham's nominees as his successor (Edward Dicconson, Lawrence Mayes, Lawrence Rigby) were acceptable to Rome, and he came to think that he 'had reason enough to apprehend a Regular' being appointed. And so it was. 'James III' nominated Thomas (Dominic in religion) Williams, a Welsh Dominican. He was educated at Bornhem, Rome and Naples; he also held various positions of authority in his order on the continent including the headship of the Dominican college at Louvain. He was the only Dominican vicar apostolic and was the only one to receive episcopal ordination directly from the Pope (also a friar). The clergy (and gentry) of the north were not best pleased to have a friar as their bishop, certainly not one without experience of the English mission. John Ingleton (a priest influential at the Jacobite court) writing from Paris predicted that:

> Tis certain the choyce of Bishop Williams will be attended with very ill consequences, and not less mortifying to him than to others. A friend of mine lately come from the North and well acquainted with the Catholic Families, assures me that not one Gentleman will give [Williams] a residence in that District. He is a stranger, a beggar ... I have taken the liberty to acquaint the King how much the Northern Clergy are offended at this choice...

Undeterred, though alone and practically penniless, Williams sailed from Flanders to North Shields, where, perhaps unexpectedly, he was greeted by George Gibson, secular missioner in Newcastle, and escorted to Durham where he stayed about three weeks at an inn, the clergy taking 'care to make the reckoning easy to him'. At first he lived with the Tunstalls at Wycliffe, then at Huddlestone Hall in Yorkshire as the guest of Sir Edward Gascoigne, 'gratis'. He died there in 1740 aged 73 and was buried at Hazlewood Hall.[6]

The Dicconson family of Wrightington Hall, Wigan, had particularly close ties with the Jacobite court at St Germain through William Dicconson, tutor to Prince James and Treasurer to Mary of Modena. Edward, his younger brother was ordained at Douai and stayed on at the college in various offices for some twenty years. In 1720 he came to the mission as a chaplain in Staffordshire and he was made vicar general in the Midland District. As 'a man of learning, application to business and much dexterity in the management of affairs', he was nominated for a mitre on several occasions, but he was suspected of Jansenism and even Stewart patronage counted for nothing in such cases. He must have proved his orthodoxy during a four-year stay in Rome for at last in 1740 when he was aged 70 he was made Vicar Apostolic of the Northern District. He took up residence near Wrightington, the first of the northern bishops to live on the western side of the District. He does not appear in the narratives of the 'Forty-five. It was not long before the old bishop began to petition for a coadjutor and Francis Petre was appointed in 1751. Dicconson died in May the following year and was buried at Standish near Wigan.

Francis Petre was a member of the well known family seated in Essex. He too had Jacobite connections in that his uncle had been chaplain-tutor in the Radcliffe family at the beginning of the century, and his promotion to the coadjutorship was partly due to the influence of 'James III'. Petre was educated at Douai and ordained priest in 1720. He remained in France pursuing further studies before returning to Essex to take up the life of a country gentleman on the family estate which he had inherited. He succeeded as vicar apostolic in the north within two years at the age of 60 and he took up residence in Showley Hall near Ribchester which he leased from the Walmesley family. He acted alone for some fifteen years but in 1767, when he was ailing, he asked for the assistance of a coadjutor. The first to be appointed died within two years but the second lived to succeed him. Petre died aged 84 in 1775 and was buried in the church at Stydd near Ribchester. Fortunately, his episcopate of twenty-three years was not in the least controversial since it came after the elimination of the Jacobite threat and before the political campaigns for Catholic relief.

The *terna* of 1767 for Petre's first coadjutor named Christopher Stonor, William Maire and Henry Tichborne Blount. The nuncio in Brussels advised Propaganda that Maire was

> a mirror of virtue, and that from his great experience as vicar-general in the northern district, where he was highly esteemed, he was the best possible person (not to mention the dignity of his birth) to select for the post of coadjutor with succession.[7]

Maire was born in 1704 at Lartington. He studied at Douai and was ordained in 1730. He returned to England five years later to be chaplain at Lartington and he later served the secular missions in Old Elvet and Gilesgate in the city of Durham. He may have displeased Petre by disclaiming any Jacobite sympathies during the 'Forty-five but it seems he was obliged to do so for his personal safety. Ill-health precluded his taking any active part in District life and he lived quietly at Lartington where he died in 1769. He was interred in the church at Romaldkirk and his memorial is at Lartington.

The *terna* of 1770 for Petre's second coadjutor named William Walton, Charles Howard and John Lodge; Walton was selected. He came from a Manchester family and was ordained at Douai in 1741 by Bishop Dicconson. He spent the early years of his priesthood in Berkshire and London and he became Richard Challoner's secretary and vicar general. Upon his appointment to the coadjutorship in 1770, Walton moved to Clayton-le-Dale to live close to Petre. The aged bishop was not easy to work with, however, and

Challoner had to persuade Walton not to resign. On his succession to the vicariate at Christmas 1775 Walton moved to York. He died there five years later, aged 64 and was buried in St Michael-le-Belfry. He was the third vicar apostolic of the Northern District to have died in the previous ten years; prudently, just before he died he had applied for a coadjutor naming Matthew Gibson, John Chadwick and Nicholas Clavering; Gibson was selected.[8] Until this point, the vicars apostolic of the north lived in relative obscurity and tranquillity, undisturbed even by activist Jacobitism which, in any case, was fast fading from memory after the 'Forty-five, and there was perhaps the prospect of a peaceful transition to ecclesiastical toleration in the not too distant future. As it turned out, those developments took place some years into Gibson's episcopate.

***

The geographical development of the mission in north-east England occurred in two, more or less distinct, phases. Of some sixty chapels to be found at one time or another during the period 1688 to 1851, half were in existence by the Revolution. Development between 1688 and 1730 was largely a change in chaplaincies. Four public missions and six new chaplaincies were inaugurated in that half century, but five chaplaincies closed, three of which were in Jacobite houses. The disposition reached by 1730 corresponded to the main locations of the Catholic population and would remain substantially unchanged for some sixty years. In 1734, however, Robert Witham, President of Douai College, lamented the shortage of priests in England, but he was never a very happy or optimistic man and, anyway, he was referring to the national situation—the north-east cannot be included in his analysis.[9] The second phase began from around the time of the Relief Acts when industrialization and urbanization gathered pace and complementary changes in missionary deployment were required.

It is somewhat surprising to find that the mission achieved a permanent structural form and comprehensive geographical deployment by 1730, given that the period was punctuated by the Revolution of 1688 and the Jacobite 'Fifteen, events which were generally considered as major disasters for the Catholic cause in England. It seems, then, that, in the north-east at any rate, the establishment and progress of the mission proceeded independently of political factors. The improving scene was exemplified in James Mickleton's account of the mission in Durham at the turn of the eighteenth century. Similarly, within a few years of the 'Fifteen, the Claverings of Berrington and the Widdringtons of Cheeseburn Grange re-instituted chaplaincies, yet both families were deeply involved in the rising. Another example would be the remarkable speed and confidence with which the missions in Newcastle reopened after the Revolution of 1688 and again after the 'Fortyfive. It may also be noted that no priest-holes or hiding-places were constructed in Catholic houses after 1680, and those found in the course of rebuilding were exhibited as historical curiosities. It was very much in a romantic frame of mind that the Swinburnes posted a servant-girl at a window of Capheaton Hall in the 1770s while Mass was being said to warn of the approach of strangers; there had been no real need to do that for some time. On the other hand, no chapel is known to have been consecrated during the period.

The explanation for how a Catholic missionary organisation was able to take root and function so freely at an apparently inopportune time lies in the fact that the Church was hardly visible. A semi-clandestine public chapel in a town was usually accommodated in a house belonging to the gentry, located in an upper room or in some outbuilding in an alley behind the house. And then, three-quarters of mission-stations were domestic gentry chaplaincies and most Catholic estates lay in remote, rural places. At first, the chaplain lived in the mansion and the chapel was in a converted room on an upper floor of the house. In an age when a landed proprietor was absolute master of his own estates and could change the landscape at will, even moving a village if it interrupted the view from his morning-room, it is hardly to be wondered at that the establishment of private chapels went unchallenged. A tight rein was kept on the chaplain; his primary duty was to the patronal family and household. Only secondarily did he minister outside those circles, and if he did, he was required to do so discreetly, and return home promptly. In short, although the religion of the squire was undeniable, the identity of the priest well known, and the existence of a chapel and its congregation common knowledge, the ecclesiastical infrastructure was kept inconspicuous so far as possible and Catholic missionary activity was calculated to cause no offence. The mission could not have survived in any other way.

Little geographical expansion of the mission took place between 1730 and 1790 which was essentially a period of consolidation. Of ten new mission stations, seven were chaplaincies; a handful of chaplaincies became public missions; and some supply missions became residential. In other places, after a period of stability, or perhaps when a congregation outgrew existing accommodation and could afford it, a chapel would be improved and enlarged. Some patrons would give their domestic chapel a more accessible position in the mansion. A public mission property might be redeveloped completely to provide a separate chapel building, or at least to make part of the house a permanent chapel. Space for more worshippers could be found by the addition of galleries, and this was done in most town-chapels. These small, simple vernacular buildings, still located in back streets and alleys, were devoid of external ecclesiastical features. Even in some strongly Catholic rural areas, chapels were disguised or given a severely plain external front and most chapels were devoid of any internal ecclesiastical features such as side-altars, confessional boxes, statues, organs, Stations of the Cross, or memorial tablets.[10]

The safety of the Catholic mission depended on its isolation and its discretion, but while those attributes allowed the mission to settle and become well-established, they also inhibited change, for most chapels and priests were deployed at the convenience of the gentry. Since the cost of any development would fall on them, having established their own domestic chapels and perhaps contributed to the support of one in the nearest town, they would be disinclined to build independent chapels which they would neither use or control.[11] Most endowments attached to town-chapels were paid to priests who travelled from country houses from time to time, often monthly, to offer Mass, hear confessions and visit the sick. Moreover, a fund providing a clerical stipend was usually strictly and non-transferably tied to a specific chaplaincy; it would prove difficult enough to persuade some families to continue honouring such a bequest, without risking its withdrawal by suggesting it be applied elsewhere.

Although these financing arrangements were beginning to change at the beginning of the eighteenth century, as urban Catholic professionals and tradesmen, as well as wealthy priests, began to leave money specifically to endow town-chapels, a shortage of priests and the insecurity of financial provision prevented urban development for many years. In 1750, of the eight market towns of County Durham (Barnard Castle, Darlington, Hartlepool, Staindrop, Stockton, Sunderland and Wolsingham), only Stockton had a fixed mission, although priests visited some of the other towns. The situation in Northumberland was somewhat better in that Alnwick, Hexham and Newcastle had residential missions, but Berwick, Morpeth and Rothbury were still non-residential. Hence, so long as the law prevented the Catholic clergy from owning property, so long would the mission be under the control of the gentry, and so long would its geographical disposition remain unchanged. Fortunately, the population as a whole was relatively settled and, once established, the missionary organisation could operate within the restraints placed upon it, at least in the short term.

Few mission stations escaped disruption arising out of lay control. Indeed, it is no exaggeration to say that the Catholic mission in the eighteenth century suffered more at the hands of its own lay leadership than anything inflicted on it by Protestants. Lay support and protection was essential to the mission in the darkest days of persecution, but when Catholicism began to be tolerated in the eighteenth century, it became more of a hindrance than a help. Most of the dozen or so missions which closed during the century were chaplaincies which came to an end because of the misfortune of the patronal family. Some estates were forfeited and others sold; and one or two families apostatised or became extinct. Few of those losses could not be compensated for by neighbouring missions and little long term damage was suffered, but difficulties arose even in those chaplaincies or gentry dependencies which did survive. The dismissal of a chaplain at the whim of a patron, or the temporary closure of a chapel when the patron was absent, made for an unpredictable and insecure ministry. The greatest effect of the closures and of dictatorial patrons was to stimulate the clergy to gain their own independence and obtain greater security for the mission.

Change became inevitable once the urban population began to grow, but the prerequisite of missionary independence was repeal of the laws that prevented Catholics from owning property and which prohibited places of Catholic worship. The first Catholic Relief Act, 1778, remedied the former grievance but it was only under the second act, of 1791, that chapels could be opened under licence. That act emancipated the mission and the clergy, and it ushered in a period of missionary development and a shift from a rural to an urban apostolate. The clergy promptly took control of existing town-chapels, registered them under the Relief Act and, funded largely by public subscription, embarked on a programme of new building. Bishop William Gibson told Propaganda in 1804 that some thirty new chapels had been opened since 1790 in the whole of the Northern District, one third of which were in the north-east. Some rationalisation also took place. Between 1807 and 1829 the two chapels in Newcastle, Hexham and Durham were reduced to one in each place. By the end of the 1850s, only twelve of the forty missions in the north-east had not been redeveloped and of those, four chaplaincies already had adequate facilities, the rest were newly-established public chapels. Bishop William Hogarth, whose episcopate lasted from 1843 to 1866 was said to have built or enlarged every chapel or church in the four counties comprising his diocese.[12]

The erection of new chapels often came about because existing buildings were in a ruinous condition, or as replacements for chapels in unsuitable or inconvenient places. The commonest reason for building a new church, however, was when an increase in the congregation meant that existing accommodation was insufficient and could not be extended further; necessity then became the justification to move to a better location. The habit of architectural discretion was hard to break, however, and the new churches at Berwick and Stella were partially disguised. William Pitt recommended the conversion of an existing building for a seminary rather than the building of a new one which would only attract unwelcome attention. The isolation of Crook Hall in northwest Durham was regarded by many as a decided advantage, just as Ushaw was selected for the site of a new college because of its inaccessibility. Thus, the supersession of the hole-in-the-corner vernacular chapels between 1791 and 1850 represented the culmination of a long process of missionary development. The Relief Acts merely legitimised a well-found organisation of missions and missioners and facilitated the construction of permanent, purpose-built churches which would be managed by the clergy.[13]

Although churches were built for various practical reasons, there were ideological considerations that should not be overlooked. It was important for the emancipated English Catholics that the proper status of their Church relative to other religious groups be clearly recognised. They no longer wished to be regarded as chapel-folk, but as church-goers, and the erection of churches clearly distinguished them from other dissenting groups. Church-building also demonstrated a sense of confidence and permanence. And, in particular, they wished to emphasise their continuity with the pre-Reformation Church. These aspirations were realised by ensuring that new churches were more spacious and imposing, built in stone to a traditional, native medieval (Gothic) style and given an Old English dedication. In these ways the Church conveyed a cluster of ideas about the recovery by the English Catholics of their ancient pedigree. Few churches of the period were built in the classical or, for many people, foreign style.

In all, some twenty-six churches were built between 1790 and 1850 across the region Most were in conspicuous locations to accommodate larger congregations, and, although a wide range of building costs were incurred, most involved an average outlay of £2,000. Catholic churches were all funded voluntarily in the absence of church-rates and other customary or statutory levies available to Anglican church-builders, and they were paid for in one of several ways.[14] A proprietary church built by a landowner on his own estate was financed wholly at his expense, as at Minsteracres. Apart from any pious motive or sense of duty, the proprietor could then always press for the appointment of a priest to his own liking. A modified form of proprietorial right could be retained when a landowner provided the site for a church and made a substantial contribution to the building costs, (perhaps including part of the priest's stipend), leaving the balance of the mission's funding to be raised by priest and people. Mostly, however, churches were built with the voluntary contributions of the laity, subscribed or collected locally or nationally. When sums raised in that way were insufficient to defray all the building costs, the balance was borrowed from vicariate funds, and paid back by the congregation over several years. Although the vicariate would endorse the project and perhaps make a contribution, it was assumed as a matter of course that the priest and congregation were financially responsible for the new building.

As might be expected, churches could not have been erected without the financial support of wealthy layfolk, but, rather than the landed gentry providing the finance, it was the newly-emergent middle class. The Revd John Barrow wrote to the vicar apostolic in 1798:

> you will not now be able to obtain as large Benefactions from the Gentry, as you might five or six years ago ... Merchants, Manufactorers, Tradesmen, etc. are the Persons to whom we must, in these days of Dissipation look up to for our chief support. These can afford to contribute largely, and will not fail to do so, if we can persuade ourselves to try their bounty.[15]

These were Challoner's 'new people'. Bishop Milner told Bishop Gibson that more reliance would have to be placed on the clergy than on the gentry. Bishop William Riddell was saying much the same thing fifty years later: 'in this District there are few monied men, and as regards the gentry, we can't get anything from them.' Churches with few or no well-to-do supporters relied on collections made elsewhere. Such means of raising funds included appeals in the *Catholic Directory,* the sale of old chapel sites, begging for donations among holiday-makers in spas and resorts such as Hartlepool and Tynemouth, and fund-raising tours by missioners ('not less painful to the feelings of the clergyman than burdensome to the public'). Offerings from Protestant well-wishers were not refused. A lack of funds nowhere prevented the erection of a church, though one or two were delayed and others were not completed.[16]

Where a church was built at the sole expense of a landowner, his role in the design and execution of the building was, of course, dominant. The choice of architect, builder and materials, the precise style and location, and the dedication were all chosen by him. In much the same way, and in most cases, a public church would be executed entirely to the requirements of the missioner. Occasionally, a committee would be formed within the congregation to agree the design. One or two priests took it upon themselves to be their own architect, with disastrous results, as at Hexham, but a church was normally designed by a professional architect. He would provide plans, perhaps a model, and estimates, so that a congregation would know the precise cost and amend its requirements if necessary. Local builders were engaged to erect the building under the general direction of the architect's clerk.

The Gothicism of Augustus Welby Pugin chimed with the desire of many clerics to build on a grander scale than any of them could have imagined possible a few years before and in a way that would proclaim the church's continuity with the Middle Ages. Pugin, however, was a purist and he proved to be exacting, even intransigent, in his dealings with employers over stylistic and artistic matters, let alone the liturgy—plainchant only was acceptable. Lingard thought the Gothic Revival simply silly and warned the Ushaw College authorities to guard against being 'bamboozled with Pugin's whims'. Pugin's relationship with Newman (who described himself as 'no aesthetic') suffered because of the former's uncompromising rejection of Oratorian style. In any case, the relatively high cost of Pugin's buildings and his unbending manner meant that he did little work in the north-east. His design for St Mary's, Stockton, (c.1840–2) never progressed beyond the nave. St Cuthbert's chapel at Ushaw (1843–8, 'one of the most satisfying buildings I have ever produced') had to be rebuilt by Dunn and Hansom fifty years afterwards. Only one building remains substantially as he designed it, though unfinished—St Mary's Cathedral, Newcastle (1842-4). True to form, however, he fell out with the Building Committee. Their request for a detailed contract led him to fancy that they saw him as an untrustworthy tradesman, and he would not be 'called in and ordered about like a pork contractor in a workhouse'. Pugin was absent from the opening, which was just as well because although it was a grand affair with nine bishops in attendance, a Beethoven Mass was to be sung and, if he had agreed to go in at all, he would have walked straight out.[17]

Hansom, Gibson, and others, were engaged instead of Pugin and their churches were successful creations, though necessarily less ambitious than many Anglican churches of a similar date. Among the earliest were St Andrew in Newcastle (1798) and St Michael at Esh Laude (1799), with the same dedication as the Anglican parishes in which they were situated. Later, St Michael in Houghton le Spring followed suit, but other dedications were not so impertinent. They were, nonetheless, carefully chosen for their local and medieval associations. Dedications to the Virgin took the old English form of St Mary; the shift to the use of 'Our Lady' and the cult of foreign saints was part of the romanising process begun under Cardinal Wiseman. In the same way, the sudden appearance of St Patrick as a dedicatee at Felling in 1842 was associated with the arrival of Irish immigrants in the region. The only exception to the choice of an English dedication came late in the period when the new church at Minsteracres was named after St Elizabeth of Hungary who was driven from her throne because her charities were ruining the state. She became a cult figure in nineteenth-century gentry circles because 'she highlighted that Victorian fascination with the high-minded self-sacrifice of the high born'. The Silvertops did not beggar themselves by any means, but they clearly associated their efforts with the Queen-Saint and wanted to remind their tenants of their family's benevolence.[18]

Roman Catholic Churches Erected in North-East England, 1790–1851
(The architect is named if known)

1790	Biddlestone
1798	Newcastle, St. Andrew
1799	Esh Laude, St. Michael
1802	Brooms, St. Cuthbert
1807	Croxdale, St. Herbert
1811	Thropton, All Saints
1813	Cheeseburn Grange, J. Dobson
1821	North Shields, St. Cuthbert, R. Giles
1827	Darlington, St. Augustine, I. Bonomi
1827	Durham, St. Cuthbert, I. Bonomi
1829	Berwick, Ss. Mary & Cuthbert
1830	Hexham, St. Mary
1832	Stella, Ss. Mary & Thomas Aquinas, J. Green
1835	Sunderland, St. Mary, I. Bonomi
1836	Alnwick, St. Mary, J. Green
1837	Houghton le Spring, St. Michael, I. Bonomi
1839	Bellingham, St. Oswald, I. Bonomi
1840	Cowpen, St. Cuthbert
1841	Swinburne, St. Mary
1841	Longhorsley, St. Thomas of Canterbury
1842	Stockton, St. Mary, A.W. Pugin
1842	Felling, St. Patrick
1843	Birtley, St. Joseph, J. Dobson
1844	Newcastle, St. Mary, A.W. Pugin
1846	Bishop Auckland, St. Wilfrid, T. Gibson
1850	Morpeth, St. Robert of Newminster, T. Gibson
1851	Hartlepool, St. Mary, J.A. Hansom

The Italian architect Giuseppe Bonomi came to England in 1767 to work under the Adam brothers. As a Catholic and a foreigner, he was black-balled from the Royal Academy in 1789 and 1790; he was only admitted an Associate member on the casting vote of Sir Joshua Reynolds. For similar reasons he obtained few official architectural commissions. His son, Ignatius, was more successful, however, and he designed five Catholic churches in the north-east (six, including a rejected design for St Mary, Hexham): St Augustine, Darlington, St Cuthbert, Durham, St Mary, Sunderland, St Michael, Houghton le Spring, and St Oswald, Bellingham. He was on close terms with clergy of Durham Cathedral, and in 1827 he was appointed Consultant Architect. Evidently, his Catholicism was no bar to Protestant patronage for he obtained four times as many Anglican commissions in the diocese of Durham but he was not strongly attached to his religion anyway and he lapsed in 1840. He became a free-mason, and in 1837 he married Charlotte Fielding, the daughter of a local Protestant clergyman and he was listed as a church-warden of St Mary-le-Bow in Durham three years later. He received no further commissions from Catholics except from the Charltons who were his personal friends and for whom he renovated Hesleyside and built St Oswald's in Bellingham.[19]

***

Catholic worship in the eighteenth century was restrained; small congregations assembled for Low Mass in tiny chapels; there was no music, no incense, and no displays of lighted candles, flowers or ornate vestments. High Mass is unlikely to have been celebrated at all, the reservation of the Blessed Sacrament was rare, and Benediction was unheard of, as was congregational singing. Occasionally, people would be invited to stay on after Mass and meditate on one of Challoner's texts. The psalms were recited around the end of the century at Lartington, but the liturgical context is not known. Banister recalled that there had been 'the hottest contest in your parts about saying Vespers in English before the congregation' in Newcastle by Charles Cordell. Bishop Hay told Thomas Eyre that if English were allowed in Vespers, 'the next step would be to ask the same for the Mass', and he 'would not expect many real conversions from it'. Bishop Challoner disapproved of such innovations and told Bishop William Walton to discourage the giving of Benediction in English.[20]

John Lingard thought the best means of gaining converts was the improvement of preaching. Sermons given in Catholic chapels, he said, were

> calculated to offend persons of any education from their incoherence and incorrectness both in point of composition and occasionally, I am sorry to say, of good sense.

William Warrilow and Charles Cordell both had the reputation of being good preachers, although their successor, James Worswick, was not thought to be effective in that respect. James Losh, the Unitarian lawyer, often went to the chapel in Newcastle and on more than one occasion he remarked on Worswick's 'poor and intolerant sermons', 'by no means well delivered'. Rutter worried about his preaching manner, having an impediment in his speech and being unable to 'speak extempore'. He could not see the necessity of 'adding to the great number of sermons that are already made' and observed that many priests thought it sufficient to read from a book of sermons rather than to write one and learn it by heart. Banister's view was simply that 'one cannot speak [but] too plain to the vulgar'.[21]

Religious practice was largely confined to Mass and Vespers on Sundays, monthly Communion and private devotion. Personal piety was sustained almost wholly by the reading of English devotional works or translations of French and Italian spiritual manuals. Even in the middle of the nineteenth century, Bishop Hogarth discouraged processions and Stations of the Cross and recommended instead the private recitation of the Rosary and the prayers of *The Garden of the Soul*. May Devotions were not introduced in Newcastle until 1841, and then they were not universally popular. Lingard devoutly wished that such foreign practices ('lights and serenading') be abandoned because they made the Catholic religion ridiculous in the eyes of Protestants. Certainly, the 'imposing ceremonies of the Romish faith' which accompanied the openings of the various new Catholic churches from the 1820s were all reported by the newspapers in awestruck tones. High Mass and Benediction were, however, to become increasingly familiar to Catholics and Protestants alike. The funeral of a priest at the cemetery in Jesmond in 1842 was preceded by a long procession of school-children, layfolk and clergy,

> accompanied with crosses and other symbols of the Roman church. The proceedings excited much notice, such a procession having been quite unprecedented for nearly 300 years.[22]

But old recusant habits died hard. No doubt he was an exception, but Thomas Witham, who died at Lartington in 1897, was said to have always read his sermons and never to have had Benediction in his chapel.

The absence of overt spiritual and liturgical warmth was due to the English temperament and to a desire to avoid unwanted attention, but it also arose out of the lack of appropriate facilities. All chapels, public and private, were poorly furnished. There may have been a holy water stoup at the door and, perhaps, an oil-painting over a plain table-altar, but there was little else to distinguish the room from any other in the house. There was barely room for the congregation let alone the accretions which became commonplace after Emancipation. Edward Norman likened Catholic chapels to Dissenting chapels in both architectural and decorative terms. The setting and tone required for Counter-Reformation Catholic ceremonial was simply lacking.

The Holy Year of Jubilee, 1750, was one occasion which showed that people would respond to the opportunity to express greater devotion. Presumably it was observed in all missions, though only the Jesuits reported it. Almost everyone in their congregations made a general confession and received Holy Communion (some on several occasions) and went monthly thereafter. Numbers of conversions were made, many people were reconciled to the Church after a long absence, and some Catholics presented themselves at the sacraments 'who had never come before'. Both Waterton in Durham and Turner in Stella remarked that people were 'more diligent than before'. Evidently, the Jubilee celebration was akin to the parochial mission of the nineteenth century, but, there were no further occasions in the period on which communal fervour could be stimulated in that way.[23]

The development of the Catholic mission during the long eighteenth century kept pace with the demands placed on it, though necessarily constrained by its resources. No large group of Catholics went without pastoral care, and the majority of mission stations were adapted or replaced as circumstances changed. Bishop Thomas Smith proudly informed Propaganda in Rome in 1823 that whereas Catholic churches:

> were once to be found hidden in private houses and in remote places, they now stand boldly in our principal cities, in full public gaze, admirable in their size and the splendour of their ornamentation. The sacred ceremonies which formerly in this region were performed quietly and in a hidden manner, now in many places are celebrated with singing and organ music.[24]

***

Opinions differed as to the income required by a priest. For some time, bequests of £400 or £500 had been made by priests and layfolk as the capital investment needed to yield a return of some £20 to £25 a year which Thomas Eyre calculated to be 'a competent maintenance' for a missioner. But Joseph Berington considered that sum

> a very handsome salary for a gentleman's chaplain; and if the rural curate have twenty more to keep himself, his house and his servant, it will be said he is very well provided for. Some may have small annuities from their own families, but this is not common.

The Durham-born Jesuit James Jenison wrote *Oeconomica Clericalis* to show that £50 a year was quite inadequate to support a priest, even one 'living in a ready-furnished house, rent-free'.

Practice varied. In 1805, Thomas Gillow, chaplain at Callaly Castle, told Eyre that Mr Clavering 'advanced my salary to 26 guineas per annum and agreed to pay my horse tax and blacksmith's bill, to both of which I was before subject'. Since he was tabled in the castle, those arrangements were probably equivalent to £50 a year.[25] In 1795, Henry Rutter, chaplain at Minsteracres, whose salary of £20 a year was two-thirds that of the butler, tried to interest Robert Banister in applying for the mission in Durham, observing that it was 'certainly the best we [secular] Clergy have in these two counties, & is even double to most of them'. He said the income of £100 a year was made up 'In Government security £65. From Mr Forcer's legacy £25. Interest of £250 from Wm. Salvin Esqr. £10. The field opposite the house. The furniture belongs the house'. He compared that with the mission in Hexham which got 'not above £45 per annum' but Banister was not persuaded.[26] Circumstances and practice therefore varied, but a secular priest could rely on a minimum subsistence income of £30 a year from his salary augmented by Mass stipends, mortuaries, gifts, an annual dividend from the Northern Brethren's Fund, and other incidentals.

The regulars adopted a similar strategy to that of the seculars, although we have more details of the Jesuit system. Jesuit missioners were required to include in their annual reports the amount and source of their incomes, and the reports of the Jubilee Year of 1750 best show how their system worked. Most Jesuit chaplains received a salary of £10 from their patrons and one or two had private annuities. Society funds were used to bring a priest's income up to about £30 a year, depending on his expenses. John Darrell, resident at Callaly Castle, received a salary of £10 plus £16 from the Society. William Newton at Biddlestone Hall got '£10 per annum, to find myself everything except diet', so he would have qualified for an allowance from the Society. In some cases, the capital of a fund established by a patronal family was held by the Procurator and was disbursed by him. Thomas Leckonby at Pontop Hall was allowed £33.3s; he also had 'from contributions £4 and coals free. From mortuaries and other helps £1.10s.' and an annuity of £5. The Widdrington fund established in 1730 'for the maintenance and support of a priest (being of the Society of Jesus) for ever, for and in the parish of Horsley', was held by the Society. Joseph Howe reported: 'No salary from the place, but £30 per annum from the Factory [Procurator] and £5 per annum to pay house rent'. In this way, the Provincial was able to equalise, even, perhaps, to impose a ceiling on the income of an individual priest. The beneficial effect that had on the soul served also to prevent unseemly competition for lucrative chaplaincies.[27]

Although the lay gentry were the principal benefactors of these funds, some resented the generosity of their deceased relatives and they occasionally tried to prevent the execution of a testator's instructions or they might retain the capital in their own hands to ensure that they had firm control over the missioner. The attitude of Edward Standish, patron at Stella Hall, was perhaps exceptional, but it is worth reproducing the substance of a letter he wrote to Bishop William Gibson in 1792. The salary of his chaplain was £60 a year, a sum which Standish thought was

> sufficient for a priest to live decently upon, as I know many examples of curates of the Church of England who not only live upon £50, but also maintain a wife and family ... I know very well that some places make a great deal more than what I could allow for Stella, but ... I do not perceive that the mission is served in a more exemplary manner than it used to be when priests had a great deal less; on the contrary I hear of their travelling all over the kingdom and sometimes out of it for their amusement, and when at home frequenting playhouses and assemblys. Although these amusements are innocent in themselves, they are expensive, and I see no necessity of contributing to them; this is the reason why I have given no answers to various applications I have received for subscriptions to chapels in this county. I am aware of the censure I shall be liable to from a certain disposition of people for this sentiment, and the interpretation which may be given to it.[28]

And, he might have added, he did not care. This was a perennial problem; fifty years later the vicar apostolic, William Riddell, asked Sir Edward Haggerston of Ellingham to increase the chaplain's salary, observing, 'I do not wish the priests to become rich, but I wish every one in the district had a hundred a year'. In the 1820s the Jesuit in Durham had a salary of £120-£130 but that was exceptional; it is unlikely that many priests enjoyed an income of that amount before 1850.[29]

Notwithstanding difficulties with one or two individuals, by the middle of the eighteenth century only one in three of missioners was entirely dependent for a living on the patrons with whom they lived as domestic chaplains. The rest had sufficient resources to maintain their own households, albeit on the patron's estate. To reduce still further the number of gentry-dependent priests, some chaplains made bequests to ensure that their successors would enjoy greater self-sufficiency. Moreover, partly as a result of Bishop Smith's reorganisation of the mission's finances, some funds were created by priests for priests to operate financially independent town-missions.

Before the Catholic Relief Acts, the funds of the secular clergy were administered by lay trustees as directed by the Clergy Agent, Treasurer of the Northern Brethren's Fund. Some capital was invested in property (at one time the mission owned ten houses in Old Elvet, Durham) and some was handed over to the laity as trustees; yet other sums belonging to the mission were retained by the gentry. These arrangements were somewhat precarious, and clerics were never entirely confident with the lay management of the mission's funds. When, however, in 1771 Bishop Walton told Bishop Challoner that the northern priests wanted to manage the funds themselves, Challoner warned him that the laity would not 'easily acquiesce to any alterations you could propose; the less as they are usually jealous of the Bishop's meddling with their temporals'.[30] The passage of the Relief Act in 1778, therefore, prompted the clergy to take control of their finances wherever possible. In 1781 the clergy of Lancashire decided to call in their

> monies which rural deans have time out of mind lent to farmers, yeomaners, tradesmen, gentlemen &c., and often lost, & often mismanaged, & place them in the stocks.

Bishop William Gibson would 'have no laick made trustee of ecclesiastical monies or lands' thereafter.[31] With the increasing availability of gilt-edged stocks, modern methods of investment were used and the use of lay trustees was abandoned. The expertise of the clergy in running their own financial affairs was not obviously

The Catholic Mission 1688–1850

superior, even in the opinion of some priests. Rutter wrote to his uncle in 1786 saying that Nicholas Clavering was

> one of our [Northern Brethren's] fund supervisors, but I think an improper one ... We have had no meeting this year, which I suspect to be a manoeuvre of his, lest he be discharged from his office.[32]

There would be the later example of William Birdsall bringing the Berwick mission to bankruptcy.

On the other hand, Bishop Gibson certainly had a point. Sir John Lawson died in 1811 and his heir, Sir Henry, could not trace the papers authorising the stipends of the priests at Hexham, Sunderland and Thropton which had been paid by Sir John. Sir Henry therefore told Bishop Smith that he had every reason to suppose that the funds had been exhausted and that it was not in his power as a responsible executor to continue making payments.[33] Remnants of the old system of gentry-controlled finances persisted long into the nineteenth century. As late as 1841 Bishop Hogarth feared that chaplaincy monies could at any time 'be taken over by the squire or his successors'. In his opinion, the mission in the north would not prosper until 'the chapels are detached from the mansion house of the squire'. It was suggested in *The Tablet* that a chaplain had become merely a status symbol for the Catholic gentry.[34]

***

In May 1691, the eleven secular priests in the north-east met and agreed the constitution and rule of a 'Fund for the relief and benefit of the Clergy of Bishoprick and Northumberland' which became known as the Northern Brethren's Fund.[35] Its origins, in fact, date to the Restoration: Thomas Eyre wrote in 1807, 'The earliest copy of the rules of our clergy funds goes back as far as 1660'. These rules are now missing but his statement is supported in the earliest list of benefactors which was headed by Sir Edward Radcliffe of Dilston

Castle, the donor of £100. Membership of the fund was confined to the secular clergy (bishops were excluded) but the rule stipulated that membership would only be granted to priests who submitted to the vicar apostolic's jurisdiction and who remained at their posts. (Exceptionally, though not full members, four French refugee priests received the annual dividend during the five years they worked on the mission.) The rule of 1691 laid down that the primary aim of the Fund was the relief of necessitous Brethren: those out of place, sick, aged or imprisoned. After that, 'the overplus of the rents rising from the fund shall be equally divided among the Brethren of the District, as often as there is, or shall be any considerable dividend to be given out'. The Treasurer, however, had to keep a reserve of £10 for emergencies. When a priest first came into the District and had signed the constitutions, he was given £1 representing two stipends for Masses to be offered for benefactors. Every Brother was to leave at least £10 to the Fund at his death and each was to offer three Masses at the decease of a member and a monthly Mass for the Fund's benefactors.

The founding Superiors were Roger Midford (Vicar General), Richard Rivers and Ferdinando Ashmall; the first Treasurer was Francis Hodgshon. The members of the Fund met every three years on 'the Tuesday after the feast of St Bartholomew'. The number of priests was never more than sixteen in the eighteenth century but, despite being accustomed to gather in quiet places without exciting comment or arousing suspicion, these meetings were perilous. Nevertheless Bishop Smith promoted the meetings because he wished the priests, normally isolated on their scattered missions, to have a sense of belonging to a corporate body, and to have an opportunity to discuss spiritual and temporal matters of common interest. In 1707 he wrote to one:

> I hope your meeting on the 27th of August will be the increase of peace, mutual love and confidence in each other;

and that every particular man zealously join in everything for the common good and honour of the whole body.

Robert Witham said in 1712, 'We do not only transact what belongs to ye fund, but confer on other matters and publish ye orders and instructions from our Bishop, and what in general related to ye Body ...'

New rules, signed in 1703, laid down that the rule and other books relating to the affairs of the Fund were to be kept by the Superiors and Treasurer in a 'private and remote place, which they shall make known to two or more of their Brethren, that in the case of death, they may not fall into the hands of our enemies'. A demand for greater secrecy was embodied in the rules of 1726. The members were also invited to leave their books to a common library and urged to tell their people about the Fund and the benefits they would receive as benefactors. An annual Mass for the faithful departed was also instituted. Another responsibility of the Fund's Superiors was to

> look after the funds that have been given by the laity or others of this District to ye Colleges abroad for the education of youth, and shall use their utmost interest with ye donors and trustees thereof that such youth as belong to this District and are the most promising, be sent upon them.

The demands on the resources of the Fund do not seem to have been heavy in the eighteenth century. In 1751 Mr Chambers, priest at Cliffe, was paid one guinea for assisting Mr Johnson at Staindrop, who was ill. In 1760, four guineas were paid to Mr John Norman, a farmer at Croxdale, because he was looking after the sick priest, Mr Warham. A dividend was paid regularly; from 1781 to the end of the century; the average was £5, and in the first part of the nineteenth century the dividend averaged £8 a year. It appears that until 1828 members were also given their *Ordo* each year. Changes have been made to the rules over the years but the essential purpose and character of the Fund remain the same. It was instituted when the English secular priest could look only to the charity of his fellow-priests and faithful layfolk for his temporal needs and help in distress. Its major role now is to provide an association for the clergy and to offer spiritual benefits to its members and benefactors alike.

***

There were two groups of Regular clergy on the mission during the period: the Jesuits and Benedictines. The formal relationship between the regulars and the vicars apostolic was controversial until 1753 when Pope Benedict XIV issued the bull *Apostolicum Ministerium*. Essentially it laid down that as regards their personal life regulars were subject to their own superiors, but in their external ministry they were subject to episcopal control. This remained the principle and practice governing the missionary work of the regulars until the issue of the bull *Romanos Pontifices* in 1881. There was always a certain amount of jurisdictional friction between the regulars and the vicars apostolic but they rubbed along together for the common good. A handful of monks served on the northern mission throughout the period without undue controversy[36] as, indeed, it was the intention also of the Jesuits, but the suppression of the Society of Jesus by the Holy See in July 1773 imperilled their contribution.

At the suppression there were eleven Jesuit priests in the two north-eastern counties with the care of half the Catholics in Northumberland and one fifth of those in County Durham.[37] John Walsh, their superior, had died in May in Newcastle and William Strickland at Alnwick succeeded him. William Warrilow, in Newcastle, was the only one to protest publicly against the suppression which he did in a letter to the local newspaper, for which he was reprimanded by his secular colleague in the town, Charles Cordell. Relations between the two priests never recovered. Henry Rutter, chaplain at Minsteracres told his uncle:

> I often see Messrs. Warrilow and Cordell at Newcastle; oftener I believe than they one another, for light and darkness are scarce more opposite than these two singular characters. The latter has *cacoethes scribende,* Warrilow has that of *loquendi.*

Rutter was advised by his uncle not to 'admire Mr W...w; a pompous man, I hear, *oia' magna loquens* I suppose.' He may have heard of Warrilow's reputation as a preacher; Mrs Siddons declared that had he taken to the stage he would have immortalised his name and realised a splendid fortune.[38]

In the event, all eleven Jesuits signed the Brief of Suppression for the vicar apostolic. He renewed their priestly faculties and they all carried on in their posts. Moreover, at a meeting at Alnwick in October 1774 they agreed that all funds belonging to the Jesuit missions would become the personal responsibility of incumbent ex-Jesuits; the vicar apostolic was thus relieved of any necessity to find money for their support.[39] To everyone's relief, then, the suppression had no immediate effect, but changes soon occurred.

There were four ex-Jesuit missioners in County Durham, two of whom were the first in the Residence to be displaced. Richard Murphy, chaplain at Stella Hall, was dismissed in 1775 when the estate changed hands and Thomas Eyre a secular priest, was appointed in his place. Stella was never again a Jesuit mission. Nor was Pontop Hall, a few miles to the south, after the death of the chaplain, Thomas Leckonby, in 1778. Joseph Howe, at Cheeseburn Grange, wound up Leckonby's affairs. It may be thought surprising that the ex-Jesuit succession was not maintained at Pontop since the vacancy came soon after the suppression and ex-Jesuits were still readily available. There was, however, a domestic problem. The patron, Thomas Swinburne, had died six years before Leckonby, leaving a 60-year-old widow and an adult son who was married to Charlotte Spearman, a Protestant. She was not amenable to a resident chaplain and would only tolerate a secular priest in the house while old Mrs Swinburne was alive.

There was, in any case, something of a glut of priests at this time and Bishop Walton, mindful of the precarious financial situation of the mission and, perhaps, seeking to increase the number of places for secular priests, said that ex-Jesuits should only:

> be employed on the mission where they can be provided for, else it would be imprudent to increase the number of priests. And this seems to be our situation at present: Messrs. Houghton, Parkinson and Marsland are out of work, another is expected from Hilton [Rome]: so that there is no want, but, on the contrary, an evident redundancy.[40]

This was a temporary situation, for demand would soon exceed supply.

The other two ex-Jesuits in County Durham were undisturbed in their places and, since they were the longest-lived in the Residence, they represent continuity between the suppressed and restored Society. Edward Walsh was missioner in the city of Durham for the whole fifty years of his priestly life. He was popular in the city where he was known as 'the thirteenth prebendary', but Rutter thought him a social climber:

> He has travelled much and passes for a very agreeable companion, is very great with all the prebendaries and constantly one of their parties. In return for which he gives a grand rout once a year to which all the gentlemen and ladies are invited and at his last was honoured with above 90 persons of the first rank of gentility in the neighbourhood.[41]

Shortly after Walsh's death in 1822 at the age of 83, the Jesuit Provincial, Nicholas Sewell, instructed John Scott to negotiate the amalgamation of the Jesuit and secular missions in Durham. Scott left in 1826 after burying Christopher Rose, the last surviving member of the suppressed Society in the Residence. Rose had been the youngest member in the year of the suppression and had served at Hardwick Hall for fifty-six years. He retired to Durham in 1824 when the mission at Hardwick was moved to Hutton House a few miles to the north under a young secular priest, Thomas Slater, who had assisted the aged ex-Jesuit since 1822.[42]

The ex-Jesuit missions in Northumberland were first affected in 1774 when Joseph Pleasington, chaplain at Callaly Castle, retired to Alnwick at the age of 59, having grown weak and 'zealously crazy'; he had objected to Mrs Clavering riding on a Sunday. Clearly this was a place the ex-Jesuits sought to retain, for Joseph Dunn, 28 years old and newly-ordained, was immediately appointed to the chaplaincy. But he left within two years and, after an interval of three years, the mission was taken over by an exiled French ex-Jesuit. That, however, was intended to be temporary, for negotiations were then proceeding between the vicar apostolic and the family about the appointment of a secular chaplain. The change of tenure here, then, seems to have occurred either as a result of differences between Dunn and the patron or because of a change of attitude towards the ex-Jesuits.

Ellingham Hall was another chaplaincy the ex-Jesuits hoped to keep. In 1779 John Richardson, aged 45, retired probably because of illness for he died three years later. He was succeeded immediately by the ex-Jesuit Matthew Joy who remained at Ellingham until his death in 1798, aged 56. His unexpectedly early death so long after the suppression might have brought a change of tenure here but William Meynell, a highly peripatetic ex-Jesuit, was quickly sent north to fill the vacancy. He was 54 years old and, no doubt, expected to hold the living for some time, but the patron, Edward Haggerston, died without issue in 1804 leaving the estate to his nephew Thomas Haggerston of Sandhoe. He and his wife had been used to Benedictine chaplains, and so Meynell was immediately replaced by Dom John Forshaw. Much the same thing happened when Joseph Howe, chaplain to the Riddells at Longhorsley Tower, who had also supplied at Felton Park until 1778, died in 1792 at the age of 81. The Riddells then engaged James Weldon, a fellow-ex-Jesuit, but he was in his sixties and did not stay long in the north. The missions of Longhorsley and Felton were separated at Howe's death and, since Riddell had known Benedictine chaplains at his home in Swinburne Castle before his marriage, both missions were handed over to monks.

Doubtless the ex-Jesuits would have liked to hold on to Haggerston Castle and Berrington Hall, missions they had occupied in north Northumberland for almost a century. Charles Hanne had been a vigorous missioner in his youth but he was 62 years old when the Society was suppressed and he lived quietly in the castle until his death in 1799. Francis Digges, the American-born ex-Jesuit chaplain at nearby Berrington Hall, retired in 1776 at the age of 63 but he too remained in residence. They were assisted for seven years by Nicholas Sanderson, who, fortuitously, had to leave Swinburne Castle when it was closed for renovation at this time. He left in 1784 to go to Alnwick and Thomas Nixon was moved up from York. William Clavering, patron at Berrington, died in 1789, aged 82, leaving less than £600. The new squire, Edward Clavering, seemingly oblivious of the limitations of such a small inheritance, began to rebuild the mansion, but he so over-reached himself that parts of the estate had to be sold off; one of his first economies was to let the residential chaplaincy lapse when Digges died in 1790. When Nixon left that year to follow Sanderson at Alnwick no more ex-Jesuits could be found and a transfer to the seculars of what had now become a unified mission was put in hand. Michael Tidyman was placed in charge and was provided with a new and furnished house and an income of £90 a year by Sir Carnaby Haggerston.

Alnwick was the one mission place the ex-Jesuits had no intention of losing if they could help it. In 1784 William Strickland was appointed President of Liege Academy (which removed to Stonyhurst in 1794) and he was succeeded by Nicholas Sanderson and Thomas Nixon, both of whom died in their late fifties, necessitating the transfer in 1793 from Richmond of the 70-year-old Francis Holme. He belied his age by completely rebuilding the chapel within three years. At his death in 1802 the ex-Jesuits found it almost impossible to find a successor. In 1797, shortly after Stonyhurst College had opened, Strickland told Warrilow that it was probable that

> some years must elapse before the college will be able to furnish successors to all the places ... Till this takes place, recourse must be had to monks, friars, [and secular] clergy.[43]

Curiously, Strickland doubted if any English secular priest would find Alnwick 'a very desirable place.'[44] Thus for ten years to 1812 the ex-Jesuit mission at Alnwick had to be put in charge of a French exiled secular, M. Vergy. The English Jesuits then resumed their tenure with John Beaumont, a newly-ordained priest in the restored Society. The last of the Northumbrian ex-Jesuits was William Warrilow, who died in 1807. Although Newcastle was one of the principal missions in the country, the ex-Jesuits were unable to provide a successor for him. In fact, this chapel had become redundant. St Andrew's, under the secular priest, James Worswick, had become the focus of Catholic life in the town.

In summary, then, the suppression of the Society of Jesus did not have as great an impact on the mission in the region as was feared. Since all the Jesuits acceded to the decision, change would depend on their own longevity and the good will of patrons. Only in one or two cases do hints of anti-Jesuit feeling emerge. Most patrons took the view that if their chaplains signed the Brief they could remain in place and continue to receive an income from the old Society's funds of which the patrons were trustees. Three-quarters of the ex-Jesuits lived on for twenty years or more and it would be over fifty years before the last of them died. In a remarkable display of flexibility they managed to maintain a presence for longer perhaps than even they dared to hope. Inevitably, though, as the younger ex-Jesuits died around the turn of the century, it became an increasingly difficult task and most missions had to be given up. After 1807, Alnwick was left in Northumberland with Durham and Hardwick Hall in County Durham; Alnwick alone remained at the time of Catholic Emancipation.

The suppressed Society was a long time dying, then, but the last of its members had the satisfaction of being succeeded by members of the restored Society. But the restoration by Pius VII in 1814 was not accepted by the English vicars apostolic for fear that it would adversely affect their campaign for emancipation. In 1817 Edward Walsh went to Rome to have their decision rescinded but a restoration could only take place where the civil government agreed and in 1819 Bishop Poynter was told that the British government 'had an insuperable objection to the establishment of the Jesuits in England'. The matter was not resolved until 1829. Until then, English members of the Society were referred to as 'Gentlemen of Stonyhurst'.

***

France, which had been the traditional refuge of English Catholics, became the enemy of religion at the Revolution, and, from 1792, Protestant England became a sanctuary both for French clerics and expatriate English Catholic establishments. Some three hundred priests landed at North Shields in October 1796. The government recommended that the priests live together for economy, and large groups were put up in government buildings in Sunderland and Berwick and in a row of newly built miners' cottages in Heddon. The Anglican Sir Matthew Ridley took some at Plessey Checks, Stannington, and others are known to have been at Witton Gilbert in Durham and Spittal, near Tweedmouth. The rest were dispersed around the region in various Catholic houses and missions: at Brooms in a half-finished chapel and priest's house; ten at Stella with Mr Silvertop; and three in Bishop Auckland. Alexis Hebert lived with John Galley, a coal-merchant in Sunderland, and M. de Buisson officiated in Mr Dunn's house in Gateshead Fell. Thus some middle-class families were given the opportunity of having a resident chaplain, an unexpected but welcome social boost. Most missions would find it difficult to support a second priest and, in any case, many of the French clerics would be excluded from pastoral work because of language. Rutter was 'for the present their interpreter and do what lies in my power to make them comfortable.' And then, the French were believed by many English priests to be 'dangerously bigotted to Gallican liberty' and that it was only prudent to keep them isolated from English Catholics. The French were invited to assist at examinations at Crook Hall, but some thought them unscholarly.[45]

For various reasons, then, most of the French exiles lived in closed communities. At the same time, however, some mission histories show that, when required, those who could speak English did fill temporary vacancies. French priests acted as stop-gaps at Croxdale, Darlington, Stella, Stockton and Sunderland in County Durham, and at Callaly Castle, Berrington Hall, Hexham, Stonecroft Farm, Witton Shields and Wooler in Northumberland. Four missions owed much more to the exiles. The French stand-in at Alnwick was in charge for ten years. The presence of the French in Berwick dispelled a great deal of anti-Catholic prejudice, and Michael Tidyman was emboldened to open a chapel in the town and appoint Louis Bigot as missioner. When Bigot returned to France in 1801 his congregation was desolate at the loss. Philip Besnier took over a year later. It is likely that Berwick would have remained a supply-station from Haggerston for many years had it not been for the efforts of the Frenchmen. The mission at Cowpen near Blyth had its origins in the appointment of a French exile as chaplain to the Sidney family in 1801. Louis Deshogues (or La Hogue) succeeded in 1801 and he remained long after the majority of his fellow-countrymen went home. A resident mission was established at North Shields at the turn of the century under two French priests. One of them, Pierre Dubuisson, having returned to France came back to England in 1802 hoping (in vain) to be appointed missioner at the new church of St Cuthbert.

It is somewhat unfair, then, as some have done, to dismiss the French contribution to the English mission. Most of the exiles were never asked to help, but those who were became successful and popular missioners, not least because they were prepared to endure conditions rejected by English priests. Acknowledging their contribution in 1801, Rutter wrote 'Some of our French priests are gone, and others are about to go. The Mission in these parts will feel the want of them.'[46] Quite so, for a shortage of priests had been developing in the wake of the French Revolution and (to a lesser extent) the Jesuit suppression. In 1792 Rutter had told his uncle:

> There are now three considerable congregations adjoining to mine which appear to me not to be sufficiently provided for. Mr Ashmal at Newhouse who is 97 years of age at least has been unable to do duty for a long time. No priest has been fixed at Pontop since Mr Johnson's death. Nor is Stella, as I hear, yet provided with a pastor. For the present indeed Mr Story from Hexham says prayers there and Mr Worswick at Pontop...[47]

In 1798 the Revd John Barrow, aged 63, told the vicar apostolic:

> The more I reflect on the present state of the Northern mission, the more plainly I see the future scarcity of Missionaries to fill our Places. More than twenty of us are far advanced in years, without the most distant prospect of a succession, though we have numerous congregations.[48]

In 1767 the average age of the clergy was about fifty. Moreover, suitable candidates for the priesthood were hard to find. William Fletcher, missioner in Sunderland, told Thomas Eyre in 1805 that he did 'not know a Catholic of this congregation that is fit for a Clerk's place.'[49]

In 1802 there were thirty-one missioners in the region (including six Benedictines) but eleven congregations in the region were without pastors. Michael Tidyman wrote to Thomas Eyre at Crook Hall on 27 February 1803:

> Supposing our numbers are likely to be still more reduced, I cannot help communicating to you an idea ... which perhaps you will laugh at as ridiculous and impracticable: it is this, to send officially and with proper recommendations a priest or two to Spain, or if you please, Portugal, in quality of recruiting officers in order to enlist a few strong and likely subjects to fight under the banner of the English Mission. ... [T]hey might at least say Mass for the people on Sundays and Holydays, and with time and pains might be competent masters of the language, so far at least as may be necessary for the administration of the Sacraments.[50]

Significantly, recruiting closer to home in Ireland was not mentioned for, although three seminaries had been established there, all the Irish priests were needed at home. In any case, the 'Irish Question' was a continuing political problem which the bishops were disinclined to aggravate. The reluctance to employ Irish priests went back, in fact, to the Restoration period when it was said that 'Not a single Irish priest is a true friend to the English' and the vicars apostolic resisted the employment of Irish priests all through the eighteenth century. In 1734, when there appeared to be a national shortage of priests in England, the President of Douai wrote that Bishop Stonor 'much contrary to the judgement of the other clergy bishops and his predecessors ... made some endeavours to get and introduce irish clergy-men, of whom he may have plenty' into the Midland District, but it would not be until Emancipation that a few carefully selected Irishmen were allowed into the presbyteries of north-east England.[51]

In a Pastoral Letter of 1813 Bishop Milner remarked on 'the distressing scarcity of Clergy'[52] but the crisis was beginning to abate; ordinations of English secular priests had begun at Crook Hall in 1794 and the number of clerical applicants began to rise when Ushaw College opened in 1808. But it was a close-run thing. The Church was fortunate in retaining the services of the ex-Jesuits and obtaining those of the French exiles which enabled it to maintain that presence across the region which it had worked so hard to achieve over the previous century, and without which the Catholic Revival of the nineteenth century would have been set back many years.

***

A thirty-year long correspondence between Robert Banister and his nephew Henry Rutter, both secular missionary priests, the former in Lancashire, the latter a chaplain in Northumberland provide an exceptional view of Catholic life in the period, particularly of the domestic difficulties of the chaplaincy system.[53] The fortunes of the mission were bound up with those of the landed gentry but they did not live in settled circumstances, subject as they were to changes in family expectations as well as political events and economic trends. Further, in an embarrassingly large number of cases a patron quarrelled with his chaplain, leading to disruptions in pastoral care. Since the majority of the missions in the north-east were chaplaincies for much of the century, the relationship between patron and chaplain became a greater influence on missionary development than the external political context.

Robert Banister was a Douatian and was ordained in 1750. He stayed on as a professor until coming to the English mission in 1769. He returned briefly to Douai but he shortly left once and for all and went to Mowbreck Hall, in Lancashire, where he would remain until he retired in 1803. His long stint at Douai made him highly influential for he trained almost all of the English secular clergy of the late eighteenth century. He was a tough, unimaginative and humourless man with rigid and old-fashioned ideas about education, and he disliked the Catholic gentry intensely. He was known to be in Bishop William Gibson's 'privy council', and he was himself regarded as *episcopabile* in 1780 and again in 1800, although (as is quite usual) he expressed delight at not being selected.

Banister's nephew, Henry Rutter, was born in 1755 and went to Douai College at the age of 13. In 1779, a sub-deacon and in his second year of theology at Douai, he was appointed tutor to John Clifton, a 15-year-old Lancastrian. Rutter was to attend the boy at Douai until his own ordination in 1780, after which they would move into the Royal College at St Omer where he would conduct the rest of Clifton's education. But Rutter's relationship with Clifton deteriorated rapidly. The boy was undisciplined and Rutter knew he could not cope:

> neither my disposition nor capacity are suited for this way of life. You know I am of a silent & dull turn of mind, & fitter to keep company with F. Bruno at the Chartreuse than young people of so contrary dispositions. Besides, the life of a Tutor seems to be a very indolent one, without any advantage either to himself or his pupil, who, considering him as an enemy to his ease, pleasure & satisfaction, keeps him out of his company as much as possible.[54]

Rutter became thoroughly alarmed at the prospect of taking Clifton, a young man in the rudest of health, on the Grand Tour because he knew perfectly well that Clifton's interests were social not cultural, and the tutorship was brought to an abrupt end. Bishop Matthew Gibson appointed Rutter chaplain to the Silvertop family at Minsteracres in Northumberland. Appalled at the idea, having had so much trouble with Clifton and not wishing to repeat the experience with four young Silvertop boys, Rutter tried to get out of it. He lobbied the clergy of Lancashire and made quite sure that everyone, including his new patron, knew that he did not want the job. The bishop was not to be coerced, however, and the appointment stood. On 23 August, 1783, then, 'in better health than spirits', Rutter arrived at Minsteracres. Despite his misgivings, in his first letter Rutter said that he was agreeably surprised with the place and regretted that he had expressed himself 'so freely and unfavourably' on it. Nonetheless he adopted a guarded approach with the family although he admitted that it was generally 'allowed that persons of our [priestly] character are no where in the county better received than here'. Banister was pleased to hear it and recommended his nephew not to cause a rupture between himself and the Silvertops, but to fall in with all their wishes.[55]

Rutter remained at Minsteracres for forty years despite a frequently expressed antipathy to the gentry imbibed from his uncle and from his experience with Clifton. He would serve three generations of Silvertops: George (I) for six years (1783–9); John for twelve years (1789–1801); and George (II) for twenty-one years (1801–22). The first George was much attached to Douai College, and would 'not suffer any thing to be said in her dispraise' and Rutter often heard 'the praises of Douay College, now raised to the highest pitch by the vigilance and superior abilities of its President' William Gibson. John Silvertop, the son and heir, was 'not so easy and amicable in his manner as could be wished'. He did, however, possess 'other qualities that make that deficiency less remarkable'. He had testified some regard for his chaplain more than once, but Rutter did 'not place much confidence in the favour of Great Ones'. Of his wife, Catherine Lawson of Brough, Rutter merely remarked that she was 'of an even temper and likewise a very good Christian but much given to ye Jesuitical devotions' (she was educated at the Bar Convent in York). There were five children and Rutter feared 'very much for them from the fondness of servants, &c., did not the father maintain his authority over them'. Rutter undertook the 'tedious task of teaching' much against his wishes; he had gone to Minsteracres 'with a resolution of declining this honour, but her Ladyship's eloquence overcame' him.[56]

All chaplains had pastoral responsibilities in addition to the duty they owed to their patrons. The returns made at the episcopal visitations in this period frequently remark on the peripatetic lives of the Catholic priests. Although the missioners were seen about, they were careful to avoid any charge of proselytising. The vicar of Edmundbyers reported that he had 'heard of a popish priest (a Mr Rutter) calling at some of the houses in the parish', but he 'did not understand that it was for the purpose of making proselytes'. On the other hand, Rutter did occasionally call on a Methodist in Muggleswick, and the vicar understood that their conversation was 'always on the subject of religion and most commonly controversial'.[57]

Rutter had more mundane matters to attend to in his early days at Minsteracres. He told Banister that 'we are all clockwork here, such regularity and exactness is observed' and his greatest need was for a timepiece 'to measure out his time to his poor people, so as not to trespass upon his family's hours'. It would not do to keep those in the big house waiting, especially as he had the use of the squire's galloway, and even occasionally 'his own horse a great favour, not often to be expected'.[58] Clothing was of great importance. Priests dressed as gentlemen, except that they always wore black. Rutter regretted not having brought his best black suit and he asked his uncle for it. That allowed Banister to give vent to a stern discourse on the proper clerical attitude to dress. He told his nephew that he could not afford 'broad cloth, or silk breeches or ruffled shirts' on a salary of £10 a year. Instead, he should wear plain clothes and patch them as necessary. Rutter was never to be ashamed of darns and patches, for they would disgrace a niggardly patron more than a humble chaplain. Therefore, 'If a coat of good plain at 9s. p. yd. displeases the eye of your quality, you can insinuate the true reason why you have no better'. Banister would not send the suit and Rutter would have to buy some cheap material and get a suit made up out of it. 'Pray do not be ashamed of such geer', Banister said, 'many a good missioner never wore better, nor perhaps as good'. Futhermore, there was no need to wear a clean shirt with ruffles every day, '2 or at most 3 in a week is sufficient'. Rutter accepted this as good but impractical advice. A patched coat would never be allowed because it would 'give ladies the hysterics'. Banister was unyielding: 'Your stipend being £20 p. annum, I expect you will save one half every year & put it out to fructify'. Rutter's response was derisive:

> You have too good an idea of my economy if you think I can do with £10 p. ann. I shall be content if I can but save two guineas, which I mean to send annually to my Mother for her tea and other little necessaries.[59]

Banister kept up the pressure and instructed Rutter never to waste his time at cards or be a 'Lady's implement to make up their parties'. Rutter, however, was confident on that score; he was not

> of a nature to gain the favour of Ladies: I have some thing too heavy, too stupid and sombre about me to enter into their light and frivolous amusements, to laugh, play with and flatter them. Indeed, I find that I am not formed for

> society and this defect I attribute chiefly to Education ... so I have one perfection, at least, requisite in a chaplain, that of being silent and a poor, stupid thing, that can't open its mouth.[60]

Banister could not take him for his predecessor William Gibson, who had

> left behind him the reputation of being an excellent marker [marksman]; an honour I don't aspire to. He always accompanied his patron in this capacity and on all other occasions showed a flexibility greater than my pride will submit to. He was indeed a most worthy man, but his humility in this respect not a little surprises me.[61]

Rutter had

> a most despicable opinion of our Catholic nobility and gentry in general, as they seem to surpass the rest of the world only in extravagance and the fashionable vices of the age.

Banister readily agreed and he reminded Rutter that they would ever consider themselves self-sufficient and would shrink from priests who 'disturb them sometimes on the spacious and flowery road on which most of them roll and dance along'. Minsteracres, however, was in many respects at the centre of north-eastern Catholic life, and Rutter was forced to associate with people he more or less disdained 'for very few see more company than we do'. He often travelled around the region meeting his fellow-priests and their patrons.[62]

His own admitted lack of the social graces, however, suggests that Rutter did not make the most of his opportunities. He seldom remained in company after dinner: 'I am as mute as a cat at table and after a bumper to the coal trade, take myself off to my room very quietly, unless the fineness of the evening invites me to a solitary walk'. Nonetheless, while keeping his distance, Rutter kept a close eye on the gentry, partly out of fascinated horror, but also because in many cases the survival of the mission depended on their fortunes. In fact, although his dislike of the gentry was so intense that it is surprising that he tolerated them at all, his expectations were often confounded. He had to admit that the Silvertops were not too bad. Sir John Lawson of Brough, 'a person of virtue and polite accomplishments', was esteemed by him above all other Catholic gentlemen. Sir Carnaby Haggerston also gained his admiration for behaving exactly as most priests wanted, which was to come to the aid of the clergy when asked, and normally by opening their purses, but not to interfere otherwise in affairs ecclesiastical.[63]

Rutter said little about his priestly duties. He remarked that 'Prayers are at 8 and a half; but I say them no oftener than I think proper'. Banister instantly urged Rutter 'most earnestly' to say Mass daily. Rutter frequently asked Banister for advice on pastoral problems, most of which seem routine, but others were unlikely to have been on the syllabus at Douai. There was the question of whether it was permissible to buy goods from smugglers and whether an alehouse-keeper could be a good Catholic. Other enquiries concerned an application for holy water from persons who imagined themselves bewitched; an Irishwoman who pretended to cure by touch persons that had 'been venomed'; and he wanted to know what he should say to a young woman who hired herself (as a domestic servant) to a neighbouring parson. He needed guidance on the best method of instructing adult converts, since the catechism was too tedious for them; how was he to deal with a priest for whom he was confessor whom he knew to attend the theatre; and whether someone who took his children to the theatre was admissible to Holy Communion. He asked how to treat servants; he alluded to an unspecified domestic incident after which he had arranged for the dismissal of the house-keeper and another person. Rutter enjoyed Lent and was not particularly impressed with the attempts at penance practised at Minsteracres and wondered if it was acceptable to take hot chocolate and buttered buns for breakfast. He needed to know what distance would excuse a healthy person from attending Sunday Mass in winter. He expressed distress about 'such as live at a distance in Protestant places and who seldom come to prayers', and was it correct

> to marry Cat. with Prot-ts? or to baptize the children of those nominal Caths. who know nothing of religion and never come to chapel? Or to church those heathenish ignorant mothers who never come near you at any other time?

Bishop Riddell complained of a related practice fifty years later. He regretted that the Catholics of Coquetdale had not yet begun to have their children baptised in a chapel but preferred 'it done in the house, as had been the practice for time immemorial' on the grounds that the chapel was too far off.[64]

None of these matters caused Banister the least difficulty. Poor sailors who brought over a few gallons of rum or a pound or two of coffee could be excused but those who trafficked in smuggled goods were not to be tolerated. Men could be excused from attending Mass if they lived over eight miles from a chapel, women somewhat less. He was unhelpful about the menus at Minsteracres and advised Rutter always to take breakfast, especially when he was to go out, otherwise his health would suffer. Buns in Lent were allowed: 'you make no scruple of eating apple-pyes or tarts, which are not made without butter in the crust'.[65] Sir Carnaby Haggerston softened the rigours of a Northumbrian Lent with sea-food from Seahouses and Craster. His chaplain clearly took a more liberal view than Rutter. John Thornton said Sir Carnaby took a lobster soop each day in Lent to keep the juices of his body from sowering in Spring; assure yourself that the sweetening diet, especially in the Spring of the year, lobsters, cockles, oysters & such sort with moderate exercise is a better remedy than fasting.[66]

With regard to dinner parties on days of abstinence, Banister remarked:

As to setting flesh meat on the table for their Prot. guests, it is coming into vogue, as I hear. It is a very unnecessary complaisance for Prots. will go to a Cath. Gentleman to dine on fish, being glutted with flesh dinners.

Banister was not so much concerned with the dietary excesses of the gentry as with their general behaviour:

as to writing for or instructing persons of quality or fortune, tis to little purpose. No way will please them, but that which is broad & easy. Yet I would venture to answer for their chocolate in the morning & their tea in the evening, their dipping a small biscuit in wine, & licking up a tea-spoonful of sweet-meats in Lent, or on other fasting days, provided they would extirpate that pride, which is ever predominant in their heart, that idle & unprofitable life of carding, visiting, dancing, going to plays & balls & making la frivolite the sole end & object of their thoughts and time.[67]

Rutter made no comment on that; indeed, he may have been a little shamefaced about his own gadding about, for he accompanied Silvertop on occasional business trips, and he went with the family on visits to relations or on holiday. The Silvertops took a house at Tynemouth in 1796. Sea-bathing was highly regarded as a cure-all and Rutter considered it most beneficial but it did not protect him from gout; indeed, at Christmas 1800, the squire, the chaplain and the butler were all down with it.[68]

Banister's approach to catechetical instruction was simple and he applied it to adults, converts and children alike. Complicated expositions of doctrine were to be avoided; nothing could be better than 'beating plain, easy, but necessary truths into the giddy, heedless, inattentive minds of poor peasants'. The literate could be given *The Garden of the Soul*, and the illiterate be taught to get the Lord's Prayer, the Hail Mary and the Creed off by heart. He added that it was also necessary to explain the ten commandments in detail because he believed that there were those who had

> no idea of the words, adultery, fornication, pollution, &c. I say the idea of those words, not of the things. 'Tis therefore requisite to explain the meaning of those words, as modestly as possible, yet so as to be understood, adding at the same time a lively description of the torments prepared for those who do such things.

On staff discipline He urged Rutter 'to hinder all kissing &c.' between servants, and that whenever he entered the kitchen he was to 'take notice of the chairs, whether they be not broken by carrying double'. His own servants gave him trouble of this kind: he was unable to protect his manservant from the importunities of the kitchen-maid, whom he was forced to dismiss. Rutter commiserated: 'I hoped you had cured her of love long ago; but this disorder, it seems, is not so easily mastered'.[69]

Rutter's long sojourn at Minsteracres was due largely to Bishop William Gibson's refusal to move him, coupled with the inconvenient fact that the family came to like him. Rutter did not apply for a change in the first ten years but the idea was never far from his mind and he made repeated requests to leave thereafter. Indeed, he and his uncle were forever suggesting that the other might apply for any vacant post that came up. Rutter suggested that Banister apply for Newcastle when Charles Cordell died in 1791 or 'perhaps York would please you better ... you will have a polite congregation indeed, but I am told rather difficult to be pleased'. Rutter tried to persuade his uncle 'to come and live among our canons at Durham' after the death of John Lodge in 1795, but Banister suggested that Rutter himself should go there. Characteristically, Rutter's reply was self-deprecating:

> I frankly own that I am not a proper person for a place of such importance and should form indeed a very striking contrast to the other priest who is there, I mean Mr. Walsh, the gregarious and popular ex-Jesuit.[70]

Rutter asked to go to Thropton and applied to fill a vacancy at Hexham, but the bishop ignored him. Rutter gave up. He would think no more of changing his situation although he thought his 'nerves may advise to the contrary'. Banister sympathised but he pointed out the advantages of a chaplaincy over a public mission:

> You wish, I suppose, to be emancipated because whilst you live in a family you seem to yourself to carry a chain; but on the other hand reflect that you have nothing to do with house-keeping, no rents to pay, no servants wages to find, nor a thousand other articles to distract you. If company and visitors do not fill your head too much with unprofitable narratives and rumours, you may retire to your garret and shut out all distractions, perplexities and anxieties and solicitudes and pursue your meditations and studies without interruption.[71]

As Banister suggested, chaplaincy life did indeed lend itself to scholarly pursuits but it seems that not many priests took advantage of the opportunity. Indeed, a lack of culture and polish was probably the principal reason why chaplains were treated so badly by their patrons. An episcopal document of 1737 said that many priests were rough and ignorant and that greater care ought to be taken when selecting candidates for the priesthood. Berington noted that the Douai clergy were 'ignorant of the world and unpleasant in their manners':

> It is the complaint of our gentry that priests are rough and unsociable: they would be less so, perhaps, if their patrons were less proud, less ignorant, and less imperious. On both sides are faults which should be corrected.[72]

Indeed, many Catholic gentlemen sought out the more cultivated and liberal priests to share their mansions. Similarly, culturally inclined chaplains seized the chance of accompanying young gentlemen on the Grand Tour as preceptor (and chaperone, although most exerted a light touch in that respect; Rutter had baulked at the very prospect). Rutter remarked that the library at Minsteracres contained a lot of history, and Banister urged him to use it. An English history was very much needed

> for the use & perusal of Catholics, who would not be led into errors & prejudices & false notions & sentiments about many important points & characters ... your squire has a valuable assortment for you & if you desire more, go to Mr Marmaduke Tunstall at Wycliffe on Tees.[73]

Rutter did not take up the proposal and it was John Lingard who would become the principal Catholic historian of the period with his multi-volume *History of England*.

Apologetics, church history, scripture and theology were the more usual topics for clerics. In the late eighteenth century some forty Catholic books were published in the north-east, thirty-five of them in Newcastle. Charles Cordell was the most prolific with at least fourteen titles to his name, many of which were translations of French devotional works. In 1786 Rutter hoped that his latest would sell 'as many of his former works are still on his hands'. Cordell was criticised for putting into practice his two-volume *The Divine Office for the Use of the Laity* (1780) at St Andrew's. Rutter began to collect books and shortly to publish his own. A *Life of Christ* came out in 1803; John Barrow told him that 'a better spiritual book never as yet has appeared in print' and it was serialised with illustrations in 1830. Rutter translated Italian and French devotional works and one or two volumes of biblical exegesis and asceticism.[74]

John Silvertop's health began to decline at the turn of the century. Rutter prayed that his life be spared 'for the sake of his family, for his death would in my opinion occasion a great change in it, not much to my satisfaction'. Silvertop died on Boxing Day, 1801, aged 51. His widow remarked that Rutter would not suit her son George, the new squire. The opportunity was therefore taken to move the chaplain out of the mansion into his own cottage. Rutter refers on one occasion to his house-keeper, and there is a local tradition that a small house about a quarter of a mile from the mansion was a presbytery. His congregation had remained stable at about one hundred, but an increase in the number of baptisms each year lifted the total to about one hundred and fifty and it held up for much of the first half of the nineteenth century. Rutter was 47 years old when he moved. He had by that time been at Minsteracres some twenty years, and he had gained the confidence of his brother-priests. He was elected Second Superior of the Northern Brethren's Fund in 1793 and in 1808 he was made First Superior. In 1810 Bishop Douglass recommended either John Lingard or Henry Rutter as President of Ushaw College in succession to Thomas Eyre (both declined).

At the beginning of 1803, aged 78, Banister retired to Dodding Green, a small mission near Kendal, 'for an easy retirement in my old age'. He enjoyed some nine years there before he died in May 1812. Rutter was growing old too; he was 65 in 1820 and 'very subject to infirmities' but, as Lingard remarked, 'he therefore wishes to have a house of his own, his own servant and to be his own master'.[75] Two years later Bishop Smith acceded to his long-held wish to leave and moved him to Yealand in Lancashire. Twelve years later he retired to Dodding Green, just as his uncle had done and he died there suddenly of a stroke in September 1838, aged 85.

The Banister-Rutter letters provide a valuable insight into the relationship between squire and chaplain and are helpful in explaining the incompatibility of priest and patron which occurred so often in the region. Rutter's tone mellows over the years, and it is clear that the Silvertops became used to him, and even came to like him, but this must have been for his priestly qualities rather than for his social attributes which, he freely admitted, were deficient. Many of the difficulties between priest and patron can be attributed to social differences as much as anything else. It is striking how often in this period a patron sacked his chaplain to make way for a priest of his own family, and priests of gentry origin were rarely treated as cavalierly as the humbly-born. Indeed, a gentry-born priest such as the Jesuit John Thornton enjoyed a much more congenial relationship with his patron than Rutter ever aspired to.

John Thornton (1675–1759) entered the household at Haggerston Castle in 1711 and his first duty was to accompany Sir Carnaby Haggerston (III), his 13-year-old pupil-patron, on the Grand Tour.[76] Thornton stayed on as chaplain at the castle on their return in 1719, and he remained there for thirty-four years. He was very much the country gentleman and a close friend of the principal Northumbrian Catholic families, among whom he associated on terms of social equality. He used the alias of Hunt, an old gentry family of Yorkshire with which he was connected. He regularly wrote to Sir Marmaduke Constable of Everingham, an uncle of Sir Carnaby, and it is from his letters that we get a few glimpses of a chaplain's life in this remote mission on the north-east coast of England.

Thornton was a keen sportsman and, it appears, a boon companion of the hunting and racing elements of the gentry. Sir Carnaby lacked a similar disposition and his chaplain expressed some exasperation at the rather boring and genteel pursuits preferred at Haggerston: 'Our diversion consists now in walks, allies, parterres, vestoes, Belvideres, grottos, and such like, so that the very name of hunting sounds barbarous'. Landscape gardening reduced the acreage available for hunting, and that was sufficient to damn it in Thornton's eyes. His enthusiasm for the chase so exceeded his patron's that 'sitting solitary upon the housetop', he sometimes wished he was in Yorkshire with Constable, who evidently shared his obsession. The birth of Thomas Haggerston in 1722 led him to hope that since the child had been born in the 'fox-hunting season, he may come to follow it more than his father'. He did; in 1743 Sir Marmaduke described Thomas as 'really a handsome well-shaped youth and does his exercises tolerably well, and riding (is) his favourite, in which he excels'. Thornton became involved in such secular matters as his knowledge, experience and continental contacts proved useful. As an authority on hunting-dogs, he was able to obtain suitable animals from Spain. He was also a connoisseur of horses, and he selected one to send down to Everingham, with the assurance that Yorkshire would 'ring with the fame of him'. He ordered wines from the continent, and he boasted that he supplied the table at Haggerston 'with as good wine as Bordeaux and the Grand Duke's vintages can produce', and he deplored Sir Carnaby's preference for port. He told Constable in 1725 that 'Your nephew's taste is entirely lost since he came from your house, for our poor maigre claret will not now go down with him … for [he] nothing now relishes but your Lisbon'.[77] Sir Carnaby had six children, and the chaplain was consulted at all stages of their upbringing; Sir Marmaduke advised Sir Carnaby to be 'sure that Thornton and no one else' was with Thomas when he went courting.

It is impossible to imagine Rutter enjoying such a companionable relationship with the Silvertops. His experience with the squireling John Clifton engendered in each of them a lifelong aversion of priest for squire and vice versa quite opposite to the intimacy Thornton developed in his tutorship of Haggerston. The two priests spent a similar length of time as chaplain, but it was enjoyed in one case and endured in the other. Thornton was comfortable in his situation, Rutter was ill-at-ease; it is hard to attribute this to anything other than a social mismatch. A comparable case is that of Dom John Naylor, chaplain at Biddlestone for fifty-four years. But, as John Bossy suggests, Naylor's tranquillity was 'partly due to the Selbys being there so little of the time'.[78]

Quite apart from any personal or social problem between chaplain and patron, there was a pastoral difficulty. A chaplain had responsibility for a congregation drawn from a wide area, not all of whom would be connected with the estate, but the chapel was in a private house and the priest was mainly beholden to his patron. In return for protection and subsistence, the chaplain surrendered much of his independence. He might dine and hunt with his squire, but that was often on sufferance and merely highlighted the chaplain's status which might be likened to that of a penurious relative. A patron demanded proper deference from all within his domain, including his chaplain who was a paid member of the establishment. From the patron's point of view, there was little to distinguish his instructions to the butler about the weekend guests from his decisions about Mass-times, which were probably conveyed to the chaplain through the higher domestic servants. A patron might alter the time of Mass without notice; close the house to go on holiday, or raise difficulties over a chaplain's wider pastoral duties. A chaplain would be hard-pressed to avoid having to adjudicate in domestic arguments, to refrain from comment on questionable behaviour, or offend the patron or his lady, perhaps unwittingly (and he was, of course, in the awkward position of being confessor to the household). Although a chaplain would naturally seek to convert spouses and estate-workers, he was circumscribed by law, and proselytism was out of the question. Whatever ambitions Catholic priests may have entertained about the conversion of England, such ideas never entered the heads of the Catholic gentry whose attentions were firmly fixed on their own political emancipation. Nor did the priests have any inclination to emulate their Anglican counterparts in becoming members of the magistracy, or of creating an alliance equivalent to that of squire and parson.

It was for social and pastoral reasons, then, that chaplains began to move out of the mansions and into cottages on the estates. The same trend occurred in the location of chapels, which were moved down from upper floors into state rooms and then out of the mansions into detached buildings on the estate. This had advantages all round. The patron would be rid of an uncongenial presence at table, the priest would be free to spend longer periods with his general congregation, and spend less time pandering to the ladies in the big house, attending social events and worrying about the state of his clothing. He would also be unaffected by any absence of the patron, and the chapel would be more accessible to outsiders. Nonetheless, the close proximity of the chapel ensured that the squire retained overall control and the priest was within reach.

Although the priest and patron were freed from the enforced daily contact neither had relished, the new pattern of chaplaincy life did not help to resolve the wider ecclesiastical problem of jurisdiction which beset the mission throughout the period. On the one hand, so as to enjoy some financial security, the clergy wished to have unfettered control over the charitable donations made for their maintenance. On the other hand, patrons sought to retain some say over the uses to which funds provided by their families were to be put, and that would include, among other things, the right of presentation to a chaplaincy. In 1782 Rutter was told that his erstwhile pupil's father would 'let none come on his premises but one of his own choosing: & the elected must likewise please the rusticks of the place'. Bishop Walmesley told Bishop Gibson in 1796 that laymen should be allowed to nominate priests to the missions they financed but the Charltons, Claverings, Haggerstons and Silvertops were prevented at one time or another from selecting their own chaplains. Mr Riddell of Cheeseburn Grange declared that he would never acknowledge a bishop's authority to have pastoral letters read out in his chapel and forbade his chaplain to do so. In 1834 William Riddell told Bishop Penswick that the Catholic gentry could be 'very ticklish and nice when dealing with either bishops or priests'. As a member of the Felton Park gentry family he was in a good position to know but Penswick too should have known since his father had been steward to the Gerard family. At any rate, Penswick became particularly keen to promote town-missions; but he was not, as suggested, the first to do so.[79] Bishop Briggs was accused by one chaplain of giving 'too much ear' to gentlemen in preference to the clergy. Clearly, a chaplain's lot was not usually a happy one. In most cases, a combination of social, financial and vocational factors made life for a priest in a gentry household uncongenial. The economic freedom a chaplaincy offered was out-weighed by the dependence required. Not surprisingly, then, most priests sought their freedom with some fervour. The Catholic Relief Acts gave them the opening.[80]

***

Rutter and Banister kept a close eye on all politico-ecclesiastical proceedings affecting the Catholic body.[81] When the agitation following the first Catholic Relief Act (1778) died down, Catholics began to plan for a second act which would extend toleration to the clergy. At first matters went well but the cisalpine tendencies of the

Catholic Committee elected to negotiate the new act put it at odds with the bishops. Matters came to a head in 1790, firstly over the terms of the oath which the Committee proposed to include in the act and, secondly, over the succession to the London and Northern vicariates which had fallen vacant. Some members of the Committee thought it appropriate to couch the oath in the most liberal terms and to elect the new bishops. At the same time, the matter of the location and management of the replacement for Douai College in England also became controversial. After what has been quoted from their letters already, it will hardly be surprising to find that both Banister and Rutter were ultra-conservative on all these matters. At the centre of these storms stood the vicars apostolic, the brothers Gibson.

The Gibson family of Stonecroft Farm gave a number of priests to the Church in the eighteenth century. Matthew Gibson was born in 1734 and was sent to Douai at the age of 13. After his ordination in 1758 he remained in the college as a professor for ten years. On his coming to the English mission, he went as chaplain to the newly-widowed Mrs Mary Maire at Headlam, near Gainford. Bishop Walton made him his vicar general in 1776, and his coadjutor in 1780; Gibson's succession to the vicariate later that year was automatic. He remained at Headlam until Mrs Maire died in 1784. She left £4,000 in charitable bequests, including £40 a year to Gibson personally 'besides a thousand pounds to him as bishop which with former benefactions should afford him a decent maintenance'. The bishop then moved up to Stella Hall where Thomas Eyre, 'his particular friend' and secretary was missioner.[82]

Gibson and John Silvertop were kinsmen and friends. The proximity of Stella and Minsteracres gave Rutter the opportunity to keep Banister informed of episcopal activity, and to pass on anything of interest which came his way at table. On more than one occasion Banister warned Rutter not to let Silvertop see their letters because he would certainly blab to the bishop. The stream of gossip they exchanged certainly lent force to the need for secrecy. Rutter reported that the servants at Stella thought that Eyre preached 'better than his RR guest'; Rutter thought Eyre had 'more the cunning of the serpent than the simplicity of the dove'; and Banister so deplored the bishop's 'ways of prescinding, arguing, splitting, doubling, &c.' that he could not easily trust him 'and never implicitly'.[83]

Much of Matthew Gibson's episcopate of ten years was taken up with the affairs of the Catholic Committee. A committee of laymen had negotiated the first Catholic Relief Act almost without the need to refer to the vicars apostolic. In 1782 the lay gentry decided to reconstitute the Committee to work for further relief. Sir Carnaby Haggerston represented the eastern half of the Northern District. Almost immediately, the Committee antagonised the bishops by claiming that the Church in England was wholly dependent on the 'Court of Rome' for even the most minor matters of discipline, because vicars apostolic did not enjoy the episcopal jurisdiction of a resident ordinary. This was a major obstacle to further political relief and the Committee invited the vicars apostolic to make appropriate representations in Rome. Bishop Gibson agreed with the Committee, but some of his brethren did not, and the proposal was dropped. The Clergy Agent in Rome did not think that a change of status would make any difference to the necessity for consulting the Roman Curia. The episode showed, however, that the seeds of cisalpinism had been sown, and it was borne in upon the bishops that the gentry were now prepared to raise issues previously considered the prerogative of the clergy.[84]

A new Committee was elected in 1787 with Sir John Lawson representing the north-east, Sir Carnaby having declined to be re-nominated. The restoration of the hierarchy was again proposed, but this time the Committee went much further by suggesting that the bishops ought to be elected 'by the flock they are to teach and direct'. Then it was suggested that there were no religious grounds for Catholics to refuse the Oath of Supremacy. On this occasion the bishops were united in opposition, and such was the Committee's dismay that a statement was issued explaining that it did not wish to interfere in matters of a purely spiritual nature. But it was too late. Sir John Lawson organised a formal protest from the north voicing strong dissent from the Committee's activities, and it was signed by almost every family in the region. It was thought that 'the greater part of the Country gentlemen' were now 'averse to the very existence of a Committee'. The Committee took fright and responded by admitting the clergy to membership. Bishop Gibson was not mollified by that, and he doubted whether priests would have enough power to prevent any mischief. Rutter reported the bishop to be 'in no great esteem with our gentlemen, nor do I think he courts much their favour and friendship'.[85] After Gibson's death, Marmaduke Tunstall told William Salvin that Gibson, whom he had known at Douai College, was

> no bad classical scholar, and I am willing to think meant well, but had extravagant notions of the power of the hierarchy, surely most strangely ill-timed and had he lived, might have embroiled his flock with many disagreeables.

Although Gibson had been 'a man of true probity, parts & learning', he 'had not a conciliating manner'.[86]

In 1788 the Committee drew up a solemn Declaration and Protestation of Catholic principles which was intended to expedite a second and full relief act. Fatally, however, the document contained the statement that 'We acknowledge no infallibility in the Pope'. Taken in its context of the time that was a perfectly orthodox statement. Indeed, some fifteen hundred laymen and priests readily signed the Protestation, including fourteen priests in the north-east and members of every gentry family in the region, except the

Silvertops. Bishop Gibson told Thomas Eyre that George Silvertop 'tho' no Divine, could discover false doctrine in it', and Sir John Lawson said he would not sign unless Bishop Gibson did so. Armed with what seemed to be an endorsement of their approach, the Committee recast the Declaration in the form of a petition to parliament. In discussion with the government about the terms of a relief bill, however, the Committee drafted a new oath to reflect the contents of the Declaration, and they also agreed to the description of themselves as Protesting Catholic Dissenters. The vicars apostolic were not consulted at any stage and when at last they saw the draft bill they immediately condemned it. Bishop Gibson issued a pastoral letter prohibiting anyone in the Northern District from subscribing the oath; he issued a further letter at the beginning of 1790, and he refused point blankly to meet the Committee to discuss the matter. He died in May that year, at the height of the controversy. Bishop James Talbot of the London District had died in January, and so the ranks of the episcopate were halved at this most critical point.[87]

Inevitably, some said that these dissensions killed Bishop Gibson, who was 59 years of age at his death, but he had been ill for some time. In 1785 Rutter wrote that Gibson had to change his ways and take exercise 'to work off the gouty humour' of which the doctors said he was full. In 1786 Rutter called for the appointment of a coadjutor, and he reported a rumour later in the year that Gibson had asked his younger brother William to accept the post. But a sealed envelope opened after his death contained the nomination of Robert Banister or Thomas Eyre as his successor. He had, however, asked Bishop Thomas Talbot to nominate his brother because he was reluctant to do it himself, which seems to show that he was unlikely to have nominated him earlier as his coadjutor. Bishop Talbot did as he was asked, but he went further and invited the clergy of the District to make their own nominations. Some priests and liberal laymen intended to elect a bishop and inform Rome. Banister and Rutter were horrified. Banister wished he could fly to Rome where he would 'strenuously advise His Holiness to send two learned and pious Italian priests' to fill the vacancies.[88]

Banister knew that he and Eyre had been recommended by the late bishop (and he shortly became aware that his name was second on the *terna*) but he realised that his or Eyre's elevation was so unlikely that the inclusion of their names can only have been meant as 'props to lift up Mr. William Gibson'. Rutter was surprised that Banister had been recommended at all: 'I can hardly believe that you are to be our Bishop, I foresee so much opposition will be raised against you by Committee men and others'. Banister said that if Rutter thought he was 'a very objectionable person, yet I apprehend that Mr. Wm. Gibson will be as much or more so'.[89]

Banister had kept up a running commentary on William Gibson's presidency of Douai College since 1781. Gibson had plans for reform, both structurally and academically but the financial resources of the college were insufficient to meet the costs of rebuilding, and many alumni resented his revision of the syllabus to include French, literature and mathematics. Banister was a leading opponent of these plans and he feared for the future of the college 'where all but a lick-spittle disapprove of the carryings-on of the polite Mr. Gibson'. Ideally, John Cotes should be made vicar apostolic, but Banister felt that the elevation of Gibson would at least get him away from Douai. Truly he said,

> the office of a president of Douai College, & of Spain & Lisbon is more important than that of Vicar Apostolic in this island. For our presidents abroad furnish our bishops with a good or bad clergy according to the good or bad choice of alumni, according to the principles, spirit & manners in which they are trained up, &c. So although Mr. W. Gibson has not been applauded everywhere for his

administration of Douai College, he may have more success in an episcopal character.[90]

Half the secular priests of Lancashire raised a petition for the removal of President Gibson in 1790. Banister warned Rutter that in the event that Gibson was dismissed, he was not to surrender his post to him, although in Banister's view Gibson would not be welcomed back at Minsteracres for Gibson would have been 'expelled' if he had not been appointed to the presidency. That seems most unlikely in view of the esteem in which Gibson was held by the Silvertops, although his absence of six years in London while holding the chaplaincy may not have pleased his patron. Rutter merely said that it 'would be high treason' to raise the problems of Douai at Minsteracres, so he never mentioned the college.[91]

William Gibson returned from Douai in July 1790, partly to bury his brother, but also to protect his own position, for he knew that he was being considered for either vicariate. He had not given up the presidency of the college, but Rutter thought 'a mitre might tempt him to do it, for inter nos I think he looks that way'. Rutter reported to Banister that Gibson had written to Christopher Stonor, Clergy Agent in Rome, resigning the presidency because of bad health, 'but finding his hopes of a mitre not so certain as he imagined, he now retracts'. It may have been that he knew he was not a nominee of the Committee or the southern clergy for the London District, nor was his name under consideration by the northern clergy. He was informed in August, however, that he had been elected to the Northern District, and he had the courtesy to tell Banister in confidence; the news was very well received but only because of its significance for Banister's beloved alma mater. Gibson had been something of a snob when President of Douai and the riots which led to the college's closure in 1793 were said by Marmaduke Tunstall to have been partly due to Gibson's 'great intimacy' with Baron Fott, governor of the town, for 'the very name of an aristocrat is much more odious there than that of the devil'.[92]

Gibson's elevation was not universally welcomed. Lord Petre remarked that 'Mr. Gibson was the most obnoxious man that could have been appointed'. Sir John Lawson ordered the Revd William Dunn 'to take at his cost and charge post horses, post chaises & ride God knows whither to prevent it'. Dunn 'wore out 4 pairs of breeches in his assiduous perambulations through the town to promote the good design'. The northern clergy sent four of their number down to London 'to concert pressures with the Committee against Mr. Gibson'. Gibson might 'go to the north as bishop, or in any other capacity [but he] will remain unheeded and unaided'. Gibson was aware of the general feeling about him and said that 'though he knew he was obnoxious, yet he meant to procure his consecration'. The clergy and the Committee soon decided to make the best of a bad job. The priests in the north now welcomed him; some even thought of sending a commendation of him to Rome. Rutter was amused 'to hear the praises they now give Mr. Gibson, whom before they condemned as the most unfit person in the world'.[93]

Marmaduke Tunstall hoped the new bishop would 'be of a more moderate turn' and 'prove more happy in that now necessary accomplishment'. Sir John Lawson wrote to Gibson to congratulate him and to reconnoitre the ground that the new vicar apostolic would hold. He hailed the prospect of 'union in the Catholic body' augured by Gibson's elevation, which, he went on 'might have been brought about by softer means sometime since, had our Ap. Vicars been more cautious & less precipitate in their measures'. Further, 'could the Catholics see you Gentlemen of ye Mitre show such good example, I have no doubt but that the effect would be salutary'. Plunging on into even deeper waters, he suggested that on the question of civil allegiance, 'the church can have no business, it is clearly a matter out of the Spiritual interference'. The real question was

> If I take the oath in the temporal sense of the Government, am I or am I not a member of the Catholic Church, or am I less so than I was before? The Vicars Apostolic owe it to us to point out the parts of the oath which are contrary to faith.

The bishop-elect replied that he reserved the right of the bishops to approve any oath tendered to the English Catholics. Clearly, he was no more prepared to deal with the Committee than his brother and indeed he would prove as obdurate in his dealings with the laity as many had expected and in the process he created lifelong enemies.[94]

Lawson, it must be remembered, was one of the conservative northern Catholics and on a number of occasions he had voiced the misgivings of the northern gentry about the Committee's proceedings. Marmaduke Tunstall, too, deplored that body's behaviour, but both men acknowledged the importance of bringing the gentry and bishops together. Henry Maire, also a conservative, was forced to tell the new bishop that the civil content of the oath was not within the jurisdiction of the bishops, and that if they could not approve the oath then they had to present an alternative. Banister and most of the northern clergy urged Gibson to stand firm. Henry Bennet was a lone clerical voice advising the bishop that 'a little dexterity, a certain maniere' would greatly contribute to the resolution of the problem. But, it proved impossible to temper the bishop's abrasive and autocratic style. He was later described by Thomas Smith, his coadjutor, as

> singularly averse to those who were plotting for the introduction of novelties in religious matters. He was a strenuous advocate for ecclesiastical discipline and for all subordination...'[95]

In the event, Gibson met the Committee with Bishop Douglass at the beginning of February 1791. The conference was unsuccessful because the Committee refused to defer to the bishops when Gibson bluntly asked them to do so. The bishops therefore approached a number of laymen not on the Committee to lobby parliament on their behalf, and John Silvertop and Henry Maire organised a petition from the north to the Privy Council. It turned out that the petition was unnecessary because the Solicitor General told the bishops that their objections had persuaded the government to replace the disputed oath. Parliamentary proceedings lasted some three and a half months and the Relief Act corresponded entirely with the wishes of the vicars apostolic; the oath used was that of the Irish Catholic Relief Act of 1774.

The crisis was over but lasting damage had been done to lay-clerical relations. Banister was so depressed at the turn of events that he entertained 'a conceit to get my picture drawn & in such a manner as to express very emphatically my sentiments & marked disapprobation of the doctrine & errors so lately diffused amongst us'. He did not say where the portrait was to hang.[96] In all these deliberations Bishop Gibson was intransigent in defence of the episcopal prerogative in matters ecclesiastical. The Committee heartily wished he had gone to the north and stayed there. After the act was on the statute book, the Committee passed a vote of thanks to the bishops, but omitted Gibson's name from it. In fact, for all that William Gibson was a highly authoritarian churchman, he was liberal enough to support the political rights of the Catholic gentry with whom he had been at odds for some thirty years.

***

George Silvertop (II) was coming towards the end of his schooldays when in May 1791 he and his younger brother Henry were withdrawn from Douai College to Louvain, 'in consequence of the commotions and disturbances' of the Revolution. George completed his education at Old Hall Green; Henry returned to Minsteracres where, with his younger brother Charles, he was tutored by another refugee from Douai, the deacon John Bell, whom Rutter described as 'a sedate young man who tho' from Douay has nothing about him of the frippery of a modern Beau'. Rutter was gratified that the college could still turn out sound and level-headed clerics, even in the 'calamitous state' to which it had been reduced under William Gibson's presidency. Bell was presently appointed prefect-general at Crook Hall.[97]

Rutter and Banister had been pleased to see Gibson's removal from the seminary, but they did not foresee that, as bishop, he would be responsible for its re-establishment in England. The location and status of a seminary in place of Douai College was to be the source of considerable apprehension in the minds of many priests in the north for several years. Banister wanted the college to be re-established elsewhere on the continent, but the bishops preferred it to be on English soil. After a certain amount of dithering over various houses, in September 1794 Gibson rented Crook Hall to serve until a permanent college could be created. Banister was invited to teach Divinity, but he would only agree if the old syllabus was brought back. He also wished the new college to be confined to church-students:

> let Gentlemen, Merchants' sons & such like found a college for themselves & according to their own ever-varying ideas & whimsical notions. There is Tudhoe & Old Hall Green & several other schools that may serve their purpose. They aim at no degree of true erudition & learning; reading, writing, speaking French, dancing & talking fluently are the grand accomplishments.

Actually the Committee had already proposed that a school be established for lay pupils only. Banister also deplored the tendency of the 'gentry, the Exs, the nigri Fratres &c.' who seemed 'to be eager, if not for a total independence, at least for an equal authority & jurisdiction with the Bishops' all of which he put down to the influence of impious gallicanism.[98]

A location for the college in the north was thought more suitable than the south of England for various practical reasons. The only objection Rutter had heard was that

> some of our very refined Douatians are afraid of children spoiling their accent in these parts. This is a weighty objection to be sure, but I should hope it might be got over if they considered that housekeeping is at least one fifth in the north, & that the proximity of Old Hall Green to the Metropolis must render it a very improper situation for a great Gen. Coll. where young men are prepared for the ministry.[99]

Moreover, the ex-Jesuits, the Franciscans and the Benedictines had established themselves in the north—'a certain proof that they consider it an eligible situation'. There was also the fact that the Northern District had the largest number of Catholics and priests. This was all eminently reasonable, but not persuasive outside the District, although Bishop Milner did chip in with an encouraging letter to Bishop Gibson:

> I own, though a Londoner myself, I have a strong partiality for Northern men to make priests of. Every one of our Bishops (that is good for any thing) are northern men & so are the choice of our Clergy throughout the Kingdom. Hence for the good of this very District, I hope you may arrange matters so that we may continue to be supplied with a certain proportion of honest healthy Northern lads to correct, when properly qualified, the defects and vices of the South.[100]

The eventual decision was for the north to have its own seminary, but it was five years before the Ushaw estate was bought, and another eight before a college was opened in 1808.

The long delay arose out of several circumstances, but principally because of Gibson's indecisiveness. Banister and Rutter found themselves in a difficult position when discussing the matter. On the one hand they held a proper respect for Bishop Gibson as their superior; they supported him in his disputes with the liberals and they agreed with him about the need for a college in the north. On the other hand, they were unwilling to allow the man who (they thought) had almost brought Douai College to ruin, to have sole control over its replacement. They deprecated his determination 'to be both Bishop & President, the sole controller of monies & funds, the pursebearer & paymaster general'. Banister held the bishop to blame for the delays, and at one point he told him that

> considering 20 chapels (& some great & magnificent ones) had been built in Lancashire, & several with a good messuage or dwelling-house, within these 20 years or a little more,

he was 'grieved that one college could not yet be erected'. Rutter advised the bishop to put a little more confidence in his clergy's advice, but to no effect. Rutter said that whatever ideas Gibson

> may himself entertain of his own transcendent abilities, I fear little will be done if all is to be left to his management, especially considering his infirm state of health which seems still declining.[101]

Gibson would not be rushed in this matter, as in any other; indeed, he avoided taking decisions until the last possible moment. He proved extremely difficult to deal with; he was autocratic, would accept no advice and he was regarded as unsound in financial matters. Nor would he pay the slightest heed to any suggestion on any matter which came within his personal jurisdiction or prerogatives. John Lingard's candidature as President of Ushaw was opposed because his views were altogether too independent. (Lingard might well have objected to his appropriation of two or three of the best apartments in the college even though Gibson was resident only occasionally.) When Gibson learned that the clergy thought that a coadjutor bishop ought to be appointed he simply ignored them, but when he later let it be known that he was thinking of proposing his brother Richard for the post, the northern clergy were appalled. Three brothers as successive vicars apostolic was one thing, but John Barrow thought Richard Gibson qualified only as a farmhand, and even the loyal Banister threatened to petition Propaganda against him. The idea was dropped.[102]

Although William Gibson had succeeded to the northern vicariate at the relatively early age of 54, he was never fully well. He was the senior bishop from 1797 and, in deference to his poor health and seniority; many of the general meetings of the vicars apostolic took place in Durham. The demands of his widespread District were heavy, and in March 1804 he reported to Propaganda: 'For many months I administered the Sacrament of Confirmation three or four times a week and as often preached sermons before Catholics and Protestants. My journeys were very long and fatiguing'.[103] He suffered a long illness in 1805 at the age of 67 and he was never again as active as before. His handwriting deteriorated and was soon illegible; it was suggested that his secretary take dictation from him. It was not until 1807, after the Ushaw business was completed, that Gibson, aged 72, agreed to take a coadjutor, nominating Thomas Smith, whom he had known for some thirty years, as a fellow North-countryman, student, professor and procurator at Douai and latterly in Durham as missioner and his compliant and mild-mannered secretary.

Smith was born in 1763 at The Brooms, Durham, into a minor gentry family. At Douai he was said to have 'genius, a facility for acquiring knowledge, and was remarkable for his piety and obedience to the rules'. He was ordained at Douai in 1787. He was at the college when it was over-run by French Revolutionaries and was imprisoned. He returned to England on his release and appeared at the General Quarter Sessions in Durham in October 1795 to make the 'Declaration and Oath' required by the Relief Act of 1791 which enabled him to practise as a priest and he took over the secular mission in Old Elvet and became Bishop Gibson's secretary. He was said to be urbane and suave, and he seems to have been popular: 'to know him is to love him', said Bishop Sharrock. He declined an invitation to become President of the English College at Valladolid and he is said to have refused a mitre twice.[104]

Although they had worked together for a very long time, Gibson wanted Smith only as a secretary and successor, but decidedly not as a partner. Indeed, Smith's *Brief* specifically prohibited him from 'interfering in the affairs' of the vicariate without Gibson's express permission, and he would not entrust Smith with any episcopal responsibility. In 1819, Gibson, 81 years old, still refused to retire though he was incapacitated by senility and paralysis. He had long since been unable to offer Mass or say his office, and he had to be carried about and fed like a child. His condition was so bad that his vicars general asked Bishop Poynter of the London District to obtain special faculties for Smith. They were granted, though Propaganda was careful to say that it was not 'intended to give umbrage' to the 'excellent Vicar Apostolic'. But it was a great relief all round when Gibson died in 1821. Smith handed over the Durham mission to William Croskell so as to concentrate on his episcopal role to which he came as a welcome contrast to his predecessor.[105]

In 1823 Bishop Smith compiled a *Relatio* on the District for Propaganda. It covers the whole District and it is not possible always to separate data relating to the western part from the eastern. Thus he simply estimates the total number of Catholics as 120,000 'though some believe it to be 150,000, most of whom live in Lancashire.' He was able to say, however, that no-one who like him had spent some thirty years on the mission could possibly doubt their piety and zeal. There were eleven mission-stations in County Durham and twenty in Northumberland. Furthermore: 'Catholic schools for young children, which had hardly existed before, are now established in very many places, insofar as the number of Catholics allows'. Ushaw College was an episcopal seminary and there were two convents: the Poor Clares at Scorton (ex-Rouen), who ran a boarding-school for girls, and the Carmelites at Cocken Hall (ex-Lierre,) who were enclosed. His greatest need was for more missionaries to work on the rapidly expanding mission in the north-east, though it is unclear why he had to appeal specifically for the services of 'some priests from the Roman Colleges, from Valladolid or Lisbon'. Smith's episcopate was dogged by ill-health and he out-lived Gibson by only nine years. He died at Ushaw and was buried there in August 1831. His obituary in the *Orthodox Journal* described him as 'peculiarly affable and conciliatory'.

Learning from his own experience, Smith had sought a coadjutor in 1824, naming John Lingard, Thomas Gillow and Thomas Penswick in his *terna*. Penswick, a 52-year-old Lancastrian was selected. He was educated at Douai and latterly at Crook Hall where he was ordained in 1797. He became missioner at Chester and then in Liverpool. In 1823 he was appointed coadjutor for the Northern District and was consecrated at Ushaw. It seems that he was 'a handsome man, affable, generous and diligent'.[106] Smith gave him responsibility for the western side of the District. He succeeded to the whole vicariate in 1831 and, given 'the great extent of the

District [and] the multifariousness of its administration', as Nicholas Wiseman put it, Penswick needed little persuasion to seek a coadjutor and in 1833 John Briggs was appointed. Penswick died three years later.

John Briggs, born in Manchester in 1788, was the first of the vicars apostolic of the District not to have been educated at Douai but received his priestly formation at Crook Hall and at Ushaw College where he was ordained in 1814. Two years later he was appointed to the mission in Chester where he remained for some seventeen years before being appointed President of Ushaw and coadjutor to Bishop Penswick. On succeeding as vicar apostolic he resigned the presidency and moved to live in Fulford House, York, presumably because it was a more convenient place from which to tour and administer the vicariate. Two years later, aged 50, he conducted an extensive confirmation tour and visitation of the District. In 1847 the Prefect of Propaganda asked the Rosminian, Luigi Gentili, to report directly to him on the state of the English Church. Gentili reported that the bishops did not and did not dare to make visitations of their Districts: 'I can assert without hesitation that they do not know a third of what is wrong in their Districts'.[107] In fact, Briggs had taken steps to do so almost a decade earlier. Having previously distributed a visitation questionnaire based on Anglican practice, he made his visitation of the sixteen missions in Northumberland and thirteen in County Durham in May and June 1839.

In April 1838, the vicars apostolic met at York to discuss a reorganisation of the vicariates. The Northern District, being the largest and most unwieldy, clearly needed reform, and in 1840 it was divided into three vicariates: Lancashire, Northern and Yorkshire. George Brown was appointed to Lancashire, and Briggs to Yorkshire, but a problem arose over the Northern appointment. Henry Weedall, President of Oscott College, was nominated. But, finding that the northern clergy would not accept him, as an outsider as well as being of weak character, he pleaded ill-health and fled 'to Rome to get off ye heavy burthen of a bishop's charge ... they say he is a very clever man, tho' little, like you, and timid...'[108] And so he was passed over.

Francis Mostyn became the first vicar apostolic of the newly created Northern District. He was born in 1800 in Oxfordshire to 'an illustrious family, wealthy, and of exceeding piety, competent learning and much zeal...' He was educated at Oscott and ordained in 1828, and he spent twelve years on the Wolverhampton mission. Friends feared that he would decline the promotion because of 'his timidity and retiring habits' but he was induced to accept. The northern clergy were as little impressed with him as they had been with Weedall and for similar reasons. Not only was he an outsider but, Lingard said, he had 'no outstanding ability' and was 'a man more likely to be led than to lead'. After seven years of poor health Mostyn died in 1847.[109]

As had now become usual practice, Bishop Mostyn had obtained a coadjutor. Coincidentally or not, in view of the clergy's objections to the existing and previous incumbents, the Northumbrian William Riddell was appointed. He was born at Felton Park in 1807, educated firstly at Stonyhurst College and then in the English College, Rome, where he was ordained in 1830. He was missioner at St Andrew's, Newcastle, from 1832 and was consecrated bishop in March 1844. From August that year he combined his episcopal duties with those of missioner in the newly opened St Mary's church. Riddell's independent episcopate lasted but three months, August to October, 1847, for he became a victim of an epidemic of typhus which raged through the town that summer. His body was interred in the newly constructed crypt of St Mary's.

William Hogarth was born at Dodding Green, Westmoreland, in 1786. He was educated for the priesthood at Crook Hall and

Ushaw College and was ordained in 1809. He held various posts in the college until 1816 when his health collapsed and he took over what was expected to be an undemanding mission, the chaplaincy at Cliffe Hall, near Piercebridge. But the chaplaincy closed because of the insolvency of the patron, Henry Witham, and Hogarth moved to Darlington in 1824. In addition to his missionary work, he served as vicar general to Bishops Briggs, Mostyn and Riddell. At the latter's death, Robert Tate, Vice President of Ushaw, was invited to become vicar apostolic but he declined and Hogarth, aged 62, was consecrated in August 1848. (Lingard regretted the selection of Hogarth as a bishop because he did not have 'the manners of a gentleman'.[110]) Just two years later, in September 1850, the ordinary English hierarchy was restored by Pius IX and Hogarth was named first Bishop of Hexham (embodying the medieval dioceses of Durham and Carlisle).

There were fifteen vicars apostolic of the Northern District between 1688 and 1850. Eleven were born in the north, six of them in the north-east. Nine had gentry origins; the others came from a mercantile background. All but one were seculars, and all but three were educated at Douai or Ushaw. One was appointed when he was 37 years old and another when he was 71 but the rest were in their forties, fifties or early sixties. Eight of them had held a previous appointment in ecclesiastical administration as an official in a seminary or as a vicar general. They were not a particularly scholarly group; nine had held teaching posts in seminaries, but only six held doctorates, and, although many of them printed their sermons and pastoral letters, only four published books (mostly translations from French works). Doubtless, the heavy administrative burden of the large Northern District did not allow time for a literary career. Seven served as coadjutors and six of them waited up to seven years before succeeding to the vicariate; the other waited eleven years. Episcopates (as coadjutor and ordinary combined) were generally lengthy: two died within a year or two of their appointment but six served up to fifteen years and six survived between twenty-one and thirty-one years. Thus despite a constant refrain of ill-health, twelve of them survived well into old age: four into their early eighties. This brief statistical analysis goes only to show that the vicars apostolic were a varied group who shared no common sociological features but their ecclesiastical role. As was remarked of Thomas Penswick, their 'talents were not splendid, but they were useful.'[111]

***

The restoration of the hierarchy proved unexpectedly controversial. The British government raised no objection when it was informed of the plan in 1847. In an unofficial diplomatic visit to Rome, Lord Minto was briefed on the negotiations in an audience with Pope Pius IX. The restoration was referred to in parliament on several occasions and the press reported it. So as not to offend Anglican sensitivities by adopting titles of existing dioceses, care had been taken to choose new or unused ancient sees for the restored hierarchy. The vicars apostolic were confident enough therefore to reassure the Holy See that the political climate was favourable for a restoration and that the nation would treat it with indifference. But when Nicholas Wiseman, the newly appointed Cardinal Archbishop of Westminster, jubilantly announced the restoration in his pastoral letter *Ex Porta Flaminia* in terms which could be construed as an assumption of temporal power, the age-old dread of triumphalist Catholicism was awakened. The *Newcastle Guardian* prophesied that the end of the world was at hand. The outraged Edward Maltby, Bishop of Durham, wrote to Lord John Russell, the Prime Minister, deploring this 'Papal Aggression' and an Act was passed prohibiting the use of any English territorial title by Catholic prelates.

In the north-east, the clamour over Papal Aggression was supported mostly by Dissenters who circulated petitions and convened public protest meetings, much as they had done in 1829. Anti-Catholic hysteria moderated when Charles Larkin gave several explanatory public lectures and Catholic priests preached conciliatory sermons; the attendance of battalions of restive Catholic Irishmen also helped to break up hostile gatherings. Most people, however, especially in 'the middle and trading classes' were satisfied that the restoration was a wholly internal Catholic matter and would make no inroads into Anglican supremacy. The agitation was short-lived and Catholics were not substantially inconvenienced by it, but the episode led to the formation of a Catholic Defence Association to protect their religious interests, which was just as well because the Protestant Alliance was formed at the same time, and it became the largest and most active anti-Catholic organisation in the region.

A meeting of clergy and laity was convened in Hexham to object to the use of the town's name for the new diocese but the Ecclesiastical Titles Act was never invoked and Bishop Hogarth is said to have been the first of the English bishops to sign documents in the proper episcopal form: + *William Bishop of Hexham*.[112] The Roman Curia had intended the diocese to be named Newcastle but Hogarth preferred Hexham:

> As to the idea of gratifying the people of Newcastle, I think it of little value. A bishop may go into Newcastle occasionally on great occasions, but no one should be condemned to live there ... [113]

He even considered building his cathedral in Hexham. Hogarth soon came to realise the importance of Tyneside, however, and he raised no objection to the renaming of the diocese as Hexham and Newcastle in May 1861, but he still declined to live in either town and remained in Darlington where he died in 1866 after a markedly energetic and expansionist episcopate.

Notes

1. For Mayes' career in Italy see B. Hemphill, *The Early Vicars Apostolic of England 1685–1750* (London: Burns & Oates, 1954) passim.
2. Stonor was Agent until his death in 1795. He was followed by Robert Archdeacon (al. Smelt, d. 1814), Paul Macpherson (resigned in 1817) and Robert Gradwell (to 1828).
3. W. M. Brady, *The Episcopal Succession in England, Scotland & Ireland A. D. 1400–1875* ([Rome, 1877–1878], Farnborough: Gregg Reprints, 1971, 3 vols), III, pp. 246/247. A recent compendium of short biographies is at N. Schofield, & G. Skinner, *The English Vicars Apostolic 1688–1850* (Oxford: Family Publications, 2009).
4. Brady, *Episcopal Succession*, III, pp. 248/249; G. Anstruther, *The Seminary Priests: A Dictionary of the Secular Clergy of England and Wales, 1558–1850* (Ware: St Edmund's College; Durham: Ushaw College, 1968–1977, 4 vols), 3, pp. 114–117.
5. Anstruther, *Seminary Priests*, 3, pp. 205–207.
6. Hemphill, *Vicars Apostolic*, pp. 124–127.
7. J. Gillow, *A Literary and Biographical History, or Bibliographical Dictionary, of the English Catholics: From the Breach with Rome, in 1534, to the Present Time* (London: Burns & Oates, c.1885–1895, 5 vols), 5, sub Maire.
8. Brady, *Episcopal Succession*, III, pp. 262, 265.
9. Anstruther, *Seminary Priests*, 3, pp. 253/4.
10. Hemphill, *Vicars Apostolic*, p. 83.
11. Edward Norman seems to have been unaware of this feature of the mission when he wrote that English Catholics were free to build churches wherever they were needed because they had 'no ancient structure of parochial administration or outmoded diocesan finance as the state church had' to inhibit its development, though it depends on what is meant by 'ancient' and 'outmoded'. E. R. Norman, *The English Catholic Church in the Nineteenth Century* (Oxford, The Clarendon Press, 1984), p. 7.
12. A list of registrations under the 1791 Act will be found at Durham County Record Office [DCRO]: Q/R/RM1.
13. B. Little, *Catholic Churches since 1623* (London: Hale, 1966), pp. 30, 50; D. Milburn, *A History of Ushaw College* (Durham: Ushaw College, 1964), pp. 44, 57, 74; Ushaw College Manuscripts [UCM], V, 452; L. Gooch, *The*

Revival of English Catholicism: The Banister-Rutter Correspondence 1777–1807 (Wigan: North West Catholic History Society, 1995), Banister to W. Gibson, 10 Feb. 1792. [Henceforth these letters will be cited by originator and date.]

14 Insofar as funds allowed, churches were built to standards comparable with those of the Anglican Church. Newcastle, All Saints, probably the largest provincial Anglican church erected in the century, was completed in 1796 at a cost of around £27,000, paid for by an annual rate of 2s. in the pound, cf. W. Parson & W. White, *History, Directory and Gazetteer of the Counties of Durham and Northumberland*, etc., (Newcastle: White, 1828, 2 vols), I, p. lxv.

15 Milburn, *Ushaw College*, p. 68.

16 Leeds Diocesan Archives [LDA]: Gibson Papers, Milner to Gibson 28 July 1798; LDA: Smith Papers, open letter to diocese, 1828; Hemphill, *Vicars Apostolic*, p. 85.

17 R. Hill, *God's Architect: Pugin and the Building of Romantic Britain* (London: Allen Lane, 2007), passim.

18 It was, however, the new (1828) Anglican church in Winlaton which was first to adopt the dedication of St Patrick. Bishop Challoner had encouraged devotion to the English mediaeval saints. St Elizabeth was one of the cults revived by Montalembert, cf. B. Aspinwall, 'Changing Images of Roman Catholic Religious Orders in the Nineteenth Century', *Studies in Church History* 22 (1985), p. 359.

19 J. Crosby, *Ignatius Bonomi of Durham, Architect* (City of Durham Trust, 1987), passim. The Bonomis became interested in the Waldensian Church in Italy through their friend the Revd Dr William Gilly. Charlotte Bonomi published an anti-Catholic novel, *Edith Grey, or Ten Years Ago* (1852) to caution young girls against rubbing brasses for the Camden Society or poring over drawings of Gothic architecture in *The Ecclesiologist*, since such interests would inevitably lead to Rome. During the course of the novel, Edith visited Piedmont to take encouragement from the persecuted Waldensians. Ignatius thought an Italian edition of her novel might buoy up the Italian Protestants; more practically, he built two churches for them.

20 NRO: RCD 1/4, 5, 6: Hogarth, 29 Aug. 1841, 5 Feb. 1842, 17 Mar. 1842; UCM: IV/306, Hay to Eyre, 27 Nov. 1797; Banister, 14 Oct. 1799; B. Ward, *The Eve of Catholic Emancipation, 1803–1829* (London: Longmans, Green, 1911–1912, 3 vols), II, p. 173.

21. M. Haile & E. Bonney, *Life and Letters of John Lingard 1771–1851* ((London: Herbert & Daniel, 1911), p. 353; *The Tablet,* 8 June 1844, p. 358; Anon., 'Some Letters of Lingard to Newsham and Tate, 1837–1850', UM 16 (1906), p. 5; Kirk, *Biographies,* p. 73; Rutter, 23 June 1782; Banister, 14 Oct. 1784; E. Hughes (ed.) *Diaries and Correspondence of James Losh,* (Surtees Society [SS] 171, 1956), Diary, 25 Dec. 1813.

22. J. Latimer, *Local Records 1832–1857* (Newcastle: The Chronicle, 1857), 18 Oct 1842.

23. Foley, *Records,* passim.

24. LDA: Smith Papers, 148A: Smith's *Relatio* or Report to Propaganda, 1823. Five more important churches were built between 1850 and 1855: Hartlepool, St Mary (1851, J. Hansom); Wolsingham, St Thomas of Canterbury (1854, Hansom); Crook, Ss. Mary & Cuthbert (1854, E. Pugin); Minsteracres, St Elizabeth of Hungary (1854, Hansom); Gainford, St Osmund (1855, T. Gibson).

25. Smith, 'Maintenance', p. 4; J. Berington, *The State and Behaviour of English Catholics from the Reformation to 1780* (London: Faulder, 1780), p. 160; J. Kirk, *Biographies of English Catholics in the Eighteenth Century* (London: Burns & Oates, 1909), p. 138; UCM: Eyre Mss No. 97, Gillow to Eyre 22 Jan. 1805; Northumberland Record Office [NRO]: Cookson Mss viii 2/5. Lady Radcliffe left her entire fortune for the maintenance of the clergy, and from it each priest in Northumberland and Durham received about £10 a year. The average annual stipend of an Anglican incumbent in the 18th century was about £150; a curate received around £50 a year; and a Methodist preacher got £30 a year, plus an allowance for board and lodging and a horse when travelling on circuit. (They, of course, might have been married.)

26. Rutter, 19 Nov. 1783 and 18 Feb. 1795.

27. H. Foley, *Records of the English Province of the Society of Jesus* (London: Burns and Oates, 1877–1883, 7 vols), passim.

28. NRO: RCD 1/347. Bishop Milner told Bishop Gibson that in future more reliance would have to be placed on the clergy than on the gentry, cf. LDA: Gibson Papers, 28 July 1798.

29. NRO: Riddell Letter Book, No. 93, 4 Aug. 1846; Farm St Archives, X, Sewall to Scott, 6 Feb. 1823.

30. Anon., 'Letters of Bishop Challoner', UM 63 (1953), p. 17: Challoner to Walton, 3 Jan. 1771.

The Catholic Mission 1688–1850

31 Banister, 21 Mar. 1784; Anon., 'Letters of Robert Banister to Thomas Eyre 1797–1801', UM 24 (1914) p. 173, Banister to Eyre, 30 Sep. 1797.

32 Rutter, 23 Oct. 1786.

33 NRO: RCD 2/105, 27 Jan. 1812.

34 NRO: RCD 1/4, Hogarth to Fletcher, 17 May 1841; NRO: RCD 1/6, Hogarth to Mostyn, 4 Apr. 1843; *The Tablet* 2 Nov 1844, p. 693.

35 This section is an edited version of W. Smith, *The Northern Brethren's Fund 1660–1960*, (privately printed, 1960). The pamphlet contains many details which are not reproduced here. There are, for example, two appendices giving the early benefactors and a complete list of the Superiors, Treasurers and Secretaries of the Fund.

36 The principal source for the Benedictines is Dom Athanasius Allanson, who, however, remarked: 'I cannot but record my deep and heartfelt regret that it has ever been my misfortune to attempt to compile the dull and uninteresting *Biography of the English Benedictines*' (1842), published at Ampleforth Abbey as Saint Laurence Papers IV, (1999). For the Jesuits see Foley, *Records*, passim.

37 Known formally as the Residence of St John the Evangelist, colloquially as 'the Durham District' or, in code, as 'Mrs Durham'.

38 Rutter, 26 Jan. 1784; Banister, 21 Mar. 1784; Rutter, 16 Nov. 1788, n3.

39 A signed copy of the Brief is at NRO: RCD 6/9. See also UCM: II/119–121, 25 Oct. 1773.

40 UCM II/124, Dec. 1775.

41 Rutter, 9 Mar. 1796.

42 Farm St Archives: VIII 26 Sep. 1825; X, 6 Feb. 1823.

43 NRO: RCD 6/9, 12 July 1797.

44 NRO: RCD 3, 1 Sep. 1802.

45 D. Bellenger, 'The French Exiled Clergy in the North East', *Northern Catholic History* [NCH] 11 (1980), pp. 20–24. See also: idem, 'The French Exiled Clergy in the North of England', *Archaeologia Aeliana* [AA] (5) (1983), X, pp. 171–177: idem, *The French Exiled Clergy* (Bath: Downside Abbey, 1986).

46 Rutter, 24 Nov. 1801.

47 Rutter, 30 Nov. 1792.

48 Lancashire Record Office [LRO]: Barrow Letters, 1 Jan. 1798.

49 UCM: No 80, 13 May 1805.

50. W. Nicholson, 'Irish Priests in the North-East in the Eighteenth Century', NCH 19 (1984), pp. 18–22.
51. Hemphill, *Vicars Apostolic*, pp. 98–100; Anstruther, *Seminary Priests*, 3, p. 253.
52. P. Phillips, 'Catholic Biblemongers: Silvertop or Copperbottom', NCH 43 (2002), p. 42
53. Rutter, 19 Nov. 1783 and 18 Feb. 1795.
54. Rutter, 22 Apr. 1782. Fr Bruno was James Finch (ob. 1821 aged 72), the last of the English Carthusians and prior of a monastery in Austria, distantly related to Rutter. See L. Gooch, '"What shall we do with the Wanton Student": Tutoring the Catholic Gentry in the Eighteenth Century', *Recusant History* [RH] 22/1 (1994), p. 63 ff.
55. Rutter, 19 Nov. 1783; Banister, 19 Sep. 1783.
56. Rutter, 11 Oct. 1784; 9 Jan. 1785.
57. Cf. Visitation Returns.
58. Rutter, 19 Nov. 1783.
59. Rutter, 1 Sep. 1783; Banister, 19 Sep. 1783.
60. Rutter, 19 Nov. 1783; Banister, 19 Dec. 1783.
61. Rutter, 11 Oct. 1784.
62. Rutter, 9 June 1786; Banister, 2 Apr. 1789.
63. Rutter, passim between Mar. 1784 and Feb. 1794.
64. Rutter, 23 Oct. 1786, 25 Mar. 1789, 17 Jan. 1790, 19 Dec. 1791, 1 Aug. 1793. NRO: RCD 1/3, Riddell Letter Book, No. 68, to T. Forster, Scrawnwood, 9 Oct. 1845.
65. Banister, 11 Feb. 1785, 14 Apr. 1788, 21 Mar. 1784, 2 Apr. 1789.
66. R. Wilton, 'Early Eighteenth Century Catholics in England', *Catholic Historical Review* 10 (1924), p. 384.
67. Banister, 21 Mar. 1784, 1 Sep. 1787.
68. Rutter, 6 June 1796, 22 June 1789, 7 Nov. 1796, 17 Jan. 1800.
69. Banister, 17 July 1786, 27 Nov. 1786, 25 Feb. 1792; Rutter, 12 Mar. 1792.
70. Rutter, 12 Apr. 1791, Nov. 1795, 9 Mar. 1796; E. Mackenzie & M. Ross, *The County Palatine of Durham* (Newcastle: Mackenzie & Dent, 1834, 2 vols), II, p. 402n; J. Gillow, *The Church during the Suppression of the Hierarchy in Newcastle and Gateshead* (Preston: Catholic Printing & Publishing Co., 1889), p. 65.

[71] Banister, 31 Jan. 1796, 1 Aug. 1793, 16 Nov. 1796.
[72] Berington, *State and Behaviour*, p. 174; Hemphill, *Vicars Apostolic*, pp. 96/97.
[73] Banister, 9 Jan. & 11 Feb. 1785.
[74] Gillow, *Dictionary*, sub nomen. LRO: Barrow Letters, Barrow to Rutter, 25 Apr. 1804. See also A. Fotheringham, 'Printing, Publishing and Bookselling in the North East before 1800' NCH 39 (1998), pp. 24–30. Rutter's only contribution to the contemporary debate over Emancipation was an 'Answer to Dr. Southey' (London, 1825), which was hardly noticed; cf. Gillow, *Dictionary*, V, p. 459, No. 10.
[75] UCM: Lingard Correspondence, No. 104, Lingard to Gradwell, 17 May 1820.
[76] This section on Thornton at Haggerston is based on R. Wilton, 'Early Eighteenth Century Catholics in England', *Catholic Historical Review* 10 (1924), and M. Joyce, 'The Haggerstons: The Education of a Northumberland Family', RH 14/3 (1977), pp. 175 ff.
[77] The chaplain at Everingham was the Benedictine John Potts who was in every sense an estate agent. Potts had been Cellarer at the Benedictine Abbey in Lambspring, and he, no doubt, was consulted on similar matters at Everingham.
[78] J. Bossy, 'Four Catholic congregations in Rural Northumberland', RH 9/2 (1967), p. 108.
[79] Brady, *Episcopal Succession*, III, p. 278.
[80] Berington, *State & Behaviour*, p. 162; S. Doherty, 'English and Irish Catholics in Northumberland, c.1745–c.1860' (Queen's University of Belfast, PhD, 1987), p.220; B. Ward, *The Dawn of the Catholic Revival in England 1781–1803* (London: Longmans, Green, 1909, 2 vols), I, pp. 88, 92; LDA: Briggs Papers, No. 375, Parker to Briggs, 13 May 1838; NRO: RCD 4/20, Riddell to Penswick, 19 Oct. 1834; RCD 1/3, Riddell to Silvertop, 21 July 1845; RCD 1/8, Hogarth to Charlton, 19 Aug. 1851; RCD 1/9a, Hogarth to Haggerston, 21 Jan. 1851.
[81] The authority on these matters remains B. Ward, *The Dawn of the Catholic Revival in England 1781–1803* (London: Longmans, 1909, 2 vols) and idem, *The Eve of Catholic Emancipation, 1803–1829* (London: Longmans, Green, 1911–1912, 3 vols). See also E. Duffy, 'Ecclesiastical Democracy Detected', in 3 parts: RH 10/4, 10/6, 12/2 (1970–1975), and, J. Connell, *The Roman Catholic Church in England 1780–1850: A Study in Internal*

[82] *Politics* (Philadelphia: The American Philosophical Society, 1984).
[82] See Schofield & Skinner, *English Vicars Apostolic*, passim.
[83] Banister, 14 Oct. 1784, 12 Jan. 1786; Rutter, 25 Apr. 1786.
[84] 18 Geo. III, c. 60. Ward, *Dawn*, I, pp. 93/94; UCM: III/243, Stonor to Gibson, 4 May 1784.
[85] Rutter, 29 Mar. 1787; Ward, *Dawn*, I, pp. 114/119.
[86] Bodleian Library, English Letters [BLEL] C.229: Tunstall to Constable 8 June 1790; 17 July 1790. See also L. Gooch, *Paid at Sundry Times* (Ampleforth Abbey: Saint Laurence Papers, X, 1997), No. 31.
[87] UCM: V/475c; UCM: Eyre Correspondence, Gibson to Eyre, 26 Jan. 1789.
[88] Ward, *Dawn*, I, p. 225; Rutter, 18 Mar. 1785, 1 Jan. 1786, 3 Sep. 1786, 24 May 1790, 27 June 1790; Banister 7 June 1780.
[89] Rutter, 27 June 1790; Banister, 3 July 1790, 5 Aug. 1790.
[90] Banister, 27 Feb. 1786, 5 Aug. 1790. See also Milburn, *Ushaw College*, pp. 16/17, 64 n3.
[91] Rutter, 9 June 1786; Banister, 17 July, 1786; UCM: Eyre Correspondence, Banister to Eyre 17 Nov. 1792.
[92] Rutter, 29 July 1790; Banister, 8 Sep. 1790; BLEL, C.229: Tunstall to Constable, 8 June 1790.
[93] E. Duffy, 'James Barnard and the Catholic Committee, or "How Horatio Held the Bridge"', UM 85 (1974), p. 45; Banister, 8 Sep. 1790, 12 Feb. 1791; UCM: PA/C14, J. Chadwick to W. Dunn, 19 Nov. 1790; Rutter, Sep. 1790.
[94] Ward, *Dawn*, I, p. 55; NRO: RCD 1/1, 21 Sep. 1790, 25 Oct. 1790; DCRO: Salvin Papers, D/Sa/C108. See also: Anon., 'Douai Papers V: Some Letters of Marmaduke Tunstall to Vincent Eyre', UM 24 (1914), p. 71.
[95] Ward, *Dawn*, I, p. 55; Gillow, *Dictionary*, sub Gibson, p. 449.
[96] Banister, 26 Oct. 1794, 13 Mar. 1795; NRO: RCD 4/4–9; Ward, *Dawn*, I, p. 280.
[97] Rutter, 10 Aug. 1791, 3 Feb. 1794, 16 May 1792.
[98] Banister, 19 Dec. 1793; 18 Jan. 1794.
[99] Rutter, 28 June 1795.
[100] Rutter, 16 July 1795; LDA: Gibson Papers, Milner to Gibson, 27 Nov. 1795.
[101] Banister, 16 Nov. 1796; Rutter, 12 May 1797.
[102] Banister, 13 Apr. 1799, quoting Barrow. Richard Gibson died in 1801 at

Mawley Hall, Shropshire, where he had been chaplain to Sir Walter Blount for 35 years, 'much respected and beloved by the family and his congregation, notwithstanding his constitutional roughness and apparent harshness'. (Cf. Gillow, *Dictionary*, II, p. 446.)

[103] Brady, *Episcopal Succession*, III, pp. 268/269.

[104] A recent biography of Smith is at J. Dunne, *The Northern Catholic Community in 1823, A Report to Rome* (Leeds Diocesan Archives, 2007).

[105] Brady, *Episcopal Succession*, III, p. 270; Dunne, *Northern Catholic Community*, passim.

[106] Gillow, *Dictionary*, V, p. 259.

[107] G. Bradley, 'Bishop Briggs' Visitation of Durham and Northumberland in 1839', NCH 3 (1976), p. 25.

[108] Sr Stanislaus to her brother George Haydock, 28 June 1840, in J. Gillow, *The Haydock Papers* (London: Burns & Oates, 1888) p. 187.

[109] Brady, *Episcopal Succession*, III, p. 344.

[110] G. Culkin, 'Lingard and Ushaw', *Clergy Review*, 35/6 (1951), p. 368.

[111] Gillow, *Dictionary*, V, p. 259.

[112] Brady, *Episcopal Succession*, III, p. 411. Hexham had not been an episcopal see since 821AD.

[113] Minute Book of the Hexham and Newcastle Cathedral Chapter, 1 Sep. 1852.

5 MISSION STATIONS IN COUNTY DURHAM

THE HUB OF the mission in the county[1] lay in the city of **Durham** where there had been a substantial Catholic population all through the seventeenth century and which probably numbered around two hundred and fifty at the time of the Revolution. There had been a resident chaplain in the Maire's family house in Gilesgate since the 1680s, perhaps earlier, and a chapel was conducted by the secular clergy at 33 Old Elvet, Mr. Forcer's house. In about 1685 the Jesuits opened a mission in Mr. Pudsey's house at 44–45 Old Elvet, comprising 'a chapel of some size' and a school in Mr. Rowell's house, also in Old Elvet. Evidently, then, the mission was well-appointed and served by more than one priest, but that extrovert demeanour proved unfortunate, for in December 1688

> A numerous and violent mob rushed into the chapel with such fury that in a few moments everything was destroyed from top to bottom. The roof, walls, floor, and altar were reduced to ruins. The cross itself was publicly burnt ... Their determination seemed to be to root out, if possible, every vestige of the Catholic religion. From the chapel the mob turned off to the houses of the Catholics ... plundering whatever furniture they could lay hands upon and sacrilegiously mutilating all sacred pictures, images and books ... The resident Fathers of Durham were compelled to fly and wander up and down in disguise, keeping to the most difficult and unfrequented roads ... They passed their days, and sometimes their nights also, in the open fields and woods ...[2]

The chapel was reopened at the turn of the century but the priests moved to live more privately and conducted themselves with greater discretion. Thomas Pearson, (d. 1732) the Jesuit missioner, is known to have lived at 'Mr Ward's woollen draper' and Alexius Tocketts (d. 1731), lived at 'Mr Clifton's in Old Street'. Thomas Waterton came to the city in 1729 but he would live at the Jesuit mission until his death in 1766. The secular mission was rebuilt in 1725 and it continued in use for the next century.

Lady Mary Radcliffe, the youngest and unmarried daughter of the first earl of Derwentwater, left home at Dilston in 1703 to live independently in Durham and she built a new house at the bottom of Old Elvet which was ready for occupation in 1706. It was confidently asserted that the house was 'really designed for a Nunnery (as at York) for entertainment of young Ladys of that persuasion'. That may well have been true since great-aunts, aunts and sisters had entered the religious life. Ferdinand Ashmall, 55 years old and who had been at Dilston some twelve years earlier, moved from the neighbouring secular mission in Old Elvet to be her chaplain. He died six years later and was succeeded by Augustine Jenison, gentry-born in Durham and 32 years old; he had been ordained in Douai in 1701. Lady Mary and her chaplain were interrogated after the 'Fifteen and in 1716 he left to be replaced by Luke Gardiner (alias Robert Carnaby or Mitford) nephew of Roger Mitford. He had been ordained priest in Paris in 1713 and had just returned to England. Lady Mary died in 1724 (and was buried at Dilston) and Gardiner, who was made vicar general, moved to live elsewhere in the city. The Radcliffe chaplaincy ceased but Lady Mary left her large fortune for the support of the secular clergy in Northumberland and Durham.

Bishop Thomas Williams confirmed around two hundred Catholics of the three chapels in the city and its environs in 1729. Three years later there were over three hundred papists in the city, including ninety-three children and three priests. The Catholic laity formed a wide cross-section of the city's social and economic structure, and they went about their daily business, accepted by the citizenry, of which they formed an integral part.

The 'Forty-five led to another sacking of the chapels in the city but the Catholics were not easily intimidated. In 1750, the Jesuit Thomas Waterton, reported that the chapel had been repaired, and extended, and that the Jubilee celebrations had been attended by a large and devout congregation:

> We had three different times set apart for it, viz. 14 days each during which we had Prayers morning and afternoon with meditations and instructions, and the shop as frequented as of H. days; and many presented themselves for goods who never had come before; almost all changed for the better, many in an extraordinary manner. Out of near 300 that then frequented me I had not above four or five who did not make a general review of their whole lives and of this number above thirty and odd that of thirty or forty years had been with nobody. Several reconciliations made; several other acts of virtue performed which still show themselves as a more diligent attendance on days of Obligation both mornings and afternoons, and particularly a monthly application to the Sacraments which I hope as it does at present will continue. In mine near twenty have or will I believe enter the true fold, drawn as I think, in great measure by the edifying comportment of the people on this occasion.

Waterton also had a school in Old Elvet, which was recommended by Sir Marmaduke Constable to Sir Carnaby Haggerston in 1740 for its high standards; it would also allow him to keep his young children 'nigh to you' to the satisfaction of his lady. Additionally, Waterton, and his successors attended the forty or so Catholics in the Bishop Auckland area, for which the stipend was two guineas a year plus one guinea to pay the rent of a room. These sums augmented his income of about £23 a year from the Durham mission and an annuity of £25 from his brother.[3]

The Jesuit mission in Durham was evidently flourishing at this time, and it seems to have eclipsed activity at the secular mission. In 1767 William Maire, 63 years old, had been resident in Durham for twenty-six years, living on £24 a year. He had moved from Gilesgate in 1741 on his appointment as vicar general and he remained there until 1768. He was consecrated coadjutor to Bishop Francis Petre but, being in poor health, he retired to his family's home, Lartington Hall, where he died the following year. At this time the priest at the Gilesgate mission was John Bamber; he was 50 years old and had been resident for sixteen years. The mission was closed in 1769, partly because it was no longer needed and partly because a greater need for a priest existed in Sunderland.[4]

The Catholic population of the city fell from over four hundred in 1767 to well under two hundred in the early years of the nineteenth century. There were Catholic dame schools, and so the population was not in absolute decline but by the beginning of the 1820s the situation was not encouraging. The Jesuit missioner, Edward Walsh, was 80 years old in 1820 and the secular priest, Thomas Smith, was almost 65. Smith had been appointed coadjutor to the vicar apostolic, William Gibson, in 1807 and both sick and ageing bishops lived together in Old Elvet until 1821 when Gibson died aged 83. Smith handed the mission over to James Wheeler, chaplain from Clints Hall who was described as 'more scholar than pastor', and he returned to the more tranquil conditions of the Yorkshire chaplaincy three years later. The much more ebullient William Croskell took over in Durham. Walsh died in 1822 and Nicholas Sewell, the Provincial, decided to close the Jesuit mission in the city since the congregation of 'about 100 or a few more' did not justify a second chapel in the city when a mission was badly needed in Wakefield or Huddersfield.[5]

Bishop Smith took the opportunity of the amalgamation of the two missions and the arrival of a new and vigorous missioner to sanction the building of a new church and house to replace the two old chapels, as well as to provide a suitable residence for a bishop. (The Jesuit property was given to the District as a contribution towards the new buildings.) The following account is probably by the architect, Ignatius Bonomi:

> The two Catholic Chapels in Old Elvet being rather small for the accommodation of the Catholics residing in Durham and being inconveniently situated for public access within the houses of the clergymen; it was considered expedient to build a new Chapel sufficiently large for uniting both Congregations with an attached residence for the Clergymen; the Chapel measures within, 70 feet long 30 feet wide and 30 high. The Building which is situated at the head of Old Elvet nearly opposite the County Courts was begun in April 1826 from a plan of Mr Bonomi and the masons work was undertaken by Mr. Jackson.

The opening of St Cuthbert's, Durham, and St Augustine's, Darlington, in May 1827 signalled the architectural emancipation of the post-Reformation Catholic Church in the north-east. New schools were provided in 1832 and again in 1847; by which time the Catholic population of the city was estimated to have reached one thousand.[6]

**

The Benedictines held the mission at **Chester le Street**, which had been established in 1696 with a fund of £300 given by William Tempest for the benefit of Catholics living around Lumley Castle. Tempest was agent for the Lumley family which had been Catholic until the reign of James II when Richard, Lord Lumley, apostatised. A monk later remarked on how his predecessors had been 'tossed about after the defection of the Lumleys', though no details are now known. The chapel and priest's residence were in a house in the eastern part of the town, possibly in that of 'Widow Tempest', one of fifty-seven named adult Catholics there in the return of 1705. The chapel was attended by a riding missioner or from Lintz Hall until about 1720 when Dom Bertram Edward Bulmer took up permanent residence. In 1732 the episcopal visitation return said that there were thirty Catholic families in the town. Bulmer died in 1745, and in the following year the new missioner, Dom Anthony Raffa, moved the mission out of the town into the village of **Birtley** some two miles to the north. There were several reasons for the move. Other prominent town chapels were sacked at that time and Chester le Street, conspicuous on the Great North Road might have become a target. The Humble family, coal merchants, had presented the mission with a plot of land in Birtley and doubtless Raffa assessed that the security of his mission would be better kept in relative seclusion. And then, in 1744 the Catholic population was larger in Birtley (twenty-five) than in Chester le Street (fourteen). A further justification for the move was that Birtley would be convenient for the thirty Catholics in Lamesley. Finally, Raffa had an indirect connection with the locality, for he had been chaplain to the Riddells at Swinburne, and they owned a large house and property in Gateshead (where nearly sixty Catholics were living in 1767).[7]

The chapel and presbytery were built at Birtley by 1751 and the mission received a legacy of £100 from Dom Placid Hutton, a Durham man.[8] A more substantial increase in its funding was provided but, in a way that was becoming commonplace, the benefaction almost became an encumbrance. Ralph Brandling and his wife Eleanor (both converts) set up house in Felling Hall around 1740. The Hall had been abandoned by his uncle Ralph when he had gone to live in Middleton Hall, near Leeds, on his marriage to Ann Legh, some forty years earlier. The Brandlings took a Dominican chaplain but when Ralph Brandling, the elder, died in 1749, the chaplain was dismissed and the Jesuits in Pontop Hall, Durham or Newcastle attended Felling Hall for the next two years.

Dom Anthony Raffa had earlier made the acquaintance of Mrs Brandling's two sons, Ralph and Charles, when they were at the Academie Royale at Angers. When, in 1751 Ralph died aged 21, Charles returned to Felling with the corpse. Raffa agreed to stay at Felling Hall pending the appointment of a 'suitable gentleman' as chaplain, but he stipulated that he must be allowed to 'say prayers for my congregation on the first Sunday in each month and attend my people in all other respects the same as if I was at Birtley'. He clearly wished to avoid being drawn into the position of full-time resident chaplain, but he had to offer some quid pro quo for the endowment of £500 made by the recently-deceased Ralph Brandling as

> a pious foundation to the honour and glory of God and the benefit of my soul in favour of the poor Catholicks of the parish of Chester le Street in the County of Bishoprick, namely for the support of a Priest there to pray, help, assist and instruct the people there and bring up their children in the fear of God.

The money was to go to Dom Anthony and after his death to the Benedictine order. Twenty Masses were to be said annually for Ralph's soul, and two Masses were to be offered at Felling monthly; Charles was executor.[9] A 'suitable gentleman' had not appeared by 1754, but Raffa was keen to move back into Birtley. Charles Brandling came of age that year and the Benedictine Provincial therefore decided to renegotiate the pastoral arrangements. It was immediately made plain that Brandling regarded his brother's endowment as a capital fund for a chaplaincy in Felling Hall, not for the support of the missioner in Birtley, and he stopped paying the priest's stipend and refused to hand over the capital to the Benedictines.

A compromise was reached in which Dom Anthony would live in Birtley but would continue to say Mass in Felling Hall twice a month for which he would receive £20 a year. Brandling was not prepared to enter into any long-term agreement which might imply his surrender of the fund's control. On the contrary, after Raffa died the interest on the endowment would be applied by Brandling for the 'use of a Priest for his own family to attend him when he should think proper'. The Provincial managed to reach an agreement that Raffa's successors would be Benedictines but Brandling would not commit himself on paper to that effect. He did, however, resume payment of the stipend in 1755 and he paid up the arrears; but he did not part with the capital until 1760, two years after Raffa's death. The money was then held in trust by Sir John Swinburne. Charles Brandling apostatized in 1771. The mission at Birtley survived the intrigues of the Brandlings and ceased to be dependent on a single patron, and an almost uninterrupted succession of Benedictine missioners would serve the mission for the next two centuries.

In 1767 there were one hundred and seventy-two Catholics in the parish of Chester le Street, and by 1780 the Catholic community was said to be 'chiefly composed of persons connected with the collieries'. The Birtley chapel was 'a small unlighted chamber' and the priest lived with 'a pious Catholic family'. These arrangements became increasingly unsuitable and so a new chapel was built in the late 1780s on land donated by the Humble family and was registered by Dom Bernard Slater on 29 October 1791. This was described as 'a plain unpresuming edifice' an indication that Catholic chapels were still being built in a discreet and vernacular manner to avoid any possibility of giving offence. In 1814, however, Dom Leo Spain was seriously afflicted with scrupulosity; the congregation lived in terror of him and great damage was done to the chapel and its fittings. He left in 1816 and the premises were then 'nailed up'. In 1837 the chapel was described as 'an abominable place, so exceedingly damp and rather out of the way, and certainly has no attractions. The House, though small, is very tolerable.' Notwithstanding that there were a hundred or so communicants, it was even considered moving the mission back to Chester le Street, it being the larger town.

In 1842, however, the Benedictines signalled their continuing commitment to Birtley. The newly-appointed missioner, Dom James Sheridan, bought a new site (for £400) on which he built the 'neat' church designed by John Dobson in the Early English Gothic style, dedicated to Ss Mary and Joseph, with a house and school, costing £1,500. Allanson remarks that the Benedictine Province was not financially burdened because 'the Cottages on the ground paid the interest of the purchase money and the public subscriptions nearly paid for the new undertaking'. The church was opened on 18 August 1843 and registered with the civic authorities on 12 May 1846 'as a place Congregation or Assembly for Religious Worship after the manner of the Church of Rome'.[10]

***

Although Eleanor Brandling was still resident in 1767 there are no references to priests officiating in Felling Hall after the apostasy and removal of Charles Brandling.[11] For some seventy-five years thereafter the Catholics of **Felling** were attended by the clergy of Newcastle or other priests in the vicinity. In 1840 William Riddell, assistant priest at St Andrew's, Newcastle, found that there were some four hundred Catholics in the Felling area, mostly Irish migrants. By the beginning of 1842, he had built, at his own expense, a chapel dedicated to St Patrick in the Early English style by John Dobson at Felling Shore on land given by Mr Caley of Saltwell. The mission could not at first support a resident priest since he 'could not calculate upon raising about £25 a year from the members of the congregation, subscriptions, etc.' Riddell therefore attended from Newcastle until 1845 when an Irish priest, Anthony McDermott, was appointed as resident missioner.[12]

***

Anne Haggerston was widowed in 1708 but she lived on at Haggerston Castle until her son Carnaby and his priest-tutor returned from their Grand Tour in 1719. Carnaby married two years later and his mother left the castle and rented a house in **Gateshead**, taking with her the missioner Francis Anderton S.J. She did a great deal of travelling, always accompanied by her chaplain. She died at St Omer in 1740 and the chaplaincy lapsed but its closure cannot have had much effect on the mission. Gateshead House, on the other hand, belonged to the Riddell family and they maintained a Benedictine chaplaincy from around the time of the Restoration until the end of the century when after a short secular tenure, it was taken over by Jesuits: Robert and William Riddell, uncle and nephew, followed by Luke Pippard, Richard Molyneux and Thomas Maire. But then, the destruction of the old chapel by the anti-Jacobite mob in 1746 forced the removal of John Walsh to Newcastle and the proximity of Gateshead to the missions in Newcastle and Birtley saved the expense of providing a chapel for the remnants of the old congregation which numbered fifty-eight in 1767 and was reduced by 1792 to only twelve 'families chiefly mechanicks, artificers and labourers. They assemble[d] for divine worship at a place in Newcastle'.

Towards the middle of the nineteenth century, however, some two to three thousand Catholics were living in Gateshead and Frederick Betham instituted a supply mission from St Andrew's in Newcastle in 1851. A temporary chapel was set up firstly in a warehouse and Betham immediately issued an appeal to raise £800 to buy land on which to build a permanent church. The chapel and warehouse were destroyed in a fire in 1854 and the mission moved to the Queen's Head Hotel since funds to buy the land were not raised until 1856. In May 1858, Edward Consitt, welcomed Bishop Hogarth to lay the foundation stone of St Joseph's. The church, by Archibald M. Dunn, ('elaborately and proudly Decorated') was opened in July 1859.[13]

***

In 1767 around seventy Catholics lived in **South Shields**, and thereabouts on the south bank of the Tyne. There were some twenty Catholic families at the end of the eighteenth century, 'none above the rank of tradesmen and including labourers and the lowest mechanics'. Until 1821 they were visited by priests from adjacent missions but for several years afterwards the Catholics ferried across the river to attend Mass in the newly-opened church in North Shields, or went down to Sunderland (1835) or perhaps across to Felling (1842). A Sunday school was opened in South Shields in 1832, staffed at first by volunteers, but its growth led to the appointment of a paid teacher. He began to organise lotteries and social events to raise funds for a chapel. On three occasions, Protestant owners of land refused to sell to the Catholics but in 1848 a disused chapel of the Bristol Brethren was bought and it became St Bede's Catholic Church in the following year. The Jarrow and Hebburn Catholics doubtless also attended the chapel.[14]

***

Sunderland became 'the most important shipbuilding centre in the country' in the course of the eighteenth century. In 1689, out of a population of around three thousand, there were thirty-two Catholics living in the town headed by Robert Hallyman, a gentleman.[15] Most of the rest were described as yeomen, but it seems odd that twenty of them were listed as single men and it is likely that many of them were, in fact, married. The priest John Wilkinson is known to have lived there in 1704 and he died in the town in April

1734, aged 64. The finances of the mission were secured by the priest Francis Hodgson. He died in May 1726 at Wycliffe leaving £800, in trust to Marmaduke Tunstall, half for the maintenance of a secular priest at 'Sunderland by the Sea and at or about South Shields or other destitute place near there unto on all Sundays and Holydays in the year'. (The other half was to be applied for the same purpose in the vicinity of Darlington.) Priests who can be identified with the mission at Sunderland in the next twenty years included William Anderson and John Girlington (who had been with the Radcliffes in Tynedale until 1729). They lived with Francis Whytehead, a Master Mariner, who also provided space for the chapel on the third floor of his house, 30 Warren Street. The number of Catholics in the town fluctuated markedly during the first half of the century: in 1705 there were fourteen, in 1736 there only two families, but in 1743 there were twenty-seven individuals.

The incumbent at the time of the second Jacobite Rising was John Hankin, the 40-year-old son of a Newcastle lawyer, but his comfortable, well-appointed and apparently secure mission was one of the few to suffer in the aftermath of the rising. On 22 January 1746,

> about three hundred men, mostly sailors and apprentices armed with pistols and cutlasses, with drums beating and colours flying, went about ten o'clock in the morning to the papist Mass-house in the town where they found several people at prayers and a couple to be married who, with Mr Hankin, their priest, all fled out, upon which the sailors immediately pulled down their altar, crucifix, together with all the seats, the priest's robes, all their books, their furniture and every individual thing in the room and burnt them in a fire in the street made for that purpose; and also a large library of books and papers belonging to the priest ...[16]

Mission Stations in County Durham 275

The fate of Mr Whytehead is not known but the unfortunate priest had to make his escape disguised as a woman. He moved to the rural mission at Witton Shields and retired in 1772; he died at St Omer ten years later.

After the sacking of the chapel the congregation was attended weekly from Durham by John Bamber who was said to have dressed as a huntsman on these journeys. His appointment as resident missioner was made possible by the closure of the Maire house in Gilesgate, Durham. Mary Maire died in 1751 and bequeathed the house to the secular clergy. Bamber, her chaplain, went on living there but as a riding-priest, attending at Headlam, Darlington and Sunderland. In 1768 Nicholas Taylor gave £100 to the mission, the interest on which was to be paid to 'a secular priest who shall be fixed and settled in the town of Sunderland to assist the Catholics of the said town and people adjacent'. Ann Pyatt also left £100 'in trust for ye annual use of ye present or future incumbent of Sunderland, of Sunderland upon ye Sea or Wearmouth, having ye charge of souls of ye Catholics in that neighbourhood'. Thus, since the Darlington Catholics could be looked after by the priests in Cliffe Hall and Stockton, and given that there were two chapels in the city of Durham, Bamber was free to move to Sunderland where the congregation numbered one hundred and thirteen. The Taylor and Pyatt bequests, together with the funds attached to the old mission in Gilesgate which were transferred with him, were sufficient financial support.[17]

On 1 August 1769 Bamber rented a house in Vine Street at £9 a year from James Galley, a coal-merchant, in which he opened a chapel for a congregation which grew to one hundred and seventy-four by 1780. Galley went bankrupt that year, however, and when the house was seized by his creditors the priest was forced to quit. Ralph Galley, James's son, offered to rent two rooms in his own newly-built house in Dunning Street as chapel and vestry;

though confined and damp, his offer was accepted and presently everything was contrived to be as convenient for the priest and congregation as so small premises were susceptible of.

The priest took lodgings nearby (where he heard confessions), but no sooner had things been settled than John Bamber died.[18]

In view of the obviously unsatisfactory arrangements he found, Bamber's successor William Fletcher decided to put the mission in Sunderland on a firm footing under the independent control of the vicariate. Land was bought in 1786 and plans for a chapel and house were prepared: 'all plain but good work for the sum of three hundred and fifty pounds'. Before the building was finished, however, the chapel was set on fire, and a reward was offered for information leading to the culprit's conviction. (It was forty years exactly after the earlier chapel had been fired.) The workmen themselves were suspected but were exonerated by the magistrates. William Scott was arraigned at the Durham Assizes but he, too, was discharged. The chapel was completed in 1788 and insured for £400, the total building costs had risen to £385.[19] As was usual at this time, church-income was partly raised through bench-rents; the scale of charges (payable on Mayday or Martinmas) was as follows:

> 1. *Gallery.* £1.1.0d. for front benches, 14s. for each of the other benches and each person that sits at the front benches to pay 10s.6d. annually, second benches 8s., third and fourth benches 6s.
>
> 2. Better benches in front of chapel, deposit 16s., pay 4s. per annum.
>
> 3. Inferior benches under gallery, deposit 8s., pay 3s. per annum.[20]

The congregation in Sunderland at the end of the eighteenth century numbered one hundred and fifty. (The missioner also visited Houghton le Spring, Washington, and Seaham Harbour.) A day-school was added around 1810. A substantial growth in the congregation in the period between the Second Catholic Relief Act and Emancipation required that the mission property be enlarged twice (at a cost of £835 and £300 for an organ). The improved arrangements were described:

> At the west end a commodious gallery is erected which, with the lower part of the chapel, will seat about 400 persons. Above the altar is a fine painting of the Crucifixion.

A new missioner, Philip Kearney, an Irishman, arrived in 1829 to find

> a fast increasing congregation, cabin'd, cribb'd, and confin'd in a dreary loft with a priest's house attached ... no feudal dungeon offered a more grim and forbidding exterior...

More generously the *Catholic Magazine* described the situation in 1832:

> The congregation is large and increasing, averaging from 3 to 400 communicants. It consists of persons engaged in the Shipping, mechanics and with few or none who live wholly independent. The chapel and house stand near the river, in a very retired situation about the centre of Bishopwearmouth. The chapel is a neat, plain brick building, but too small for the congregation.

Kearney proposed to build a large and prominent church. The architect Ignatius Bonomi was engaged, and land on the principal north-south highway through the town (within sight of Bede's monastery at Monkwearmouth) was bought from the earl of Durham. The local newspaper reported that the completed church would 'stand unrivalled as the finest public building in these towns' and would accommodate fifteen hundred worshippers. *Vindex* was prompted to write to the local newspaper to remind the citizens of Sunderland of the errors of Rome, and to deplore the erection of the new church. That was the only objection, however, and St

Mary's, Bonomi's largest church, was completed at a cost of £5,000 in 1835.[21]

Since the school was on the same site as the old chapel, it too had to be replaced, and a two-storey building to accommodate three hundred boys (not all of them Catholics) was erected next to the church in 1836. Kearney went over to Ireland to persuade Edmund Rice, founder of the Christian Brothers, to provide two teachers for the new school. Rice was reluctant to overstretch his commitments in England, but he eventually agreed. Kearney wrote in 1836 to say that the school was ready and to tell Rice that he could pay the Brothers '£100 a year with house and coal'. The local newspaper shortly reported that 'Two Irish monks were teaching 250 Protestant boys and converting them to the Popish religion'. If true, (and Catholic boys were probably in a minority since the school could accommodate three hundred pupils) the boys' parents were unconcerned. At Kearney's request, the Brothers left in 1848, having declined to accept government regulation and inspection of the school and were replaced by the Presentation Brothers. In 1843, with the approval of Bishop Mostyn, Kearney recruited a group of five Irish Sisters of Mercy to come to Sunderland. He had bought a house close to the church and school with money left by Lady Peat. (She also bequeathed £1,000 for a new convent.) The newspaper reported:

> Sunderland Nunnery. The house lately occupied by Mrs Mesnard, Green Street, in the town has been appropriated by the Roman Catholics to the purpose of a nunnery for the order of Sisters of Charity [sic]. Six ladies from Cork have already taken the veil, four of whom are young, the remaining two advanced in life. They engage themselves in visiting the sick, in serving the destitute. An accession of numbers is shortly expected.

They also opened a school for girls and they would take over from the Brothers in 1858. Kearney's ambitions for the mission were soon justified, for in the fifteen years following the opening of the new church, the Catholic population of the town was said to be four thousand—a twentyfold increase, and perhaps an over-estimate. In 1846/7 one of the first conferences of the Society of St Vincent de Paul was erected in the town and it became a crucial part of the church's social mission in Sunderland.

***

Houghton le Spring on the river Wear was the most substantial township between Durham and Sunderland, and four or five Catholic families lived there during the eighteenth century. When the Carmelite community's lease of St Helen's Hall in Auckland expired in 1804, they moved into Cocken Hall, near Houghton le Spring, of which the nuns' patron Sir Henry Lawson was part lessee from the Carr family. It had been monastic property and an eighteenth-century engraving shows a seventeenth-century house set amid a gracious park overlooking the ruins of Finchale Priory on the opposite side of the river. Notwithstanding its attractive location, the Hall was difficult to let because it was reputed to be haunted and the nuns therefore got the lease very cheaply. Between 1810 and 1820, however, when coal-pits began to be sunk in the locality, the annual rent of the Hall increased steadily and it became clear to the nuns that they could not afford to go on living there much longer. They therefore bought Cockerton Field House near Darlington, a seventeenth-century property in twenty acres of land, which became their permanent home in 1830.[22]

The Catholic community grew with the opening of the new collieries although in 1817 Houghton le Spring was described as a place of 'all pervading bigotry' by the new missioner Thomas MacDonald. Even before he arrived, a Methodist preacher had sought to blacken his character describing him as an atheist and ignorant of the scriptures and the standard prayers.[23] When the convent closed, the missioners in Hutton House and Sunderland attended for a short time before James McEvoy was appointed resident missioner in 1832 with a salary of £40 a year. He rented a house and opened a mission in a converted Baptist chapel for a congregation of eighty to one hundred people. He also began to collect funds for a church, making use of the Catholic press for his appeals. The 1833 *Catholic Directory* carried a piece which was intended both to stimulate readers to support his 'little flock being composed exclusively of the poor' who had difficulty meeting the running-costs of the mission, and to motivate readers to recover something of the pre-Reformation Age of Faith represented by the local Norman church of St Michael and All Angels now in Anglican usage: 'The fine old Cruciform Church, which is still the chief ornament of the village, attests at once the Faith, the zeal, and religious magnificence of our Catholic ancestors'. Presently, he told the vicar general:

> our Mission here is assuming an aspect so very imposing and our numbers have so far out-grown our means of accommodation that I have made up my mind to put on a brazen front and try my fortune next summer.

He also said that he had approached the local coal-owners for financial assistance, pointing out that he had over one hundred children to educate. The Protestant schools

> have robbed me of some children—so much so that I undertook 6 months back by way of opposition to pay for the education of a few of the most destitute females, some of whom are orphans. Oh! that some benevolent mortal would just give us one thousand pounds what an oasis would then spring up in this moral wilderness.

McEvoy went on:

There are a great number of nominal Catholics in this part of the country who are exceedingly fastidious in their notions of accommodation, and who under more favourable conditions would attend at least occasionally and thus enable me to secure their children. With a new chapel erected on the noble site we have in view, I think I could safely calculate on the regular attendance of 200 Catholics, Sunday after Sunday.

In 1837 Bishop Briggs opened St Michael's, a dual-purpose building to designs by Ignatius Bonomi; the chapel, seating for four hundred people, was on the upper floor and the ground floor became a school-room.[24]

***

The Catholics of north-west Durham had always been well provided with pastoral care. The Tempest family acquired a former Benedictine convent in the parish of Ryton in the late sixteenth century and Nicholas Tempest rebuilt it as **Stella Hall** soon after 1600 but a succession of chaplains can be traced only from 1688. Sir Francis Tempest died abroad in 1692 and the estate passed to Jane Tempest his sister. In 1700 she married William, fourth baron Widdrington. Dom John Wilson was their chaplain and he headed the roll of one hundred and eighty-three papists listed in 1705. They were mostly pitmen working in Widdrington's collieries and living in Stella, Blaydon and Winlaton.[25]

Lady Jane Widdrington died in 1714 bequeathing funds to produce a chaplain's salary of £28 a year (the capital was held by the family to ensure control over the appointment). For some years after the death of Dom John Wilson in 1725, however, the Benedictine tenure became increasingly precarious because Widdrington would not pay the monk's stipend.[26] Presumably at the invitation of the patron, the seculars took over in 1732. In 1748, shortly after his accession to the estate, Henry Francis Widdrington commissioned James Paine to make substantial alterations to Stella Hall. But he also dismissed the secular priest Thomas Greenwell from the chaplaincy and installed the Jesuit Richard Murphy (alias Turner) in his place. No explanation for this change is known. Whatever the reason, many in the congregation objected to the removal of the priest who had served them for twelve years for one brought in at the will of the patron, and they formed a breakaway congregation at Blaydon, supporting Greenwell with their voluntary contributions as Murphy himself made clear in his Jubilee report of 1750:

> Customers to Shop on Days required commonly 170, though few Patients of mine, as most make use of another gentleman maintained by them for years for that purpose.

The rival congregation was short-lived, however, for Greenwell caught an infection while attending a sick person and he died after a short illness in 1753. But then in 1775 the estate passed to Thomas Eyre and Murphy was dismissed to make way for the new patron's kinsman, Thomas Eyre, a secular priest. Murphy was 'out of place' in Newcastle for eighteen months before he was appointed chaplain to Lord Arundel in Salisbury.[27]

There were some four hundred and fifty Catholics in the parish of Ryton in 1767, and around four hundred at the end of the Napoleonic Wars. Eyre acted as the bishop's secretary and treasurer for much of his time at Stella Hall, and Bishop Matthew Gibson also lived there between 1784 and 1790. The estate changed hands again in 1792, when it passed into the possession of the Towneley family. Eyre left to go as chaplain to the recently-widowed Mrs Silvertop at Wooler, a move deprecated by his near neighbour, Henry Rutter at Minsteracres:

> I cannot indeed well justify this step in my friend, leaving an old and numerous congregation to bury himself in a

> desert country where there is nothing to do. There are now three considerable congregations adjoining to mine which appear to me not to be sufficiently provided for. Mr Ashmal at Newhouse who is 97 years of age at least has been unable to do duty for a long time. No priest has been fixed at Pontop since Mr Johnson's death. Nor is Stella, as I hear, yet provided with a pastor. For the present indeed Mr Story from Hexham says prayers there and Mr Worswick at Pontop but many things I fear are omitted when priests are not fixed and supply only for a time.[28]

Notwithstanding his remoteness in north Northumberland, however, Eyre remained at the centre of vicariate affairs (he was now vicar general) and he kept closely in touch with all developments in the area. He had supplied for a time at Pontop Hall before he went to Wooler and he would return to north-west Durham within two years.

The Towneleys leased Stella Hall to Mr Clayton, Town Clerk of Newcastle and, since the availability of the chapel was reserved only until Mayday 1794, new premises had to be found. Eyre had been considering building a new chapel and he had obtained £500 for the purpose (some of which had come from the proceeds of a sale of the contents of the Hall) and Stella House, belonging to the Silvertops, was taken. Despite some misgivings about his security of tenure, William Hull accepted the appointment as missioner and he moved into the new premises with some exiled French priests. Silvertop soon built a new chapel (Eyre's fund was not used) and it remained in use for about forty years. Its replacement became necessary partly because it had become inadequate for the growing congregation but also because it lay on the intended track of the Newcastle and Carlisle Railway.[29]

In 1827 Hull was afflicted with 'the stone' and three years later, approaching his eightieth year, he retired and was succeeded by the newly-ordained 24-year-old Thomas Edward Witham, nephew of George Silvertop of Minsteracres, and brother of the principal Catholic in the congregation, Mrs Emma Dunn (neé Witham) of Hedgefield House. The well-connected priest was clearly the best available man for this large and prominent mission which was ripe for further development. Investment of the Eyre fund had by this time increased the capital to £950, and that was brought up to £1,500 by 'a number of sums contributed by the Catholic and Protestant Ladies and Gentlemen in the neighbourhood', which was sufficient to build a new church. The 'neat' church, dedicated to Ss Mary and Thomas Aquinas, designed by the local architect John Green to seat three hundred people, was opened in October 1832 by Bishop Penswick. A contemporary gazetteer remarked that 'economy in more instances than one seems to have been carried too far in this erection'. Alterations were effected by John Dobson in 1847.[30]

***

A few miles to the south-west of Stella there was a Catholic farming and mining community centred on the villages of Tanfield, Hamsterley and Ebchester in the northern part of the parish of Lanchester. In the early years of the eighteenth century, the Catholics of the area could attend 'Prayers at different gentlemen's houses, where there happened to be a priest'. Stanley Hall, described in 1834 as standing 'on a wild hill top', belonged to the Tempests who supported a Jesuit. Lintz Hall was owned by the Hodgsons who had a Benedictine chaplain in 1698. Other Catholic houses in the locality included Hamsterley Hall, belonging to the Swinburnes, **Pontop Hall** (the Meaburnes) and **The Brooms** (the Smiths). In 1732, about one hundred and fifty Catholics were associated with, or dependent on these estates. Changes in family circumstances, however, led to a reorganisation of pastoral arrangements. Sir Nicholas and Lady Tempest were dead by 1742; their Jesuit chaplain, Joseph Howe, remained at Stanley Hall but the chaplaincy lapsed on his transfer to Longhorsley Tower in 1745. The house later passed into the ownership of the Towneley family. The Benedictine moved out of Lintz Hall around 1713 when it was let after the death of Ralph Hodgson. The last of the family, another Ralph, died in 1773 but since his only daughter was married to Thomas Selby of Biddlestone, there was no need to engage a second chaplain for this house. Augustine Walker, a Benedictine monk, was at 'Mr Swinburne's at Tanfield' between 1750 and 1753, but that is the only evidence of a resident priest at Hamsterley Hall until the end of the century when a French exiled priest signed the register; it is probable that Walker moved between the halls at Lintz and Hamsterley. Walker was a Jacobite, and of a scientific turn of mind; he wrote papers on the coal trade, electricity, heat and light and the rising of vapours. He would go on to become Prior of St Edmund's, Paris and, successively, Procurator and President of the English Benedictines. He died aged 73 in January 1794 in a French prison. At mid-century, then, only Pontop Hall remained available as a mission station in the locality.[31]

Anthony Meaburne bought the manor of Pontop in 1600, and his descendants established themselves as minor coal-owners on this and the Crook Hall estate close to Iveston nearby. The family prospered notwithstanding the penalties suffered for their recusancy and they were able to build the imposing Pontop Hall in 1700. The mansion incorporated a chapel on the top floor. Anthony Meaburne died a bachelor in 1712, aged 84, leaving £500 to the Jesuits for Mass to be said in the hall monthly. It is likely that Joseph Howe was the first beneficiary of this fund and he attended from Stanley Hall until his departure in 1745. The estate passed to another Anthony Meaburne; he died in 1732 leaving two adult daughters. Mary, the elder, widow of Thomas Thornton of Netherwitton, married, secondly, Thomas Swinburne, third son of Sir

William Swinburne (II) of Capheaton, and carried the estate into that family. They lived at Pontop Hall throughout their married life, and in 1748 they took over the Jesuit chaplaincy previously maintained by the Tempests in Stanley Hall. The first resident Jesuit was Thomas Leckonby; in 1750 he reported: 'My salary from factory £33.3s., contributions £4 and coals free, other helps about 30s., customers to shop 145'. His death in 1778 marked the end of the Jesuit tenure for he was succeeded by James Johnson, a secular priest.[32]

The patron, Thomas Swinburne, had died six years before Leckonby, leaving a 60-year-old widow and an adult son Thomas Anthony who had married Charlotte Spearman, a Protestant. The new patron kept the chapel open and he accepted a group of repatriated students from Douai College until Crook Hall, another imposing late seventeenth-century house, was got ready for them. But his wife would not have a resident chaplain after the deaths of old Mrs Swinburne in 1786 and the 45-year-old Revd James Johnson in 1790. The congregation of one hundred and sixty was then attended by Thomas Eyre of Stella (before he decamped to Wooler) or John Worswick, the priest at Lartington, but that could only be an emergency arrangement.

In 1791, pastoral arrangements were reviewed. Eyre, faced with the effective discontinuation of the chaplaincy, together with the inconvenient location of the chapel on the upper floor of Pontop Hall, and emboldened by the Catholic Relief Act passed that year, proposed to create an independent mission.[33] In May 1793, on behalf of the vicar apostolic and John Silvertop, trustee of the Meaburne fund, Eyre accepted the offer of John Smith of High Brooms to make over to the mission a plot of freehold land of between four and five acres, 'immediately adjoining on to the Pontop Estate; with a view to a house and chapel being built there for the benefit of the Pontop congregation'. Eyre was very happy that the new chapel would be in a 'pleasant spot and infinitely more engaging than the ruinous hall', even if it was in a high and exposed location, and he wrote to several Catholic families in the locality for their approval of the plan but also to solicit subscriptions towards the chapel. Eyre had little hope of receiving a contribution from Henry and Martha Swinburne of Hamsterley Hall although he informed them of the plan, 'to keep them, if possible, in good humour'; in fact, they were hardly ever at home. John Silvertop was prepared to be a trustee of the new mission, to which he subscribed £70, and he agreed to superintend building operations, which were to be carried out by the men of the congregation.

In May 1793 Eyre thought the buildings at Brooms would soon be completed and he returned to north-west Durham from Wooler in 1794. Work proceeded slowly, however, and it was not until 1796 that the chapel was finished. The priest's house was not ready but Eyre nonetheless offered it to a group of fifteen exiled French priests who had arrived at North Shields in October that year. The house was made habitable for them and they lived in it for the next six years.[34] The French occupation of the property at Brooms made it unavailable for public use, however, and so the mission remained in Pontop Hall for the time being attended by the French priests. Thomas Eyre had taken charge of the seminary in nearby Crook Hall which opened in October 1794 for the students who had returned to England from Douai following the revolution in France; they would remain there until Ushaw College opened in 1808.

The house and chapel at Brooms became available to the mission when the French priests left in June 1802 and in September John Lingard, Vice President of Crook Hall, formally opened the chapel; it was dedicated to St Cuthbert and was described in the local newspaper as 'a small but remarkably neat building'. John Bell was appointed missioner to the congregation of around one hundred. He had been tutor in the Silvertop household at nearby

Minsteracres, and then Prefect of Discipline at Crook Hall. On one occasion in 1807, John Smith had to remonstrate with Bell who had forbidden the congregation to enter his house and stand by the fire in the parlour to discuss politics before Mass, as they were wont to do with Eyre. Bell was taken to task for being so unfeeling to people who needed to be warmed up: 'Nowhere else did such a thing happen'.[35]

A priest was resident at The Brooms until 1819, but none was available after that, and the mission was served from Esh Laude. In 1832 the *Catholic Magazine* reported that the mission's income was 'not sufficient to support a pastor'. In 1836, when still no resident priest had been appointed, John Smith, elder brother of the recently-deceased vicar apostolic, and son of the mission's founder, asked that William Fletcher at Esh be moved to Brooms and serve Esh Laude on a supply basis (that is, to reverse the existing arrangements). Fletcher did not want to move and suggested instead that Smith petition for a resident priest at each place since it was almost impossible for one person to give 'the attention necessary to so wide a District'. Apart from Smith's keen personal desire to have a priest living in the mission-house which his father had taken such pains to provide, there were other considerations, much the most important of which was the increase in the population due to industrial development in the Derwent valley.[36] Smith outlined the situation at the mission in Brooms in letter which is worth quoting at length as an illustration of the problems facing the mission in the expansionary period after Emancipation.

> Mr Fletcher had begun in December 1834 a fortnight Sunday school here which appeared to be doing good. Since then the numbers have increased and on Mr F's last Sunday here I counted 54 children come from the [Communion] rails. From 12 to 13 was the normal number. One third at least of the 54 are children of protestant parents, many of

whom have not once been in Chapel themselves yet voluntarily send and seem quite pleased that Mr F should teach their children. From that, the Railroad and a new Colliery beginning at Medomsley, the chapel is generally filled and sometimes too crowded so that more room (probably a Gallery) must be provided. Dr. Briggs spent a day with me last week when I stated the above adding that our case was most extraordinary for whilst the numbers in the great towns were increasing prodigiously, the county congregations had been on the decrease ['in these two counties' deleted] although by the deaths, removals and falling off in fervour of many of our old C. families we were threatened with the fate of our neighbours till all on a sudden this singular and unlooked for change took place. I concluded by saying that if he cd. conveniently spare a priest it wd. be well, as the two were rather much for 1 priest. Dr. B appeared to listen without saying more than that Mr F had told him part: but that he had had petitions for priests from 5 new places and 2 or 3 old ones were to be filled: that he was afraid that neither place had sufficient funds to support a priest and we made out that Brooms at present had £64.8.6 and Esh £58.16.4. neither of which were sufficient.[37]

Smith decided to try other tactics. He wrote to Briggs pointing out that if action was not taken and the congregation at Brooms did fall, then no priest would be appointed anyway. He would not bequeath money to maintain 'a Pastor where there is no Flock' and he would be forced to move to the vicinity of another chapel. He wrote again a little later to tell the bishop that the chapel had again been completely filled on Sunday and to make explicit an earlier hint about his support of the mission. Smith wanted to alter his will in favour of 'this mission as well as a little for the College', but he would not do so until a resident priest was appointed to Brooms. 'The uncertainty of life', he pointedly added, particularly at his age, made him very desirous of having the will 'amended and executed as soon as possible'. He kept up the pressure; in September 1836 Smith reminded the bishop that a new gallery had been erected and that the chapel had once again been filled to overflowing.[38]

Bishop Briggs informed Smith in December 1836 that he had hoped to appoint a priest to Brooms that Christmas, but the difficulty was the insufficiency of the Brooms fund. Smith's response was that the congregation at Esh was very much the same as it had been the last thirty years, consisting of 'old Catholic families', whilst Brooms, 'from a rather declining state has all on a sudden as to numbers in the Chapel, and particularly as to Children at the rails is increased'. He went on:

> it is becoming so fashionable to attend the Chapel that we are never without several of the neighbouring Protestants with all of whom as far as I can learn Mr Fletcher is in high favour. Indeed, his impressive manner of preaching and his clear and copious explication of the Catechism can hardly fail to edify and please them.

He did not say, however, whether they were prepared to contribute the additional funds to keep a priest at Brooms which was what the bishop was concerned about. Nonetheless Fletcher moved to Brooms in January 1837, though whether this was due to Smith's pestering, his promise of further endowments, or because it was desirable pastorally, is not clear. There were, however, resident priests at Brooms thereafter. John Smith altered his will that year to add twenty-five acres to his existing bequest of land, the rent of which was to be paid to the priest at Brooms. He died in 1839.[39]

The history of the mission at Brooms in the first half of the nineteenth century illustrates the difficulties faced by the Church in providing effective pastoral care. The adjacent missions of Esh Laude and Brooms, each with a new chapel, competed for scarce priests. Esh Laude was a settled farming community; the mission was established on land donated by the patron, a baronet, and he controlled the priest's stipend which was intended to finance that mission alone. It was given precedence over Brooms, an expanding working-class mission, notwithstanding that the patron was a brother of the late bishop. The bishop was in a difficult position; his reluctance to accede to Smith's request was partly due to the inflexibility of the financial arrangements as well as because of the lack of priests. But it is all the more difficult to understand given that a priest from Ushaw College could so easily have supplied at nearby Esh Laude, thus freeing the missioner to move to the more distant Brooms. Briggs did come to the right pastoral decision in the end, even if it looked as if Smith helped him to make up his mind with the promise of a further endowment.

It is worth recording a further attempt by a layman to influence the appointment of a priest to the mission at Brooms. In May 1841, George Silvertop called on Bishop Hogarth to urge the settlement of the mission on the Revd Thomas Danson, who had been chaplain at Minsteracres for seventeen years. The bishop was nettled by Silvertop who had said that he understood that

> the Brooms was vacant and as Mr Danson liked solitude and there was little or nothing to do at Brooms, he thought that would do. I told him that it was not vacant and that there was a great deal to do and that I thought we had no places that would do for Mr D.

Silvertop, Bishop Hogarth rightly concluded, had some 'strange notions of what a missionary should do'. The chapel at Brooms had to be extended in 1845 but the massive influx of people then attracted by the expanding coal and iron industries in the area required a much greater pastoral effort—Danson could not have coped; at any rate, he left for the south of England shortly afterwards.[40]

***

Francis Kearney became missioner at Brooms in 1849 and he took the next steps in the development of the mission in this locality. He bought land at **Blackhill** overlooking the Derwent valley, and in August 1854 the foundation stone of a church to his own designs was laid. But when the building was almost complete it was destroyed in a violent storm. A. M. Dunn, a professional architect, was engaged and the new church (St Mary's, 'cathedral-like' in its proportions) was opened in July 1857 by Bishop Hogarth; Cardinal Wiseman gave the inaugural sermon.[41]

***

Esh is a chapelry in the parish of Lanchester five miles west of the city of Durham. The manor had belonged to the Smythe family from the middle of the sixteenth century, when Margaret Esh married William Smythe of Nunstainton, and they had supported priests in the manor house. In 1651, shortly before his death, the elderly but determined recusant and royalist George Smythe granted a ninety-nine-year lease of sixteen acres at **Newhouse** in the Deerness valley below Esh Hall, so that a

> Pr. of ye Sec. Cler. of Eng. may for ye comfort of our Neigh. have a convenient lodging with provision for fire & meat for 1 horse and 2 kine in ye most convenient place for ye purpose…

and a chapel with a priest's house were built. The priest was also provided with a stipend of £10 a year, which, if he got nothing else, hardly seems sufficient, given that this mission-station covered the whole of the western part of the county.

The heir, Edward Smythe, was aged 26 when he was created a baronet at the Restoration in 1660. In 1687 he rebuilt the mansion and provided a domestic chapel on the upper floor; a priest-hole was discovered when the house was demolished in 1857. The

Catholic community survived the Revolution and John Simpson (*vere* John Torbett), ordained at the English College, Valladolid, came to Newhouse around 1697, the first named priest known to be there. Edward died in 1714 and Smythes were not involved in the 'Fifteen although it appears that Simpson went abroad for a while. The Smythes moved to Acton Burnell in Shropshire, an estate acquired through marriage. The family retained possession of their ancestral Durham estates, however, and maintained the Newhouse mission, through their Durham agent. (This was one of the very few missions in the region to remain free of interference from the patron, but, of course, that was only because he was an absentee landlord.)[42]

At his death in 1727, Simpson left £550 to the mission and money to increase the priest's stipend to £30. The 50-year-old Hartlepool-born Ferdinand Ashmall was appointed and at the same time Sir Edward renewed the lease

> of that dwelling house with the garden etc called or known by the name of Newhouse, together with a close or parcel of ground there, now divided into two fields commonly known as the Priest's Field with common right upon the moor or common called Moor Gate Moor for one Horse and Two cows. All which premises are situate in the Chapelry of Esh and now in the possession or occupation of Ferdinand Ashmall, Gent. together with one Annuity or Rent charge of Fifteen Pounds a year... to have and to hold them for 99 years from the first day of May next, [1745] ensuing and paying Sir Edward Smythe his heirs and assigns the rent of Forty Shillings.

At that time Ashmall had some one hundred Catholics in his care. Of the sixty-six families living in Esh in 1792, twenty-seven were Catholic. Ashmall was then ninety-seven years old and he had to be assisted by fellow-priests in the locality; John Yates lived in with him from 1795. The latter found the chapel in a ruinous condition but he could not persuade the old priest to do anything about it. Nor could Thomas Eyre, who told the bishop he had endeavoured to persuade Ashmall

> to remove but with doubtful success. Have however stopt Mr Shepherd's grounds of complaint respecting the chapel, which indeed is falling in so much that it appears very dangerous to be in it. We have about forty of a ninety nine years lease to come. Sir Ed. Smith allows besides about £13 p. ann. also perhaps ten or twelve acres of ground, so we cannot expect him to do much and how to raise money for such a building I know not, it cannot be repaired it must be entirely new built. The buttresses as well as timber seem all to have failed. Yet forty years is not a term to induce us to build upon. I can not have a good heart about this as I have about Stella and Pontop which both will be very snug and comfortable.

Doubtless Eyre discussed the problem with Sir Edward and Mr. Taylor, the estate manager, but everyone realised that little could be done until the old priest died, which he did in 1798.[43]

Sir Edward Smythe had already thought of moving the mission up the hill, where there would be 'a chapel and house ... on a more permanent footing, with a view to its becoming a fixed incumbency for a clergyman.' and he immediately offered to exchange the dilapidated property at Newhouse for Salutation Field on the fell top west of the village of Esh. The vicar apostolic promptly agreed. The location came to be known as **Esh Laude.** A new chapel dedicated to St Michael (the same as that of the pre-Reformation church at Esh) was opened on 1 January 1799. The chapel, 'a neat edifice, plain and simple in its appearance without any pretensions to grandeur and magnificence, and suits well with the nature of the congregation', had no external ecclesiastical features. The domestic buildings (a Gothick cottage, a coach-house and a stable block) date from 1804. The whole was designed to give the impression of a farm-house with the usual outbuildings: the more obvious churchly feature of an apse was not added until 1850.[44]

According to the visitation return of 1810 'about two thirds of the 276 inhabitants of the chapelry' of Esh were reputed Papists, which was a marked increase on the number in 1792. A new school was opened in 1814 to supersede a dame school in existence from at least 1767; it was also endowed by the Smythes, and Lady Smythe was patroness. Because no priest was available, the missioner supplied at Brooms for over fifteen years from 1819, making this appointment one of the most demanding in the region; the number of communicants at Esh Laude alone around this time was one hundred and twenty. In 1832, the *Catholic Magazine* said that, in addition to Brooms, the missioner at Esh Laude also had in his district

> the town of Wolsingham, eight miles in an opposite direction, and so on, if need be, to the confines of Westmorland and Cumberland. On the south, to Witton le Wear, &c.

Fletcher was 'constantly on the move attending sick persons at Wolsingham and Pontop'. His life was not made any easier in 1835, as John Smith explained:

> Poor Mr Fletcher has unexpectedly got into an unpleasant business. For many years our neighbouring parsons have been most quiet and friendly with Catholics, but a few months ago a Mr. Chevallier was presented to the Incumbency of Esh and is quite an Ultra-Zealot which he has shown [in] different ways.

The Revd Temple Chevallier's presentation to the Curacy of Esh was coincident with his appointment as first Professor of Mathematics and Astronomy in the University of Durham, of which he was also Registrar. Soon after his arrival in Esh he reported to Bishop van Mildert that he had been much put out at having found a flourishing Catholic community: the principal land-owners were Catholics; of the population of the chapelry, two hundred and fifty-five were Protestants and three hundred and seventy-seven were Catholics, and half of the latter were in residence at Ushaw College; there was a chapel to which a school was attached. It was essential, Chevallier advised his diocesan, 'that this growing and permanent influence should be counteracted as much as possible'. He did two things; firstly, he became resident in the chapelry. Because there was no church property, however, he had to rent Flass Hall which belonged, as it happened, to Lady Jane Peat, a Catholic. The bishop had to raise the income of the curacy by £100 a year to allow Chevallier to build or buy a glebe house. Secondly, Smith said, Chevallier opened

> a school in opposition to Sir Edward's and solicited scholars and subscriptions all over the neighbourhood in which he has been so successful as to take away all the Protestants from the Mistress and threatens to take off by his Master some of the more advanced children. Mr F. thought he might not submit without some attempt to oppose his career and instead of the Mistress has engaged a superior Catholic Master from Sedgefield. How this Master's £50 a year is to be made up (as Sir Edward's to the Mistress is only £20) is not yet known.[45]

The outcome of the rivalry does not appear, but doubtless the Smythes came to the rescue. There were two hundred and seventy-eight Catholics in Esh in 1851.

***

Croxdale Hall, the ancestral seat of the Salvin family, lies in a chapelry in the parish of St Oswald, Durham. The house has Tudor origins and was altered in the mid-seventeenth century to include 'a chapel chamber'. Like many other northern gentry (Catholic and Protestant) the Salvins rebuilt their mansion in the latter half of the eighteenth century. Work began around 1758 but the internal furnishings were not completed until the end of the century. In 1807 the chapel was redesigned by Ignatius Bonomi in a 'thinly Gothic' style. In 1823 Surtees remarked of the house: 'Without the least attempt at display, everything wears the quiet air of ancient possession. The house is hospitably plain and spacious…'

Priests were resident from the reign of James II, and they also served Tudhoe and Sunderland Bridge. William Errington was missioner for some forty years until his death in 1733 and he was 'particularly zealous and indefatigable in paying weekly visits to the three villages under his care, preaching, exhorting, instructing, and visiting the sick, etc.' For much of the eighteenth century there were two priests in the locality: the chaplain for Croxdale Hall, and a missioner for Tudhoe. The 'Croxdale Fund' was made up by bequests from the Revd William Errington (£500), Frances Kennett (£100), Lady Maria Radcliffe (£100) and Catherine Salvin, who died in 1754 (£100), enough to support both priests, and it seems that they lived in Tudhoe Hall.

The priests were therefore largely independent of the Salvins domestically and financially but they were, nonetheless, subject to the patron's over-riding control. Thomas Talbot, a 25-year-old newly-ordained priest went to Croxdale straight from the *Venerabile* in Rome in 1762. But in 1771,

> some differences taking place between him and the late Wm. Salvin Esqr he was sent to Marton near Burton Constable. At the request of Wm. Salvin the Rt Rev Bishop Petre … appointed Rev. Arthur Storey

in his place. The cause of the dispute is not known but the ease with which Salvin got rid of a priest is another example of how powerful a lay patron could be. The Catholics of Croxdale would only get missioners of whom their landlord approved, and there would be no mutiny as there had been at Stella ten years earlier in similar circumstances.[46]

In 1767 the congregation in Tudhoe numbered seventy and there was about the same number in Croxdale. The latter was headed by William Salvin, his wife and five children, and ten household servants. Some in the Croxdale congregation were more exuberant than many of their co-religionists. The Anglican curate complained in 1774 that the Catholics often rang a hand-bell when they left their chapel on Sunday mornings 'as if in defiance'. In 1792, during the rebuilding of Croxdale Hall, the curate noted that

> the chapel in Mr. Salvin's house which used to be resorted to by a numerous congregation ... is now shut up and I am informed it is confined to the occasional use of the family alone; which family upon Sundays generally resort to the Popish chapel at Tudhoe or at Durham. There is no Popish Priest at Croxdale but Mr. Arthur Storey occasionally attends from Tudhoe who keeps a Popish School in that village, but I do not find any Protestant children are admitted.

There was, in fact, an exiled French priest in Croxdale Hall around the end of the century, and he seems to have taken care of the Salvins' pastoral needs while Storey concentrated on his school.

In 1778 (after the first Catholic Relief Act) Storey had taken a large house in Tudhoe belonging to the Catholic Lawsons of Brough in the North Riding, in which he opened a preparatory boarding school, which he named Tudhoe Academy, for boys aged eight to fourteen. The venture was not viewed optimistically by some of his fellow-priests who felt that he could not manage both a school and a mission at the same time. An assistant priest-schoolmaster was appointed, however, and the Academy provided a valuable service to the gentry who were able to keep their children in England before they were old enough to be sent abroad to complete their education. Storey was a Latinist and his Academy offered, at £22 a year, a wide classical education with particular attention being paid to 'morals, behaviour and mental improvement'. Dancing was two guineas a year extra. In March 1794 six of the students expelled from Douai arrived at Tudhoe pending their resettlement in a new seminary. At one point the Academy was considered for that role, being 'for cheapness of fuel and provisions, healthiness of climate and other considerations ... an eligible situation', and in June 'zealous and opulent members' of the Catholic body were invited to subscribe the necessary funds. But nothing came of it and the students moved out to Crook Hall in October.

In 1807 Storey wrote, 'For many years I have been employed in the arduous important task of educating our Catholic youth. I rather wish now to retire to more easy employment'. Ushaw College opened the following year and Tudhoe Academy became redundant. In May 1808, therefore, it and the mission were closed. The Salvins' chaplain 'succeeded to the charge of Tudhoe Congregation which was once more allowed to go to Croxdale Chapel'. Storey lived in extreme poverty in his retirement and he died at Thirsk in July 1825 aged 82.[47]

The visitation return of 1801 showed the Croxdale Catholics to be more discreet than before, for they did not 'in any degree interfere with the members of the regular church'. Thomas Smith came as missioner in 1802 and he lived temporarily in Croxdale Hall officiating in the chapel which was reopened for public use in 1807, just as Storey was thinking of leaving Tudhoe. The *Catholic Magazine* of 1832 described the situation at Croxdale as it had been for several years, and as it would remain until the 1850s. The chaplain had 'a wide tract of country' over which the one hundred and eighty communicants were scattered:

The large and populous places of Sedgefield, Bishop Middleham, Bishop Auckland, &c. are within the range of his pious labours, and his frequent attendance at those places, situated nine or ten miles apart and from his residence, makes this mission no sinecure. He does not reside in the Hall, but in the village of Sunderland Bridge, about a third of a mile distant. The house stands pleasantly situated at the east end of the village, possessing an excellent garden and orchard, and about seven acres of land.

***

In 1752 the Durham Jesuit Thomas Waterton recorded 'for assisting at **Bishop Auckland** £2.2s. and a guinea. Mrs Durham [the Jesuit district] pays [the rent] for my shop [chapel] there'. In 1767 around thirty Catholics lived in the area and they assembled for Mass in the house of Lancelot Bradford, a tailor, but the congregation was in decline: it had halved by 1780 and, although priests continued to attend, it was on the point of extinction. Several expatriate religious communities had been assured by the Dukes of Cambridge and York, then serving in the army, that in the event of their expulsion from France they would be welcomed back to England. In 1794, a community of Discalced Carmelites (founded in 1648 at Lierre in Brabant) fled as the French advanced. Their *Annals* recorded their flight:

> On 2nd July we proceeded to Breda and thence to Rotterdam. Here we beheld a moving sight: several different communities, all on their way to England, among them the Carmelite community of Antwerp. On the 4th we took shipping to England.

The group of twenty-three nuns stayed for nine weeks in the London house of Charles Butler, at his expense, before moving north. They were received en route at the Bar Convent and were put up by Sir John Lawson at Brough Hall for two weeks until St

Helen Auckland Hall was readied for them. The Jacobean house had been rented from the Carr family by Sir John as a college for the students of Douai College, but Bishop Gibson's irresolution about accepting it for that purpose 'so disgusted Sir John that he made a tender of the house to the Lierre Nuns who were glad to accept of it and are now established to their great satisfaction'. Presumably, their chaplain, James Roby, ministered to the few Catholics of the town.

The nuns attracted a great deal of sympathy and support. In June 1802 Benedict Rayment, chaplain at Lartington, wrote to Giuseppe Bonomi (father of Ignatius):

> I am going tomorrow to preach at your acquaintances the good ladies of St Helen's Auckland for the glorious feast of the sacred heart. I have heard them speak in raptures of you'.

Quite why they thought so highly of him is unknown, but it shows how widely the community was known. Even the vehemently anti-Catholic Bishop of Durham, Shute Barrington, gave them alms. When the community left the town he insisted on their driving through his grounds, a privilege he reserved for his friends, he said, among whom he counted the nuns.[48]

The Carmelites moved to Cocken Hall in 1804 leaving the handful of Catholics in Bishop Auckland without a resident pastor. (Three exiled French priests lived in the town from 1796 to 1802 but they confined themselves to 'their own private devotions' and do not seem to have attended the local Catholics.) Edward Walsh, the Jesuit in Durham, then aged 65, was unable to resume the supply mission so the missioner at Croxdale took it on. Otherwise the people would travel the seven miles to Croxdale for Mass. The residential mission in these parts of the county therefore lapsed and it was some forty years before it was resumed.[49]

New coal-mines were sunk in south-west Durham from 1825 and the Stockton and Darlington Railway was extended north towards Bishop Auckland to carry coal down to the Tees. The industrialisation of the area led to an increase in the population but it was not until 1840 that the missioner in Darlington began to visit the town. William Hogarth went on Sunday afternoons to recite Vespers and to give instruction to a small group who at first gathered in the house of Mrs Elizabeth Newton, and then, as numbers increased, in a room of the Shepherd's Inn, Fore Bondgate. In 1841 Thomas Peacock lent a room in the same street, free of charge, and Hogarth began to say Mass there. A permanent mission was required, of course, and Luke Curry was appointed in 1842; but he left within the year and James Gibson took over. He immediately issued an appeal in the *Catholic Directory* for donations to establish the new mission:

> In consequence of the numerous coal mines opened in the neighbourhood, and the establishment of several public works, the influx of population has been very great, and many of the new residents are Catholics. These, with the Catholics who for years have been scattered among the villagers of the mining district, amount to not less than 400 souls ... There is no provision for the priest, except what may arise from the contributions of these poor people.

Sufficient money having been collected by 1845, Gibson bought land from Peacock and the foundation-stone of a church was laid by the bishop. St Wilfrid's, in the Early English style by Thomas Gibson of Newcastle, costing £1,000 and designed to seat three hundred people, was opened 'with unusual pomp and ceremony' by Bishop Riddell in 1846. The industrial development which had led to the rapid increase in the Catholic population of Bishop Auckland was paralleled elsewhere in west Durham. Missions were established in Wolsingham, Crook and Tow Law around mid-century to serve the large number of Irish immigrants attracted to the new ironworks and coal mines of the area.[50]

***

Francis Maire married Anne Clavering in 1726 and they went to live in **Hardwick Hall** which had belonged to the family since 1587. Since there was a hide in the house and a cave accessed through an underground passage, priests were probably in residence from Elizabethan times. Henry Allan, who had been a riding-missioner in the locality for some time, became resident chaplain to the Maires. Except for a seven-year period in which the secular priest Nicholas Clavering, nephew of the patroness, was chaplain, Jesuit priests served at the Hall continuously from 1743 and received a salary of £10 a year as well as board and lodging. The congregation came from the coastal villages north of Hartlepool and in 1750 numbered 'about 53 that have learnt trade', (that is, adults). The Hardwick estate, as well as that of Hutton Henry, a village about midway between Stockton and Sunderland, came into the possession of Catherine Silvertop-Maire in 1811, but she had to sell both properties to clear the debts of her son, Henry Thomas Witham. He was born a Silvertop but changed his surname at his marriage. In addition to Hardwick, Witham inherited his mother's estate at Lartington and he also held the estate of Cliffe Hall through marriage. At the turn of the century, then, in addition to several small properties, Witham possessed three major Catholic estates, each having a longstanding chaplaincy.[51]

Witham was thriftless, not because he spent lavishly, but because he was a gambler. His great-grandson put it well when he said, 'That Harry Witham did not keep racehorses seems not to have prevented him from losing large sums on the turf'. On one occasion, it seems, Witham arranged a ball at Lartington Hall to celebrate the anticipated win of *Doctor Syntax*, a well known racehorse owned by the Catholic Ralph Riddell of Felton Park, which would restore his shattered fortunes. News arrived, however, that the horse had lost; the dance was cancelled and Witham fled to Scotland to escape his creditors. He spent the next six years in Edinburgh pursuing his other, less extravagant, interest in fossils and geology. Nonetheless, his financial difficulties could only be rectified by the sale of real estate. His mother agreed to the disposal of the Hardwick estate, which went to the Earl of Darlington in 1819. Within a year, Darlington had cut enough timber to recoup his capital outlay. The estate, moreover, shortly began to yield a fabulous quantity of coal.[52]

Disastrous as that sale was for the family, it was almost as bad for the mission. Darlington permitted the chapel in Hardwick Hall to remain in use for the time being but notice to quit was eventually served to take effect on Mayday 1824. Thomas Slater, the secular priest who had been there since January 1822 assisting the 80-year-old Jesuit Christopher Rose, wrote to George Silvertop, trustee of the mission, asking for his help in its relocation. The letter was returned unopened (Silvertop was hardly ever at Minsteracres at this time, involved as he was in the campaign for Catholic Emancipation) and Slater gave vent to his frustration and anxiety of the moment:

> The Mission had been at Hardwick from time immemorial and Harry Witham's extravagances forced him to sell it to Lord Darlington. George Silvertop, Harry's brother had the management. No provision was made to continue the Mission and if I had not come forward with my private means, this Mission had been lost ... Hy Witham and Silvertop did nothing. Ld. Darlington sold me the moiety at the same price he gave for it 11 acres more or less. Thus proving that Harry Witham and George Silvertop had less feeling than the heretic Ld. Darlington who always and after when [Duke of] Cleveland, showed his goodness to me in the H[artle]pool Chapel. Give me such as Ld. Cleveland before 10,000 of your H. Withams and Geo. Silvertops although they professed themselves Catholics and the duke was what was called a Heretic.

In a postscript Slater lamented how foolish he had been to write to Silvertop.[53]

Lord Darlington allowed Slater to remain at Hardwick until a new house and chapel could be built at **Hutton Henry**. Slater recorded that he 'In 1824, built the Chapel and Residence at Hutton House and removed to it the 5th day of April 1825'. (Rose had retired to the Jesuit house in Durham.) The chapel, dedicated to Ss. Peter and Paul, was 'a brick building, finished in the interior in a neat Gothic style'. It was, as Sir Henry Lawson observed, 'in a tolerably central situation' for the congregation of about eighty communicants. It was also advertised as convenient for visitors to the watering places of Hartlepool, Seaton and Carewe.[54] The *Catholic Magazine* noted in 1832 that

> the large and increasing villages of Easington &c. to the north will, on account of the advancing coal works in that direction, soon become very populous, and afford additional numbers to the congregation.

***

From the middle of the eighteenth century the mission at Hardwick Hall included **Hartlepool** ten miles away on the coast. Amerston Hall nearby had long been the residence of the Ashmall family, and in 1743 Mrs Ashmall supported a priest: 'her son, who goes to Owton in the parish of Greatham, to say Mass at a farmer's house which belongs to Mr Salvin'. That was Ferdinando Ashmall the last of the family. When he became missioner at Esh in 1745 his trustees sold the Amerston Hall estate in 1762 for £1,330. In 1767 the chaplain at Hardwick Hall attended sixty-seven Catholics in the Hartlepool area in 1767 and sixty in 1780. A house-chapel was registered in 1791 but the congregation was in slow decline: in 1831 there were only twenty Catholics in a population of 1,330. The staff and students of Ushaw College spent part of their summer holidays in Hartlepool in the 1820s, to take the 'sea-bathing cure', and Mass was said in their hotel. Similarly, priests who accompanied 'R. Catholic families during the Bathing season' said Mass in the town.[55] A small chapel dedicated to St Hilda was opened in January 1834. A stone over the doorway declared

> This building was erected by John Wells and presented to the Roman Catholics for the use of their religious exercises at the request of Mary, his wife, A.D. 1834.

Wells was not a Catholic, and it was only because of his devotion to his wife, that Hartlepool had a chapel at all at this time. His use of the term 'presented' was ambiguous, however, for in April 1838 Thomas Slater told Bishop Briggs that '£250 was paid to John Wells in consideration of all claims he might have upon the chapel, land, house, etc. in Hartlepool'. Presumably, then, Wells had retained some rights to the ownership of the property but had lost interest in it now that his wife was dead.

The 25-year-old Lancastrian William Knight went to Hartlepool in 1834 within a year of his ordination at the English College in Lisbon, and he would remain there as missioner for the whole forty years of his priestly life. His income was partly secured by a bequest of the Revd William Coghlan, who left £400 in 1836 to the missioner in Hartlepool, provided he was a secular priest. Nonetheless, the mission was extremely poor; the furnishings of the house were listed as '8 chairs, 1 clock, 1 table, 2 blankets'. There were no wealthy patrons, as the *Catholic Directory* was careful to make clear:

> Hartlepool, Rev. Wm. Knight. Divine Service 10.30 on Sundays and 10 on holy days; afternoon service at 3.0.
>
> N.B. There will be several sittings kept for the accommodation of those who frequent this and the neighbouring watering places, and it is hoped that those who occupy them will not forget the necessities of this new mission.

A small school was provided in 1837 by a lay benefactor. At first, twenty pupils were instructed by one teacher but two years later a young woman was employed to teach the girls separately. On the occasion of Bishop Briggs's visitation in 1839 Knight reported that forty-six children attended his catechism class of whom twelve were not Catholics; the school was attended by one hundred and twenty-three pupils. The bishop confirmed thirty-four adults and twelve children.[56]

The congregation grew rapidly to fifteen hundred by 1851, largely as a result of an 'influx of Irish workmen and others connected with the improvements' in the railways (1834) and the docks (1847). A new church was required and, although the profit made on the sale of a plot of land was substantial, the balance had to be made up from the weekly contributions of the congregation. The church, dedicated to St Mary, by J. A. Hansom and costing £4,000 was opened in August 1851 by Bishop Hogarth in the presence of Cardinal Wiseman. This was the latter's first engagement in the north as cardinal, and he was nervous at appearing in the Anglican diocese of Bishop Edward Maltby who had done so much to fan the No-Popery agitation when the Catholic hierarchy was restored the year before. Wiseman wrote to Knight about his visit:

> I should wish it to be as little known as possible: if you can have me met at the station as quickly as possible, & conducted to my place of abode, I shall be glad. I have heard that great excitement prevails at H. as yet; and many have advised my not going; I trust therefore that on our side nothing will be done to attract attention beyond what our business requires.[57]

The visit passed without incident and Wiseman left for Ushaw unembarrassed by the attentions of any except perhaps those of the Catholics themselves. (St Mary's was the first Catholic church in the north of England to have a peal of bells, and they were first rung to welcome the cardinal.)

***

For over a century a group of some forty Catholics in **Sedgefield** were visited occasionally by the missioners of Stockton or Croxdale. In 1792 Mass was celebrated 'about five or six times in the year in a private house in the town (belonging to one Rowntree)'. Rowntrees were listed in the 1767 Papist Return. Such was the situation for fifty years, until, that is, the opening of the coalfield in east Durham. In 1839 the Revd T. S. Irving was appointed resident missioner and he built a chapel dedicated to St Joseph but it rapidly became evident that it would not suffice. **Thornley** was a village a few miles to the north of Sedgefield with some fifty inhabitants in 1831. A colliery was opened in 1835 and the population rose to almost two thousand seven hundred and fifty by 1841; the Catholics among them attended Mass at Sedgefield. In 1850 the missioner opened a chapel 'of very plain character' which had previously been a dissenting chapel in Thornley and dedicated it to St Godric. The *Catholic Directory* of 1851 informed its readers that the priest in Sedgefield 'resides alternate weeks here and at Thornley'. A school was attached by 1854 and the congregation, which numbered one hundred and fifty in 1852 almost quadrupled by 1855.[58]

***

South Durham was the slowest part of the county to develop a settled missionary structure and the Catholics were poorly provided for in the eighteenth century. This was partly because few of the local Catholic gentry families had survived, hence there were no chaplaincies on the north side of the Tees. The Jenisons of Walworth Castle, the Ashmalls of Amerston Hall, the Withams of Preston upon Tees, the Cloptons of Sledwich Hall had either died out or moved away by mid-century. Sledwich became a Witham residence but the family moved to Cliffe Hall in 1703. Westholme at Winston, as well as Low Dinsdale Manor, home of the Surtees family, had also long since passed from Catholic ownership. For much of the eighteenth century, then, the Catholics of south Durham had to be served from four chaplaincies in the North Riding: Cliffe Hall[59], Lartington Hall, Wycliffe Hall and The Friarage, Yarm, (fore-runners of the missions in Barnard Castle, Darlington, Gainford and Stockton). Moreover, the financial foundations of the missions at Stockton and Darlington were provided by three Yorkshire priests, each of whom left £400 for the purpose.[60]

The Wapentake of Gilling West held the largest number of Catholics in the North Riding and the focus of recusancy was **Wycliffe Hall**, home of the Tunstall family, south of the Tees below Whorlton. The domestic chapel, which was rebuilt in 1748, served a sizeable congregation of Durham Catholics until the middle of the nineteenth century.[61] The Revd Anthony Metham, who was at Wycliffe for a time, died in 1694 leaving a legacy to the mission which was applied by the vicar apostolic James Smith to fund a priest in **Stockton**. In 1695 the Revd Marmaduke Dalton bequeathed £400 for the support of a priest to serve the 'poor Catholics in the area of West Pits and the south side of the Bishopric' By 1740, both funds had depreciated substantially and were amalgamated to yield £27 a year, but the recipient had to look after Darlington as well as Stockton.

The first beneficiaries of the fund lived in the manor house of Preston upon Tees, which had been seized in the 1650s as the home of one of the Sayer family, 'a papist delinquent'. The estate came into the possession of the Withams of Cliffe in 1673 but it was sold in 1723 by William Witham to Sir John Eden of Windlestone and the priest moved to Stockton. The priest probably lived either in a rented house (perhaps in Playhouse Yard) or in the home of one of the twelve property-owning Catholic inhabitants listed in 1723 among whom were the late owners of Preston, Catharine Witham, a widow, and her son William. Acting also as a riding-missioner and in conjunction with the chaplain at Hardwick Hall, the priest attended small groups of Catholics in Billingham, Greatham and elsewhere in south-east Durham. He was also committed to saying a monthly Mass in Darlington, and it is likely that he served the fifty Catholics in Yarm, where he could well have been resident for part of the time.

In 1743, Mrs Elizabeth Grainge, the convert widow of a Stockton brewer and maltster, entered into a bond with the vicar apostolic to give the mission £200 to supplement the Metham fund. The priest was to say Mass in Stockton every Monday, Wednesday and Friday, all holydays, and three Sundays in the month. There were some fifty Catholics in the town when the newly-ordained John Hawarden arrived in 1754 to take over this well-endowed mission. The children of Mrs Grainge, left the church, however, and stopped paying the interest on her bond. Although attempts were made to get them to honour it, the bond was effectively rescinded by 1763.

In 1767 there were sixty-three Catholics in Stockton, with their priest Robert Jackson. Although the congregation was in decline, John Daniel, missioner from 1783, began to collect funds for a new chapel to replace the century-old premises in a back alley close to the quay and the Playhouse theatre: 'in a most inconvenient part of the town, the approach to which was awkward and disagreeable'. Notwithstanding the disreputable locality, the new chapel, 'a plain brick building', was built on the same site and was opened and registered in 1791. An exiled French priest was in Stockton at the end of the century, and he gained the approbation of the mayor, as a teacher of French and for his publication of a French-English dictionary. Thomas Storey, nephew of Arthur, was missioner from 1803; he opened a preparatory school for five or six young gentlemen aged from seven to ten years, at fifty guineas a year. The school was advertised regularly in the *Catholic Directory* and was, no doubt, Storey's principal means of support for in 1810 there were only ten Catholics in Stockton 'composed chiefly of inferior persons'.[62]

Stockton was in the forefront of railway development in the 1820s, and the Catholic population began to increase. There were seventy, mostly 'mechanics &c.' in 1832 and numbers grew to two hundred and fifty within the next four years. The chapel was extended 'as funds would not yet allow for the erection of a more commodious place of worship' but it was shortly decided to 'build a new chapel and residence in a more appropriate situation'. Joseph Dugdale, missioner from 1830, began to collect money but it was slow to come in from the impoverished but still expanding congregation. It was clear that a new church had become essential and the foundations of St Mary's, designed by A. W. Pugin in the Early English style, were laid in May 1841. The church was only partially completed and not fully to design, when it was opened in the summer of the following year by Bishop Mostyn; the need for larger premises had outweighed any aesthetic considerations. Pugin's design would never be fully realised.

From around 1838 Dugdale began to visit Middlesbrough which was a newly-emergent industrial town with a small Catholic community. A resident priest was appointed in 1841 and the supply mission from Stockton was discontinued. In 1851 it was reported that five hundred Catholics lived in the town.[63]

***

For many years **Yarm** was the principal port on the river Tees. The Dominican Friarage at Yarm had come into the possession of the wealthy merchant Nicholas Mayes on his marriage to Cecily Sayer in 1620. The Mayes were Lords of the Manor thereafter and remained Catholic, which accounts for the relatively large number of fifty Catholics living there at the beginning of the eighteenth century. A visitation return of 1735 by Henry Bradley, the Anglican curate reported that

> There is a reputed Popish priest who constantly resides in Mr Maye's family, his name is ... Syddal [Charles, *vere* Hodgkinson]. Mr Maye's house is the place of resort where great numbers of Papists assemble every Sunday, and there Mass is understood to be perform'd. There hath been a visitation, and Confirmation suspected to have been held (as well as I can remember) about 5 or 6 years ago by a Popish Bishop. There is no Popish school within this parish that I ever heard of. There have been two persons (within these 10 years) perverted to the Popish religion, the one a youth John Coulson, about the age of 21, the other a widow Mary Harperley, about the age of 60—but by whom I know not.

Lawrence Mayes (1673–1749), younger brother of Nicholas, spent much of his priestly life in Rome as Agent of the English vicars apostolic. John Mayes (1670–1742), the elder son, entered the legal profession: his tombstone in churchyard at Yarm describes him as 'a prominent Roman Catholic counsel'. He married Mary Meynell of North Kilvington and the estate passed to the Meynells at her death in 1770. In 1767 there were one hundred and eight Catholics in Yarm. Edward Meynell had built a new mansion by 1775, to which a chapel was added in 1795. Jesuits served as chaplains for much of the period: Charles Hodgkinson (alias Siddle), Thomas Nandyke, and Thomas Meynell.[64] The seculars took over following the death of Meynell. in 1804. The return in 1851 gave the Catholic population as one hundred and fifty.

***

Cliffe Hall, south of the Tees near Piercebridge, had been a Witham chaplaincy since the reign of Charles II. The small Catholic communities in Darlington, Gainford and Piercebridge as well as a large swathe of north Yorkshire were served from Cliffe. Late in the eighteenth century, however, the chaplaincy began to develop symptoms of the tensions between priest and patron which occurred elsewhere. In December 1775 Bishop Walton feared that the Withams did not intend to take another chaplain after the death of Henry Maire; even then, as he had already calculated, 'unless they make a better allowance and more regular payments, there does not appear to be a sufficiency for an incumbent to subsist upon'. John Billington went there as chaplain in 1784 but he took some time to settle down; two years later it was said that he 'was in good spirits and at last reconciled to his situation and it to him'. In 1789, however, it was feared that Billington would 'not long be able to do the duty of a missioner: he is indeed very pious ... but so troubled with scruples as to be almost unfit for any of his Ecclesl. functions'. He stayed three more years, but then he became 'incapax and so quit Cliffe'. Another young priest, William Coghlan, son of the Catholic publisher, went to Cliffe Hall in 1792 but he had resigned by 1804 since, as Henry Rutter remarked, he did 'not seem calculated to live in a Gentleman's family'. Coghlan moved into Darlington for a short time but he returned to Cliffe for a few months before finally leaving for Scarborough. Between 1766 and 1811 there were eight chaplains at Cliffe Hall and the congregation fell by two thirds over the same period. The closure of the chaplaincy, however, did not come about as a result of clerical dissatisfaction. The Cliffe estate was sold because, as the *Catholic Magazine* coyly put it, 'untoward circumstances alienated it from its late inheritor' Henry Witham. As we have seen, the circumstances were hardly untoward. At any rate, William Hogarth, who had been chaplain since 1816, removed to Darlington in 1824.[65]

***

As a Quaker and non-industrial town, it is not surprising that of the several major centres of population in the county, **Darlington** had fewest Catholic inhabitants. In 1726 the Revd Francis Hodgson left a bequest of £20 a year to support a priest in Darlington and the surrounding locality although it would be many years before a resident priest could be appointed; meanwhile a supply-mission was maintained from Stockton, Durham or Tudhoe. There were sixteen Catholics in Darlington in 1705, twenty-one in 1743 and eighty-four in 1767; they were said to comprise ten families in 1774. That slight but encouraging rise in the population went into reverse thereafter; there were forty-three in 1780 and there were 'not more than 40' in 1814. The Ridsdales, a family of craftsmen, seem to have led this community throughout the century and Mass was celebrated monthly in their house by the missioner of Stockton. In 1786, despite the small congregation and the infrequency of Mass, it was decided to acquire an independent property for the mission and two adjoining houses in Bondgate were bought for £110 from a Quaker banker and a chapel was created. For some time after 1792 the Ridsdales supported a French exiled priest, Pierre Tassou. It seems that the optimism was justified, for over the next fifteen years the congregation was swollen by Catholics in outlying villages and the accommodation became increasingly inadequate. In 1805 the missioner, Thomas Storey, borrowed £300 from the vicariate to buy a plot of land behind Ridsdale's house to build a new chapel to accommodate a congregation of around one hundred and fifty drawn from the town and district. Notwithstanding its rapid transition to independence, however, the mission remained under the care of the Stockton priest and it only became a residential misson in its own right as a result of the closure of the chaplaincy in Cliffe Hall which occurred shortly after the death of Storey in 1822.[66]

William Hogarth, erstwhile chaplain at Cliffe, moved into Ridsdale's house next to the new chapel in 1824 to become the first 'Incumbent of the United Congregations of Cliffe and Darlington' only to find that the mission was effectively bankrupt. Nonetheless, the energetic 37-year-old priest immediately launched an appeal for donations towards the cost of replacing the old chapel which was

> much too small, being incapable of accommodating more than one hundred and fifty persons, while the united congregations will amount to upwards of four hundred. It is the more necessary that a chapel should be erected on a scale proportioned to the numbers of Catholics, because the maintenance of the Pastor must, in this instance, depend upon the rent of the place by the seats, and, should the spot be abandoned for want of funds necessary for its support, a wide extent of ground will be left destitute of a pastor and the people, in most instances, at a distance of twelve miles from any place of public worship.[67]

In June 1825 land contiguous to the existing church property, and more prominently situated, was bought from the Earl of Darlington and Viscount Barnard, and in 1826 a new chapel, designed by Ignatius Bonomi, was begun. In April 1827 Hogarth wrote to Bishop Smith to tell him that he had decided to have the chapel named 'in the style and title of St Augustine's' and invited the bishop to perform the opening ceremony at the end of May. He forbore to mention that the church would not be finished for the formal opening. Commentators described the style of St Augustine's as 'debased Gothic' or as 'combining strength with elegance'; yet another said:

> It is in the gothic style, yet simple and unadorned. It may not, perhaps, be improper to state that Darlington, considering the forbidding circumstances in which it has been placed, furnishes an extraordinary instance of the increase of catholics.

The congregation was not convinced that a new church was required at all, despite the unification of the two missions, and notwithstanding Hogarth's impatience to open the church before it was completed. Some people thought it too large and that there had been unnecessary expenditure on its construction. This was a short-sighted view because the mission was bound to prosper. In the first place, Hogarth had 'received 30 into the church' in 1828 and he had '25 more who if all be well will be received at Christmas'. Then, as the *Catholic Magazine* pointed out in 1832, 'The great increase of trade opened out by the rail way will shortly make this one of our principal missions in the county'. On the other hand, the same writer noted that the income of the mission was but 'moderate'; Hogarth would have large debts for some time. He told the bishop that 'we have not a very great number of *very* poor, but we have no opulent people among us and the living here is but scanty'.

It was also at this time that the community of Carmelite nuns arrived in the town from St Helen Auckland. They bought the late eighteenth-century Cockerton Field House on what became known as Nunnery Lane, which was altered for conventual purposes in 1830–1832. A small stone chapel in simple lancet style by George Goldie, and windows by the well known Newcastle-born glassmaker William Wailes, were added in 1848–1854. A community of Poor Clares came to the town in 1855 and a Tudor-Gothic red brick convent was built for them on the same property by J. and C. Hansom.

Hogarth was given the opportunity to move to Hull in 1830 but, although the income would have been three times that of Darlington, he decided to stay because 'poor as it is it is of my own making as it were and I felt if I left it much serious injury would have been done'. Certainly, Hogarth seems to have been successful and popular. He had a small school and he provided a library of almost three hundred books. There were two hundred and eighty Easter communicants; the record of baptisms was healthy and Bishop

Briggs confirmed sixty-five persons on Trinity Sunday 1839 of whom eighteen were English converts gained within the previous three years. The church was enlarged to seat four hundred and fifty and accommodate the expanding congregation. 'Such is the continued increase in converts', it was said, that very soon the church would again be thought too small. In 1842 a mixed school with thirty-two pupils was rebuilt to take up to one hundred and twenty pupils.[68]

***

The Catholics of Barnard Castle and upper Teesdale crossed the Tees to attend Mass in **Lartington Hall** in the parish of Romaldkirk in the North Riding. This is one of the oldest missions in the present diocese of Middlesbrough; its recusant ownership can be traced to the early seventeenth century when the house was built. The first residential chaplain seems to have been Thomas Liddell who was there from 1693 to 1713 and Lancelot Pickering was chaplain for the next fifty years (1713–63). Thomas Maire (d. 1752) added the west wing to the house in which the chapel was located. Henry Maire (born Henry Lawson in 1751, he changed his name to Maire after inheriting the estates of John Maire in 1771) later extended the house and rebuilt the chapel. Edward Kitchen was chaplain for over twenty years (1772–93); he died at Lartington, insane. Attempts to recruit a satisfactory replacement were not at first successful. Thomas Ferby was not 'agreeable to Mrs Maire' and quickly returned to Crathorne; John Worswick was 'found asleep at 10 o'clock [and] stayed only a few months'. But Benedict Rayment then went to Lartington, and he stayed eighteen years. In June 1802 he wrote to Giuseppe Bonomi, who had done him a favour, inviting him to call if he was ever in the vicinity to 'gratify your exquisite taste for architecture with a sight of the most beautiful correct and chaste Gothic Chapel in England...' Evidently the priest was unaware that the elder Bonomi regarded Gothic architecture as a 'contagion'.[69]

This estate was the last remaining property of the Witham family which had been impoverished by Henry Witham. He inherited Lartington at the death of his mother in 1832 and he returned from Scotland to take over the estate. He was greeted with a parade through Barnard Castle: the band, banners and bells proclaiming his popularity and people's expectations of his former largesse. He was then in his fifties, however, and he had entered a more sober phase of life, that of the responsible and benevolent squire. He founded the Mechanics Institute in Barnard Castle and he supported the Dispensary Society which provided the poor with medicine. He commissioned Ignatius Bonomi to build a museum at Lartington to house his geological specimens, his paintings and his library of three thousand books He was pricked for High Sheriff of Durham in 1844, but he died before his year of office was over. The estate passed to his eldest son George but he died three years later and Lartington Hall came into the possession of the only surviving son, the Revd Thomas Edward Witham, 41 years of age, then serving at Berwick.

Witham came to Lartington Hall as missioner, with a congregation of around one hundred, but also, and apparently just as important, as squire, a role for which he might have been born and one which he much enjoyed. He once remarked of himself that if it had not been for the extravagance of his father, he would have been the richest commoner in England. As it was he did not do too badly. He was something of a *bon viveur* and he kept a good cellar although he had the village inn closed down. He was friendly with the Duke of Cleveland, with whom he dined frequently at Raby Castle. He was also a railway entrepreneur and he became a director of the Tees Valley Railway. Witham acted as missioner in **Gainford** from 1847, where in 1852 he built (entirely at his own expense and

Mission Stations in County Durham

on which he endowed £4,000) St Osmund's church by J. Gibson in the Early English style as a chapel of ease to St Augustine's in Darlington. He continued to minister there until 1861 when Michael Ellis, chaplain at Lartington, died, and Witham returned home.[70]

***

In 1767 almost forty Catholics were living in **Barnard Castle** and they were served from Lartington. At the beginning of the nineteenth century the congregation numbered some twenty-five Teesdale families. Owen Longstaffe, born in Lincoln and married to Lucy Ullathorne (aunt of the bishop), had been taken into partnership by his father-in-law, Francis, to manage

> the extensive flax, tow and spinning wheels of Messrs. Ullathorne and Longstaff, established in 1798 and whose manufacture of shoe threads gives employment to between 400 and 500 hands

in Startforth and Barnard Castle. In 1847 Owen Longstaffe rented the Union Hall in Ware Street and adapted it for use as a chapel; he also provided the stipend for a resident priest. Three years later he bought the property for £400 and gave it to the mission. In 1851 the Catholic population of the town was given as one hundred and seventy. Longstaffe set apart a room in a mill as a Catholic schoolroom and he later financed the building of a separate school.[71]

Notes

[1] The histories of the missions in this and the next chapter have been pieced together from a wide variety of formal and informal sources. Ushaw College Manuscripts [UCM]: W. V. Smith Papers, comprise an invaluable collection of genealogical and historical notes on Catholicism in the north east, to which students will be indebted for many years, notwithstanding Fr Smith's frequent omission of his sources. The diocesan archives in the

Northumberland Record Office [NRO: DIO] yield useful, though not extensive information on the mission history of the period. The most useful printed sources include: G. Anstruther, *The Seminary Priests: A Dictionary of the Secular Clergy of England and Wales, 1558–1850* (Ware: St Edmund's College; Durham: Ushaw College, 1968–1977, 4 vols); D. Bellenger, OSB, *English and Welsh Priests, 1558–1800* (Bath: Downside Abbey, 1984); H. Foley (ed.), *Records of the English Province of the Society of Jesus* (London: Burns & Oates, 7 vols., 1877–1883); P. R. Harris, *Douai College Documents, 1639–1794* (Catholic Record Society [CRS] vol. 63, 1972); G. Holt, SJ, *The English Jesuits, 1650–1829: A Biographical Dictionary* (CRS vol. 70, 1984); B. W. Kelly, *Historical Notes on English Catholic Missions* (London: Kegan Paul et al, 1907); M. Morris & L. Gooch, *Down Your Aisles: The Diocese of Hexham & Newcastle 1850–2000* (Hartlepool: Northern Cross, 2000). CRS volumes containing mission registers also provide essential material. A great deal of information on Catholic families has been obtained from J. C. Hodgson (ed.), *Northumbrian Documents of the 17th and 18th Centuries, Comprising the Register of the Estates of Roman Catholics in Northumberland* (Surtees Society [SS] vol. 131, 1918); C. R. Hudleston (ed.), *Registrations of Durham Recusant Estates, 1717–1778* (SS vols 173 & 175, 1962 & 1965). R. Welford, *Records of the Committees for Compounding, etc., 1643–1660* (SS 111, 1905), is also useful on estate matters. The periodicals *Northern Catholic Calendar* [NCC] (1872 et seq); *Northern Catholic History* [NCH] (1975 et seq); *Northern Cross* [NC] (1956 et seq); and *Ushaw Magazine* [UM] (1891 et seq) are also important.

2   J. M. Tweedy, *Popish Elvet* (Durham, St Cuthbert's Church, 1981, 2 parts), I, p 64.

3   W. V. Smith, '18th Century Catholic Education in County Durham', in UM 73 (1963), p. 25. Tweedy, *Popish Elvet*, I, p. 84.

4   Mrs Mary Maire died in 1751 leaving the property in Gilesgate to the mission (Tweedy, *Popish Elvet*, p. 69). Another Mrs Maire died in 1784 leaving some £4,000 to the mission (UCM: III/102).

5   Farm Street Archives, X, Sewall to Scott, 6 Feb. 1823; VIII, Sewall to Walsh 26 Sep. 1825. The salary at that time was £120–£130 p. a.

6   W. Fordyce, *The History and Antiquities of the County Palatine of Durham* (Newcastle: Fordyce, 1857, 2 vols), I, p. 331.

7   G. Scott. 'The Benedictines in the North East in the Eighteenth Century'. In: NCH 32 (1991), p. 41. The Humble family had owned Ryton House

in the 18th century. The estate passed out of the family when the Humble heiress married Joseph Lamb (d.1800).

8 NCC 1884 and 1919; *Catholic Magazine* [CM] II, No. 14 (1832), p. 113.

9 E. Walsh & A. Forster. 'The Recusancy of the Brandlings'. In: *Recusant History* [RH] 10/1, (1969), pp. 35ff. Much of the following is derived from Downside Abbey Manuscripts, 'Record Book of the EBC'; *Northern Cross*, Apr. 1985.

10 Scott, 'Benedictines In the North East', pp. 40 ff.; G. Scott, 'A Brief History of Birtley Catholic Mission and Parish' in NCH 35 (1994), pp. 46ff.; A. Allanson, *Biography of the English Benedictines* ([1842] Ampleforth Abbey, Saint Laurence Papers IV, 1999), p. 394; G. Scott, *St Joseph's Roman Catholic Church, Birtley: A Short History and Description* (Birtley: St Joseph's, 1993). R. Welford, *Men of Mark 'Twixt Tyne and Tweed* (London & Newcastle: Scott, 1895, 3 vols), I, sub Brandling; R. Welford, *A History of the Parish of Gosforth* (Newcastle: Welford, 1879), pp. 16/17; B. Little, *Catholic Churches since 1623* (London: Hale, 1966), p. 76; NC, Mar. 1988; J. Latimer, *Local Records 1832–1857* (Newcastle: The Chronicle, 1857), Aug. 1843.

11 The hall was sold and in due course it became The Mulberry public house, cf. *Proceedings of the Society of Antiquaries of Newcastle upon Tyne* [PSAN] (3) VIII, (1918), p. 104.

12 W. V. Smith, *Catholic Tyneside* (Newcastle: C. T. S., 1930), p. 81; NC Apr. 1985; Fordyce, *Durham*, II, pp. 749, 766.

13 Smith, *Catholic Tyneside*, p. 90; A. Forster. 'An Outline History of the Catholic Church in North East England'. In: NCH 10 (1979), pp. 14/15.

14 Smith, *Catholic Tyneside*, p. 85; M. J. Young, *A History of Catholic Jarrow* (n. p. n. d., c. 1940). In 1856 the priest from South Shields began to visit Jarrow to say Mass in a private house. A new church, dedicated to St Bede, was opened in December 1861. Hebburn became a separate parish and a school-chapel was opened in 1872.

15 Hylton Castle, west of the town, was occupied by the Catholic family of Hylton until 1758. A chaplain was maintained in the castle at the end of the sixteenth century but it is not known when the mission was discontinued. Sunderland here includes Bishopwearmouth and Monkwearmouth. Care is required when looking at old records to avoid confusing the town with the village of Sunderland Bridge, near Durham.

16 L. Crangle. 'The Roman Catholic Community in Sunderland from the 16th

Century'. In: *Antiquities of Sunderland* (Sunderland Antiquarian Society 1969), XXIV, p. 66.

17   K. Devlin et al, *St Mary's Jubilee (1835–1985)* (Sunderland: St Mary's, 1985), passim. See also NCC 1885 and 1936.

18   UCM: DIO 11, 24 Aug. 1780; NRO, RCD: 2/56.

19   In 1792 it was said that the Catholics had 'lately built a chapel at some expence'.

20   In the post-Emancipation period bench-rents would become a matter of considerable controversy in many places. One Sunderland parishioner left funds in 1831 for a bench 'to be free to five poor people to kneel at that are not able to pay for a bench'. Vestiges of the practice can still be seen on benches in older churches where brass plates identify the licensed occupant.

21   *Orthodox Journal* (1835), I, p. 142; Little, *Catholic Churches*, p. 76; E. Mackenzie & H. Ross, *The County Palatine of Durham* (Newcastle: Mackenzie & Dent, 1834, 2 vols), I, p. 293.

22   Fordyce, *Durham* I, pp. 493, 600; The Community, *A History of Darlington Carmel 1619–1982* (Darlington: The Community, 1982). There were 16 nuns and 6 lay-sisters originally.

23   J. Hagerty. 'Notes on the Northern District under Bishop Thomas Smith'. In: NCH 27 (1988), p. 27.

24   NRO: RCD, McEvoy to Penswick, 26 Oct. 1835; LDA: Smith Papers, McDonald to Smith, 9 July 1817.

25   NCC 1914; Fordyce, *Durham*, II, p. 680; R. Surtees, *The History and Antiquities of the County Palatine of Durham* (Durham: Andrews, 1816–1840, 4 vols), II, p. 272; J. Galletly & T. Yellowley, *Ss. Mary & Thomas Aquinas, Stella, 1831–1981* (Stella, 1981).

26   Allanson, *English Benedictines*, No. 563.

27   UCM: DIO 41. Henry Francis Widdrington (de jure fifth baron) died s. p. in 1774 and the estate passed to his nephew Thomas Eyre, with remainder to his cousin Edward Standish, cf. W. Hedley, *Northumberland Families* (Newcastle: Society of Antiquaries, 1968, 2 vols), II, p.106.

28   L. Gooch, *The Revival of English Catholicism: The Banister-Rutter Correspondence 1777–1807* (Wigan: North West Catholic History Society, 1995), Rutter, 3 Mar. 1793. These letters will be cited henceforth by originator and date. Two thirds of the congregation made their Easter Duty in 1792.

29 LDA: W. Gibson Papers, Eyre to Gibson, 25 Feb. 1793; Fordyce, *Durham* II, p. 680; Lady Mary Eyre gave £500 to Eyre for a chapel, but he was then at Pontop Hall; Little, *Catholic Churches* p. 66.
30 Mackenzie & Ross, *Durham*, I, p. 193.
31 NRO: RCD 4, pp. 46–59; Surtees, *Durham*, II, p. 732; G. Scott. 'A Monk's View of the Coal Industry in 1750'. In: NCH 15 (1982), pp. 3ff.
32 T. Matthews, *History of Brooms Parish, 1802–1969* (Consett, 1969); NCC 1920; NC, Dec. 1985; J. W. Fawcett, *A History of the Parish of Dipton* (Durham: Fawcett, 1911), pp. 35–42.
33 Rutter, 30 Jan. 1791. Crook Hall belonged to the Baker family which had strong Catholic connections. See D. Milburn, *A History of Ushaw College* (Durham: Ushaw College, 1964) for a history of the Durham collegiate establishments and Fordyce, *Durham*, II, pp. 660f; UCM: Smith of Brooms Papers, OS/D1, Eyre to Smith, 8 May 1793.
34 UCM: Smith of Brooms Papers, OS/D2, Eyre to Smith, 24 Mar. 1794; LDA: W. Gibson Papers, II, Eyre to Gibson, 9 May 1793; Hedley, *Northumberland Families*, I, p. 113.
35 Mackenzie & Ross, *Durham*, I, p. 226; UCM: Smith of Brooms Papers, OS/D3, Smith to Bell, 1807.
36 UCM: Smith of Brooms Papers, OS/D20d, 11 Mar. 1836, Smith to unnamed addressee.
37 Ibid.
38 UCM: Smith of Brooms Papers, OS/D20d, 11 Mar. 1836; OS/D20g, 20 Sep. 1836; NRO: RCD 4, 25 July 1836.
39 UCM: Smith of Brooms Papers, OS/D20i, 16 Dec. 1836
40 NRO: RCD 3/371, Hogarth to unnamed addressee, 27 May, 1841.
41 Anon., *St Mary's* (Centenary Booklet, 1957).
42 N. Emery. 'Esh Hall, County Durham'. In: *Durham Archaeological Journal*, 3, (1987), pp. 83ff; Fordyce, *Durham*, I, pp. 418ff; II, p. 657; NCC 1937.
43 NRO: RCD, Gibson Papers, II, Eyre to Gibson, 9 May 1793.
44 UCM: DIO 9; *Catholic Magazine*, 1832, p. 117.
45 UCM: Smith of Brooms Papers, OS/D20c, 11 Dec. 1835. W.R. Wiggen, *Esh Leaves* (Durham: Caldcleugh, 1914), pp. 54ff; W. B. Maynard, 'The Ecclesiastical Administration of the Archdeaconry of Durham, 1774–1856', (Durham PhD, 1973), p. 218.

46 NCC 1907; *Catholic Magazine*, 1832, p. 117; A. Coia, *Tudhoe St Charles Parish 1858–1983* (Tudhoe, 1983); Fordyce, *Durham*, I, pp. 382, 392; J. F. Heyes. 'Education at Sunderland Bridge'. In: UM 81 (1971), passim.

47 Rutter, 23 Aug. 1787; *Catholic Directory* 1794; J. Lenders, *Minsteracres* (Rochdale, Orphans Press, 1932), p. 78 n2.

48 Anon., *A History of Darlington Carmel 1619–1982* (Darlington, Carmel, 1982), passim; J. Crosby. 'Joseph Bonomi (1739–1808)'. In: NCH 25 (1987), p. 31.

49 NCC 1884; Anon., *St Wilfrid's 1846–1996* (Bishop Auckland, 1996); Little, *Catholic Churches*, p. 76; J. Bossy, *The English Catholic Community 1570–1850* (London: Darton, Longman & Todd, 1975), p. 321; NC Oct. 1983. Anon. 'St Helen's Auckland and Escomb'. In: PSAN(3) vol. 1, No. 28, pp. 261ff; Rutter, 30 Sep. 1794.

50 Fordyce, *Durham*, I, p. 553.

51 A. Forster. 'The Maire Family of County Durham'. In: RH 10/6 (1970); M. Hodgetts. 'Elizabethan Priest-holes: V—The North'. In: RH 13/4 (1976); CM (1832); Fordyce, *Durham*, II, pp. 374/375.

52 Fordyce, *Durham*, II, p. 40; Latimer, *Local Records*, 1 Mar. 1833; W. Parson & W. White, *History, Directory and Gazetteer of the Counties of Durham and Northumberland*, etc., (Newcastle: White, 1828, 2 vols), II, p. 131n; G. Silvertop, *Memoirs* (Newcastle: privately published, 1914), p. 19.

53 Silvertop, *Memoirs*, pp. 15–17.

54 *Laity's Directory*, 1826; Farm Street Archives, X, folio V, Lawson to Scott, 15 Sep. 1823.

55 T. A. Dunne, *The Catholic Church in Hartlepool* (n.d., n. p. [1934]); P. Fitzpatrick, *The Catholic Church in Hartlepool and West Hartlepool 1834–1964* (Hartlepool, 1964); Fordyce, *Durham*, I, p. 419n; II, p. 317; DRO: Q/R/RM1.

56 NRO: RCD 4/254–258, Slater to Briggs, 14 Apr. 1838.

57 Dunne, *Hartlepool*, prints a facsimile of Wiseman's letter dated 'Everingham, Tuesday'; Fordyce, *Durham*, II, pp. 258/259; Latimer, *Local Records*, July 1850.

58 NC Apr. 1986; Fordyce, *Durham*, II, p. 382; Latimer, *Local Records*, 29 Sep. 1850.

59 Cliffe's congregation 'resided chiefly in Bishopric': UCM: DIO 11, 5 Nov. 1775.

60 M. Dalton (1695), A. Metham (1694) and F. Hodgson (1726), cf. Anstruther, *Seminary Priests*, 3, sub nomen.
61 A. W. Dodds, 'Catholicism in Wycliffe and Gilling West', unpublished notes at the chapel (n.d.).
62 W. V. Smith. 'St Mary's Parish, Stockton on Tees, to 1900'. In: NCH 9 (1979), pp. 13 ff.; NC Jan. 1984; Fordyce, *Durham*, II, p. 164; H. Heavisides, *The Annals of Stockton on Tees* (Stockton: Heavisides, 1865); Mackenzie & Ross, *Durham* II, p. 30; *Catholic Directory*, 1816.
63 R. Carson, *The First 100 Years: A History of the Diocese of Middlesbrough 1878-1978* (Middlesbrough Diocesan Trustees, 1978), p. 105.
64 H. T. Dickinson (ed.), *The Correspondence of Sir James Clavering*, (SS vol. 178, 1967), pp. 184, 188; J. W. Wardell, *A History of Yarm* (Yarm: Wardell, 1957), pp. 134ff; S. L. Ollard & P. C. Walker (eds), *Archbishop Herring's Visitation Returns, 1743*, (Yorkshire Archaeological Society, 75, 1929), p. 219.
65 UCM: II, 124, Bishop Walton, Dec. 1775; Rutter, 25 Apr. 1786, 22 June 1789, 12 Mar. 1792; Anstruther, *Seminary Priests*, 4, p. 68; J. Laurenson. 'Catholic Chaplaincies and Families in the North during the Eighteenth Century'. In: CRS 4 (1907), p. 256; Mackenzie & Ross, *Durham*, II, p. 135.
66 The registers begin in 1783. G. Wild, *The Darlington Catholics: A History up to 1866* (Darlington, Wild, 1983) supersedes all previous articles.
67 Wild, *Darlington*, p. 52.
68 Fordyce, *Durham*, I, p. 469; J. Sykes, *Local Records* (Newcastle: Sykes, 1833, 2 vols), 29 May, 1827; UCM: Smith of Brooms Papers, OS/D13, Hogarth to Smith, 15 Oct. 1828; OS/D14, same to same, 3 Feb, 1820; *Orthodox Journal*, IX, No. 213 (1839), p. 65.
69 Carson, *Middlesbrough*, p. 85; V. Chapman, *Lartington* (Lartington, 1985); J. Crosby, *Ignatius Bonomi of Durham, Architect* (City of Durham Trust, 1987), pp. 30–36.
70 H. Dix. 'An Old Time Pastor of the Diocese of Hexham and Newcastle, 1806-97'. In: UM 59 (1949), p. 16; Silvertop, *Memoirs*, p. 15. The estate passed out of Catholic ownership at the death of Mgr. Witham in 1897. For Gainford see Fordyce, *Durham*, II, p. 131, and Latimer, *Local Records*, 26 June 1855. Witham turned the first sod for a railway between Barnard Castle and Darlington on 20 July 1854 as Chairman of the Board of Directors. He is said to have built the church at Gainford 'for personal reasons', cf. W. V. Smith. 'The 1851 Census of Worship and the Irish

Immigration into County Durham'. In: NCH, 7 (1978), p.23; D. Milburn. '"A Kinder Man or Better Master Never Lived": Monsignor Thomas Edward Witham of Lartington (1806–1897). In: NCH 39 (1998) pp. 31ff., passim.

[71] NCC 1881.

6 MISSION STATIONS IN NORTHUMBERLAND

IT HAS BEEN remarked earlier that relations between priest and patron in chaplaincies were usually strained and that other difficulties were endemic.[1] **Stonecroft Farm** was a chaplaincy in which everything that could go wrong did, and which therefore provides a model of all that was amiss with the chaplaincy system. The farm was a property of some three hundred acres on the Stanegate, six miles north-west of Hexham in a remote corner of the parish of Warden. In 1680 it was bequeathed by Ursula Mountney to Lord William Widdrington, a kinsman. She charged the estate with a yearly payment of £20 to Ralph Clavering, the purpose of which she explained in the private instructions attached to her will. Considerable acrimony and confusion arose out of her request that Stonecroft

> may always be let to farm to some discreet Catholic qualified to entertain a priest for the help of poor Catholics in Hexham and Warden parishes and other places adjacent; And whereas my dear brother John Widdrington late deceased did by his last will order to appoint that a Dominican or Franciscan priest should be kept at Stonecroft, the which I do hereby order and desire may be performed accordingly if a priest of any such order can conveniently be had; And I do give £20 per annum to the priest that shall serve at Stonecroft for his maintenance.[2]

Although the Dominicans had provided chaplains at Stonecroft for several years, Mrs Mountney preferred Franciscans, and at the retirement of the Dominican William Bertram in 1684 she declined a Dominican replacement and appointed a Franciscan instead. Mrs

Mountney died in 1686 and her chaplain died six months afterwards. The Franciscans immediately sent George Goodyear to take over but the Dominicans objected.[3] Ralph Clavering, trustee of the annuity, convened a meeting at Hesleyside, the outcome of which was that Goodyear would be left in place for a year and that a Dominican would then take over. Widdrington, however, took it upon himself to appoint the Franciscan, Constantine Jackson, to the post when Goodyear's time was up and Clavering raised no objection. So things stood until 1693 when Widdrington sold the estate to Thomas Gibson.

Now, the ownership of Callaly Castle changed at the same time, a combination of circumstances that would not normally have any connection. John Clavering, the new owner of Callaly Castle, however, was married to Anne Widdrington, and she wanted her Jesuit brother to be chaplain at the castle. Clavering therefore dismissed his late father's Dominican chaplain, George Thomas Gibson, brother of the new owner of Stonecroft Farm. Being out of place, he turned to his family and Thomas Gibson discharged Jackson to make way for him. Jackson complained to the vicar apostolic, James Smith, who declined to become involved because, as he said, 'Mr Gibson is master of his own house and may or may not admit Mr Jackson as he pleases'.

An extraordinary situation now developed. George Gibson was elderly and infirm, and unable to carry out the full duties of a missioner. In 1696 it appeared he was dying and a petition was addressed to the vicar apostolic outlining what had been going on during the three years since Constantine Jackson's removal:

> Father Gibson ever since his entry to his place at Stonecroft hath been very much incapacitated to perform his office by reason of his infirmity of body, that when any of your Petitioners or other neighbouring Catholicks do at any time apply themselves to the said Father Gibson (he) alleges his

infirmity and doth direct them to apply themselves to the said Father Jackson who ever since Father Gibson's entry to Stonecroft assisted and helpen the Catholicks in the parish of Warden and elsewhere. And the said Father Jackson hath ever since his removal from Stonecroft been destitute of any certain abode or maintenance. May it please your Good Lordship therefore ... to grant your Petitioners that our former Spiritual Pastor may succeed the said Father Gibson in the place of Stonecroft.

The petition was signed by a highly respectable group of Tynedale Catholics including such names as Widdrington, Charlton, Errington, Selby and Haggerston, but Bishop Smith was not impressed and he wrote instead to the Franciscan Provincial to have Jackson removed from the area. He was probably more shrewd than callous acting in this way, for he would know, as the petitioners might not, that another Gibson had been ordained as a Dominican priest shortly before, and that he would secure his family's patronage, as in fact it turned out.

William Thomas Gibson, O. P., arrived at Stonecroft Farm in 1698, and he would have remained there for the rest of his life except that he had to flee to escape arrest for illegally solemnising a marriage in 1712. Nonetheless, the Dominican tenure of the chaplaincy seemed secure. Peter Thompson arrived in November 1714. Almost immediately he was caught up in the Jacobite Rising, in which the Gibsons were enthusiastic participants. The rebel George Gibson died before his father, and so the farm escaped forfeiture, and it passed, in 1720, to his 9-year-old son George, for whom William Charlton acted as trustee. During George's minority Stonecroft Farm became the residence of his great uncle Jasper Gibson who married Margaret Leadbitter in October 1720.[4]

The chaplain Peter Thompson did not get on with Jasper Gibson, the de facto patron of the chaplaincy, and Thompson declared that he had suffered a great deal at Jasper's hands over many years. The chapel and priest's rooms were in a farmyard building and Thompson alleged that geese and hens were driven 'promiscuously' under the chapel where they made such a noise that he was much disturbed and could scarce hear himself speak. Thompson also said that early one Sunday morning in May 1721 before Mass, Gibson 'fell upon me like a hell dog, in the presence of his Protestant servants and others that were come to prayers'. Within a year of the change of ownership, Thompson wrote in his journal: 'after more than usual abuse perceiving I could not live easy at Stonecroft, I went away on 4th October 1721, and left the Gibsons'. He moved into Hexham and lodged at 'Mr. Rymer's merchant'. It should be said that Jasper Gibson was not anticlerical; four of his twenty-one children became priests, two of them bishops. Moreover, his wife's family had strong Dominican associations and they provided chaplains at Stonecroft later in the century. At any rate, the farm became a supply mission, attended by Peter Thompson for the following thirteen years.[5]

Franciscan priests had continued to serve in the area after their exclusion from the Stonecroft Farm chaplaincy at the beginning of the century. Jackson died in 1717 and he appears to have been succeeded by Bonaventure Hutchinson, alias Joseph Clark, the name by which he was best known; he was at Swinburne Castle when Thompson left Stonecroft. In 1725 Hutchinson was appointed Praeses of Hexham, a promotion that apparently emboldened him to reopen the question of the tenure of the Stonecroft Farm chaplaincy. He would have known of the vacancy and he would have been well aware of the terms of Ursula Mountney's will. It must have seemed to him an ideal opportunity to recover the chaplaincy for his order.[6]

Accordingly, in 1725 Hutchinson held a series of meetings with the trustee, the vicar apostolic and others connected with the family and the chaplaincy. After an encouraging conversation with Ralph Clavering (grandson of the original trustee), he appeared at Mr Rymer's house in Hexham early in September and announced that Clavering had conferred the chaplaincy on him and that he would leave Swinburne Castle for the farm at Martinmas. Thompson immediately arranged to see Clavering. The latter explained that all he had told Clark was that he would listen to both sides of the argument. A meeting of all interested parties was convened a week later in the Newcastle offices of the Catholic lawyer John Hankin. Clavering settled the matter once and for all by declaring for the Dominicans. There the matter rested, and in 1734 a resident Dominican chaplain was appointed since Thompson, then 60 years old and ill, was unable to travel regularly out to the farm. The Franciscans registered their continued interest in the chaplaincy, but no notice was taken.[7]

Dominican priests served at Stonecroft Farm throughout the century although, in what would become the usual practice, in later years the priest lived in his own cottage on the estate. In 1767 William Houghton ministered to fifty-eight Catholics in Warden. He was a tall, athletic man and it is said he was seized by the press-gang in Liverpool but escaped from them by treating them to a glass of grog. He was a scientist (controversially espousing the theories of Descartes and Newton), a classical scholar and a poet. He edited and wrote for the short-lived *The Catholic Magazine and Reflector* (six numbers of which appeared in 1801).

The Stonecroft chaplaincy came to an end in 1815 when the Gibson family fell on hard times. George Gibson (1770–1834) had mortgaged the farm for £5,000 at the beginning of the century but he could not redeem the mortgage and he sold the property to his kinsman Jasper Gibson of Newburgh Lodge. He too got into financial difficulties and his affairs were put into the hands of trustees. The first economy was to dispense with the chaplain, and the chapel was served from the Dominican chapel in Hexham from 1816. That was not sufficient to save the farm, however, and six years later the trustees sold it for £6,805. The new owner, John Todd, was a Protestant and he refused to pay the rent-charges to the priest in accordance with the Mountney will. Nicholas Leadbitter, a Catholic lawyer of Hexham in whom the fund had been vested in trust, took the case to the Court of Chancery in September 1831. The Master of the Rolls decided that under the old law the bequest was void because it was intended for superstitious uses but under existing law it could be termed a charitable gift. The rents should therefore be handed over together with any arrears. The fund was later transferred to the mission in Hexham. Thenceforth, the congregation of the Stonecroft Farm mission, which numbered around fifty for much of its existence, travelled to Hexham for Mass. In 1828 it was reported that there were 'few Dissenters and fewer Catholics' in the parish of Warden.[8]

The history of the Stonecroft Farm chaplaincy is important in that it exemplifies all the disadvantages of the chaplaincy system. It illustrates the difficulties that could arise over badly drafted wills and when patrons became involved in politics. It shows that the power of the lay patron over the chaplain was supreme, and that the security of tenure of a chaplaincy depended entirely on goodwill and on the solvency of the patron. Finally, it demonstrates that when clerical rivalries arose, and particularly when the regular orders were involved, the ecclesiastical jurisdiction of the vicar apostolic was limited. Indeed, he was effectively impotent in chaplaincy matters, yet the majority of his priests were chaplains. The Stonecroft Farm case is perhaps exceptional, but in the course of the eighteenth century one or more circumstance of a similar kind arose in almost every chaplaincy in the north-east.

***

Dilston Castle passed into the Radcliffe family upon the marriage of Anne Cartington to Sir Edward Radcliffe in the late fifteenth century. Radcliffe of Dilston became the most prominent Catholic and royalist, then Jacobite, family in north-east England during the seventeenth and early eighteenth centuries. In March 1688 Sir Francis was created Baron Tynedale, Viscount Radcliffe and Langley and Earl of Derwentwater following the marriage of his son Edward Radcliffe to Lady Mary Tudor, (the non-Catholic daughter of King Charles II by Moll Davis). But the family's seemingly impregnable social position was reversed at the Revolution. The first earl refused the oaths to William and Mary and was briefly imprisoned in 1691; he was feared as the most dangerous Jacobite in the north-east. The second earl lived safely in London but James, the third earl, was executed in 1716 for his resolute adherence to Jacobitism to the point of rebellion and effectively brought the family down. This, however, is not the place to relate that history but only to treat of Dilston as the headquarters of Catholicism in Tynedale.

There is evidence of a chaplaincy at Dilston from the early 1660s although the chronology in subsequent years is not always clear.[9] It was not unusual for wealthy recusant families to support more than one priest and the Radcliffes followed the practice, engaging a family chaplain and tutor for the children as well as supporting a second priest for the household and tenantry, though both were usually boarded in the mansion. The employment of two priests avoided any pastoral difficulties when the patron and family were absent since one priest was always left behind. In 1666 Lady Elizabeth Radcliffe gave £600 to support two Benedictine missioners: one to serve the family at Dilston and the other to minister near Lake Derwentwater. The fund was entrusted to the Claverings at Callaly, but the money was not invested wisely so that little or nothing was paid till 1706. On the breaking up of the estate, the interest of the fund was paid to the monks serving at Beaufront and later to the monks serving at Swinburne Castle and Whenby in Yorkshire. Among the dispositions of Sir Edward (II) was a bequest of £400 to found a studentship at the English College, Lisbon, for the training of a priest for the English mission. Robert Sutton (al. Salisbury) the son of a Yorkshire gentleman was ordained at Lisbon in 1662 at the age of 21 and went immediately to Dilston where he spent his whole priestly life. Around 1666 he was joined by William Ducket, whose origins and education are unknown.

Roger Mitford, only son of a substantial gentleman of Thropton, Northumberland, and who was ordained at the English College, Douai, around 1663, first appears at Dilston in 1672 and he spent the rest of his priestly life with the Radcliffes, as chaplain-tutor. The second priest at Dilston for much of Mitford's time was Ferdinand Ashmall, of Amerston in south-east Durham. He was educated for the priesthood at the *Venerabile* in Rome, and he was ordained at the Lateran in 1674, aged twenty-four. Ashmall received an annual salary of £12 (which was insufficient for him to live independently and indicates that he lived in the main house).

In August 1687 Bishop John Leyburne confirmed four hundred and eighty-one Tynedale Catholics at Dilston. The following year James Smith, vicar apostolic appointed Mitford Vicar General of Northumberland and Durham. In 1694 Mitford was made Archdeacon of Northumberland in the Old Chapter. He stayed on at Dilston after the first earl's death in 1696 but he died within the year and was buried in Corbridge church. Among his bequests was £400 to educate a priest at Douai, and £400 to support that priest while serving at Rothbury. Ashmall meanwhile had left Dilston around 1686/1687 to become public missioner in Old Elvet, Durham; he also became a superior of the Northern Brethren's Fund and he followed Mitford as Archdeacon of Northumberland.

Two new priests now entered the service of the Radcliffes. Robert Riddell, son of Sir William Riddell of Gateshead, had been ordained in Rome in 1668 and had served as chaplain to the Benedictine nuns in Pontoise before arriving around 1681, aged 53, as missioner at Dilston and in the Radcliffes' Newcastle townhouse in Newgate Street (which had been in The Close initially). He died in Tynedale in 1702. The newly-ordained, 25-year-old Benjamin Petre became family chaplain and tutor to the earl's sons. He had all the attributes of the ideal nobleman's chaplain. He was the youngest son of a wealthy and well-connected esquire in Essex who had married, thirdly, a daughter of the first earl of Portland whose sister had served Mary of Modena; Petre was neither learned nor ambitious but was rather, 'gentle, pious, humble, timorous and affectionate'. In view of all that, it seems remarkable that he was prepared to serve at all in such an intractable and restive Jacobite family and there was another difficulty. The earl's marriage broke down in 1700 because the countess remained implacably opposed to becoming a Catholic. (They did not like the north and spent much of the time at his London residence in Arlington Street.) No doubt to her further displeasure, in 1702 Derwentwater sent his three sons James aged 13, Francis, 11, and Charles, 9, to the Stuart court at St. Germain, at the request of Queen Mary, widow of James II, to be companions and fellow-pupils of Prince James Francis Edward, their cousin. The earl, moreover, left a fund of £400 for the support of a general missioner at Dilston.

A list of chaplaincies compiled at about the time of the second earl's death in 1705 included that of Derwentwater, but it also listed separately 'Mr Thomas Radcliff ... The Hon[ble] William Radcliff ... Mr Arthur Radcliff' without giving their places of residence. These were the remaining brothers of the earl and all were bachelors (Francis, the other, had died in 1704) and, since his four sisters were either in convents or living elsewhere, they were the only members of the family who could have been resident at Dilston before the 'Fifteen. They all had estates in the north from which they derived their incomes and on which they may have lived though there is no record of any of them supporting a chaplain. Had the chaplaincies been listed in 1706, it would have included that of Lady Mary Radcliffe. Three years earlier she had left home to set up independently in Durham and she built a new house in Old Elvet which was ready for occupation in 1706. The household was dispersed at her death in 1724.

None of the family lived at Dilston after 1704 although one or more of them may have lived in the family's town-house in Newcastle. Petre continued as family chaplain and remained with the widowed countess at Hatherop and London after her husband's execution in 1716. They parted in 1720 when she retired to Brussels where she died of small-pox in August 1723. She bequeathed Petre a chalice and paten 'with some church stuff that he had for many years in his keeping'.[10] John Radcliffe, de jure fourth earl of Derwentwater, died in London in December 1731, a month after writing his will in which he bequeathed Petre £100 a year 'which my father intended to settle upon him'. Petre was the last family chaplain to serve the Radcliffes. He became coadjutor vicar apostolic of the London District, in the see of Prusa *in partibus infidelium* with right of succession to Bonaventure Giffard.

The second earl's bequest in 1705 of £400 to support a priest was for a general missioner at Dilston and, at Colonel Thomas Radcliffe's request, the first beneficiary was the 40-year-old John Girlington (Riddell's successor) a Lancastrian. He had been ordained at Lisbon and was chaplain to the Withams at Sledwich in Durham from around 1685. He moved to Dilston in 1702 but his tenure was marred by complaints from the start. In 1722 Charles Busby, the agent at Dilston told the countess:

> Mr Garlingtons behaviour has given scandall near 20 year, but much more publique within this Six Months; the originall began from an Attache he tooke to one Mich: Bell and

his Wife, the man a mean blockheady ffellow, and the Woman of no good Character. Howsoever [they] have so deluded him as to spend £400 or 500 of his moneys, and w'n y't would not do to support their extravagances he has borrowed other considerable Summs...

rendering Girlington insolvent. Busby went to Durham in December 1722 to ask Mr Carnaby to get the bishop to remove the priest. Busby was confident that the people would 'not be destitute this holy time' for he would send for Mr Thompson, the missioner in Hexham, 'who is acquainted in y't Country to do the Duty'. In any case, Girlington was no longer required at Dilston when the countess closed the chapel and he lived in Hexham but Busby reported that he did

> not value the reflections y't are cast upon him by all people, so not likely to alter his Course of life, continually shuffleing f'm place to place, and never abideing where he should be.

Arthur Radcliffe, whose mental health gave increasing cause for concern, was living at Capheaton and Girlington was sent for on several occasions to attend him, and in June 1726 the priest accompanied Radcliffe to London. Radcliffe died in 1729 and Girlington removed to Sunderland where he died shortly afterwards.[11]

After Girlington's departure, the Northumbrian Arthur Bede Halsall, a Benedictine whose principal mission was at Beaufront from 1721, looked after the dozen Catholic families at Dilston where Mass was said in the house of a Mr Swinburne. He was there when Bishop Williams confirmed sixty-four people in 1729 but the Dilston estate passed out of Catholic ownership in 1731 and the chapel was converted to Anglican usage two years later. Halsall died in 1737 and was buried in the choir of Hexham Abbey under the alias of Edmund Tait. The Dilston Catholics were probably included in the total of sixty-three Catholics listed in the 1767 return from Corbridge. At the time of Emancipation, the Catholic population had fallen to fourteen persons.[12]

***

A large number of Catholics lived in **Hexham** and thereabouts, and they supported priests more or less continuously during the penal era. Except for the city of York, Hexham was the strongest centre of Catholicism in the Diocese of York. Bishop Leyburne confirmed nearly five hundred people at Dilston in 1687 but at the beginning of the eighteenth century the pastoral situation was not encouraging. William Gascoigne, a secular priest, was indicted at the General Sessions in July 1690 as 'a reputed popish priest' and he was bound over to appear at the next Assizes but he died at the end of the year. A Franciscan mission closed down in 1706 at the death of its patron, Benoni Carr, an attorney and Bailiff of Hexham. In May 1715 an appeal was addressed to the Vicar Apostolic and to the local gentry:

> We the Catholic Inhabitants of this town and other adjacent neighbours having for too long experienced the sad want and necessity of a priest to remain in this place; Do now as much as in us lies and express our utmost endeavours for encouraging the constant abode of some worthy person— and at the same time humbly implore the charitable assistance of all well disposed Christians for the said end.[13]

The petition was badly timed, for the year of the Jacobite Rising was not the best time to recruit a priest for such a conspicuous post, only a mile or so west of Dilston. It was only afterwards, and as a consequence of the 'Fifteen, that Hexham got its missioner, indeed, it got two.

The first was Peter Thompson, the Dominican who opened a chapel in Hexham after his departure from Stonecroft Farm. Anne Brandling of Middleton Hall, near Leeds, whose own chaplain was a Dominican, bought a house and field on Battle Hill in Hexham for the mission. To safeguard the property she merged it with the estate of William 'Bowrie' Charlton, a Jacobite rebel and ruffian. Thompson must have feared that his new patron was going to be no more congenial than the last, but he had no trouble. The second priest was John Girlington, who 'had his chapel in a house of Mr Thomas Jefferson, tanner, facing the tan pits at Cockshaw Bridge End'.

The Catholic population of Hexhamshire grew to around two hundred and fifty by mid-century. The Anglican episcopal visitation of 1743 showed that there were sixty-three Catholic families, most of which were living in the township of Hexham. In 1735 there had been one hundred and five individuals. The secular chapel at Cockshaw was served by George Gibson for some twenty years from 1757. He was the eldest son of Jasper Gibson of Stonecroft Farm, and he immediately set out to make his mark when he arrived in the town. Firstly, he established a wool-spinning factory to provide work for poor children. Then he set about building a new chapel. Lawrence Hall, a husbandman, had died in 1750 leaving the residue of his estate to the mission. Thomas Riddell of Swinburne and John Gibson of Great Whittington invested the bequest for ten years and bought 'two Burgesses and a little close or garden' behind the existing chapel at Cockshaw. They also 'laid out in repairing the said house and fitting up the commodious chapel there the further sum of £120, making together £360'. Hall's bequest did not cover the whole cost, as Gibson's brother later made clear:

> My brother spent above £100 upon the house and chapel out of his own pocket. Kirsopp said that the chapel had been built by the contribution of Gentlemen. This I know to be false in great measure. Some indeed did open their purses but my brother was a bad beggar and there happened to be no profusion of a liberal spirit upon the Earth in those days.[14]

That was to be a continual theme in the clerical correspondence of the period. The gentry were no longer to be relied upon as the principal benefactors of the mission; priests, tradesmen, artisans and the lesser orders generally, such as Jefferson and Hall of Hexham, were to provide most of the funds for mission development in the future. The location of the new chapel in Cockshaw was consonant with the need for the discretion still necessary at that time in the towns. The chapel, in a converted malt kiln, was approached through an archway off the street and down a side lane. The chapel was enlarged and improved as time went by. A description of it in 1823 said it was 'neatly fitted up and well seated with a small gallery at the south end. Above the altar is a fine painting of the Crucifixion'.[15]

The Dominican chapel on Battle Hill was served for most of the period by locally-born priests among whom were Nicholas Leadbitter (1754–62) and Jasper Leadbitter who took over in 1782 and was in charge for forty-five years. The old building was no longer watertight at the end of the century and a new house and chapel became necessary. Ralph Riddell, acting as trustee, used a legacy of £100 left by John Shaftoe, to buy land and a house in Hencotes on the outskirts of the town. After the necessary alterations, the new mission was opened in December 1797. The chapel was on the upper storey and ran the full length of the house, occupying over one thousand square feet and could seat around two hundred and fifty people. Despite having an organ gallery and choir, this was hardly an ambitious post-Relief chapel. Many priests in the north-east were considerably more adventurous by this time.

In 1822, Jasper Leadbitter ('of venerable appearance and primitive simplicity of manner') was 72 years of age and overdue for retirement. There was no possibility of finding a Dominican successor; the Province had been devastated by the loss of its college at Bornhem in the 1790s, and no Dominican novices had since come forward. In 1817 the Province could muster only nine priests, five of whom were too old for active work, and one of them was Jasper Leadbitter. As it happened, the 70-year-old secular missioner, Matthew Sharp, died first. He was buried in the old Lady Chapel of Hexham Abbey in December 1826. Hexham was about to experience the ardent missionary zeal of a young, newly-ordained priest, anxious to reanimate the mission in the town which had coasted along under the benign care of the two ageing priests for the previous twenty years.

Michael Singleton, 35 years of age and fresh from the seminary at Lisbon, arrived in Hexham in April 1826 to assist Matthew Sharp, who died at the end of that year. Within nine months an agreement was reached in which Jasper Leadbitter was to retire and the chapels were to be amalgamated under Singleton on the site of the Dominican chapel, with the stipulation that either a secular or a Dominican might hold the incumbency.[16] The chapel at Cockshaw was sold for £600 and an appeal was issued for subscriptions towards a new chapel to seat six hundred people:

> Till last year there were in this town two Catholic chapels, but such have been our losses that these cannot any longer be supported and though the wrecks of both properties have been united, the strictest economy will be requisite for one priest to support himself and his servant. The old chapel has for many years threatened to bury its congregation in its ruins, and that which is called the new one is so circumscribed in its dimensions that it will neither admit of enlargement nor accommodate more than half the present members many of whom come from a distance of seven miles, and some from a distance of twenty miles.[17]

A building committee was formed from the congregation to raise funds and to plan the new church. About £1,000 was collected locally and Singleton laid the foundation stone in April 1828, almost two years to the day of his arrival. This was to be no hole-in-the-corner establishment but was to have a frontage on to the main east-west road running through the town facing the abbey. Ignatius Bonomi was invited to design it, but his plans were shortly returned with a note to the effect that it had been 'determined to carry into execution the plan originally furnished by Mr Singleton'. Bonomi's reaction to Singleton's effrontery is not known, but in November 1828 the bell-tower (sixteen bells) of the new

> chapel, then building at Hexham, fell with a tremendous crash, which did considerable damage. Fortunately no lives were lost as it occurred during the workmen's dinner hour. No blame was attached to the builder, Mr. William Oliver, of Durham, as the part that fell was under the direction of the Rev. Mr. Singleton, a difference having taken place between Mr. Oliver and the committee.[18]

The project was delayed for a while but the builders and the committee were no doubt greatly relieved that Singleton spent most of 1829 travelling the country (and Ireland) soliciting funds. That was common practice at the time; indeed, the inconvenience caused to colleagues and congregations by a priest's absence on a begging tour, led to the formation of the Catholic Missionary Society which sought contributions nationally for mission development.

The new church in Hexham, dedicated to St Mary, was opened by the vicar apostolic in 1830, three months after the 81-year-old Jasper Leadbitter died ('in an attitude of prayer'). Mr. Singleton immediately turned his energies towards building a school, and that was completed in 1832 at a cost of £400.[19] In his appeal of 1828, Michael Singleton had mentioned that more than half his congregation came from a distance of seven to twenty miles away. Some would have been in the old Dilston congregation, some from the

Stonecroft area, and others would have attended two other recently defunct Tynedale missions Beaufront Castle and Capheaton Hall.

***

Originally, **Beaufront Castle**, in the Hexhamshire parish of St. John Lee, was a mediaeval tower and, in the reign of Elizabeth, the seat of the Carnaby family. The estate then passed to the Erringtons who built a new mansion in the eighteenth century. They maintained Benedictine priests at Beaufront from 1685, beginning with Dom John Gregory Skelton until 1721. When Ralph Errington died about 1699, he left money to the monk-missioner for masses to be said for his soul and for the local Catholics to attend Mass on his anniversary. A fund of £300 bequeathed by Lady Radcliffe in 1666 for the support of the Benedictine missioner at Dilston was transferred wholly to Beaufront after the closure of the Dilston chaplaincy in 1721. An uninterrupted succession of ten Benedictine missioner-monks serving Beaufront can be traced from 1726.

The Erringtons were keen to maintain their allegiance to the Stuarts although they had nothing to show for their participation in the 'Fifteen. In 1737, the Benedictine President brought the young Errington, then on his Grand Tour, to the attention of 'James III' in Rome. The family customarily called in at the English Benedictine monasteries on their travels. Ominously, however, John Errington, a bachelor and the last of his line, became Provincial Grandmaster of the Freemasons in 1776. Nonetheless, a year later, wishing to replace the domestic chapel, he wrote to Dom Augustine Walker in Rome about procuring 'a plan of a chapel to hold a large congregation. I would have it neat, light, of the Gothick construction, the less ornamented the better, with a place for a Bell if required'. This chapel was erected at Beaufront Woodhead nearby. By 1780, however, Errington, was voicing strong objections to his chaplain's desire for independence in ecclesiastical matters and in 1787 the Northern Benedictine Provincial was prevailed upon to remove him because

> Mr. Errington tells me he requires prayers [i.e., Mass] daily. I informed him I could not with any degree of propriety insist upon any subject saying Mass every day, but that if he thought proper, he might have morning prayers when the Gentleman did not think proper to say Mass.

Moreover, the Provincial feared that Errington was 'so whimsical' that it would 'be difficult to retain him as Patron' for, as Henry Swinburne observed, Errington was

> as cracked as ever man was. I wonder he is still allowed to be at large and to see company. He has the mania of fancying he has been created Duke of Hexham. He has erected a pillar in his grounds with ducal arms, supporters and coronet, on Stagshaw bank; a most public station as it is the rendezvous of an annual fair. A foreign title is his idea for a foreign crown is over his door.

When Errington wrote 'some letters of an extraordinary nature to the first lady of the kingdom' and others to the king requesting confirmation of his dukedom, a Commission of Lunacy was appointed in 1787 to take over his affairs.

There had been three changes of missioner within the previous few years, but a newly professed monk, Dom James (Alexius) Pope managed to survive from 1788 to 1793 though that was probably only because he kept out of the way. But eventually he too felt compelled to move out. The residential mission closed in 1795, and the registers stop upon the retirement of the last Benedictine chaplain, Dom Richard Simpson in 1796. The chapel at Beaufront Woodhead fell into ruin. Thereafter, the chaplain at Swinburne Castle said Mass for a declining number of Beaufront Catholics in a private house in Corbridge, two miles to the south-east.[20]

***

The Swinburnes of **Capheaton Hall** were notoriously recusant throughout Elizabethan and Jacobean times. Sir John Swinburne, 'the auld carle of Capheaton', was rewarded with a baronetcy at the Restoration for his services in the Civil War. Robert Trollope rebuilt the Jacobean mansion: its style 'provincial and endearing Baroque indulged in between 1630 and 1675 by those who would not give in to the academic virtues of Jones, Pratt and Wren'. Pevsner went on to describe it as one of the most interesting houses in the county and 'Trollope's most individual work and most successful design'. The new house (with a hide in the roof) was needed to accommodate his growing family—his wife Isabella (neé Lawson) gave birth to twenty-four children in all. People would throng around her carriage to gaze at and prod the mother of so many babies.

The Vicar of Kirkwhelpington's Return of Papists of 1705 was one of those that simply gave the name of the local Catholic squire and the value of his estate, which, as near as he could 'compute by the Booke of Rates is about 228lb. per. ann.' Sir John (the 'lost heir of Capheaton' who was sent abroad during the 'Fifteen under an assumed name and was only identified much later) maintained a Benedictine mission, with a succession of nine monk-chaplains during the century (five Swinburne girls became Benedictine nuns). The house-chapel was used by the family, servants and tenants; in 1725 there were 'about 50 hearers' and by 1750 there were around seventy-five in the congregation. The vicar complained to the Bishop of Durham about the Catholic chaplain baptising a child in the parish but the mission quietly flourished; Dom John Holderness had eighty-nine in his congregation in 1767. The chaplain at Capheaton was very well off compared to other missioners; he enjoyed £80 a year but he did undertake a number of supervisory duties on the estate.[21]

Sir Edward Swinburne (V) (1733–86) was a wine merchant in Bordeaux. The Governor of that town described him as 'Edw. Swinburne du Northumberland fils cadet du baronnet John Swinburne d'une famille catholique et zelee pour les Stuarts'. He was closely involved with the Catholic Committee which negotiated the Catholic Relief Act of 1778. He engaged 'Capability' Brown to landscape the grounds at Capheaton and he rebuilt the chapel in the west wing in 1759, incorporating 'pillars' or pilasters, a cornice and a 'great window'. The congregation rose to one hundred and six in 1780. The vicars apostolic always included the hall in their confirmation tours. Towards the end of Sir Edward's life it was said, gnomically, that he 'did not practise his religion but kept the faith'. At any rate, he moved the chaplain out of the mansion into the village and instructed him that he was 'to have no concern at the Hall but to say prayers [Mass] when he was expressly invited'. In 1785 the chaplain reported that Swinburne refused to allow him the use of a horse, not even when called out to his congregation. He also complained of the great discouragement he met with in the discharge of his pastoral duties. It was all too plain that Sir Edward was not 'much burthened with religion', an attribute which also applied to his son.

Sir John Edward Swinburne (VI) was born at Bordeaux in 1762. He was educated by the Benedictines in France and he became a friend of Mirabeau and Wilkes. Swinburne never left France until he succeeded to the baronetcy at the age of 25 upon which he took over his Northumbrian estates. He immediately renounced Catholicism and conformed to Anglicanism. Although Swinburne closed the mission at Capheaton and even refused to allow the chaplain to minister to the tenantry of the estate, Dom Andrew Bernard Ryding was allowed to remain until a new place could be found for him and he left in 1788. The vicar of Kirkwhelpington reported in 1792 that the chaplain at Cheeseburn Grange occasionally visited Capheaton but that the number of Catholics was declining year by year. Later the Hexham missioner also visited the small group of Catholics, 'all of inferior rank' in Capheaton. In 1814 there was a Catholic schoolmistress in the village who taught 'a few children but it is not known that she instructs them in the religious tenets peculiar to her church'.[22]

***

In 1664, Henry Widdrington, an ardent royalist and papist inherited **Cheeseburn Grange**, one mile from Stamfordham. Presumably he and his successors kept priests but named chaplains cannot be identified until Ralph Widdrington reopened the chaplaincy around 1718 when he returned from the continent after a self-imposed exile following the 'Fifteen. The Franciscan Bonaventure Hutchinson was said to be 'much at Cheeseburn Grange' around 1722, but five years later the Jesuits took the chaplaincy over and they remained until the death of Ralph Widdrington in 1752. He died without issue and left the estate to his nephew Ralph Riddell, brother of Thomas Riddell, squire of Swinburne, Felton and Longhorsley.[23]

The residential chaplaincy was discontinued at this point, probably because the new squire did not live permanently in the Grange, and for the next twenty years the chapel was served by neighbouring priests. In 1774 the Dominicans reinstituted a residential mission (and began to keep registers of births, marriages and deaths) but the order could not provide priests after 1792 and the post was filled by Franciscans until 1815 and thereafter by seculars. The Catholic population of Stamfordham numbered no more than fifty during the eighteenth century and, in 1792, they were described as chiefly servants or dependents of Mr Ralph Riddell (1771–1831) 'who has a considerable estate'. In 1813 Riddell had the eighteenth-century house substantially enlarged and remodelled in the Gothic manner by John Dobson and, in

1818, Dobson worked on the domestic chapel and priest's quarters on the first-floor of the mansion. In 1828, in a parochial population of 1,827, 'Of Catholics, with the worthy Mr Riddell of Cheeseburn Grange at their head, there are 70'. In 1830 the congregation numbered one hundred and forty. In 1841 a presbytery and a substantial Gothic chapel, contiguous with the mansion but with external access, were built by Dobson. Further additions by J. A. Hansom around 1860 were later demolished.[24] The chaplain for some thirty-three years from 1817 was Thomas Cock who could be delightfully vague in his registers:

> A child about 3 months old, I think it was a boy, was baptised by me, I think it was in the year 1828, and to the best of my recollection in one of the spring months...[25]

***

Hesleyside, some two miles west of Bellingham, is the seat of the Charlton family. A classical wing was added to the fourteenth-century tower-house in 1631 (to include a secret hide in the wall of the south front behind a carved stone between the second- and third-floor windows. The mansion was rebuilt in 1721; the grounds would be landscaped by 'Capability' Brown later in the century. The Charltons maintained a chapel at the top of the house for a small congregation of family, servants and tenants served by Benedictine chaplains whose names are known only from the middle of the century. Thirty-seven Catholics and their priest Thomas Bolas were listed in 1767, the year in which Edward Charlton died and William Charlton came into possession of the estate at the age of 14. According to the later *Recollections* of the redoubtable Barbara Charlton, however, 'what with the penal laws, cockering up the Pretender, ancestral extravagance and, alas! the undying vice of drink', the estate then teetered 'on the verge of ruin'. In 1778 the 'inebriate and hardly responsible Squire of Hesleyside' married Margaret Fenwick, and in a very short time she 'grasped the intricacies and the entanglement of the estate's affairs' and immediately set about their recovery.[26] One of the first economies was the closure of the domestic chapel in 1781 thus saving the chaplain's salary. The mission moved into Tone Hall, a Hodgson house some six miles away, which had shared the Benedictine chaplain since 1767. The arrangement had been that the Hesleyside incumbent would receive

> £20 a year, the use of the garden, fireing and grass for his horse. From Mrs Charlton of Reedsmouth £6 yearly. From Mrs Hodgson of Tone 5 guineas yearly. Reedsmouth and Tone to have each prayers one Sunday in the month and half the holydays. The rest at Hesleyside.

At that time the congregation at Hesleyside numbered fifteen, though it grew to fifty-three by 1780.

Tone Hall came into the possession of William Sanderson in 1784 and he assumed the name of Hodgson. The house was closed in 1793 because of his insolvency, and he went to live abroad; he died at Calais in 1820.[27] The mission was therefore moved into 'a loft or upper chamber formed out of two or three dwelling houses' in the village of Bellingham, close by Hesleyside Hall. The missioner, Dom John Sharrock, under the patronage of the Charltons of Sandhoe, no doubt thought he was doing the right thing since the domestic chapel had been closed. But Mrs Charlton was not best pleased at this display of independence, or of the priest's recourse to her relations, but matters were left as they were until the death of the squire in 1797 when she sent the monk packing. An income of £60 a year was settled instead on the Carmelite, William Clarkson, and he served at Bellingham between 1798 and 1803.

The new squire, having reached his majority began a series of building renovations including a new south front in the Palladian style—distinctly old-fashioned by this time—executed by the leading Northumbrian master-builders, William Newton and William Burnop. The main work was completed in 1800 three years after William Charlton's death and W. H. Charlton engaged Bonomi to complete the decoration. Charlton also revived the Benedictine chaplaincy. The mission was centred on the domestic chapel at Hesleyside for the next thirty years although the priest continued to live in the village, perhaps to guard against any difficulty he might have with the family in the future. In 1810, the vicar of Simondburn was pleased to say:

> Thank God there is no Popish school or Seminary in my parish. I hope the number of Papists does not increase with us: and I am happy that I have converted one large family to the Communion of our Church.

In 1814 there were no more than twenty Catholics in the parish, and perhaps two families in the chapelry of Bellingham; there had been a congregation of around eighty in 1780. It was reported in 1828 that out of a parochial population of nine hundred, there were 'two or three Roman Catholic families'. That was clearly a reference to gentry families rather than the total, for an official return gave the whole number in the congregation as one hundred.[28]

The Benedictines withdrew in 1832, and the mission was taken over by seculars. Nicholas Brown, chaplain from 1834, wished to move the chapel out of Hesleyside into the village of Bellingham where he proposed to build a new church which he estimated would cost £1,000. In March 1838 the Hesleyside Charltons agreed with the plan, though Mr Charlton was reluctant and had to be persuaded by his wife. He would give an acre of land, £300 towards the building costs, and provide the incumbent's salary of £60 a year. The land was situated exactly halfway between the village of Bellingham and Hesleyside Hall, just to remind all concerned at whose expense and for whose convenience the church was to be built. The Charltons of Sandhoe and the vicar apostolic would each match the Hesleyside contribution and the balance could be made up from local donations. Brown was delighted to tell Bishop Briggs that

> The Charltons here are desirous of having the chapel finished during the summer. If Mr Charlton could afford it, I feel convinced he would erect the chapel at his own expense, such is their enthusiasm but especially that of Mrs Charlton.[29]

But then the Charltons of Sandhoe recollected that the old chapel in the village was still standing. They gave Brown permission to make what he could 'of the old premises at Bellingham and the furniture therein', and reduced their contribution to the new church to £50. Brown was left in an embarrassing position, for the property was practically worthless; it was certainly insufficient security on which to raise a mortgage, and he would have to borrow £350 to make up the short-fall. Furthermore, the church, designed by Ignatius Bonomi in the lancet style, and dedicated to St. Oswald, cost £225 more than Brown had anticipated. In response to Bishop Briggs's enquiry about the financial state of affairs after the church's opening in 1839, Brown said that £288 was outstanding and 'As to the Question "Whence I expect to obtain the means of paying off what yet remains to be unpaid?", I do not know'. Mrs Charlton helped by donating £100, but in annual instalments of £10.[30]

Brown's problems were increased when William Charlton told him that he would only provide half his salary because Charlton of Sandhoe was obliged to pay the other half, and bickering over that went on until 1874. In May 1838, moreover, Jasper Gibson, the Hexham lawyer, drew up the Articles of Agreement, which Brown looked over before sending them on to the bishop for approval. He objected to the sixth clause which gave the Charltons the sole right of presentation to the living. Brown urged the necessity of the bishop having unfettered powers of appointing priests. The Charltons agreed but wished to ensure that no priest would be appointed who 'would make himself obnoxious to the family' and the clause was amended to that effect. The next generation of Charltons was more accommodating; Francis Charlton, third son of William, and County Surveyor of Northumberland, provided a school in 1849 at his own expense. In 1852, however, Mr Brown ran off with Mrs Drury the schoolmistress.[31]

***

In 1678 the estate of **Swinburne Castle** in the parish of Chollerton was bought from William, Lord Widdrington (III) by Thomas Riddell a coal-owner of Fenham. Riddell died in 1704 bequeathing his estates to his son Edward (who registered them in 1717). In 1726 his son Thomas married Mary, heiress to Cheeseburn Grange, a union commemorated in a door-head dated 1728 with the initials T. M. R. In 1760 their son, also Thomas, who had succeeded to Swinburne in 1754, married Elizabeth, heiress of Edward Horsley Widdrington of Felton Park and Longhorsley, who died in 1762. He immediately began to build a new mansion, incorporating what was left of the decaying castle and connecting it with the manor house.

Swinburne was for long a Benedictine chaplaincy. Bishop Leyburn confirmed one hundred and twenty-three people there in August 1687. Dom John Elphege Skelton served at Swinburne from 1695 to 1705. At his marriage, Thomas Riddell took up residence at Felton, though the mission at Swinburne stayed open in the manor house. In 1767, the Riddells and their four children together with their chaplain William Thompson, and Allen Hodgson and his four sisters headed the list of thirty-six papists in Chollerton. In 1785 the Benedictine President was asked for a monk to serve Swinburne and Felton, though Riddell did not want 'a fat unwieldly man' because 'it might be unpleasant to have a person of that description' along with him on the frequent journeys between the two houses. The presumably fragrant Jerome Marsh was chaplain at Swinburne from 1790.

There were ten or twelve Catholic families in Chollerton in 1792, a number that remained static: in 1810 it was reported that the congregation comprised 'some Cottagers in the two adjoining villages belonging to R. Riddell, Esq. but little or no alteration in numbers'. The report of 1814 was: 'No particular alterations except a small number of the young persons have lately come to [the Anglican] church ... The Protestants and Papists are taught in the same schools'. James Higginson, chaplain for thirty-three years from 1795, was dismissed by his patron in 1828 for reasons probably having to do with Higginson's 'testy, sarcastic turn of mind, warm in his attachments and bitter in his antipathies.' He treated his Benedictine superiors 'contumeliously' and it could have been the Provincial who arranged for his retirement to Birtley, where he died at the altar in 1835. St Mary's, Swinburne, was built by Dobson a few hundred yards away from the mansion in 1841.[32]

***

Longhorsley Tower is a sixteenth-century house. Edward Horsley Widdrington inherited the estate in 1690 and he continued with the Jesuit chaplaincy which can be traced to 1678.[33] He built **Felton Park** in 1732, and the domestic chapel was served from Longhorsley—an extension of the mission without an increase in the number of clerical posts. In her will of 1730, Elizabeth Widdrington left '£20 to my spiritual director, Mr John Smith', the 60-year-old Jesuit who had been with her for four years and who moved away after her death. She also left £400 'to keep a Jesuit at Horsley', and he was required to serve a small congregation in Morpeth as well. This busy post was occupied in 1750 by Joseph Howe who reported a total of one hundred and twenty-five Catholics attending the three chapels. Howe died in 1792, aged 81. At about the same time the estate passed into the ownership of

Thomas Riddell and since he had been used to Benedictine chaplains at his patrimonial home in Swinburne, monks were now appointed to Longhorsley. Riddell went further; he split the missions of Felton Park and Longhorsley Tower and placed a priest at each.

Strangely, for a family with such strong Catholic antecedents, Thomas Riddell was not so devoted to his faith to allow it to interfere with a local scheme he obviously cherished. In 1788 he applied for a market day to be held at Felton. It would have been allowed, it seems, on condition 'that he would change his religion from Catholic to Protestant. He was willing but Mrs Riddell made an objection, so [it] was at an end'. The congregation at Felton was never large; in 1830 there were seventy Catholics and in 1839 the priest said that there were forty-three communicants. Gilbert Blount built St Mary's church at Felton in 1857 for Sir Thomas Riddell who had also funded St Mary's at Swinburne.[34]

In 1793, Mrs Riddell bequeathed a new endowment of £600 for the support of the mission at Longhorsley and two years later Dom Dunstan Sharrock became missioner. He died at Longhorsley in 1831 and the mission, which served fifty-three people, was taken on by the seculars to facilitate its amalgamation with the adjacent, almost defunct, mission at Witton Shields. This reorganisation, which took place in 1833, did not please the patron, Thomas Riddell, for in April 1834 the chaplain, Nicholas Brown told the vicar apostolic that Riddell had refused to pay his salary. When Brown reminded Riddell about the endowment made in 1793, he was told that it could be considered as intended 'for superstitious purposes and illegal'. Brown, however, was confident that Riddell could be cajoled into honouring the bequest, but that was not the end of his difficulties for his plan to build a new church was sabotaged by Riddell.[35]

Riddell would not agree to Brown's proposal unless he was given the sole right of presentation to the living; even then he 'could neither give nor sell the estate, being entailed, and of course the chapel would become the property of the family' if it was built on Riddell's land as was intended. He reiterated his position two years later when the vicar apostolic moved Brown to Hesleyside (and into a similar situation) without consulting him. Riddell told Bishop Briggs that in future his permission would be required 'for a new priest to occupy the house and land on the same condition as the last incumbent'. Matters seem to have been resolved only after Briggs had been translated to the Yorkshire District and at the intervention of a younger brother, William Riddell, who was then missioner in Newcastle. A new church, dedicated to St Thomas of Canterbury, was built by Dobson in 1841.[36]

***

For much of the eighteenth century the Longhorsley missioner said Mass weekly in **Morpeth** where there was a growing Catholic congregation. At some point in the early years of the century, a chapel was established in a house in Buller's Green belonging to Robert Widdrington. In 1748, the property passed to his niece Elizabeth Hewit and his nephew Widdrington Bourne. The Vicar of Morpeth reported to the Bishop of Durham in 1764 that Bourne was a Popish schoolmaster who had a great number of scholars and who 'brought them on' extremely well; Bourne was 'the more dangerous by being so clever in his profession'. The number of Catholics in Morpeth steadily increased: in 1725 there were 'about 30 hearers'; in 1767 there were eighty-six of all ages, and in 1792 'between 50 and 60—chiefly tradesmen'. Clearly, the supply mission from Longhorsley (for which the missioner was paid two guineas a year until 1770) was inadequate for the expanding congregation, and the Riddells decided to rectify the situation.[37]

Lady Mary Haggerston (neé Silvertop), who died in 1773, bequeathed £300 for the support of a priest in Morpeth, and that sum was increased to £400 by her husband Sir Thomas, who died in 1777. A further endowment came from the estate of Basil Forcer, which had been left in 1774 for such charitable purposes as his executors saw fit. Thomas Riddell of Felton Park, a trustee of these funds, persuaded his fellow-executors to unite both bequests and to establish a permanent mission in Morpeth. In 1777 a monk wrote that there was

> a proposal on the carpet for having one of ours at Morpeth, a good town in the North. A gentleman of fortune in that County ... has made some overtures. The Fund is intended to be made at £60 p. an. ... but if he keeps the power and the direction of it in his own hands, it may be with the Incumbent as with his own domestic chaplain: Turn out at an hour's warning, and consequently not worth accepting.

In 1779, notwithstanding these fears, an old house in Oldgate was bought and converted into St Bede's chapel and presbytery at a cost of £1,537. The mission was taken by Dom Thomas Turner in 1779. The endowment of £1,200 was entrusted to Sir John Lawson, and all went well until his death in 1811, when the fund could not be traced in his papers. But Sir Henry, his successor, made good half the loss from his own resources, and obtained the rest from an estate of a York surgeon who died in 1814, for whom Lawson was executor. His efforts to repair the financial damage may have had something to do with the fact that at that time the Morpeth missioner was his kinsman Henry Lawson who had moved up from Bath in 1802.[38]

The parochial return of 1792 mentioned 'a school for the education of young girls—taught by two Ladies Roman Catholics to which children of Protestant parents are admitted'. The school had closed by 1810, but it is not known whether that was because there were no teachers, a lack of funds, or official disapproval. In 1829 the Catholic community numbered ninety-one. The mission continued to languish in its small and increasingly decrepit premises; in 1839 there were one hundred and seven communicants, but still no school. The appointment of Dom George Augustine Lowe in August 1836, however, inaugurated a more vigorous period, for he immediately began collecting for a new church. Meanwhile he did what he could to improve

> St Bede's chapel which was in great need of improvement. I changed the altar rails, got a new carpet for the sanctuary, a new set of cards and candlesticks for the altar, new stools and kneeling cushions for the body of the chapel ... the next step was to bring gas into the chapel and house, this I did in the year 1840, it cost me about thirty pounds. In the same year I bought a sweet little organ (five stops) the cost was under sixty pounds.

A choir was formed and, with the housekeeper as organist, the liturgy was henceforth enhanced by music. Such changes, trivial in themselves, as a whole indicate the confidence and zeal of the post-Emancipation generation. As in many other places, however, it was well understood that such improvements did not go far enough and that the full benefits of Emancipation would not be achieved until a new and substantial church had been erected in place of the old chapel. But that would take Dom Augustine some fourteen years. The new church, by T. Gibson, sporting a spire, cost £2,400, was dedicated to St Robert of Newminster (a twelfth-century abbot of the local Cistercian abbey). It was opened in 1850 for an estimated congregation of three hundred, and a school was built at the same time, costing £331. It should be noted, however, that all new churches were essentially bare for a number of years. The organ, the bell, statues and Stations of the Cross would all be installed but it would take time; it would not be for ten years that St Robert's was complete.

***

The Thorntons supported a secular priest in **Netherwitton Hall** after the Restoration. In 1680 there were seventy Catholics in the parish and the only school in the locality was taught by a Catholic. In 1687, Bishop Leyburn confirmed two hundred and eighty-three persons from the district there. The estate and mission survived John Thornton's participation in the 'Fifteen and in 1736 the overall population of the parish was fifty-four families, of which thirty-five were Catholic. Bishop Chandler estimated the congregation at 'about 60', by which he probably meant adults. A fund of £400 to support the priest-chaplain was established from a bequest made in 1711 by Isabella Thornton, a 'Nun of ye Visitation'.[39]

The Alnwick-born John Cotes came as chaplain in 1737 and he remained for fifty-seven years, during which time he witnessed the slow disintegration of the mission. John Thornton (the Jacobite) died in 1742, and, his eldest son Thomas having pre-deceased him in 1740, the estate passed to his next son James, who died five years later. The estate was then divided between his two daughters, Margaret and Mary, an arrangement disputed by their aunt Catherine, daughter of Thomas Thornton and wife of William Salvin. They took the sisters to law in an attempt to eject them but the suit failed. The dispute was compromised in 1769 at the Newcastle Assizes, when the defendants agreed to pay Salvin one third of the value of the estate (less £6,000 which he had already received as his wife's dowry) and he got £12,504. The settlement was confirmed by act of parliament.[40]

Margaret Thornton married Walter Trevelyan in 1772 and they took over the Netherwitton estate. But Trevelyan was a staunch Methodist and the priest was told to remove himself and his chapel (which served a congregation of one hundred and eight in 1767) out of Netherwitton Hall into an old Thornton tower-house in **Witton Shields**, about a mile and a half distant. The tower was three storeys high and there was an old chapel on the second floor. It had served a congregation of fifty-four during the previous century when the secular priest John Hankin had been in residence following the sacking of the chapel in Sunderland. The visitation return of 1774 from Netherwitton remarked on the effect of the priest's expulsion: the Catholic 'Interest is now on the decline and some converts have been made'. Cotes was not cowed, for in 1780 and 1792 the vicar complained about Protestant children being baptised by him; one father had been 'assured by the Priest that nothing should be wanting in the way of a good education for his children at free cost.'

Hankin retired in 1772 but it was not until Cotes' death in 1794 that the closure of the mission became inevitable. There had been rumours that Trevelyan's heir might become a Catholic, to 'the great vexation of his father who, during his stay with him this summer has had two clergymen in his house to dissuade the young man from such a resolution'. The vicar apostolic, William Gibson, also called on Trevelyan, but the conversion did not take place; instead he became 'a red-hot Methodistical preacher' and shortly afterwards he closed the chapel. Thomas Witham, his brother in law, tried to prevent the closure because it would be 'a hardship upon those poor people who had settled in the neighbourhood as in a place where in all probability a priest would always be maintained' but Trevelyan was adamant. Firstly, he knew of no fund for the maintenance of a priest and, secondly, 'the very few Roman Catholics (for no one can call them a congregation with propriety) legally settled here may go to Longhorsley', as he himself was obliged to do to attend his own chapel. Not surprisingly, the congregation at Witton Shields-Netherwitton, which had fallen to seventy in 1792 continued to decline; a report of 1827 said 'few

Catholics are now remaining here'. The mission was served from Thropton until 1828; thereafter the remaining twenty Catholics attended the chapel at Longhorsley, with which the Witton Shields mission merged in 1833.[41]

***

The mission at **Thropton**, two miles west of Rothbury in the Coquet valley, had its origins in **Cartington Castle**, a little further to the north. The castle was extensively modernised in the Elizabethan period and it was thought one of the largest and finest mansions in the county. It passed to Roger Widdrington in 1601. Depredations suffered in the civil wars were repaired and the castle was referred to as a 'handsome seat on top of a hill well planted with trees'. Chaplains were supported here after the Restoration and Bishop Leyburne confirmed one hundred and forty-three people in 1687. John Haggerston S. J. and James Gardiner were resident missioners around the turn of the century but the fabric of the castle had again fallen into considerable disrepair, and concern for its future led Clare Ord, daughter of Roger Widdrington (the last of that line) to move the mission into the village of Thropton and the castle was left to fall into ruin.

'At Thropton is a house lately purchased by the executors of Madam Ord of Cartington for ye maintenance of and entertainment of a Popish priest'. This was Thropton Old Hall bought in 1701/1702 with monies left by Mrs Ord and the Revd Roger Mitford. A public chapel, dedicated to All Saints, was built in the grounds and the benefactors also left a capital fund to provide the priest with £20 a year. James Gardiner served there until 1750. In 1736 there were eighteen Catholic families (numbering, it was said, one hundred and seventy-eight persons, which is surely a mistake for seventy-eight, since there were only sixty-four individuals in 1767). There were nineteen Catholic families out of five hundred and twenty-nine in Thropton in 1774, and the missioner was described as 'one Luke Potts, a sober, quiet, inoffensive man'. As well he might be, for he had been imprisoned at York in 1746, following the Jacobite Rising, and he was, no doubt, happy to spend the rest of his days quietly in rural Northumberland. By 1792 there were one hundred Catholics, a total which remained roughly constant until the Emancipation period. The property was rebuilt in 1811 by the priest Thomas Stout; the chapel, a 'discreet, simple and unassuming' building, was enlarged in 1842.

The mission at Thropton was unique in having only four pastors between its creation and Emancipation in 1829. It was also very well-endowed: several funds had been left for its support and the mission owned five cottages in the village and seven acres of land. It was presumably due to its independence, financial security, seclusion and the long tenures of the priests that the Catholic population remained stable throughout the period.[42]

***

Biddlestone Hall, originally a tower-house, stood at the top of a slope commanding the Coquet valley. The Selby family remained Catholic throughout the penal era although the identity of chaplains before the eighteenth century is not known. The first named chaplain was Thomas Collingwood (al. Durham), S.J., and he was here in 1701. In 1736 it was reported: '28 papists meet at Biddlestone, a mile from the church at Mr Selby's. Robert Widdrington, priest'. In his Jubilee Year report of 1750 the new chaplain, William Newton, S.J., told his superiors 'Customers here as near as I can guess about 50 or 60'. That was an under-estimate, because in 1767 there was nearly three times that number. His uncertainty was understandable because the mission area was extensive and the post had been vacant for three years. Moreover, there were seven incumbents of the mission in the first half of the century and those discontinuities in pastoral care doubtless had an adverse effect on the congregation. At first the chaplain lived with the family and got a 'salary of £10 and diet', but later on the priest fended entirely for himself: 'Mr Selby allow[ed] the incumbent £40 a year, the use of his garden and a cow, and feeding for one horse'.[43]

Dom Laurence Hadley arrived as chaplain in 1764 but it is not known why the Jesuits were succeeded by monks. Thomas Selby was described as 'a gentleman of fortune' in 1767, but he was compelled to leave the country in 1784 'being much in debt and the servants all discharged'. Selby died three years later, aged 78, and was buried in the parish churchyard. Dom Ambrose Naylor was chaplain for fifty-four years from 1767, apparently unaffected by Selby's insolvency. Clearly the family's fortunes recovered, for the hall was rebuilt for Thomas Selby in 1790, possibly by John Carr of York. The house was two-storied and almost square with six by five bays. A fine Tuscan porch was added in 1796. John Dobson made alterations to the house in 1820 for Walter Selby, and a small Gothic church was later built on the remains of the old tower adjacent to the new house. The congregation numbered around one hundred for much of the period after 1767. That life in the mission at Biddlestone (like that at Esh) was largely uneventful and did not suffer from the bad relations between patron and chaplain which existed in so many other northern chaplaincies, was due largely to the patrons being absentee landlords—preferring to spend much of their time at their Yorkshire residence. But, ominously, on returning to Biddlestone in 1828, Mr Selby told Bishop Smith that he expected the 'performance of the religious duties in the house' to be continued even if the chaplain was replaced. In 1837 the congregation comprised eighty-two communicants and ten converts, 'all of a humble class'. In 1841, probably coincident with the coming of age of a new patron, a secular chaplain was appointed, and he remained at the hall for forty-five years.[44]

**

Callay Castle near Whittingham, seat of the Catholic Claverings, was modernised for Sir John Clavering in the early seventeenth century, at which time the Great Hall and a new wing were added and when a priest-hide (a false flue in a chimney) was provided. Substantial rebuilding was carried out in 1676 for Robert Clavering and additions were made for John Clavering in 1707 and in 1727 for Ralph Clavering. Ralph Peter Clavering was 20 years old when he succeeded to the estates (worth about £1,000 a year) on the death of his father Ralph in April 1749 and he embarked on a major re-building of the castle the following year. Italian plasterwork medallions in the drawing room depict George II and his grandson in ridiculous fancy dress; two other medallions were left blank pending the return of the Stuarts. A spacious chapel in the classical style by Thomas Paine was completed in 1750, although it was ostensibly a ballroom.[45]

In 1677 it was reported that 'Mr Collingwood and Mr Clavering of Callile are seducing Papists and keep priests. There are also many other Papists and sectaries'. In 1687 Bishop Leyburne confirmed two hundred and ninety-two persons of the locality at Callaly. A Dominican, George Thomas Gibson, was in place between 1680 and 1693 and he was followed by the Jesuit Henry Widdrington to 1729. Named Jesuit chaplains served at Callaly until 1781 when seculars took over; the tenure was held by a Carmelite from 1792–6. In 1716 only fourteen Catholics were listed for Callaly but in 1750 John Darrell, the Jesuit chaplain, reported that

> all my customers seem to take the affair of the Jubilee so much to heart ... My salary from this place is £10.10s ... Mortuaries and perquisites £1. The number of my customers, including all ages about 280 ...

He had made about half a dozen converts.

When Darrell left in 1752 to become rector of the Jesuit college at St Omer he was succeeded at Callaly by Joseph Pleasington who was listed in 1767 along with his congregation of one hundred and ninety-eight. He was withdrawn in 1774 at the age of 59, having grown weak and 'zealously crazy'; he had objected to Mrs Clavering riding on a Sunday. Bishop Walton had confirmed two hundred and one people in the chapel the year before. After two brief Jesuit incumbencies, the seculars took over in 1781. The change in tenure required a revision of the formal terms of the chaplaincy. In 1780 Clavering settled a trust fund, which provided the chaplain with a yearly salary of £50, or £20 if the priest was boarded and fed by the family. Clavering also stipulated that the family was to have the power to change the chaplain whenever they pleased with the concurrence of the vicar apostolic.

Clavering had become so indebted after thirty years of building costs, that in 1784 he was forced to flee abroad. Henry Rutter remarked that Clavering had gone to Liege, leaving 'his affairs in the greatest confusion'. The trustees of the estate managed to bring the creditors to a settlement and thus save the estate, but economies were required. Thomas Storey, the chaplain, was dismissed and Ralph's brother Nicholas, the secular missioner in Old Elvet, Durham, moved up to Callaly to take over the mission and to act as caretaker of the estate. Rutter was not wholly convinced that the 56-year-old priest would be able 'to manage both the temporal and spiritual affairs at Callaly', which were 'an undertaking too great for him in the opinion of some who are well acquainted with him'. Clavering seems to have taken the task in his stride, notwithstanding his own reservations on the dual role he had to fulfill. The squire died at St Omer in 1787, aged 60, and the estates passed to his son John Aloysius, who was 22 years old, but it was five years before Nicholas Clavering was prepared to hand the estate over to him. Nicholas left Callaly for London around 1793 so as to help the repatriated Benedictine nuns of Pontoise, of whom his sister Anne was abbess, to find a home. In December 1794 Clavering is described as 'now of Hammersmith' and in May 1795 the nuns took a large house there.[46]

At the end of May 1796, James Peters, chaplain to Mrs Biddulph at Midhurst in Sussex, was told he was to be replaced by an acquaintance of hers. Peters wrote to Bishop Douglas saying that he wished to be placed in an independent mission rather than another chaplaincy. He was, however, offered the vacancy at Callaly Castle. After asking Clavering's terms he declined the post, saying that the northern climate would be bad for him. The secular priest Thomas Stout was therefore sent north from St George's, Southwark, but he was at Callaly for less than a year before moving to Thropton. It was then rumoured that Clavering was thinking of taking a Benedictine chaplain. Stout queried this and was told that since a chaplain was needed, Clavering 'would have a regular if no secular was available'. Stout therefore urged the bishop's secretary, Thomas Eyre, to do all he could 'to please the squire'. Within the month a newly-ordained Lancashireman, Thomas Gillow, was appointed to Callaly, despite the pleas of his cousin James Worswick who wanted him to relieve him of the burgeoning mission at North Shields.[47]

An Anglican return of 1828 gave the number of Catholics in the parish as one hundred 'grown persons', most of whom lived in Whittingham, 'their stronghold'. The congregation had fallen by about one hundred and fifty since 1780, showing that the Catholic community did not recover entirely from the difficulties encountered by the Claverings at the end of the previous century. Certainly, at only ten per cent of the population, Catholics were no longer the dominant group in the parish. John Aloysius Clavering died without issue in 1826 and the estate passed to his half-brother John Edward (son of Ralph Peter and his third wife). Mrs Clavering dismissed the chaplain within a year for reasons which are not known. She also quarrelled with the Revd Andrew Macartney in

1837. He counter-attacked by carving out a small cave on the side of Callaly Crag to which he could retreat for some peace and quiet; he did not have the use of it for long, however, because he was replaced within the year. In 1839 the priest said there were fifty-six communicants but there was 'no school, no library'.[48]

***

Shortly after the Restoration 'many Papists and schismaticks' were reported to be living in **Alnwick**, but it is not known where they assembled for Mass. From the early years of the eighteenth century, however, one or other of the priests at Callaly Castle Biddlestone, Ellingham, or Widdrington Castle said Mass monthly, on a weekday, in a house belonging to Mr Cotes in Bondgate Without, next to the Plough Inn. His wife appears in the recusant lists of the day and in 1681 she was indicted for high treason for sending her son, John, to the college at St Omer; her grandson, John, was at Douai from 1715 and he would become a priest. The house was registered by John Clavering in 1717 as 'let to Winifred Cotes'. In 1750, Mary Butler (a relative of the Ord family of Sturton Grange, near Warkworth), bequeathed tithes in Tweedmouth and Ancroft, worth £1,200, for the support of a Jesuit priest in Sturton Grange or in some convenient place in the neighbourhood. Sir Henry Lawson, the principal trustee, and John Walsh, the local Jesuit Superior, agreed that the priest should be stationed in Alnwick, six miles from the Grange, where there already was a Catholic congregation under Jesuit auspices. But two objections were raised by the family. A Protestant half-sister of Mary Butler threatened to go to law to nullify the bequest since it was intended for 'superstitious uses'; she was bought off with an annuity of £10, arranged by John Maire, the Catholic lawyer of Gray's Inn. William Ord then claimed that the priest should reside in the Grange and not in Alnwick; he, too, was induced to take an annuity of £10 in lieu (which he relinquished in 1757 for a lump sum of £120). Only then could the bequest be executed; the tithes were sold and the capital was invested with Ralph Clavering, in trust, to produce £48 a year. Sir Henry Lawson wrote to Walsh,

> all I beg and desire in consideration of the trouble I have had in this jumbled affair is that I may have a zealous and prudent man and one that will do his duty and not a very young man.

Shortly afterwards the 40-year-old Jesuit, John Parker, was appointed missioner.[49]

In 1757, Clavering bought a house for £157, discreetly 'situated about the middle of Bailiffgate on the north side' in trust for the Society, and Parker took up residence; he opened a chapel on the premises which, with several alterations, served for some eighty years. He was succeeded uninterruptedly by Jesuits until they relinquished the mission to the seculars in 1855. The salary of the missioner was £70 a year in the 1770s, and William Strickland said that he did 'not conceive that any man can live there with tolerable comfort upon less'. In 1802 he told the Jesuit William Warrilow that he doubted if any secular priest would find Alnwick 'a very desirable place'.

The congregation (led by Francis and Eleanor Clavering) numbered around seventy in 1767, and eighty-three in 1780; the number of communicants was given as fifty in 1783. From 1794 to 1828 the number of baptisms never exceeded three a year, and it is clear that the congregation was in slow decline. Nonetheless, the chapel was completely redesigned by the then incumbent, Francis Howard, and was reopened on 14 August 1796; a week later twenty-seven people were confirmed in it by Bishop William Gibson. From 1802 to 1812 the missioner was Peter Vergy, a French exile. In 1809, to accommodate a group of fourteen new residents, he obtained permission to extend the chapel, at a cost of £25. Even then the chapel could seat a congregation of no more than twenty-five (the rest stood at the back). Hence the following year the vicar happily reported that there were but 'some' papists in Alnwick, who possessed a chapel and a small dame school. He carefully noted, however, that there was

> a stipend of £60 per annum and a house for the priest who must be of a particular Order, of which I understand there are very few in England. The last Popish priest here was of the Howard family.

If the reference to the Howards was meant to be insidious it was misplaced, for the priest was using an alias; he was Francis Holme, a Lancashireman of minor gentry origins. The vicar probably meant one of Howard's recent predecessors, William Strickland, of the recusant family seated at Sizergh Castle, who was a frequent guest at the table of the Duke of Northumberland.[50]

The Anglican return of 1814 noted that the congregation had fallen to 'nearly 40 chiefly of low rank, except two widows who are lately come to reside here and a linen and woollen draper. They have made no converts here.' The school had closed. After Emancipation, however, the situation improved greatly; there were one hundred and fifty Catholics, the number of baptisms increased to over ten a year, and thirteen children attended catechism classes, clear signs of growth. John Fishwick, newly-ordained in the restored Society of Jesus, was appointed missioner in 1832 and, like many zealous young priests entering upon their first incumbency, he immediately decided on a rebuilding programme. The old chapel and house were razed and four years after his arrival the local newspaper announced:

> A new Roman Catholic chapel dedicated to the Virgin was opened at Alnwick when Mass was performed by the Rev. G. Fisher [Fishwick] assisted by the choirs of Newcastle and North Shields. The chapel is a handsome Gothic building designed by J. Green Junior of Newcastle.

Mozart's Mass No. 12 was sung and the preacher was Philip Kearney, missioner in Sunderland. St Mary's cost some £2,100, three-quarters of which had been raised locally. A picture of the Epiphany in the Italian Baroque style was bought as an altarpiece at a cost of £65. The congregation quadrupled in the first half of the nineteenth century, and in 1855 a two-room school was bought from a dissenting sect for £450; in 1864 the roll numbered fifty-eight. In the following year the mission was handed over to the secular clergy.[51]

***

There had been a secular priest at **Haggerston Castle** around 1660, but from 1688 the resident chaplain was always a Jesuit. Two sons of Sir Thomas Haggerston (II), who died before 1710, became Jesuit priests, and another became a Franciscan. Henry Haggerston S. J. was at home and acting as chaplain from 1701 to his death in 1714. In 1710, Lady Jane Haggerston (neé Carnaby), widow of Sir Thomas, bequeathed £340 to maintain a Jesuit priest in Northumberland or North Durham, and the first recipient was John Thornton S. J. who entered the household in 1711 as tutor to Sir Carnaby Haggerston (III). Thornton's first duty was to accompany his 13-year-old pupil-patron on the Grand Tour. (Francis Anderton S. J. ministered at the castle during this absence.) Judiciously, the tourists remained abroad until 1719 thus avoiding the Jacobite rising and its aftermath. Thornton then served at the castle for the next thirty-four years. Shortly before his death in 1777, Sir Thomas Haggerston built a new two-storied, seven-bayed mansion to a very plain design. He probably acted as his own architect for, as his uncle remarked, Sir Thomas's greatest inclination was 'designing either in regard to these lovely or agreeable sciences, Architecture, Painting or Fortification'. (An etching by Quarenghi ('Palladio's shadow') dated 1777 exists of a highly ambitious but unexecuted mansion.)

In 1736 there were some fifty Catholic families in the area but in 1742 Constable remarked that 'Thornton has grown old and his high spirits quite extinguished'. Consequently in 1750 Thornton reported only '110 customers to shop', which represented about half the potential attendance. The 1767 returns from the north-eastern corner of Northumberland listed two hundred and thirty-six Catholics, and this increase can be attributed to the evangelism of Charles Hanne, S.J., chaplain at Haggerston for forty years from 1758. As well as being identified as a priest in the 1767 return, he is described as 'a domestick in Sir Thos. Haggerston's house'. Michael Tidyman, a secular priest, went to Haggerston in 1790, initially to assist, but then to take over from the aged Jesuit (who retired and died in Ellingham Hall in 1799, aged 88). Tidyman began the registers on his arrival.[52]

In 1795, since the family was not in permanent residence, the castle was given over to a group of forty-one Poor Clares who had been ejected from their convent in Rouen. Sir Carnaby Haggerston (V) forgot to tell the chaplain but when the nuns arrived on Christmas Eve they were very well received by everyone. People brought them little presents and the estate-workers gave them much help. They feature briefly in the papers of Thomas Adams, an Alnwick attorney, because his property, Eshott House, untenanted for some time, might have been suitable for the nuns. He wrote to his brother in Newcastle:

> I see no objection to treat with them except the whimsicality or oddity of such tenants [but] they as well as other reasonable Creatures should be at full liberty to procure happiness.

Thomas's brother concurred and added: 'many societies of this sort have been fed, clothed & lodged by the benevolence & humanity of the Catholic gentry of this country'. The Jesuits had been especially helpful although 'in their temporal concerns I scarce know any order so dark, designing and I had almost said so tricky in their commerce with people of different persuasions'. Negotiations with the community's agent were not successful, possibly because Adams required a security and because the nuns would not be allowed 'to attempt to convert any Man Woman or Child'. In the event, then, the nuns occupied Haggerston Castle as was initially intended. They opened a school for poor children and 'in a large porch of the castle, attend[ed] to any poor people who sought their assistance'. It was in that way that small-pox was introduced into the Community and two nuns died from it. The nuns, 'all dressed alike in plain black gowns and white caps', according to Adams, did 'not sleep in Beds, each of them ha[d] a Crib or Hammock like on board a Man of War'.[53]

Having recovered some of their funds from France in the early years of the nineteenth century, the community began to look around for a house of their own and it appears that Stella House was considered in 1805. The intention to move was just as well for Sir Carnaby wanted to begin major building works at the castle. In 1806 Tidyman told Thomas Eyre that he had detected a changed atmosphere caused by the nuns staying in the castle 'two whole years against the wish and inclination of the proprietors'. When they were still there after ten years, Sir Carnaby lost patience and sent his architect up to begin the re-design. Mother Superior did not take the hint so Sir Carnaby sent the workmen in. When it became apparent that the roof was about to be replaced, Mrs Jane Silvertop of Wooler offered to buy umbrellas for the nuns. At this point Sir John Lawson intervened and obtained alternative premises. In 1808 the nuns moved into Scorton Hall, near Catterick in the North Riding, where they established a boarding-school for girls; they then moved to Darlington in 1857.[54]

Sir Carnaby added three-storey wings of three bays on either side of the central block of the castle, as well as domestic offices, built (and probably designed) by Luke Moody. At the same time the chaplains were provided with a new and furnished house in the village by Sir Carnaby who 'annexed to it an annual income of £90'. A slight decline in the congregation to around two hundred at the beginning of the nineteenth century was noted by the vicar in his return of 1810 from Kyloe. He also remarked on the impending closure of the mission in Berrington Hall and the effect that would have on the Catholic population:

> they will soon disappear in that quarter, and as the Haggerstone family do not scruple to take a good Tenant from among the Protestants, they are I think upon the decrease in both parishes.

Incidentally, the intense concern of some clergymen with interdenominational education was reflected in other comments by the vicar of Kyloe in 1810:

> There is no regular Popish school in either parish, but in the town of Fenwick there is a school kept by a Papist but most of the scholars are Dissenters; and upon conversing with him, I find he hears the children of three different Catechisms, that of the Church of England, Dr. Watts, and of his own communion, honestly enough (I believe) confining the children to that of their own church.

The vicar, however, was not one to take risks and he 'got a young man of the Church of England to commence a school in Kyloe to whom I give every encouragement'.

Michael Tidyman died in 1832 a year after his patron Sir Carnaby Haggerston (V), who was the last in the male line. Haggerston's daughter Mary married Sir Thomas Massey Stanley, Bt., and they lived at the castle and continued to maintain chaplains (William Birdsall, James Anderton, Richard Tyrer, George Corless and Robert Smith) although there were the usual difficulties and they did not stay long. In 1834 the chaplain was summarily dismissed (without consultation with the vicar apostolic) because he rarely visited his flock or preached; he regularly spent half the day in bed and drank so much that he was often seen to fall off his horse. Bishop Mostyn was advised that an older and more experienced priest was needed because Lady Stanley dominated the chaplain to such an extent that he only said Mass when she told him to. (She did, however, support a small school of twenty-four children.) Ten years later, his coadjutor, Bishop Riddell, told Mostyn that the Revd Robert Smith had expressed an 'anxious desire' to leave Haggerston and, if the bishop agreed to remove him, Smith 'would take all the blame on himself'. The cause of the disagreement is not explained but the character of Riddell's proposed replacement gives a broad hint: Joseph Cullen

> would suit Lady Stanley very well, he is quiet, and would not interfere where he has no business; he has been on the mission some little time and therefore has some experience which Her Ladyship likes.

She died in 1857 and the estate passed to John Massey Stanley, but it had to be sold within the year to cover his massive gambling debts and so Haggerston passed out of Catholic hands.[55]

***

Edward, sixth son of Sir Thomas Haggerston (II), bought the **Ellingham Hall** estate in 1698–9; his and his wife's initials with the date 1703 were carved above the front door, thus dating the completion of their rebuild of the seventeenth-century house. A chapel was attached to the west wing and Haggerston instituted a Jesuit chaplaincy, the first incumbent of which was his elder brother John who single-handedly created a Catholic community at Ellingham. There were thirty-one Catholic families there in 1736 and in 1750 the chaplain, William Pemberton, reported a congregation of one hundred and five. He spent all his priestly life in the service of the Haggerstons. He had accompanied his pupil William on the Grand Tour between 1742 and 1745 before settling down in his Northumbrian chaplaincy, though he did not seem altogether satisfied with the financial terms:

> My salary from Factory £30, and from my landlord a field valued at £8 per annum. No helps unless a little beef or the like from Haggerstone or the tenants, which Latter I repay with interest.

Sir Carnaby Haggerston (III) died in 1756 (a memorial to him was placed in the parish church), and the Ellingham estate passed to his youngest son, Edward.

In 1767 the vicar reported that the Catholics refused to answer any questions and that he was unable to identify the priest living with the family (actually the mission was vacant: Augustine Jenison had left and his successor Daniel Needham had not arrived) but, after naming one hundred and eight Catholics, 'according to the best information which could be obtained', he went on:

> John Barton is yet living in the village of Ellingham who remembers when the late Edward Haggerston Esq. purchased the Estate, at which time, he says, there was not one Papist in the parish, but now, all the persons as yet mentioned are tenants or sub-tenants to the present Edwd. Haggerston Esq.

Only four of the Catholics were not tenant-farmers or in some other way dependents of the Haggerstons, although there is no evidence that the squire made Catholicism mandatory, and it should be noted that there were five hundred Protestant families in the parish.[56] Twenty-two people were confirmed by Bishop Gibson in 1783. In 1792 the vicar reported that

> the only Papists of Distinction in my Parish: four substantial farmers are of the same persuasion and a few Cottagers.

> They have a place in my parish where they assemble for Divine Worship which place is a Chapel within the dwelling-house of ... Edward Haggerston Esq. A Popish Priest doth reside within the aforesaid Edward Haggerston Esq.'s House who is known by the name of Mr. Joy. There is one Popish school in my Parish kept by a Woman.

His disparaging comment may indicate that he was not fully aware of the size of the Catholic community. In 1796 there were eighty-three Easter communicants and twenty-five confirmands. Mr Joy died unexpectedly in 1798 aged 56, and was succeeded by William Meynell, S. J. The squire was by this time an old man and, fearing for the future of the mission, he bequeathed £140 for the support of the chaplain. He died two years later, 'much respected and a model of piety'.

His nephew Thomas Haggerston succeeded to the estate; his wife was Winifred Charlton, whose family at Sandhoe had normally supported Benedictine priests. Inevitably, then, the Jesuit was replaced by a monk. For the first thirty years of the nineteenth century the chaplaincy at Ellingham was filled by Benedictines, Jesuits or seculars, depending on the availability of priests, but the post became a permanent secular chaplaincy thereafter. In March 1828 in the normal course of events, the vicar apostolic wished to move the chaplain but Haggerston wrote:

> I am extremely sorry that I cannot oblige you. At my time of life it is impossible for me to consent to remove Mr Maddox. He suits me enormously well and is much liked by the congregation. He has now got himself comfortably settled here that I cannot think of changing him.

In September the following year, however, he accepted the proposed change and told the bishop, 'The mission is an easy one', and if the new chaplain, Mr Crane, 'will only not be on too familiar terms with the servants, I can conceive he may be happy and contented'. The outgoing chaplain, Mr Maddox, thought he had 'never met a gentleman of so unkind a temper' as Thomas Haggerston.[57]

***

The origins of the **Berwick** mission can be attributed to the Haggerstons. At the beginning of the eighteenth century, William, second son of Sir Thomas (II), and his wife Anne went to Berwick to live in the Haggerston's town-house. They took with them his brother Francis, a Franciscan, as domestic chaplain. By 1710 Sir Thomas, William and Francis were all dead and Anne Haggerston returned to the castle. She left to live in Gateshead after her son's marriage, and she later moved to Pontoise, where two of her daughters were nuns. She died at St Omer in 1740 bequeathing funds to the Society of Jesus 'with the obligation of serving Berwick unless otherwise apply'd in urgent necessity'. The Jesuit account-books for 1749 show that two guineas were paid to Francis Digges for assisting at Berwick, and until the end of the century, the chaplain at Haggerston Castle or Berrington Hall supplied in the town.[58]

The indigenous congregation in Berwick and Tweedmouth, numbering around fifty in 1767, was attended by Charles Hanne, S. J., from around 1777 until 1790 when the 80-year-old had 'become so infirm as to be incapable of that duty'. He was relieved by Michael Tidyman, the new chaplain at Haggerston Castle. The military garrison swelled the congregation at the outbreak of the Napoleonic Wars but it was fortunate that a hundred or more French exiled priests were accommodated in the town and in 1792 the congregation of around thirty-five was served by them under Tidyman's supervision. Five years later Tidyman wrote to Thomas Eyre proposing to buy property for the mission in the town. The French priests, he said, 'by residing there for a considerable time have partly done away with the prejudice that otherwise might have impeded so good an undertaking'. In 1798 Tidyman took a short lease on an old Assembly Room, but after a year he paid £350 for 'a new house built within these last nine years and used at present for a printing office' and installed Louis Bigot as missioner. When Bigot returned to France in June 1802 with most of the other exiles the congregation was desolated at 'the loss of so suitable a pastor'.

William Hurst went to Berwick as missioner in 1803 to find some seventy very poor people struggling to support the priest. He was no better off than them; the house was practically bare, the income 'too uncertain to be relied upon', and he was unable to keep himself or his servant. Hurst wrote to Thomas Eyre: 'I am not yet settled nor do I live in the Chapel-house as yet, as I am waiting for several persons who propose to come from Richmond and live with me'. The boarders did not arrive and when Tidyman went up from Haggerston, he found Hurst 'quite bewildered and absent[-minded] in his parochial functions'. Though Hurst liked Berwick, he was unable to cope with the difficulties and he left within a year.

Philip Besnier, another French exiled priest, took over and he made strenuous efforts to serve the Catholics in Berwick and the villages on the Scottish border. After a year *en poste* he gave Eyre a summary of his experiences:

> I have been under the necessity of taking a room in the town which, you understand, I am to pay for. There is a house belonging to the chapel but there is nobody in it; there is no furniture in it but a bed, a little table, a drawer, a chair, no linen, nothing else. The expense of the lodging is nothing in comparison to what I am at for the wearing of shoes and clothes. During these last twelve months I have walked no less than 1,000 miles, not to say more, and by all kinds of weather.
>
> The number of communicants is about 110, should they all come. The congregation is very much scattered. I am

> obliged to go to Scotland several times to baptise children and to visit sick people. I have been called twice to Norham, which is at a great distance from Berwick, and to many other places in the country where the road is shocking.
>
> Had I not seen a considerable change for the better amongst the congregation, although not yet as I wish, I would have given up long ago. Last year there were only 43 who received at Easter; this year I had eighty.[59]

Despite his evident poverty Besnier scrupled to accept additional financial assistance since he received a small pension from the British government; Tidyman told Eyre that Besnier's

> purse is emptied, his clothes are worn out, shoes are very dear etc. And yet he will not take a shilling as a consideration for his necessary expenses. What strange geniuses there are in the world. M. Besnier for his whims and unaccountable ideas stands hitherto unequalled.[60]

The return of 1810 reported that the Catholic congregation was 'about 60' and that M. Besnier taught in school. M. Menard, another French priest, kept a boarding school, to which both Protestant and Catholic children were admitted. Besnier died later in 1810, and there seemed little likelihood of attracting a residential missioner to so poor a position, and so in 1811 a petition was presented to the vicar apostolic by the representatives of forty-seven local families and forty private soldiers and their families of the Aberdeenshire Militia in the garrison. The writer described the need for a resident priest in Berwick. Although the road had been improved,

> he and his family on their return from Haggerston the other Sunday were fatigued to such a degree that they were actually obliged to go to bed instead of taking their dinner ... For want of more practical means of assembling on Sundays and Holydays of Obligation we fear our number

has already greatly reduced and will still more rapidly decline ... Several of the Catholic Laity in this neighbourhood say they would willingly contribute a guinea a year each ... 20 such subscribers or more might be immediately procured.[61]

The vicar apostolic could not appoint a resident missioner at that time, but the chaplain at Berrington visited the town weekly from 1812.

When the 80-year-old Scottish Benedictine William Pepper went to Berwick as missioner in 1816 he found nothing in the house except 'an old chest of drawers for the vestments, which are in tolerable good condition, 2 chairs—one in the chappel, the other in a room, one mirror, a bason stand and a broken table.' He had to spend £40 on furnishing the house and he was obliged to live 'like a hermit' ... 'very sparingly indeed'. In 1817 he described his health as good 'despite an inveterate pain in my jaw' and his 'memory and faculties much failing'. In 1824 he was succeeded by the first English resident secular missioner, William Birdsall, who moved from Ellingham Hall. He decided to build a church, but it took him five years to collect the money. The church, dedicated to Ss Mary and Cuthbert, on Ravensdowne, was opened in June 1829 with the usual grand ceremonial. No school was provided although fifteen children attended catechism classes after Mass on Sundays.[62]

Birdsall died suddenly, and intestate, in 1838. It emerged from his papers that he had debts of £2,000. (Thomas Parker, chaplain at Ellingham, had warned the bishop about Birdsall's financial position the previous year.) The immediate problem was to settle with Birdsall's brother who, as heir-at-law, claimed the property. The contents of the house were sold and they raised £400, which satisfied Mr Birdsall, and the bishop could turn to the greater difficulty of settling with Birdsall's other creditor. The cause of the late priest's situation was that some years before he had bought a cottage and a small garden next to the Catholic chapel

> for £400, which is more than it is worth but it was purchased at the time to prevent it being bought by some Moravians or Methodists who wished to have it to build a Chapel upon the property, which would have been an immense nuisance to our Chapel.

Birdsall had been paying £31 a year for the cottage, and he got that by mortgaging the chapel and house. In order to redeem the mortgage, then, the whole property, chapel, house and cottage, would have to be sold. It was valued at £1,500 and put on the market. The Revd Joseph Orrell offered to pay £1,400 for it out of his own pocket, but Bishop Briggs would not hear of it. He had decided on a scheme to drive the price down and then buy the property himself. In May 1838 he told Henry Sharples, the new incumbent, to leave the presbytery and live with neighbours, and to neglect the property. Sharples told the bishop that he felt 'ashamed and almost disgraced by being forced to hang upon my neighbours for a living', but he did what he was told. In August he reported to Briggs that he had done all he could to 'conceal your intention of buying the property'. In January, when the property presumably looked its worst, Sharples made an offer of £1,000 for it, but there was a counter-offer of £1,125. The priest's next offer of £1,150 was sufficient to secure the property, and the mission in Berwick was saved. Sharples had found the whole business so distasteful that, considering his position in the town to have become untenable; he asked to be moved, and he was.[63]

Thomas Edward Witham became missioner in 1843 and he decided to build a new church. In 1846 he issued an appeal for funds in the pages of the *Catholic Directory*; the new church would be neat, but not gaudy, and of the early style of Gothic architecture. When executed the Church will accommodate 500 people on the ground floor. Its estimated cost, including a quantity of material upon the place, is £800.

But Witham left Berwick before the project could be implemented because, as the last male of his line, he had inherited the family's estates at the death of his brother George in September 1847. Witham became squire-priest at Lartington.

***

In 1662 it was reported that in **Berrington Hall**, 'Masses are openly and publicly said and warning given to the people to come thereto'. However, a permanent chaplaincy was not established by the Claverings until 1721. The American-born Jesuit, Francis Digges was chaplain in 1750, and he reported 'about 120 customers that go through all kinds of business'. William Clavering died in 1789, aged 82, leaving less than £600, one third of which had been bequeathed by his aunt Margaret to maintain the chaplain. When Digges died two years later, the residential chaplaincy was allowed to lapse, and the mission was served from Haggerston Castle for fourteen years. The new squire, Edward Clavering, was something of a spend-thrift, despite his depleted inheritance, and he so over-reached himself in rebuilding the mansion that from 1807 parts of the estate had to be sold off. He died in 1816 and the estate was dissolved. The congregation merged with that at Haggerston.[64]

***

Minsteracres south-east of Hexham, was a farmstead owned by the Swinburne family from Elizabethan times until 1721 when it came into the possession of Albert Silvertop whose forbears had lived in Ryton and whose father William was listed as a recusant in 1674. No chaplaincy was provided, or required, since the family's main residence was in Dockendale Hall, Blaydon, and Minsteracres was effectively their summer retreat. The Silvertops steered clear of Jacobitism and their fortunes rose in contrast to those of the old Catholic families. By mid-century Albert's son George had raised the family from the ranks of colliery manager to country gentleman: he had married (twice) into the minor Catholic gentry; he obtained a grant of arms in 1758; and in 1765 he was in a position to engage his kinsman William Gibson, the future vicar apostolic, as chaplain at Minsteracres and as tutor to his son John. (Gibson was not listed in the 1767 return among the thirty-five Catholics in Bywell and Slaley.) The chapel, however, did not reflect the higher social status of the patron or the more relaxed times for Catholics. In June 1784 John Rutter, Gibson's successor but one, described the arrangements:

> [T]here is a shocking little chapel and the way to it is through my room, which indeed makes part of it on Sundays and Holydays. Moreover, there is no Sacristy, which makes it very inconvenient at times, and as an additional recommendation, it is in the garret.

Rutter was delighted to learn that a new mansion was to be built. Although the wing comprising the 'Chapel, offices and servants rooms' was the last to be completed, in 1788, the dining room on the ground floor (with painted gilded coffered ceilings and carved chimneypieces by Anton Bulletti) was made into the chapel and it served until it was transferred to a room in the outbuildings. Dobson made some additions to the house in 1816 and he is credited with the chapel which was completed in 1834.

Apart from the family and the domestics, Rutter had charge of 'a small but dispersed flock' of estate workers and other farmers numbering around one hundred and was as many as he could manage given the demands of the patronal family. When Rutter retired in 1822 the Catholic population of the district had grown to some one hundred and sixty, probably by natural means rather than conversions. But, at the Religious Census of 1851, the population had fallen back to about seventy. That decline should not be put down to any neglect by the then chaplain, John Rogerson, who, as it happens, was a keen huntsman and an expert marksman, but was due to the drift from the country into the newly industrialising towns (in this case Consett nearby to the east) which was the common experience of many rural missions. The final ecclesiastical development at Minsteracres was the erection of a church in 1854 when the architect Joseph A. Hansom was asked for 'Something nice; no matter the cost'.[65]

***

George Silvertop's widow Jane (neé Selby) returned to her native place of Earle near **Wooler** in October 1792, taking with her Thomas Eyre as chaplain. She bought a house and named it St Ninian's, the top floor of which became the chapel and priest's accommodation. Eyre left after a year or so to take charge of the repatriated church-students of Douai College in Pontop Hall, afterwards in Crook Hall and ultimately in the new college at Ushaw. Mrs Silvertop took in four French exiled priests, Charles Macquet, Charles Gicquet, Louis Bigot and Nicholas Alain Gilbert, her chaplain, who all had 'leave to say Mass and *audire confessiones Gallorum pro uno anno*'. Gilbert was known as 'The Dean' and he became friendly with the local Presbyterian minister, the Revd J. Kennedy: he taught Mrs Kennedy French, and Mr Kennedy taught him English.

In 1797 the chapel was registered at the Quarter Sessions as 'The Roman Catholic Chapel of St Ninian, Wooler, The Reverend Thomas Eyre, Clerk'. (Either the registrar was unaware of Eyre's earlier departure or Eyre was deemed to be the priest in charge because the law could not officially recognise a Frenchman as such.) In 1802 Gilbert moved to Whitby (where he would serve until 1815) and the others returned to France. Richard Whalley, a

70-year-old Franciscan priest, was in Wooler from 1805, but in 1808 he was 'infirm and suffering from rheumatism' and considered unable 'to perform the necessary duties of a missionary' though he seems to have remained in Wooler until his death in 1811. Thomas Gillow, chaplain at Callaly Castle visited Wooler 'for prayers once in three weeks' until 1816.

The aged Mrs Silvertop became anxious to bequeath money for the support of 'an able priest equal to the cure of souls and the instruction of youth; she also wished to leave St Ninian's to the vicariate but it was thought that the house was too expensive to maintain by the small Catholic population of the area which had fallen from thirty-eight in 1767 to twenty in 1814. At her death in December 1818 Gillow was consulted about the precise details of her will and he confirmed that she had wanted her bequest to be devoted to founding a mission-station in Wooler:

> She was frequently importuned by Bishop Gibson and Mr Eyre to leave the property to some other place where it would have been more beneficial, but this she would never consent to do, saying that it was her decided resolution that a Mission should be established at Wooler for the purpose of giving her family a chance of returning to the Church. The family property is at Earl near to Wooler. She declared the same to me many times. The property therefore can never under any pretence be removed to any other place. It was her wish that the money arising out of the bequest should accumulate till there should be sufficient sum to purchase or build a Chapel and House, and support a priest.... The sum left to them in money amounted to £2,200.

St Ninian's was let and a small property in Corby Knowe, an alleyway off the main street, was bought as a Mass-centre; and later Tenter Hill House was leased from the earl of Tankerville. The mission ceased to be residential, and the priests at Ellingham Hall, Callaly Castle or Berwick attended.

The congregation began to grow after Emancipation and was almost forty strong by 1840 though it was still too small to support a priest. The vicariate resumed the occupancy of St Ninian's around 1847 and, in 1850, in addition to its function as a presbytery; it became a Diocesan Missionary Establishment from which a small group of priests gave conventual retreats and parochial missions across the diocese. But towards the end of 1854 the house burned down and the enterprise came to an end. Responding to the Census of Religion in 1851, Edward Consitt, missioner, had noted that the chapel was 'small and inconvenient'. It was therefore decided to build a church but it was not until 1855 that Consitt had collected some £900 and could report on 'the actual beginning of the long talked, long prayed for *Church* ! I laid the first stone on 23 May'. The architect was George Goldie (a relative of Ignatius Bonomi), who supervised Mr Richardson, mason and builder of Wooler. The church, in the early English Transitional style, costing £1,305, and dedicated to St Ninian, was opened by Bishop Chadwick five years later.[66]

***

In 1700, **Newcastle upon Tyne** was the fourth largest town in England and 'the great Emporium of all in the Northern Parts'. Catholicism had flourished in the town since the Restoration, but it was not until the 1680s that what was expected to be a permanent missionary organisation was established. From 1681 the Jesuits kept 'a sufficiently spacious chapel and a well-frequented school' in the back buildings of the White Hart Inn. At about the same time Robert Riddell, a secular priest, was appointed chaplain to the Radcliffe household in Bell's Court, Newgate Street. In 1684 the vicar of Newcastle remarked that Catholics 'had begun to nestle more in and about the town than formerly'. The following year a

Benedictine chapel also opened. Bishop Leyburn confirmed three hundred and sixty persons in August 1687 but the world changed abruptly at the revolution in 1688. While the Benedictine chapel closed, the secular chapel remained open under the protection of the Radcliffes; Sir Francis left £400 to maintain the priest, but the chapel closed as a consequence of the 'Fifteen and the missioner rented a house in The Nuns close by. The Jesuit mission was hastily transferred to the privacy of Gateshead House, south of the river, belonging to the Riddells. The chaplain from the turn of the century was the 30-year-old Lancastrian George Pippard (*vere* Brown). He attended the Earl of Derwentwater on the scaffold in 1716 but he immediately retired to the continent for safety; he returned around 1720 and ministered in the north until 1734.

The incomplete Return of Papists for 1705 listed some fifty Catholics in the town, and there were eighty-five in 1736. The chapels in Gateshead and Newcastle were sacked by the mob in January 1746 in the aftermath of the second Jacobite rising, but the civic authorities did not countenance such acts of vandalism even though the properties belonged to supposed rebels and papists. The Town Clerk of Newcastle offered a reward of £50 for information leading to the conviction of the offenders. In any event, a redisposition of the Tyneside mission became necessary. The Gateshead mission was not reopened and, after taking refuge briefly with Ralph and Eleanor Brandling at Felling Hall, John Walsh, the Jesuit missioner, moved into Newcastle late in 1746 and took a house in The Close, on the top floor of which he opened a chapel and he quickly became well-established. In his report for the Jubilee Year, 1750, Walsh said that of some two hundred and fifty Catholics in the town, one hundred and fifty attended his chapel. He had also gained about thirty converts and four or five others were 'in a hopeful way'. His success in such a short time was exceptional; of the other Jesuits in the county, only Joseph Howe reported as many as ten converts, the others made only one or two. He added, in the customary code:

> My customers, on this occasion, gave convincing proof of their having a true sense of the affair from their constant attendance to instructions, their punctual compliance with all requisites - the subsequent fruits a more exemplary life. Of 250 that have learnt the trade not above 4 or 5 that did not enter upon business with passing first their private accounts as a proper introduction, to complete what they afterwards did, a general review, and the other necessary conditions. Above 20 that had not visited anybody for nigh 30 years, and 4 or 5 that had not for above 40, made up in a true and edifying manner their accounts on that occasion. several who nominally belonged to others chose to take merchandise of me, and by a right use of them ever since showed they knew thoroughly the value of them.

Walsh was Superior of the Jesuits in the north from 1752 until 1773 when he died, 'greatly regretted by all his acquaintance', as the *Newcastle Journal* reported.

Thomas Gibson, who had been the secular missioner since 1716, moved back into the old Radcliffe mansion in 1746 and he lived there quietly on an income (largely from Radcliffe endowments) of £36 a year with £10 more from the vicariate. (Correspondence was occasionally addressed to him as 'Mrs Anne Lawrence at the Nuns Gate'.) The house was then owned by Mary Silvertop, and Gibson was, in effect, her chaplain until she died in 1756. He died in 1765 and a brief obituary in the *Newcastle Journal* described him as 'a gentleman of very fair character'. In 1767 the mansion was occupied by Elizabeth and Bridget Silvertop. The secular clergy bought the house, and it remained in use until 1798, with Charles Cordell as the resident missioner for much of the period.

The secular mission did not prosper, and this was partly because Cordell was more a controversialist and translator than a pastor, but also, his was a quasi-public chapel in a less-populated area of the town which did not attract as much support as the wholly independent Jesuit chapel in the heavily inhabited riverside area. The number of baptisms recorded by Cordell was very low, and the Anglican returns do not record any growth in the Catholic population. In 1767 there were around two hundred Catholics in the town; in 1774 the vicar of All Saints believed there had been no increase, and in 1792 he gave it as his opinion that the Catholics were 'a declining sect'. At the same time the vicar of St Andrew's reckoned that the number of Catholics had 'rather decreased than increased'. Cordell's house was threatened by the mob at the time of the Gordon Riots in London, but the civic authorities intervened to protect the property. Cordell was offered an academic post at St Omer but he declined it and he died in Newcastle in 1791. Henry Rutter remarked,

> His death will not be so severely felt at Newcastle as he had been for some time past unable to do any duty. As Newcastle is one of the most important places in these Northern parts, I hope it will be supplied by some able person.[67]

It was James Worswick, aged 24 and the newly-ordained son of an eminent banker of Lancaster, arrived in the town to inaugurate a radically different mission.

Meanwhile, the Jesuits had rented premises in the more respectable part of the town shortly after the arrival of the Dublin-born William Warrilow. He had served at Ellingham since 1769 and was moved to Newcastle in 1773 at the death of John Walsh. (His annual allowance, like other Jesuits at that time, was some £60 a year, provided by the Society.) He immediately moved the mission from the Close to Westgate Street. His arrival in the town virtually coincided with the suppression of the Jesuits by Pope Clement XIV, but, after a brief tussle with Charles Cordell in the local newspaper, he accepted the papal decree and was allowed to remain in place. In 1803 he wrote of his deteriorating health, a decline in his intellectual powers, his difficulty in saying Mass, and his 'drooping spirits as he drops down the eventide of life'. At his death in 1807, the *Newcastle Chronicle* described him as 'much esteemed by a numerous circle of friends for his extensive information, his urbanity as a gentleman and his erudition as a scholar'. His clerical colleague John Lingard was not so impressed: 'He lived here at great expense', he said, 'besides other servants he kept a footman and two horses'.[68] By this time James Worswick had been in the town for twelve years and he had come to dominate the mission to the extent that the closure of the Jesuit chapel at Warrilow's death had little effect. (Worswick complained: 'Not a farthing have I received for the additional burden of that congregation'. In fact, he signed a receipt on 7 December 1807 for £200 given by the Society for the enlargement of the chapel in Pilgrim Street, and £50 left for the poor by Warrilow.)[69]

In 1796 Worswick had bought a house with a large garden at 73 Pilgrim Street, in the better part of the town, and he issued a public appeal for funds to complete the construction of a new chapel:

> It has often been lamented that the Catholic inhabitants of Newcastle are not possessed of a spacious and convenient chapel, suitable to the dignity of the divine worship, and proportioned to the numerous body of Catholics. The two chapels in present use, which are held under a precarious tenure, are inconveniently situated, one of them also entirely excluded from the benefit of daylight, and neither sufficiently capacious to contain the congregations. As all the places in both chapels are appropriated to the inhabitants of Newcastle, it is impossible to accommodate either the numerous Catholics of Shields, and those on the banks of the Tyne, to the amount of four hundred, or the many

strangers who are continually passing and repassing through the town, or the several families, not of our persuasion, who have expressed a desire of being admitted into our chapels, and of becoming more immediately acquainted with our religion. To remedy this inconvenience, it has been proposed to erect a chapel on a more extensive plan. For this purpose a situation universally approved of as unexceptional has been purchased. The building is begun, and it is hoped will soon be completed. In the meantime, as the great majority of the Catholics belonging to the congregation are mechanics, or such as earn their bread by working on the river, and are consequently unable to defray the expenses of the building themselves, it has become necessary to solicit the benefactions of those whom the Almighty has placed in easier circumstances ... [70]

Allowing for any exaggeration Worswick had to use, his appeal does help to illustrate the importance of the project, not just for the Catholics of the town itself and visitors to the regional capital, but also for those on Tyneside as a whole; there was, moreover, a consideration not to be dismissed, that the chapel would be a showpiece to the Protestant population.

The only site available for the chapel was a secluded spot at the far end of the back garden of the priest's house, but what was lost in the location was made up in the 'romantic' Gothic of the church's interior. Some £900 was contributed, and the large brick chapel, dedicated to **St Andrew** (in which Anglican parish it was situated), was opened on Sexagesima Sunday, 1798. Schools were provided in 1800 and the chapel was extended in 1808, to accommodate the congregation of the late Jesuit chapel. Further extensions were required in 1826, when an assistant priest was appointed, and again in 1830, by which time the chapel could hold a thousand people. A Catholic Library was established in 1822. In October 1829, the *Catholic Magazine* reported that over four thousand Catholics were under Worswick's pastoral care (which he estimated to be half the Catholic population of the county). In 1833 a new school was built at a cost of £1,500 and it was 'kept warm by a very ingenious apparatus of pipes containing warm water'. In 1849 the School Inspector noted that 'more than 1,100 children have passed through these schools in the course of a single year'.[71]

As Worswick had predicted, St Andrew's became prominent in the ecclesiastical life of Newcastle. All major events at, and visitors to, the church were reported in the newspapers. Protestants regularly went to hear sermons and solemn Masses: James Losh, the leading Whig and Unitarian, often attended. The anniversary of the king's coronation was celebrated in 1831 'with great solemnity' at St Andrews:

> The Rev. Mr. Worswick preached an eloquent and impressive sermon on the duty and obligation of loving one's country, after which he invoked the blessings of heaven on this beloved country, and its patriotic and reforming sovereign, and the coronation anthem was sung.[72]

Worswick's missionary labours were fully appreciated by his congregation. In 1830 his old scholars gave him a public dinner and in 1835 he was presented with a bust of himself and a silver tea and coffee service.

The success of Worswick's missionary zeal is evident from the growth of the Catholic population. The baptismal register for 1795 has thirteen entries; in 1829 there were one hundred and fifty and in 1840 there were three hundred and sixty-four. A meeting of the town's Catholics in July 1838 resolved that it

> behove[d] the Catholic body to endeavour to erect a large and handsome Church that may be at the same time an honour to their religion, an ornament to the Town, and capable to afford sittings for about twelve hundred persons.

A building-fund was opened and when £6,500 had been collected the architect Augustus Welby Pugin was commissioned to produce the design and he went for his favourite 'triple roof and [high] gables' elevation and three-aisle plan of the late mediaeval preaching or hall-church, in this case the London Austin Friars. Pugin thought the committee's preferred and cheaper design for lean-to aisles was too countrified: 'it is completely surrounded by lofty houses [so] that a low church would appear crushed & mere aisles without high gables would never answer'.[73] The church, dedicated to **St Mary**, was opened in 1844 to Pugin's design but without his intended tower and steeple. They would be added by Dunn and Hansom in 1872. Worswick did not live to see its opening, for he died in 1843 aged 72. He was, however, buried in the chancel of the unfinished church which, in due course, would become the diocesan cathedral. His obituary in the local newspaper was effusive: 'His liberal expenditure amongst the poor, extensive acquirements and prepossessing manners, made him beloved and respected by all classes'. The street in which St Andrews stands was named after him.[74]

***

In 1767 there were thirty-six Catholics living on the north bank of the Tyne from Wallsend to **North Shields** and **Tynemouth**. In March 1784, Henry Rutter and William Warrilow dined onboard John Silvertop's collier *Good Luck* at North Shields, which Rutter described as 'the port of Newcastle and consequently a very great trade' was carried on there. He went on, however, to wish that there was

> a good foundation made for a chapel; for there is a rising congregation, which, if properly encouraged, would soon become very numerous. Mr Johnson indeed attends there, but only now and then; for he has business enough on his

hands at home, whereas one of the Gentlemen at Newcastle might easily be spared.

But it was not until around 1790 that funds were provided for a mission in the locality, firstly by Sir John Lawson out of the proceeds of a colliery lease, and secondly in a bequest made by Bridget Silvertop. A disused Protestant chapel was rented and Mass was celebrated regularly by French exiled priests (three of whom were buried in North Shields in 1796) or James Johnson, missioner at Pontop Hall. Tynemouth came into vogue as a resort around this time, and visiting priests said Mass when there by themselves or with their patrons. Tynemouth Castle was garrisoned and the (mainly Catholic) Second Royal Lancashire Militia was quartered there from 1807 to 1810.[75]

James Worswick, who began to visit North Shields and Tynemouth monthly (on a Tuesday) after the war, had long since tried to put the mission in the busy seaport on a more substantial basis. In 1797 he had asked the newly-ordained Thomas Gillow, his cousin, to go to North Shields instead of Callaly Castle; Gillow had replied, 'build me a church and then I will come'. Worswick had just finished St Andrew's in Newcastle and took up the challenge, but there was a problem in getting Gillow away from Callaly, for as he said,

> the Bishop will not consent to my removal. He never has upon any one occasion consulted my inclinations or wishes—he seems resolved that I should both live and die under the chilling shade of grizzly Cheviot ... I have been for some time under a private engagement to Mr. Worswick of Newcastle to go to N. Shields if the Bishop's consent can be obtained. He has long wished to see a new Chapel built at the above place and is now exerting every nerve to raise the necessary funds for the undertaking. But before he took the business in hand he required my consent to become the

Incumbent declaring to me that unless I would comply (with the approbation of the Bishop) he would never engage himself in so difficult and troublesome an undertaking.[76]

Worswick persevered notwithstanding Bishop Gibson's intransigence. He bought land and by 1817 he had collected £1,400 in subscriptions, and work began on a church in North Shields on the turnpike road from Tynemouth to Newcastle. The *Catholic Directory* for 1818 contained an appeal for money for the chapel, observing that the number of Catholics in 'the town and vicinity amount, independently of foreign Catholic seamen and others, to several hundreds. It is one of the first and most improving seaports in the kingdom'. The Gothic church ('of some ambition') by the local architect Robert Giles, dedicated to St Cuthbert, designed for six hundred people, was opened in 1821 by Bishop Thomas Smith.[77] Thomas Gillow, who had recently been appointed as the first incumbent, preached at the inaugural Mass. It was only with the death of Bishop Gibson that he had gained his release from Callaly Castle, and he was to spend the remainder of his life at North Shields, assisted by his nephew Richard Gillow from 1842. In 1829 an official return put the Catholic congregation at nine hundred and sixty, and in 1839 there were three hundred and sixty Easter communicants. The first conference of Society of St Vincent de Paul in the region was erected in North Shields in 1846 to alleviate the poverty of Catholics and help to protect the faith from attack.

***

The small port of Blyth became increasingly important as an outlet for the coalfields of south-east Northumberland which were developed in the first half of the nineteenth century. Catholics in these parts attended the chapel in Morpeth until a new mission was created. **Cowpen Hall** passed to Marlow Sidney in 1804. He was a convert and he founded the new mission which initially, consisted of 'a House and Chapel with an endowment of £80 a year for the Priest ... [Sidney] made over this property to the Benedictines for the benefit of Religion.' In 1834, his son, Marlow John Sidney, had John Dobson build 'an exceedingly elegant' church, dedicated to St Cuthbert in 1840, at a cost of £1,623; a school was added in 1844.[78]

Notes

1. See Chapter 5, note 1 for the general references to the Durham mission histories which are also used here for the missions in Northumberland.
2. Quoted at W. Nicholson, *St. Mary's Hexham, 1830-1980* (Hexham: St Mary's, 1980), p. 14. The Stonecroft history has been reconstructed from Nicholson and the historical notes by J. R. Baterden: 'The Catholic Registers kept by Fr. Peter Antoninus Thompson, OP, at Stonecroft as Chaplain to the Gibson Family from 1715'; 'At Hexham and Stonecroft, from 1721'; 'At Hexham alone from 1734 and by other Dominicans from 1754 to 1826'; 'The Catholic Registers kept by the Dominicans after its Separation from Hexham, 1737 to 1821'. In: (Catholic Record Society [CRS] vol. 26 1926), pp. 180-187; Northumberland County History Committee, *A History of Northumberland* [NCoH], (Newcastle: Reid, 15 vols), X, pp. 156/157; J. Hodgson, *A History of Northumberland* (Newcastle: Pigg, 1820-1858, 3 parts, 7 vols), II/2, pp. 393ff.
3. Revd Fr Thaddeus, O. F. M., *The Franciscans in England 1600-1850* (Leamington: Art & Book Co., 1898), pp. 195, 241.
4. NCoH, III, p. 302.
5. The chapel was in a garret, but had been over a hen-roost, where 'the cackling of the hens drowned the voice of the preacher'. B. Jarrett, O. P., *The English Dominicans* (London: Burns, Oates and Washbourne, 1921), p. 239. Thompson left Stonecroft on the eve of Jasper Gibson's wedding anniversary, but whether that is significant is not apparent.
6. Thaddeus, p. 256. Hutchinson also seems to have ministered to the remnants of the Dilston congregation, cf. CRS 26, p.132.
7. The meeting in Newcastle was attended by the Revv. Thompson, Clark, Gibson (secular missioner in Newcastle, and Jasper's brother), and Messrs. Thomas Riddell and John Hankin.

8   'Archdeacon Singleton's Visitation 1826-8' at Northumberland Record Office [NRO]: ZAN M.15/A.72; J. Gillow, *A Literary and Biographical History, or Bibliographical Dictionary, of the English Catholics: From the Breach with Rome, in 1534, to the Present Time* (London: Burns & Oates, 1885–1895, 5 vols), 3, p. 416.

9   The literature on the Radcliffes of Dilston is large and growing though most is concerned with Jacobitism. The sources dealing with the chaplaincy include: W. S. Gibson, *Dilston Hall* (Newcastle: Robinson, 1850); J. Gerard. 'Catholic Chaplaincies in the North during the Eighteenth Century'. In: CRS 4, (1907), p. 247f.; R. Stanfield. 'Particulars of Priests in England and Wales 1692'. In: CRS 9, (1909), p. 106; J. C. Hodgson (ed.) *Northumbrian Documents of the 17th and 18th Centuries, Comprising the Register of the Estates of Roman Catholics in Northumberland* (Surtees Society [SS] 131, 1918); F. Skeet, *The Life of James Radcliffe, Third Earl of Derwentwater &c.* (London: Hutchinson, 1929); R. Arnold, *Northern Lights* (London: Constable, 1959); W. V. Smith. 'The Chaplains of the Radcliffe Family of Dilston'. In: *Northern Catholic History* [NCH] 11 (1980); L. Gooch, *The Desperate Faction* (The University of Hull Press, 1995); L. Gooch, 'The Radcliffes of Dilston in the Long Seventeenth Century', *The Dilston Papers* No.1 (Durham: Friends of Historic Dilston, 2007).

10 T. Stephens (contr.). 'Radcliffe Papers'. In: *Proceedings of the Society of Antiquaries of Newcastle upon Tyne* [PSAN] (3), VI, (1915) et seq., pp. 97, 134.

11 PSAN (3), VII (1916), passim

12 NRO: Q/R/RM, January 1830.

13 Much of the Hexham story is told by W. Nicholson, *St Mary's, Hexham*. See also S. L. Ollard & P. C. Walker, *Archbishop Herring's Visitation Returns, 1743*, (Yorkshire Archaeological Society, vols 75 & 77, 1929/1930), Appendix. A, pp. 194–196; R. Trappes-Lomax (contr.). 'Archbishop Blackburn's Visitation Returns of the Diocese of York, 1735'. In: CRS 32 (1932), pp. 204–388.

14 'Radcliffe Papers', PSAN (3), VII/10, p. 128; NRO: RCD 4/16, Gibson to Eyre, 17 Jan. 1782.

15 Nicholson, *St Mary's, Hexham*, p. 37.

16 Ibid. Agreement between Singleton (for the vicar apostolic) and the Revd J. A. Woods, at Hinckley (for the Dominicans), 5 Sep. 1827.

17 *Catholic Directory*, 1828, pp. 44–45.

[18] J. Sykes, *Local Records* (Newcastle, Sykes, 1833, 2 vols), I, 13 Nov. 1828.

[19] Leeds Diocesan Archives [LDA], Smith Papers: Circular of August 1828 (by the Revv. Gillow, Slater and Hogarth). It has been suggested that the church was 'probably by J. Green ... with queer battlements and bell-cote in a castle fashion', cf. N. Pevsner, *The Buildings of England: Northumberland* (London: Penguin Books, 1957), sub Hexham.

[20] NCoH, IV, p. 182; W. Parson & W. White, *History, Directory and Gazetteer of the Counties of Durham and Northumberland,* etc., (Newcastle: White, 1828, 2 vols), I, p. 416; A. Forster. 'An Outline History of the Catholic Church in North East England'. In: NCH, 10 p. 16; G. Scott. 'The Benedictines in the North East in the Eighteenth Century'. In NCH 32 (1991), pp. 35/36. For named monks see A. Allanson, *Biography of the English Benedictines*' ([1842] Ampleforth Abbey: Saint Laurence Papers IV, 1999).The Beaufront estate was sold at the death of John Errington.

[21] NRO: Swinburne Manuscripts. 6/95 (Sir William's account of the family's history); Allanson, *English Benedictines* (1999) pp. 210, 362; J. Baterden. 'The Catholic Registers of Capheaton, Kirkwhelpington, Northumberland, A Chaplaincy of the Swinburnes, 1769–85'. In: CRS 14 (1914), pp. 237–239; Forster, 'Outline History', NCH 10, p. 13; W. Hedley, *Northumberland Families* (Society of Antiquaries, Newcastle, 1968, 2 vols), I, p. 112; Scott, 'Benedictines in the North East,' pp 36–39; P. Henderson, *Swinburne: The Portrait of a Poet* (1974), ch 1; C. Y. Lang, *The Swinburne Letters* (New Haven: Yale University Press, 1959–1962, 4 vols), I, p. 11.

[22] Henderson, *Swinburne*, pp. 6/7; E. H. Burton, *The Life and Times of Bishop Challoner, 1691–1781,* (London: Longmans, 1909, 2 vols), II, pp. 190ff. Swinburne's certificate of taking the oaths of allegiance and supremacy is at NRO:, Swinburne, 612.1, 23 May 1786; L. Gooch, *The Revival of English Catholicism: The Banister-Rutter Correspondence 1777–1807* (Wigan: North West Catholic History Society, 1995), Rutter to Banister, 9 June 1786 (henceforth cited by originator and date).

[23] NCoH, XI, pp. 2, 128; XII, p. 328; Anon. 'Derwentwater Manuscripts'. In: PSAN (3), 7/11, p. 157.

[24] Pevsner, *Northumberland*, p. 114, misdates the chapel. Dobson's drawings (at the Grange) clearly show the chapel in the rebuilding of 1813.

[25] A. Durkin, *A History of St Francis Xavier, Cheeseburn, and St Matthew, Ponteland* (Ponteland: for the parish, 1996), p. 25.

[26] J. S. Hansom (ed.). 'The Registers of the Catholic Mission of St. Oswald,

Bellingham, Northumberland, formerly called Hesleyside'. In: CRS 2 (1906), pp. 355ff; J. Bossy. 'Four Catholic Congregations in Rural Northumberland 1750-1850'. In: RH 9/2 (1967), pp. 88ff.; Forster, 'Outline History', p. 13; *Northern Catholic Calendar* [NCC] 1882; NCoH, XV, pp. 223/233. L. Charlton, *The Recollections of a Northumbrian Lady 1815-66* (London: Cape, 1949), passim.

27   NCoH, VI, p. 174; Hodgson, *Northumbrian Documents*, p. 120n.

28   The visitation return from Birtley (a chapelry in Chollerton), in 1814, reported ten or twelve papists who, the incumbent said, 'I believe resort to Bellingham for divine worship'. See also NRO: QRR 2/3 (1830).

29   The visitation return from Bellingham in 1814 noted that 'seldom any divine worship [is] performed in' the old chapel. NRO: RCD 4/1, Brown to Briggs, 24 Mar., 2 Apr., 14 May, 9 Jul., 1838 and 2 Jan. 1839.

30   Charlton, *Recollections*, p. 158, has a different set of figures to that in RCD; Brown is more likely to be right about the salary; J. Latimer, *Local Records 1832-1857* (Newcastle: The Chronicle, 1857), Jan. 1839.

31   Charlton, *Recollections*, p. 209: their 'infatuations were a subject of gossip'.

32   NCoH, IV, pp. 282/283; Hedley, *Northumberland Families*, II, p. 107; *The Tablet*, 23 Oct. 1841, p. 685; Allanson, *Benedictines*, p. 335.

33   M. Culley. 'Two Northumbrian Missions'. In: *Ushaw Magazine* [UM] 7, (1897), p. 168.

34   J. C. Hodgson (ed.), *Six North Country Diaries*, SS 118 (1910), p.299; NRO: ZAH M15/72 gives the total parochial population as 2,000 of which 50 were Catholics in 1828.

35   NRO: RCD 4/20, Brown to Briggs, 29 Apr. 1834.

36   NRO: RCD 4/20, Riddell to Briggs, 27 Jan 1837; *The Tablet*, 27 Nov. 1841, p. 765; 4 Nov. 1848, p. 564.

37   K. Stewart, *A Short History of St. Robert's Church, Morpeth*, (Morpeth: for the parish, 1969); W. V. Smith. 'Widdrington Bourne of Morpeth, A Papist Schoolmaster in 1764'. In: NCH 35 (1994), pp. 16/17.

38   NRO: RCD 2/65; Downside Abbey Manuscripts: 'Record Book of the EBC', p. 122; Scott, 'Benedictines in the North East', pp. 41/42.

39   Culley, 'Two Northumbrian Missions'; Forster, 'Outline History', p. 12.

40   NRO: RCD 2/500; Hodgson, II (1), p. 319; *Newcastle Courant*, 1 & 6 Aug. 1768. The act was passed in 1770; See NRO: Trevelyan Manuscripts, ZTR I/84 and XI/4 for the legal decision and a copy of the act.

41 Rutter, 7 Nov. 1796; NRO: Trevelyan Manuscripts, ZTR XXIII/1/7, 3 & 31 Dec. 1794; NRO: ZAH M15/A72.

42 NCoH, XV, pp. 373/374; Bossy, 'Four Congregations', passim; W. V. Smith. 'Thropton: 250 years old'. In: UM 62 (1952); M. Culley. 'Thropton'. In: UM 11 (1901).

43 Bossy, 'Four Congregations', passim; NCC 1884; J. R. Baterden (ed). 'Catholic Registers of Biddleston Hall', Northumberland, 1767–1840'. In: CRS 14 (1914) pp. 249ff. Biddlestone Hall is reputed to be the model for Osbaldistone Hall in Scott's *Rob Roy*.

44 NoCH, XV pp. 427/428; Hodgson, *North Country Diaries*, p. 261; J. O. Payne, *Old English Catholic Missions* (London: Burns & Oates, 1889), pp. 10/11. T. Fordyce, *Local Records, 1833–67*, (Newcastle: Fordyce, 1867), 11 Dec. 1845, observes that when William Selby came into possession of the Biddlestone estates he found an accumulation of heavy debts and 'immediately put into operation a system of the most rigid economy and, after some years of self-denial and sequestration, he paid off the debts in full'. It is possible that William was confused for Thomas or, vice versa. See also J. M. Robinson, *Biddlestone Chapel, Northumberland* (London: Historic Chapels Trust, 2009), passim. (The house was demolished in 1957 but the chapel remains and is in occasional use.)

45 J. Gillow (ed.). 'Catholic Registers of Callaly Castle, Northumberland, 1796–1839'. In: CRS 7 (1909), pp. 319–352; NCoH, XIV, p. 499; Hedley, *Northumberland Families*, I, pp. 167ff; Bossy, 'Four Catholic Congregations,' passim.

46 J. Laurenson, S.J. 'Catholic Chaplaincies and Families in the North during the Eighteenth Century'. In: CRS 4 (1907), p. 250. Rutter, 23 Oct. 1786; 12 Mar. 1792; Hodgson, *North Country Diaries*, p. 260; NRO: Cookson Manuscripts, ZCO VIII/8/2, Clavering to Silvertop, 22 Feb. 1788. Rutter criticised Clavering for being an improper superior of the Northern Brethren's Fund probably unaware that Bishop Walton had included Clavering on the terna he sent to Rome requesting a coadjutor (cf. W. Brady, *The Episcopal Succession in England, Scotland & Ireland A. D. 1400–1875* ([Rome: 1877–1878], Farnborough: Gregg Reprints, 1971, 3 vols), III, p. 265.

47 G. Anstruther, *The Seminary Priests: A Dictionary of the Secular Clergy of England and Wales, 1558–1850* (Ware, St Edmund's College; Durham, Ushaw College, c.1968–1977, 4 vols), 4, sub Peters; UCM: Eyre Mss, No.

264, Stout to Eyre, 6 Aug. 1797.
48 NRO: ZAN M.151A.72; D. Dixon, *Whittingham Vale* (Newcastle: Redpath, 1895), p. 156; NCoH, XIV, pp. 531/532; LDA: Penswick Papers, Smith to Penswick, 5 Dec. 1825 & 7 Sep. 1827.
49 G. Holt, *The English Jesuits 1650–1829: A Biographical Dictionary* (CRS 70, 1984), has John Parker *vere* Buck but he is called George in the 1767 Papist Return and in the parish register. A. Chadwick, *St. Mary's Church, Alnwick* (Alnwick, 1936); F. O. Edwards. 'Residence of Saint John 1717–1858, Part I: The Alnwick Fund and Chapel'. In: NCH 3 (1976), pp. 17ff; Hodgson, *Northumbrian Documents*, p. 83.
50 Holt, *English Jesuits*, p. 120.
51 NRO: RCD 3/28 and 6/9: Strickland to Warrilow, 31 Sep. 1802. Latimer, *Local Records*, Sep. 1836.
52 J. Bossy. 'More Northumbrian Congregations'. In: RH 10/1 (1969) pp. 11 ff.; M. B. Joyce. 'The Haggerstons: The Education of a Northumberland Family'. In: RH 14/3 (1978) pp. 175ff; R. C. Wilton. 'Letters of a Jesuit Father in the Reign of George I'. In: *Dublin Review* 158 (1916), pp. 307ff.
53 The citations from the papers of Thomas Adams are taken from a catalogue of the Northumbrian antiquarian bookseller, Alex Fotheringham, in whose possession the papers were in April 2009.
54 The Community, *A History of Darlington Carmel 1619–1982* (Darlington: Carmel, 1982), passim.
55 LDA: Penswick Papers, Briggs to Penswick 15 Mar. 1834 and 19 Jul. 1834; NRO: RCD 1/3, Riddell Letter Book, Riddell to Mostyn, 15 Jan. 1845. The altar rails, statues and other artefacts were transferred from the chapel in the castle to the church of St Edmund, King and Martyr, opened in 1861.
56 NCoH, II, pp. 223, 261; NCC 1938; Bossy, 'More Catholic Congregations', passim.
57 LDA: Smith Papers, Albot to Smith, 6 Nov. 1825; Haggerston to Smith 9 Mar. 1828 and 30 Sep. 1829. J. Hagerty. 'Notes on the Northern District under Bishop Thomas Smith, 1821–1831'. In: NCH 27 (1988), pp. 27/28.
58 NCC 1883; T. G. Holt. 'Berwick upon Tweed: The Story of a Legacy'. In: NCH 18 (1983), pp. 3ff; Bossy, 'More Northumbrian Congregations', passim.
59 UCM: Eyre Correspondence, Tidyman to Eyre, Nos. 38, 113/4, 298, 304, 307, 322; Besnier to Eyre, 26 May, 1805. Besnier's income was £19 per

Mission Stations in Northumberland 401

year.
60 W. Nicholson. 'Nicholas Alain Gilbert, French Émigré Priest, 1762–1821'. In: NCH 12 (1980), pp. 20/21
61 The petition is copied in UCM: Smith Papers, I (Berwick), no source is given.
62 LDA: Smith Letters, Pepper to Smith, 14 Aug. 1817. Hagerty, 'Northern District,' p. 26; Pevsner, *Northumberland*, p. 90; Sykes, *Local Records*, Jan. 1829.
63 LDA: Briggs Papers, No. 219, Parker to Briggs, 28 Feb. 1837; NRO: RCD 4/2, Sharples to Briggs 29 Mar. and 4 May 1838.
64 Bossy, 'More Northumbrian Congregations'; Hedley, *Northumberland Families*, I, p. 171; F. O. Edwards. 'Residence of Saint John, 1717–1858, Part II: The Jesuits outside Alnwick and Durham City'. In: NCH 5 (1977), pp. 13ff. The last of the Claverings of Berrington died in Old Elvet, Durham, in 1825, cf. Parson & White, *Directory*, II, p. 337; Hodgson, *Northumbrian Documents*, p. 31n.
65 J. Lenders, *Minsteracres* (Rochdale, Orphans Press, 1932); F. Dobson, *George Silvertop of Minsteracres* (Consett: Minsteracres, 2004); H. Bronski, *Minsteracres: From Mansion to Monastery* (Newcastle: Minsteracres, 2000), passim (reissued as *Coal to Soul* (Minsteracres 2012).
66 UCM: Eyre Correspondence, Nos. 214, 217, 227, Silvertop to Eyre (1808/1810); NRO: RCD 4/42, Gillow to Hogarth, 20 Mar. 1838; D. Halliday, 'The Diocesan Missionary Establishment at St Ninian's, Wooler, 1851–4' in NCH 12 (1980), p. 36, describes its role at the end of this period.
67 Rutter, 30 Jan. 1791.
68 UCM: Lingard Letters, No. 27, to Orrell, 9 Jan. 1808.
69 G. Holt. 'William Warrilow and the Jesuit Mission in Newcastle upon Tyne'. In: NCH 47 (2006), p.4
70 W. V. Smith, *Catholic Tyneside* (Newcastle, C. T. S., 1930), p. 74. See also, T. C. Nicholson, *Catholic Churches and Chapels of Newcastle-on-Tyne'*, (privately published, Newcastle 1891), passim.
71 B. Little, *Catholic Churches since 1623* (London: Hale, 1966), p. 50; *Orthodox Journal*, I/47 (1835) p. 378; B. Currer. 'Catholic Education in the North-East 1833–1860. In: NCH 37 (1996), p. 32.
72 Sykes, *Local Records*, 10 Dec. 1815, 11 Sep. 1831; E. Hughes (ed.), *The Diaries and Correspondence of James Losh* (SS, 1956/1959, 2 vols), I: Diary,

25 Dec. 1813; 25 Mar. 1821; 7 Nov. 1830.

[73] P. Atterbury & C Wainwright, *Pugin* (New Haven and London: Yale University Press for the Victoria and Albert Museum, 1994), pp. 68/69.

[74] P. McGuiness. 'Saint Mary's Cathedral: The Early Years, I'. In: NCH No 5 (1977), p. 25; Little, *Catholic Churches*, pp. 97/98; *The Tablet*, 5 Aug. and 31 Aug. 1844.

[75] J. Stark, *St. Cuthbert's Church, North Shields* (North Shields, St Cuthbert's, 1902); Rutter, 14 Mar. 1784; NRO: RCD 2/61; UCM: Eyre Correspondence, pp. 375ff

[76] UCM: Smith Papers, I, p. 62, Gillow to Penswick, 26 Jan. 1816.

[77] Little, *Catholic Churches*, p. 61.

[78] NCC 1936; M. Sidney, *One Hundred Years Ago* (London: Burns & Oates, 1877); W. Whellan, *History, Topography and Directory of Northumberland* (London: Whittaker, 1855), p. 457.

CONCLUSION

THE ESTABLISHMENT OF the vicariates apostolic in 1688 effected a transformation of the English Catholic Church. Most mission-stations in the north-east had been created on an ad hoc basis in the last fifteen to twenty years of the seventeenth century but the regenerated episcopal regime formalised those arrangements, regularised their finances and introduced the first stage of centralised clerical administration. As a result, a spirit of confidence was engendered among the laity and the clergy which inspired a revival of the mission. Individuals began to bequeath substantial capital sums for the support of missionary priests on a permanent basis in given localities. Priests were appointed to specific ministries, either in a chaplaincy or, more rarely, in an independent mission. Incumbents began to be succeeded as a matter of course at their death or removal elsewhere, and congregations came to expect continuity of pastoral care. Because of legal constraints, however, priests went about discreetly, chapels were inconspicuously sited and modestly furnished, and liturgical practice was restrained. This unemphatic character of English Catholicism was fashioned in part to avoid inflaming incipient anti-Catholicism. Indeed, the quiet spirituality of the '*Garden of the Soul* Catholics', as they were to be described later, would persist well into the nineteenth century, and the more demonstrative continental devotional style would take a long time to gain hold. At any rate, by 1730 a permanent network of priests and chapels could be found across the region and the achievement of such a widespread deployment at this time is remarkable given the Church's status as a proscribed body. Moreover, the geographical distribution reached at that point could remain more or less unchanged for almost a century.

Notwithstanding the cooperation between priests and lay patrons in reviving and sustaining the mission, however, their partnership had largely broken down by the end of the eighteenth century when emancipation was in sight. The administration of the mission was bedevilled by squabbling over jurisdictional matters. The balance of power lay with the gentry who demanded an over-riding control of the chaplains and chapels which they financed. Advanced though missionary development was, further progress was inhibited because of their reluctance to allow the mission to adjust to changing sociological circumstances. Problems over the continuity of priestly tenure also arose when the apostasy, bankruptcy or extinction of a patronal family occurred. In short, the Church suffered more at the hands of its own gentry at this time than it did from Protestants.

The dictatorial manner of patrons was much resented, and increasingly restive chaplains began to seek domestic liberation. By the end of the eighteenth century the majority of patrons had been brought to recognise that their priorities differed from those of their chaplains, and they agreed to sever the irksome residential ties. Most priests moved out of the mansions and into houses or cottages nearby to lead lives having a wider pastoral reach. The use of house-chapels was largely discontinued, though often replaced by estate-churches. At the same time, despite its limited resources, the Church resolutely consolidated its presence in the towns, taking every opportunity after the Catholic Relief Act of 1791 to improve its independent mission properties; it even embarked on a programme of prestigious church-building in the major towns of the region. The costs were borne almost entirely by the layfolk of the newly-emergent middle- and working-class for whose benefit the developments were intended. In these ways, the Church's centre of gravity moved out of the rural mansions of the gentry into the villages and towns. Although the seigneurial system could still be detected in several places, the lay gentry lost control of the mission to the vicar apostolic. Without such a fundamental change in its organisation and management, the Church would not have had either the ethos or the urban base from which it could begin to meet the challenge of the 1840s when the Catholic population began to soar.

Substantial change also came about in the socio-political character of the northern Catholic laity. They were well integrated socially and economically at the beginning of the eighteenth century, and, provided they did not challenge the ecclesiastical or political status quo, they were left in peace. That understanding was not seriously undermined by the outbreak of activist Jacobitism. Although their loyalties were not in doubt, and despite their close kinship and social ties, most Catholics were reluctant rebels and restricted their involvement in the risings to a minimum. The Jacobite fervour of heads of families was tempered by dynastic and financial considerations. For the most part, those who did go out in 1715 comprised a small group of young gentlemen motivated by their friendship with the leaders, the Earl of Derwentwater and Lord Widdrington. Hence, few Catholic families of the region were penalised; in any case, forfeitures were boldly resisted to the end and, in the event, were negligible. The affected families resumed their normal lives almost immediately. The 'Fifteen was the last occasion on which the English Catholics threatened Crown and Church (although it was always assumed that that was the *raison d'etre* of popery). Few became involved in the 'Forty-five, and most quietly dropped their Jacobitism to attend to the more pressing problem of their emancipation without having to bother about what a Stuart Pretender might be saying or doing to further his own cause but hinder theirs. The mission also demonstrated great resilience, for the events of 1715 and 1745 caused no more than a brief suspension in its activity.

The poverty of the Northumbrian Catholic gentry of the eighteenth century has been greatly exaggerated, as they themselves intended. A superficial reading of their estate-registers shows them to have been heavily indebted and close to insolvency, but a close analysis reveals a thriving and creditworthy group of land-owners and coal *rentiers*, well able to bear the financial commitments common to all gentry families: dowries, jointures, and so on. The ruination suffered by some Catholics later in the century was generally the consequence of heavy expenditure on new mansions, or the lack of alternative sources of income with which to arrest the progressive fragmentation of small and marginally profitable estates which were their only resource. Furthermore, the extinction of some Catholic families was the natural consequence of a failure to produce male heirs to continue the dynasty—a misfortune common to all social groups.

The equivocal situation of formal proscription and informal toleration (or persecution without martyrdom) in which Catholics found themselves, is particularly evident in the results of the many surveys on them carried out during the second half of the century. All investigations showed that there was nothing to differentiate the Catholics of the north sociologically from the rest of the population. They lived in almost every part of the region and they were present in all age groups of both genders. They could be found in all classes, and they were employed in much the same way as everyone else, save for their exclusion from official places. Through the skill of their lawyers and the good offices of non-Catholic friends and neighbours, Catholic gentlemen developed their estates and engaged in commercial and industrial enterprises without interference. Moreover, their political exclusion permitted a number of them to apply themselves to artistic and scientific study through which they made significant contributions to the cultural life of the nation.

In only one sociological respect did the Catholics differ, and that was their failure to increase as a proportion of the population. The number of Catholics in the region fell after reaching a maximum around mid-century. Paradoxically, this fall was an unintended consequence of their social and economic integration. Since the Catholic population was widely and thinly spread, its communal character was fragmented so that maintaining the faith by the necessarily self-effacing and discreet missioners was difficult. Inter-marriage with non-Catholics became commonplace and, in a large number of cases, this led to losses immediately or in the next generation. Additional factors, which affected other Churches too, such as war, and the geographical mobility associated with industrialisation and urbanisation, also took their toll of an already tiny Catholic community. It was only after 1815 that Catholic numbers began to rise. Further growth became easier after Catholic Emancipation in 1829 when the Church was more active and visible.

The thesis that there was a continuous growth in the English Catholic population during this period is not borne out in the north-east. The high level of Irish migration into England at the beginning of the nineteenth century was sufficient to offset the overall decline in the indigenous Catholic population, but that simple aggregate conceals an important distributional feature. The majority of the Irish migrants were concentrated in north-west England, and it was only in the 1830s that significant numbers crossed the northern Pennines. Certainly, it was not until the closing years of the period covered here that the English Catholics of north-east England were out-numbered by the Irish. At that point the Church was precipitated into an age of new and difficult pastoral demands.

Although the northern Catholics were fully integrated sociologically from the beginning of the eighteenth century, they were denied religious freedom, excluded from public office and debarred from the franchise. The Catholic Relief Act of 1791, granting ecclesiastical freedom, satisfied the clergy since it represented emancipation as much from gentry control as from the penal law. The vicars apostolic recovered those episcopal jurisdictional rights which had hitherto been monopolised by the gentry. The independence of priest and chapel accelerated from this point, although the process had begun a little while before. Political exclusion, however, remained a mortifying deprivation for the laity who wished to take their places on the bench, in parliament and the corporations, and to place their sons in the Royal Navy and the Army. It became a matter of some concern to the vicars apostolic that the gentry seemed so intent on gaining those rights that they were ready to sacrifice a number of clerical prerogatives and to associate the Catholic cause with that of the Radicals. Of course, in principle the clergy regarded civil liberty as highly desirable, but enfranchisement and the right to sit in parliament or to take public office, held no particular attraction for them and after 1791 they were less active in the campaign leading to full emancipation.

Newman's portrayal of late eighteenth-century English Catholic life has proved exceptionally difficult to modify, and it lingers in some quarters. As has been shown, by the time of the Relief Acts the Claverings, Haggerstons, Maires and Withams were unrecognisable as members of Newman's *gens lucifuga*. It is impossible to fit Callaly Castle, Hesleyside or Stella Hall into Newman's picture. The Catholics had by then emerged from the shadows. They had put up with the persecution of their religion and their exclusion from professional and public life, but the majority of them became vigorous and resourceful champions of their ecclesiastical and political emancipation, and they were welcome participants on the hustings in Whig election campaigns. In the event, Catholic Emancipation was enacted entirely for pragmatic reasons of state, and almost without reference to constitutional or doctrinal considerations. As had been feared by their ecclesiastics, however, the urban Catholics had associated their emancipation with parliamentary reform and other liberal issues, and were radicalised as a result. Indeed, so far had the Catholics shed their Jacobite and recusant past that, far from desiring a restoration of the Stuarts, many of them had become advanced Liberals, even republicans.

This book has traced the history of Catholicism in north-east England from the Revolution of 1688 to the Restoration of the Hierarchy in 1850, that is, from persecution to liberty, when almost every aspect of its life was transformed. At the beginning of the period the Catholic mission was housed largely in the private country mansions of the gentry who, for all practical purposes, directed it for their own benefit and that of their families and immediate dependents. At the end of the period, most Catholics freely attended episcopally controlled missions in the towns, and congregations were comprised largely of the new working-class. The transition was largely achieved peacefully without undue violence on either side: the Crown did not want to create martyrs and Catholics did not seek martyrdom. Indeed, for most of the period governments simply wished the Catholics would go away and be content that they were no longer being executed, and Catholics were just as pleased to be left alone. The unintended consequence of this *modus vivendi* was that the Catholics gradually consolidated their position in civil society and in the process convinced their fellow-countrymen that the British Constitution would not be imperilled by their emancipation but strengthened: they were law-abiding not seditious, Catholic not Papist, tolerant not fanatic. But it took a century and a half for the strategy to pay off.

Appendix

Mission Station & Incumbent's Remarks	Accommodation Sitting/Standing	Attendance on Census Sunday am/pm	Average Attendance am/pm	No. of Scholars	RC population estimated
HIGH WORSALL, NRY, The Friarage, pre 1800, John Bradley	100/20	85/30-40	152		152
MIDDLESBROUGH, St Mary, 1848, Joseph MacPhillips. 'About 500 Catholics in the parish of Middlesbrough.'	308/-	160/160	160		500
WYCLIFFE, since 1800, John Bradshaw.	190/-	130/60			130
ALNWICK, St Mary, pre 1800, rebuilt 1836, John Fishwick.	300/50	160/100	1 yr: 160/100		160
BARNARD CASTLE, St Mary's, first used as a chapel in 1847, William F. Allen.	194/100	143/140	150/170		170
BELLINGHAM, St Oswald, 1839, N. Brown. 'Those who can afford it are expected to pay a small sum quarterly for their sittings'.		54/36	75/-		75
BERWICK, Ss. Mary & Cuthbert, 1829, A. McDermott.		200/60			200
BIDDLESTON, 'very ancient', Thomas Hoggett.		120/20			120
BISHOP AUCKLAND, St Wilfrid, July 1845, John Smith. 'If it be desired to know how many persons are able and do attend from time to time during the year the stating of the average number of persons attending on a Sunday will not be satisfactory as many persons from distant residence or other causes are impeded and only come to church on the Sunday occasionally. The number of persons so able will not be less than 900'.	240/60		240		900
CALLALY CASTLE [Thos. Ord].	120/-		35		35
CHEESEBURN GRANGE, pre 1800, Thomas Gillett.	170/-	170/50	180	None	180
COWPEN, St Cuthbert, 1840, James Burchall. 'There are in this congregation about 400 Catholics including children. About 100 are from 4 to 6 miles from Cowpen; the rest are within 3 miles'.	245/30	220/95			400
CROXDALE, 1808, attached to the house, Thomas Smith.		130/30	3 mths: 130		130
DARLINGTON, St Augustine,' pre 1800' (church erected in 1827) 'A separate and entire building used exclusively as a place of worship. ' + Wm. Hogarth Catholic Bishop officiating	100 free	400	350/400		400

Mission Station & Incumbent's Remarks	Accommodation Sitting/Standing	Attendance on Census Sunday am/pm	Average Attendance am/pm	No. of Scholars	RC population estimated
DURHAM, St Cuthbert, 1827, William Fletcher. 'According to a census lately taken of Roman Catholics belonging to the congregation of Durham, the number is 1,220. The chapel being too small to contain them, many do not come to chapel on Sundays'.	430/150	580/500			1220
ELLINGHAM, George Meynell.	70/20	51/12			51
ESH LAUDE [LANCHESTER], St Michael, pre 1800, William Thompson.	274/-	278/207			278
FELLING, St Patrick, 1841, John Kelly.	250/50	480/550	400-500	150	650
FELTON, pre 1800, domestic chapel, Samuel Davy. 'This chapel is a private one for the use of Thomas Riddell Esqr & family, & the family does not reside here at present. The mansion is let. All sittings free those excepted which the family when at home require'.		50/25			50
GATESHEAD, J. Betham, Rector. 'Temporary chapel of Our Lady & St Wilfrid, Hillgate, used for two months. Top flat of a bond warehouse now empty. Flats all empty except this. Also used as a Boy's Day School. At first there were no seats. The Mass or Morning Service is the only obligatory service in the Cath. Church. The Catholic parochial District is coextensive as to boundaries with those of the Township. Number of Catholic parishioners 3,000 of whom the greater portion are either Irish or born of I. parents.'	300/400	a.m. 380, p.m. approx 80	a.m. 500 (over 2 months)	120	3,000
HAGGERSTON, Ss. Mary & Cuthbert, Charles Eyre.			120/30		120
HARTLEPOOL, St Hilda, 1832, William Knight.	370/60	460/300		130	590
HESLEDON, Ss. Peter & Paul, 1825, Thomas Augustine Slater, Catholic Clergyman. 'Never counted' the number of sittings or standings.	100/-	70/80	1 yr: 80		80
HEXHAM, St Mary, c. 1830, Rev Mr Singleton. Built 'in lieu of 2 smaller chapels'	200/186	441/267	477/267		477
HOUGHTON le SPRING, St Michael, 1837, Arsenius Watson.	270/222	394/172			394
LARTINGTON, domestic chapel, pre 1800, Michael Ellis. 'The persons enumerated in the afternoon are the same as attended in the morning'.	150/30	131/[131]	1 yr: 86		131

Mission Station & Incumbent's Remarks	Accommodation Sitting/Standing	Attendance on Census Sunday am/pm	Average Attendance am/pm	No. of Scholars	RC population estimated
LONGHORSLEY, St Thomas, 1841, James Hubbersty. 'Sometimes we have considerably above 100 at chapel and sometimes about 100 but perhaps taking one time with another we may call the average about 90 or between 90 and 100.'	100/-	56/13/30	1 yr: 90		100
MINSTERACRES domestic chapel, J.S. Rogerson. 'No scholars'.		60/20			60
MORPETH, St Robert, 1849	200/200	250/150			250
NEWCASTLE, St Andrew, c.1801, Joseph Cullen. 'There are 10,000 Roman Catholics in Newcastle, 6,000 of whom are served by one priest attached to the chapel. About 1,000 labourers having families in Ireland attend the chapel. 2 services in the morning. J. Cullen, 73 Pilgrim St.'	844/200	1689/604			10000
NEWCASTLE, St Mary, 1844, Joseph Humble.	900/500	1700/900			see above
NORTH SHIELDS, St Cuthbert, 1821, T. & R. Gillow.	500/-	2 services: 700/550		168	868
SEDGEFIELD, St Joseph, Purchased by the Bishop about 12 or 14 years ago as far as I remember and built a few years previously. Separate but adjoining the priest's residence. I am the Parish Priest but strictly speaking am Administrator of the parish until certain ecclesiastical arrangements are completed.' Robert Suffield. 'Chapel ... I have termed them all free sittings as everyone has a seat whether he can pay or not, but all who can pay something more or less... NB. As I have two chapels, D. Service is alternately at the two morning and evening.'	100 comfortably		6 mths:100/60		100
SOUTH SHIELDS St Bede, Cuthbert St., Westoe, came into possession in 1849, Richard Singleton	370/-		430/110		430
STELLA, Ss. Mary & Thomas Aquinas, 1831, Ralph Platt.	325/100	318/124	310/120		318
STOCKTON, St Mary, 1842, Robert A. Cornthwaite.	c.300	250?/200?			250
SUNDERLAND, St Mary 'Copied from letter sent by Registrar'.	80/-		950		950
SWINBURNE, Peter Allanson 'Swinburne Hermitage'. '120 whole number that ever attends'.	100/-	50/-	120		120

Mission Station & Incumbent's Remarks	Accommodation Sitting/Standing	Attendance on Census Sunday am/pm	Average Attendance am/pm	No. of Scholars	RC population estimated
THORNLEY, Ferryhill, St. Godric, purchased in 1850. Robert Suffield, Administrator. 'Though virtually Parish Priest, we are only administrators until certain Hierarchical arrangements are completed. I have called all free sittings as there is access to all without payment, but payment is expected of all competent.'	250/-		6 mths: 250/150		250
THROPTON, All Saints, pre 1800, G.A. Corless DD - Dean.	106/-	70-80/20-25			80
USHAW, St Cuthbert's College, 1808, Michael Gibson. 'The numbers include our own community and casual attendants. We have no regular congregation from without as we perform no parochial duty, and those who do attend, attend only on sufferance, the chapel being erected solely for the private use of the inmates of the College.'	150/100	190/160			190
WOLSINGHAM, St Thomas of Canterbury, 1849. [T.W. Wilkinson] 'The numbers attending Divine Service in this congregation cannot be fairly represented in a return of this kind because very many, 1/5th of the men, are at work every second Sunday at Mr. Francis Attwood's Iron Works [in Tow Law] and thus are only able to attend alternate Sundays.'	159/30	150/40	1 yr: 150		150
WOOLER, St Ninian, pre 1800, Ed. Consitt. 'Chapel small and inconvenient.'	85/20	63/48	1 yr: c.80/80-90	30	120
Total					24,829
Missing returns (Birtley & Brooms)					2,000
Overall total					26,829

BIBLIOGRAPHY

I. Manuscript Sources

Downside Abbey: Record Book of the English Benedictine Congregation

Durham County Record Office [DCRO]:
>Londonderry Papers (D/Lo)
>National Coal Board Papers (D/NCB)
>Salvin Papers (D/Sa)

Durham University Library [DUL], Archives and Special Collections:
>Auckland Castle Episcopal Records, Clergy Visitation Returns, 1774 (to Bishop Egerton); 1792, 1810, 1814 (to Bishop Barrington)
>Grey Manuscripts
>Mickleton and Spearman Manuscripts
>Sharpe Manuscripts

East Yorkshire County Record Office [EYCRO]: Burton Constable Archive

Farm Street Archives (S.J.): X. Residence of St. John the Evangelist

Gateshead Public Library (GPL):
>Cotesworth Manuscripts (CH/...)
>Carr-Ellison Manuscripts (ZCE)

House of Lords Records Office: Main Papers, Returns of Papists, 1705, 1767, 1780, (Dioceses of Durham and York).

Lancashire Record Office: Barrow Letters

Leeds Diocesan Archives [LDA]:

>Briggs Papers
>William Gibson Papers
>Penswick Papers
>Smith Papers

Northumberland Record Office [NRO]:

>Allgood Manuscripts (ZAN)
>Archives of the Diocese of Hexham and Newcastle (RCD)
>Cookson Manuscripts (ZCI)
>Haggerston Manuscripts (ZHG)
>Ridley Manuscripts (ZRI)
>Swinburne Manuscripts (ZSW)
>Trevelyan Manuscripts (ZTR)

University of Oxford, Bodleian Library: English Letters [BLEL], C.229

Ushaw College Library:

>Diocesan Topography & Mission Papers (DIO)
>Eyre Manuscripts and Correspondence
>Lingard Letters
>President's Archives (PA)
>Smith of Brooms Papers (OS/D)
>Ushaw Collection of Manuscripts (UCM)
>W. V. Smith Papers and Transcripts
>Wiseman Papers

II. Printed Collections of Records and Papers

British Parliamentary Papers:
Census of Great Britain 1851: Religious Worship (1853)

Journals of the Houses of Lords and Commons, 1705–1709, 1765–7, 1825–9

Catholic Record Society:

Occasional Publications:
No. 2, *Returns of Papists, 1767, Vol. 2, Dioceses of England and Wales except Chester*, ed. E. S. Worrall, 1989

No. 5, *Catholics of Parish and Town 1558–1778*, ed. M. B. Rowlands, 1999

Records Series:
Vol. 2, 'The Registers of the Catholic Mission of St Oswald, Bellingham, Northumberland, formerly called Hesleyside, 1794–1837', ed. J. S. Hansom, 1906

Vol. 4, 'Catholic chaplaincies and families in the north during the eighteenth century', contrib. J. Gerard, 1907

Vol. 7, 'The Catholic Registers of the Domestic Chapel at Callaly Castle, Northumberland, 1796–1839', ed. J. Gillow, 1909

Vol. 9, 'Particulars of Priests in England and Wales, 1692, from the Archives of the Old Brotherhood', 1911

Vol. 13, 'Account Book of Mr Ralph Clavering, 1763–1764', 1913

Vol. 14, 'The Catholic Registers of Capheaton, Kirkwhelpington, Northumberland, a Chaplaincy of the Swinburnes, 1769–85', ed. J. R. Baterden, 1914

'The Catholic Registers of Biddleston Hall, Alwinton, Northumberland, the seat of the Selby family, 1767–1840', ed. J. R. Baterden, 1914

Vol. 26, 'The Catholic Registers kept by Fr. Peter Antoninus Thompson, O. P., at Stonecroft, as Chaplain to the Gibson Family, from 1715; at Hexham and Stonecroft, Northumberland, conjointly, from 1721; at Hexham alone from 1734; and by other Dominicans from 1754–1826', ed. J. R. Baterden, 1926;

'The Catholic Registers of Stonecroft, Northumberland, kept by the Dominicans after its separation from Hexham, from 1737 to 1821', ed. J. R. Baterden, 1926;

'Catholic Registers of the Secular Mission of Hexham at Cockshaw, Northumberland, 1753–1832', ed. J. R. Baterden, 1926

Vol. 32, 'Archbishop Blackburn's Visitation Returns of the Diocese of York, 1735', ed. R. Trappes-Lomax, 1932

Vol. 35, 'The Catholic Registers of the Secular Mission of Newcastle-upon Tyne, which ultimately became St. Andrew's, from 1765; Notes on the early Jesuit Missions in Gateshead and Newcastle, 1688–1807', eds J. Lenders & J. R. Baterden, 1936.

Vol. 63, *Douai College Documents, 1639–1794*, ed. P. R. Harris, 1972

Vol. 70, *The English Jesuits 1650–1829, A Biographical Dictionary*, G. Holt, S. J., 1984

Surtees Society:

Vols. 93 & 101, *Extracts from the Records of the Merchant Adventurers of Newcastle upon Tyne*, eds J. R. Boyle & F. W. Dendy, 1895/1899

Vol. 105, *Extracts from the Records of the Company of Hostmen of Newcastle upon Tyne*, ed. F. W. Dendy, 1901

Vol. 111, *Records of the Committees for Compounding etc., with Delinquent. Royalists in Durham and Northumberland during the Civil War, etc., 1643–1660*, ed. R. Welford, 1905

Vols. 118 & 124, *North Country Diaries*, ed. J. C. Hodgson, 1910/1915

Vol. 131, *Northumbrian Documents of the 17th and 18th Centuries, Comprising the Register of the Estates of Roman Catholics in Northumberland*, ed. J. C. Hodgson, 1918

Vol. 165, *Letters of Spencer Cowper, Dean of Durham 1746-74*, ed. E. Hughes, 1956

Vols 171 & 174, *Diaries and Correspondence of James Losh*; vol. 1, Diary 1811-1823; vol. 2, Diary 1824-1833 and Correspondence, ed. E. Hughes, 1956/1959

Vols 173 & 175, *Registrations of Durham Recusant Estates, 1717-1778*, ed. C. R. Hudleston, 1962/1965

Vol. 178, *The Correspondence of Sir James Clavering*, ed. H. T. Dickinson, 1967

Vol. 180, *Selections from the Disbursements Book (1691-1709) of Sir Thomas Haggerston, Bart.*, ed. A. M. C. Forster, 1969

Vol. 197, *The Letters of Henry Liddell to William Cotesworth*, ed. J. M. Ellis, 1967

Vol. 216, *The Religious Census of 1851: Northumberland and Durham*, ed. A. Munden, 2012.

Yorkshire Archaeological Society: Records Series:

Vols 75 & 77, *Archbishop Herring's Visitation Returns, 1743*, eds S. L. Ollard & P. C. Walker, 1929/1930

Vol. 136, *Constable of Everingham Estate Correspondence 1726-43*, ed. P. Roebuck, 1976

III. Contemporary Periodicals:

British Critic

Catholic Directory

Catholic Magazine

Catholic Miscellany

Clergy List

Durham County Advertiser

Edinburgh Review

Gateshead Observer

Gentleman's Magazine

Laity's Directory

New Annual Register

Newcastle Courant

Newcastle Journal

Northern Catholic Calendar

Orthodox Journal

The Tablet

IV. Contemporary Pamphlets & Poll Books

Anon., *Proceedings of the Durham County Meeting on Monday 1st June 1807* (Durham: Walker [1807]).

Anon., *By-Election Poll-Book: Durham City, 1813* (Durham, s. n., 1813).

Anon., *The Durham Election 1820* (Durham: s. n. [1820]).

Anon., *Northumberland By-Election Poll-Book (1826), Including a Complete Collection of Papers, Speeches, etc.* (Alnwick: s. n., 1826).

Anon., *Northumberland General Election Poll-Book (1826), Including a Complete Collection of Speeches, etc.* (Alnwick, s. n., 1826).

Barrington, S. *A Charge delivered to the Clergy of the Diocese of Durham* (Durham: s. n., 1806).

Barrington, S. *The Grounds on which the Church of England Separated from the Church of Rome* (Durham: s. n., 1807).

Barrington, S. *The Grounds ..... Reconsidered* (Durham: s. n., 1809).

Barrington, S. *A Charge Delivered to the Clergy of the Diocese of Durham* (Durham: s. n., 1810).

Barrington, S. *Vigilance, A Counterblast to Past Concessions and a Preventive of Future Prodigality Recommended* (Durham: s. n., 1812).

Garnet, W. *A Collection of Papers, Speeches, etc., Relating to the Northumberland Election of 1807* (Newcastle: s. n., 1807).

Lingard, J. *Tracts Occasioned by the Publication of a Charge Delivered to the Clergy of his Diocese, by Shute Barrington in 1806* (Newcastle: Walker, 1813).

V. Selected Secondary Sources: Books:

Allanson, A. *Biography of the English Benedictines*. Ampleforth Abbey: Saint Laurence Papers IV, 1999.

Anstruther, G. *The Seminary Priests: A Dictionary of the Secular Clergy of England and Wales, 1558–1850.* Ware: St Edmund's College; Durham: Ushaw College, 1968–1977, 4 vols.

Arnold, R. *Northern Lights: The Story of Lord Derwentwater.* London: Constable, 1959.

Aveling, J. C. H. *Northern Catholics: The Catholics of the North Riding of Yorkshire 1558–1790.* London: Chapman, 1966.

Aveling, J. C. H. *Catholic Recusancy in the City of York 1558–1791.* Catholic Record Society Monograph No. 2, 1970.

Aveling, J. C. H. *The Handle and the Axe.* London: Blond & Briggs, 1976.

Ayling, S. *John Wesley.*(London: Collins, 1979.

Bates, C. J. *History of Northumberland.* London: Eliot Stock, 1895.

Beck G. (ed.) *The English Catholics 1850–1950*. London: Burns Oates, 1950.

Bellenger, D. *English and Welsh Priests 1558–1800*. Bath: Downside Abbey, 1984.

Bellenger, D. *The French Exiled Clergy in the British Isles after 1789*. Bath: Downside Abbey, 1986.

Bence-Jones, M. *The Catholic Families*. London: Constable, 1992.

Berington, J. *The State and Behaviour of English Catholics from the Reformation to the year 1780*. London: Faulder, 1780.

Black, J. *The British Abroad: The Grand Tour in the Eighteenth Century*. Stroud: Sutton, 1992.

Blundell, M. (ed.) *Blundell's Diary and Letter Book 1702–28*. Liverpool University Press, 1952.

Bossy, J. *The English Catholic Community 1570–1850*. London: Darton, Longman & Todd, 1975.

Brady, W.M. *The Episcopal Succession in England, Scotland & Ireland A. D. 1400–1875*. [Rome: 1877–1878.] Farnborough: Gregg Reprints, 1971, 3 vols.

Burke, J. *A Genealogical and Heraldic History of the Commoners of Great Britain and Ireland*. London: Colburn, 1836–1838, 4 vols.

Burke, J. *Genealogical and Heraldic History of the Landed Gentry*. London: Harrison, 1952.

Burton, E. H. *The Life and Times of Bishop Challoner, 1691–1781*. London: Longmans, 1909, 2 vols.

Butler, C. *The Reminiscences of Charles Butler*. London: Murray, 1824.

Cadogan, P. *Early Radical Newcastle*. Consett: Sagittarius Press, 1975.

Carson, R. *The First 100 Years: A History of the Diocese of Middlesbrough 1878–1978*. Middlesbrough Diocesan Trustees, 1978.

Chadwick, O. *The Victorian Church*. London: Clack, 1966–1970, 2 vols.

Charlton, L. E. O. *The Recollections of a Northumbrian Lady 1815–66.* London: Cape, 1949.

Chinnici, J. P. *The English Catholic Enlightenment: John Lingard and the Cisalpine Movement 1780–1850.* Shepherdstown, USA, The Patmos Press, 1980

Clarke, J. C. D. *English Society 1660–1832: Religion, Ideology and Politics during the Ancien Regime.* Cambridge University Press, 1985.

Clarke, J. C. D. *Revolution and Rebellion: State and Society in England in the Seventeenth and Eighteenth Centuries.* Cambridge University Press, 1986.

Connell, J. *The Roman Catholic Church in England 1780–1850: A Study in Internal Politics.* Philadelphia: The American Philosophical Society, 1984.

Cooper, L. *Radical Jack.* London: Cresset, 1959.

Crosby, J. *Ignatius Bonomi of Durham, Architect.* City of Durham Trust, 1987.

Currie, R. et al., *Churches and Churchgoers: Patterns of Church Growth in the British Isles since 1700.* Oxford: The Clarendon Press, 1977.

Deane, P., & Cole, W. *British Economic Growth 1688–1959.* Cambridge University Press, 1964.

Dixon, D. D. *Whittingham Vale.* Newcastle: Graham, 1895.

Dobson, F. *The Life and Times of George Silvertop of Minsteracres.* Newcastle: Minsteracres, 2004.

Dunne, J. *The Northern Catholic Community in 1823, A Report to Rome.* Leeds Diocesan Archives, 2007.

Edwards, D. L. *Christian England.* London: Collins, 1981–1984, 3 vols.

Estcourt, E. & Payne, J. *The English Catholic Non-jurors of 1715.* London: Burns & Oates, 1885.

Foley, H. *Records of the English Province of the Society of Jesus*. London: Burns and Oates, 1877–1883, 7 vols.

Fordyce, W. *The History and Antiquities of the County Palatine of Durham*. Newcastle: Fordyce, 1857, 2 vols.

French, A. *Art Treasures in the North: Northern Families on the Grand Tour*. Norwich: Unicorn Press, 2009.

Gay, J. D. *The Geography of Religion in England*. London: Duckworth, 1971.

Gibbs, V. (ed.) The Complete Peerage by G. E. C. London: St Catherine Press, 1910–1959, 13 vols.

Gibson, W. S. *Dilston Hall*. Newcastle: Robinson, 1850.

Gilbert, A. D. *Religion and Society in Industrial England 1740–1914*. London: Longman, 1976.

Gillow, J. *A Literary and Biographical History, or Bibliographical Dictionary, of the English Catholics: From the Breach with Rome, in 1534, to the Present Time*. London: Burns & Oates, 1885–1895, 5 vols.

Gillow, J. *The Haydock Papers*. London: Burns & Oates, 1888.

Gillow, J. *The Church during the Suppression of the Hierarchy in Newcastle and Gateshead*. Preston: Catholic Printing & Publishing Co., 1889.

Gooch, L. *A Bibliography of Periodical Literature Relating to the Post-Reformation Roman Catholic History of North-East England*. Privately published, 1977.

Gooch, L. *The Desperate Faction: The Jacobites of North-East England 1688–1745*. The University of Hull Press, 1995.

Gooch, L. *The Revival of English Catholicism: The Banister-Rutter Correspondence 1777–1807*. Wigan: North West Catholic History Society, 1995.

Gooch, L. *Paid at Sundry Times: Yorkshire Clergy Finances in the Eighteenth Century*. Ampleforth Abbey: St Laurence Papers X, 1997.

Bibliography

Gooch, L. 'The Radcliffes of Dilston in the Long Seventeenth Century'. *The Dilston Papers* No.1. Durham: Friends of Historic Dilston, 2007.

Graham, F. *The Old Halls, Houses and Inns of Northumberland*. Newcastle: Graham, 1977.

Gwynn, D. *The Second Spring 1818-1852*. London: Burns Oates, 1942.

Gwynn, D. *Father Dominic Barberi*. London: Burns Oates, 1947.

Haile, M. & Bonney, E. *Life and Letters of John Lingard 1771-1851*. London: Herbert & Daniel, nd [1911].

Hansard, T. C. *The Parliamentary Debates from the Year 1803*. London: Hansard, 1803-1829.

Haydon, C. *Anti-Catholicism in Eighteenth Century England c. 1714-1780: A Political and Social Study*. Manchester University Press, 1993.

Hedley, W. P. *Northumberland Families*. Society of Antiquaries of Newcastle, 1968, 2 vols.

Hemphill, B. *The Early Vicars Apostolic of England 1685-1750*. London: Burns & Oates, 1954.

Hempton, D. *Methodism and Politics in British Society, 1750-1850*. London: Hutchinson, 1984.

Henning, B. D. *The History of Parliament: The House of Commons, 1660-90*. London: Secker & Warburg, 1983, 3 vols.

Henriques, U. *Religious Toleration in England 1787-1833*. London: Routledge & Kegan Paul, 1961.

Hill, R. *God's Architect: Pugin and the Building of Romantic Britain*. London: Allen Lane, 2007.

Hilton, J. A. (et al. eds.), *Bishop Leyburn's Confirmation Register of 1687*. Wigan: North West Catholic History Society, 1997.

Hodgson, J. *History of Northumberland*. Newcastle, Pigg, 1820-1858, 3 pts, 7 vols.

Holmes, D. *More Roman than Rome: English Catholicism in the Nineteenth Century.* London: Burns & Oates, 1978.

Holt, G. *The English Jesuits in the Age of Reason.* London: Burns & Oates, 1993.

Holt, G. *William Strickland and the Suppressed Jesuits.* London: British Province of S. J., 1988.

Hughes, E. *North Country Life in the Eighteenth Century: The North East 1700–1750.* Oxford University Press, 1952.

Hughes, P. *The Catholic Question 1688–1829.* London: Sheed & Ward, 1929.

Hutchinson, W. *The History and Antiquities of the County Palatine of Durham.* Newcastle: Hodgson, 1785–1794, 3 vols.

Jarrett, B., O. P. *The English Dominicans.* London: Burns, Oates and Washbourne, 1921.

Jones, E. *John Lingard and the Pursuit of Historical Truth.* Brighton: Sussex Academic Press, 2001.

Kelly, B. W. *Historical Notes on English Catholic Missions.* London: Kegan Paul, 1907.

Kennedy, P. (ed.) *The Catholic Church in England and Wales 1500–2000.* Keighley: PBK Publishing, 2001.

Kirk, J. *Biographies of English Catholics in the Eighteenth Century.* London: Burns & Oates, 1909.

Lancaster, M. *The Tempests of Broughton.* Broughton: H. Tempest, 1987.

Lang, C.Y. *The Swinburne Letters.* (New Haven: Yale University Press, 1959–1962, 4 vols.

Latimer, J. *Local Records 1832–57.* Newcastle: *The Chronicle,* 1857.

Lee, S. (ed.) *Dictionary of National Biography.*London: Smith & Elder, 1903–1913, 63 vols.

Leys, H. *Catholics in England 1559-1829*. (London: The Catholic Book Club, 1961.

Little, B, *Catholic Churches since 1623*. London: Hale, 1966.

Machin, G. *The Catholic Question in English Politics*. Oxford: The Clarendon Press, 1964.

Machin, G. *Politics and the Churches in Great Britain, 1832-68*. Oxford: The Clarendon Press, 1977.

Mackenzie E. & Ross, M., *The County Palatine of Durham*. Newcastle: Mackenzie & Dent, 1834, 2 vols.

Matthew, H. & Harrison B. (eds) *Oxford Dictionary of National Biography*. Oxford University Press, 2004, 61 vols.

McCord, N, (ed.) *Essays in Tyneside Labour History*. Newcastle Polytechnic, 1977.

Milburn, D. *A History of Ushaw College*. Durham: Ushaw College, 1964.

Milner, J. *Supplementary Memoirs of the English Catholics*. London: Keating & Brown, 1820.

Mitchell, W.C. *History of Sunderland*. Sunderland: The Hills Press, 1919.

Morris, M. & Gooch, L. *Down Your Aisles: The Diocese of Hexham & Newcastle 1850-2000*. Hartlepool: *Northern Cross*, 2000.

Nicholson,T. C. *The Catholic Churches and Chapels of Newcastle on Tyne*. Newcastle, privately published, 1891.

Norman, E. R. *Anti-Catholicism in Victorian England*. London: Allen & Unwin, 1968.

Norman, E. R. *The English Catholic Church in the Nineteenth Century*. Oxford: The Clarendon Press, 1984.

Northumberland County History Committee, *A History of Northumberland*. Newcastle: Reid, 1893-1940, 15 vols.

Page, W. (ed.) *The Victoria History of the County of Durham*. London: Constable, 1902-1926, 3 vols.

Parson W. & White, W. *History, Directory and Gazetteer of the Counties of Durham and Northumberland.* Newcastle: White, 1828, 2 vols.

Payne, J. O. *Old English Catholic Missions.* London: Burns & Oates, 1889.

Payne, J. O. *Records of the English Catholics of 1715.* London: Burns & Oates, 1889.

Pevsner, N. *County Durham.* London: Penguin Books: The Buildings of England 9, 1953.

Pevsner, N. *Northumberland.* London: Penguin Books: The Buildings of England 12, 1957.

Phillips, P. *John Lingard, Priest and Historian.* Leominster, Gracewing, 2008.

Purcell, E. S. *Life of Cardinal Manning.* London, MacMillan, 1896, 2 vols.

Rose, M. *The Economic History of Britain since 1700, Volume 1, 1700–1860.* Cambridge University Press, 1972.

Schofield, N. & Skinner, G. *The English Vicars Apostolic 1688–1850.* Oxford: Family Publications, 2009.

Scott, G. *Gothic Rage Undone: English Monks in the Age of Enlightenment.* Bath: Downside Abbey, 1992.

Sedgwick, R. (ed.) *The House of Commons 1715–54.* London: History of Parliament, 1970, 2 vols.

Shea, D. F. *The English Ranke: John Lingard.* New York: Humanities Press, 1969.

Sidney, Mrs *One Hundred Years Ago.* London: Burns & Oates, 1877.

Silvertop, G. *Memoirs of the Silvertops of Minsteracres.* Newcastle, privately published, 1914.

Singleton, F. J. *Mowbreck Hall and The Willows.* privately published, 1983.

Skeet, F. J. A. *The Life of the Rt. Hon. James Radcliffe Third Earl of Derwentwater.* London: Hutchinson, 1929.

Smith, W. V. *Catholic Tyneside.* Newcastle: Catholic Truth Society, 1930.

Smith, W. V. *The Northern Brethren's Fund, 1660–1960.* Privately printed, 1960.

Sterne, J. *The Danger Arising to our Civil and Religious Liberty from the Great Increase of Papists.* York and London, s.n., 1747.

Surtees, R. *The History and Antiquities of the County Palatine of Durham.* Durham: Andrews, 1816–1840, 4 vols.

Swift, R., & Gilley, S. (eds) *The Irish in Victorian Britain.* Dublin: Four Courts Press, 1999.

Sykes, J. *Local Records.* Newcastle: Sykes, 1833, 2 vols.

Thaddeus, Revd Fr. *The Franciscans in England 1600–1850.* Leamington: Art & Book Co., 1898.

Todd, J. *John Wesley and the Catholic Church.* London: Hodder & Stoughton, 1958.

Tomlinson, V. *History of Northumberland.* Newcastle: Reid, 1895.

Tweedy, J. M. *Popish Elvet.* Durham: St Cuthbert's Church, 1981, 2 parts.

Ward, B. *The Dawn of the Catholic Revival in England 1781–1803.* (London: Longmans, Green, 1909, 2 vols.

Ward, B. *The Eve of Catholic Emancipation, 1803–29.* London: Longmans, 1911–1912, 3 vols.

Ward, B. *The Sequel to Catholic Emancipation, 1830–50.* London: Longmans, 1915, 2 vols.

Ward, W. R. *Religion and Society in England 1790–1850.* London: Batsford, 1972.

Welford, R. *Men of Mark Twixt Tyne and Tweed.* London & Newcastle: Walter Scott, 1895, 3 vols.

Whellan, W. *History, Topography and Directory of Northumberland.* London: Whittaker, 1855.

VI. Selected Journal Articles

Anon. ['H. H.'] 'A Description of the Catholic Missions in the County of Durham'. In: *Catholic Magazine*, 2/14 (1832), pp. 113–121.

Bellenger, D. 'The French Exiled Clergy in the North East'. In NCH 11 (1980), pp. 20–24.

Bellenger, D. 'The French Exiled Clergy in the North of England'. In: AA (5), X (1982), pp. 171–177.

Bossy, J. 'Four Catholic Congregations in Rural Northumberland, 1750–1850'. In: RH 9/2 (1967), pp. 88–119.

Bossy, J. 'More Northumbrian Congregations'. In: RH 10/1 (1969), pp. 11–34.

Brown, W. 'Crook Hall'. In: UM 4 (1894), pp. 1–31, 125–162.

Cooter, R. 'On Calculating the Nineteenth Century Irish Catholic Population of Durham and Newcastle'. In: NCH 2 (1975), pp. 16–25.

Crangle, L. 'The Roman Catholic Community in Sunderland from the 16th Century'. In: *Antiquities of Sunderland* XXIV (1969), pp. 63–78.

Culley, M. 'Two Northumbrian Missions' [Longhorsley, Netherwitton]. In: UM 7 (1897), pp. 168–184.

Culley, M. 'Thropton'. In: UM 11 (1901), pp. 264–273.

Dix, H. 'An Old Time Pastor of the Diocese of Hexham and Newcastle 1806–1897'. In: UM 59 (1949), pp. 16–21.

Duffy, E. 'Ecclesiastical Democracy Detected: (1779–1787)'. In: RH 10/4 (Jan. 1970), pp. 193–209.

Duffy, E. 'Ecclesiastical Democracy Detected: II (1787–1796)'. In: RH 10/6 (Oct. 1970), pp. 309–331.

Bibliography

Duffy, E. 'Ecclesiastical Democracy Detected: III, 1796–1803'. In: RH 13/2 (Oct. 1975), pp. 123–148.

Duffy, E. 'James Barnard and the Catholic Committee, or "How Horatio Held the Bridge"'. In: UM 85 (1974), pp. 39–49.

Edwards, F. O. 'Residence of St. John 1717–1858, Part I: "The Alnwick Fund and Chapel"'. In: NCH 3 (1976), pp. 17–23.

Edwards, F. O. 'Residence of St. John 1717–1858, Part II: "The Jesuits outside Alnwick and Durham City"'. In: NCH 5 (1977), pp. 13–20.

Forster, A. 'A Durham Family: Jenisons of Walworth'. In: *Biographical Studies*, 3/1 (1955), pp. 2–15.

Forster, A. 'Catholicism in the Diocese of Durham in 1767'. In: UM 72 (1963), pp. 68–92.

Forster, A. 'The Maire Family of County Durham'. In: RH 10/6 (1970), pp. 332–346.

Forster A. & E. Walsh, 'The Recusancy of the Brandlings'. In: RH 10/1 (1969), pp. 35–64.

Gooch, L. 'The Vicars Apostolic of the Northern District, Part I: 1688–1790'. In: NCH 16 (1982), pp. 11–15.

Gooch, L. 'The Vicars Apostolic of the Northern District, Part II: 1790–1850'. In NCH 17 (1983), pp. 20–23.

Gooch, L. 'The Northern Brethren's Fund'. In: NCH 21 (1985), pp. 6–12.

Gooch, L. '"Incarnate Rogues and Vile Jacobites": Silvertop v. Cotesworth, 1718–1723'. In: RH 18/3, (1987), pp. 277–288.

Gooch, L. 'The Last Recusants of the North East: The Reports of 1780 and 1787'. In: NCH 27 (1988), pp. 7–11.

Gooch, L. 'Priests and Patrons in the Eighteenth Century'. In: RH 20/2 (1990), pp. 207–222.

Gooch, L. '"What shall we do with the Wanton Student": Tutoring the Catholic Gentry in the Eighteenth Century'. In: RH 22/1 (1994), pp. 63–74.

Gooch, L. 'The Religion for a Gentleman: The Northern Catholic Gentry in the Eighteenth Century'. In: RH 23/4 (1997), pp. 543–568.

Hagerty, J. M. 'Notes on the Northern District under Bishop Thomas Smith 1821–1831'. In: NCH 27 (1988), pp. 20–30.

Hexter, J. H. 'The Protestant Revival and the Catholic Question in England, 1778–1829'. In: *Journal of Modern History* 8/3 (1936), pp. 297–319.

Joyce, H. B. 'The Haggerstons: The Education of a Northumberland Family'. In: RH 14/3 (1978), pp. 175–192.

Linker, R. W. 'English Catholics in the Eighteenth Century: An Interpretation'. In: *Church History* 35 (1966), pp. 288–310.

Linker, R. W. 'The English Roman Catholics and Emancipation: The Politics of Persuasion'. In: JEH 27/2 (1976), pp. 151–180.

MacDermott, T. P. 'Charles Larkin, Radical Reformer, 1800–79'. In: NCH 28 (1988), pp. 13–17.

McGuiness, P. 'Saint Mary's Cathedral; The Early Years', Part 1. In NCH 5 (Spring, 1977), pp. 21–25.

McGuiness, P. 'Saint Mary's Cathedral; The Early Years'. Part 2. In: NCH 6 (Autumn, 1977), pp. 21–25.

Milburn, D. '"A Kinder Man or Better Master Never Lived": Monsignor Thomas Edward Witham of Lartington, (1806–1897)'. In: NCH 39 (1998), pp. 31–56.

Milburn, G. 'The Census of Worship of 1851'. In: DCLHSB 17 (1974), pp. 3–20.

Milburn, G. 'Catholicism in Mid-Nineteenth Century Northumberland'. In: *Tyne 'n Tweed* 32 (1978), pp. 16–21.

Nicholson, W. 'Ralph Peter Clavering of Callaly [1727–87]'. In: NCH 1 (1975), pp. 18–24.

Purcell, P. 'The Jacobite Rising of 1715 and Roman Catholics', *English Historical Review* 44 (1929), pp. 418–432.

Reed, M. C. 'George Stephenson and W. T. Salvin: The Early Railway Capital Market at Work'. In: *Transport History* 1 (1968), pp. 10–20.

Rounding, J. A. 'William, 4th Baron Widdrington of Blankney, c.1675–1743'. In: NCH 22 (1985), pp. 24–30.

Scott, G. 'The Benedictines in the North East in the Eighteenth Century'. In: NCH 32 (1991), pp. 28–42.

Smith W. 'The Maintenance of the Clergy of Northumberland and Durham in Penal Days'. In: UM 47 (1937), pp. 1–14.

Smith, W. 'Thropton: 250 Years Old'. In: UM 62 (1952), pp. 186–198.

Smith, W. '18th Century Catholic Education in County Durham'. In: UM 73 (1963), pp. 20–27.

Smith, W. 'The 1851 Census of Worship'. In: NCH 7 (1978), pp. 20–30.

Smith, W. 'St. Mary's Parish, Stockton on Tees, to 1900'. In: NCH 9 (1979), pp. 13–19.

Smith, W. 'The Chaplains of the Radcliffe Family of Dilston Castle'. In: NCH 11 (1980), pp. 11–19.

Treble, J. H. 'The Attitude of the Roman Catholic Church towards Trade Unionism in the North of England, 1833–42'. In: *Northern History* 5 (1970), pp. 93–113.

Vaughan, F. J. 'Bishop Leyburn and his Confirmation Register of 1687'. In: NCH 12 (1980), pp. 13–18.

Wilton, R. C. 'Letters of a Jesuit Father in the Reign of George I'. In: *Dublin Review* 158 (1916), pp. 307–323.

Wilton, R. C. 'Early Eighteenth Century Catholics in England'. In: *Catholic Historical Review* 10 (1924), pp. 367–387.

VI. Unpublished Theses:

Armstrong, G. G. *The Life and Influence of Shute Barrington (1734 to 1826), Successively Canon of Christ Church, Oxford, and Bishop of Llandaff, Salisbury and Durham.* Durham M.Litt., 1937.

Child, M. S. *Prelude to the Revolution: The Structure of Politics in County Durham, 1678-88.* Durham PhD, 1972.

Daykin, C. *The Parliamentary Representation of Durham, 1675-1832.* Durham, M.Litt., 1961.

Doherty, S. *English and Irish Catholics in Northumberland, c.1745 – c.1860.* Queen's University of Belfast, PhD, 1987.

Gooch, L. *The Durham Catholics and Industrial Development 1560-1850.* York, M.A., 1984.

Gooch, L. *From Jacobite to Radical: The Catholics of North-East England 1688-1850.* Durham PhD, 1989.

Maynard, W. B. *The Ecclesiastical Administration of the Archdeaconry of Durham, 1774-1856.* Durham, PhD, 1973.

VII Locally Printed Parish Histories

[These are often published without regard to bibliographical convention: anonymous, unpaginated, undated and without place of publication.]

Alnwick: A. Chadwick, *St. Mary's Church, Alnwick.* 1936; *Guide to St. Paul's R.C. Church.*

Barnard Castle: *St. Mary's Church, Barnard Castle*; V. Chapman, *Lartington.* 1985.

Berwick-upon-Tweed: J. M. Rowley, *A History of the Church of Our Lady and St. Cuthbert.* 1992.

Bellingham: W. Nicholson, *St. Oswald's Church, 1839-1989.*

Biddlestone: J. M. Robinson, *Biddlestone Chapel, Northumberland*. Historic Chapels Trust. 2008.

Birtley: *Chronicles of St. Joseph's Mission*; G. Scott, *St Joseph's Roman Catholic Church, Birtley, A Short History and Description*. 1993.

Bishop Auckland: F. Hickey, *St. Wilfrid's (1846–1996)*.

Blackhill: *St. Mary's*. 1957; *St. Marys*. 1986.

Brooms: T. Matthews, *History of Brooms Parish, 1802–1969*. Consett, 1969.

Cheeseburn Grange: A. Durkin, *A History of St Francis Xavier, Cheeseburn & St Matthew, Ponteland*. 1996.

Darlington: The Community, *A History of Darlington Carmel 1619–1982*. 1982; *St. Augustine's (1827–1977)*; G. Wild, *The Darlington Catholics: A History up to 1866*. Darlington, 1983.

Esh Laude: W. Beavis, Newhouse and Esh Laude (A Short History).

Esh Winning: *St. John Boste and the Continuity of Catholicism in the Deerness Valley*. 1993.

Felling: J. Geraghty, *Parish History*.

Gateshead: V. Carney, *Corpus Christi Parish History 1936–1986*; *St. Joseph's Church*.

Hartlepool: T. A. Dunne, *The Catholic Church in Hartlepool*. Hartlepool, 1934; P. Fitzpatrick, *The Catholic Church in Hartlepool and West Hartlepool 1834–1964*. Hartlepool, 1964; A. E. Brown, *St. Joseph's Church (1895–1995)*.

Hexham: W. Nicholson, *St. Mary's Hexham 1830–1980*. Hexham, 1980.

Houghton le Spring: D. Lincoln, *St. Michael's Parish History*.

Hutton House: *Sts. Peter and Paul (1825–1975)*.

Jarrow: M. J. Young, *A History of Catholic Jarrow*. 1940.

Minsteracres: J. Lenders, *Minsteracres*. Rochdale, Orphans Press, 1932.

Morpeth: K. Stewart and N. Cassidy, *A Short History of St. Robert's Church*. 1969.

Newcastle: *St. Andrew's Parish History*; V. Bartley, *A History and Guide of the Cathedral Church of St. Mary*. 1998.

North Shields: J. Stark, *St Cuthbert's Church, North Shields*. 1902.

South Shields: W. Fee, *The Story of the Catholic Church in South Shields*. 1976.

Stella: J. Galletly & T. Yellowley, *Ss. Mary & Thomas Aquinas, Stella, 1831–1981*; Anon., 'The Opening of the New Chapel at Stella in the County of Durham'. In: *Catholic Magazine* 1/12 (1832), pp. 773–782.

Stockton on Tees: *St. Mary's (1842–1992.)*

Sunderland: Srs M. Wilfrid & M. Michael, *The Story of the Sunderland Sisters of Mercy 1843–1993*; Sr. M. Stanislaus, *St Anthony's, Sunderland (1883–1983)*; *St. Mary's*; K. Devlin et al, *St Mary's Jubilee (1835–1985)*; St. Benet's parish history notes; St. Patrick's parish history notes.

Tudhoe [Croxdale]: A. J. Coia, *St Charles's Parish (1858–1983)*.

Tynemouth: A. Pickering, *The Story of Our Parish* (Our Lady and St Oswin).

Wooler: W. Nicholson, *St Ninian's Parish History*.

INDEX OF PERSONS

Adams, Thomas 370–1
Allan, George 124, 126
Allan, Henry 303
Allanson, Dom Athanasius 271
Allen, Cardinal William xix
Allgood, Lancelot 65
Anderson, William 274
Anderton, Francis, S.J. 272, 369
Ashmall, Ferdinand (Ferdinando) 204, 264, 293–4, 305, 334
Ashmall, Mrs 305

Baker, George 124–5
Baker, John 62
Bamber, John 23, 266, 275–6
Banister, Robert 195–6, 199, 217
   correspondence with Rutter 216–29, 235, 237–8
   retirement 228
   views on Douai 243–4, 245
Banks, Joseph 72
Barrington, Bishop Shute 301
   anti-Catholic campaigning 107, 109, 114–17
   career 115–16
   charity 117–18
   dispute with Lingard 114–20, 166n
Barrow, Revd John 191, 214–15, 228, 246
Beaumont, Colonel 122
Beaumont, John 211

Beaumont, T.W. 127, 133, 135, 136–7, 140, 142, 144
Beaumont, Wentworth 164
Bell, John 243, 287–8
Bell, Matthew 133, 134–5, 141, 142–3, 144, 145
Bell, Robert 150
Benedict XIV 206
Bennet, Henry 241
Berington, Joseph 34, 39, 60, 116, 199, 226–7
Bertram, William 327
Besnier, Philip 214, 377–8
Betham, Dr John 178–9
Betham, Frederick 41, 272
Biddulph, Mrs 365
Bigot, Louis 214, 377, 383
Billington, John 313
Birdsall, William 203, 379–80
Birkhead, George xix
Bishop, Bishop William xix
Blackburne, Archbishop 51
Blackwell, George xix
Blakiston, Mrs 9
Blundell, Nicholas 54
Bonomi, Giuseppe 195, 301, 317
Bonomi, Ignatius 83, 118, 195, 267, 277, 281, 297, 315, 318, 342, 351
Bourne, Widdrington 355
Bradford, Lancelot 300
Bradley, Henry 312
Bradley, John 83
Brandling, Anne 338–9

Brandling, Charles 27, 68, 77, 270
Brandling, Charles (II) 78–80
Brandling, Charles John 133, 134–5, 141
Brandling, C.J. 127
Brandling family 77–80, 95, 268–9, 386
Brandling, John 150–1
Brandling, Ralph 77–8
Brandling, Ralph (II) 78
Briggs, Bishop John 161, 233, 249–50, 281, 306, 307, 317, 355, 380
Brown, Bishop George 249
Brown, Lancelot 'Capability' 74, 346, 348
Brown, Nicholas 350–1, 354–5
Bulmer, Bertram Edward 268
Burchall, James 43
Burdett, Francis 130, 132
Burnop. William 350
Burton, Edwin xiii
Busby, Charles 336–7
Butler, Charles 117, 300
Butler, Mary 366
Butler, Revd Alban 59, 60
Byres, James 62

Carr, Benoni 338
Cartington, Anne 333
Castlereagh, Lord 152
Challoner, Bishop 196, 202
Chambers, Mr 205
Chandler, Bishop Edward 20–1, 24, 358
Chapman, W. 151
Charlton, Barabara 69
Charlton family 348–52
Charlton, Francis 352

Charlton, W. 156
Charlton, W.H. 350
Charlton, William 74, 339, 351
Chevallier, Revd Temple 295–6
Clark, J. 151
Clark, Joseph (Hutchinson) 330
Clarke, Jonathan xviii
Clarkson, William 349
Clavering, Ann 303
Clavering, Anne 364
Clavering, Edward 210, 381
Clavering family 333, 363–6
Clavering, James 5
Clavering, John 8, 17, 139–40, 328
Clavering, John Aloysius 364, 365
Clavering, John Edward 365
Clavering, Margaret 381
Clavering, Mrs J.E. 365
Clavering, Nicholas 203, 303, 364
Clavering, Ralph 17, 327, 328, 331, 363, 367
Clavering, Ralph Peter 363, 364
Clavering, Sir John 363
Clavering, William 210, 381
Clayton, Mr 283
Clement XIV 388
Cleveland, Duke of 318
Clifton, John 217–18
Cock, Thomas 348
Coghlan, Revd William 306, 313
Collingwood, George 8
Collingwood, Mr 363
Collingwood, Thomas, S.J. 361
Consitt, Edward 385
Constable, Amey (née Clifford) 87, 88
Constable, Cecily 86

Index of Persons

Constable, Cuthbert *see* Tunstall, Cuthbert
Constable, Marmaduke Cuthbert (Tunstall) 88–93
Constable, Sir Marmaduke 53, 55, 265
Constable, William 60, 65–6
Constable, William (b 1721) 87–8
Conyers family 13
Cordell, Charles 196, 206–7, 225, 227, 387–8, 389
Cotes, John 238, 358, 359, 366
Cotes, Mrs Winifred 366
Cotesworth, William 72
Cowper, Lady 5
Crane, Mr 375–6
Creagh, Sir William 3
Crewe, Bishop Nathaniel 4, 13
Croskell, William 247, 266
Crowley, Ambrose 4
Cullen, Joseph 42, 373
Cumberland, Duke of 22
Curr, Joseph 160
Curry, Luke 302

da Cugna, Luigi 14
Dalton, Revd Marmaduke 309
Daniel, John 310
Danson, Revd Thomas 291
Darlington, Earl of, anti-Catholicism 148
Darrell, John 200, 363
Davison, Thomas 35
Defoe, Daniel 20
Derwentwater, Countess, property and wealth 17
Deshogues, Louis 214
Dicconson, Edward 182

Dicconson family 182
Dicconson, William 182
Digges, Francis 210, 376, 381
Dobson, John 271, 347–8, 353, 355, 362, 382, 395
Douglass, Bishop 242, 365
Dubuisson, Pierre 214
Ducket, William 334
Dugdale, Joseph 311
Dunn, Archibald M. 273
Dunn, Joseph 209
Dunn, Revd William 240

Eden, Sir John 309
Eldon, Lord, dispute with Grey 150–1
Ellis, Michael 41–2, 319
Ellison, Cuthbert 127, 133
Errington, Edward 8
Errington family 343
Errington, Henry 64
Errington, John 3, 343–4
Errington, Nicholas 8
Errington, Ralph 343
Errington, Thomas 3
Errington, William 8, 18, 297
Esh, Margaret 292
Ewbank, John Wilson 157
Eyre, Francis 93, 196
Eyre, Thomas 73, 199, 203–4, 207, 215, 282–3, 286–7, 294, 365, 371, 376, 377, 383

Fenwick, Dr J.R. 69, 121, 137–9
Fenwick, Margaret 348–9
Ferby, Thomas 317
Fiennes, Celia 6
Fishwick, John 368

Fletcher, William 42, 215, 276, 288, 290, 295–6
Flounders, Benjamin 83
Forcer, Basil 13, 356
Forcer family 55
Forcer, John 9
Forshaw, Dom John 210
Frazer, Simon, Lord Lovat 5

Galley, James 275
Galley, Ralph 275
Gard, Robin xxi
Gardiner, James 360
Gardiner, Luke 264
Gascoigne, Sir Edward 53, 55
Gascoigne, Sir Edward (IV) 65
Gascoigne, Sir Thomas (VIII) 62–3, 68
Gascoigne, William 338
Gentili, Luigi 249
George III 114
George IV 152
Gibbon, Edward 57
Gibson, Bishop 112, 119, 374, 393–4
Gibson, Bishop Matthew 184, 234–5, 236, 237–8, 282
Gibson, Bishop William 74, 189, 191, 202–3, 217, 220–1, 233, 238–42, 243–6, 266, 359, 367, 382
Gibson, George 131, 181, 329, 331, 339
Gibson, George Thomas 328–9, 363
Gibson, James 302, 319
Gibson, Jasper 329–30, 331, 339, 351
Gibson, John 339
Gibson, Richard 246
Gibson, T. 156, 357
Gibson, Thomas 302, 328, 387

Gibson, William Thomas 329
Gicquet, Charles 383
Giffard, Bonaventure 336
Giffard, Thomas 93
Gilbert, Nicholas Alain 383
Giles, Robert 394
Gilley, Sheridan xxi
Gillow, Richard 394
Gillow, Thomas 199, 365, 383–4, 393–4
Girlington, John 274, 336–7, 339
Goldie, George 316, 385
Goldwell, Bishop Thomas xix
Goodyear, George 328
Gordon, Lord George 107
Grainge, Elizabeth 310
Green, J. Jr 368
Greenwell, Thomas 282
Gregory XV xix
Grey, Charles, Lord Howick 108, 109, 112, 127, 128–9, 136, 143, 148
  dispute with Eldon 150–1
  election, 1807 122–3
Grey, Henry George, Lord Howick 130
Grey, John 108, 144
Grey, Sir George 163

Hadley, Dom Laurence 362
Haggerston Mr (Ellingham) 122
Haggerston, Anne 272, 376
Haggerston, Edward 8, 18, 64, 201, 210, 373, 374
Haggerston family 369, 376
Haggerston, Francis 376
Haggerston, Henry, S.J. 369
Haggerston, John, S.J. 360, 373

Index of Persons

Haggerston, Lady Jane 369
Haggerston, Lady Mary 356
Haggerston, Sir Carnaby (II) 8, 61, 68, 156, 211, 222, 223–4, 235, 265
Haggerston, Sir Carnaby (III) 18, 369, 374
Haggerston, Sir Carnaby (V) 370, 371–2
Haggerston, Sir Thomas 3, 356, 369
Haggerston, Thomas 64, 67, 141–2, 210, 230, 374–6
Haggerston, William 64, 376
Haggerston, Winifred (née Charlton) 374
Hall, Lawrence 339
Hallyman, Robert 273
Halsall, Arthur Bede 337
Hankin, John 274, 331, 359
Hanne, Charles, S.J. 210, 370, 376
Hansom, J. and C. 316
Hansom, J.A. 307, 348, 383
Hardinge, General Sir Henry 127, 130, 152–3
Hardwicke, Lord 51–2
Harrison, William xix
Hawarden, John 310
Hay, Bishop 112, 196
Headlam, Dr 150
Heneage, Elizabeth 88
Higginson, James 353
Hodgkinson, Charles 312
Hodgshon, Francis 204
Hodgson, Allan 352
Hodgson, Anthony 158
Hodgson, Francis 274
Hodgson, Ralph 285
Hodgson, Revd Francis 313–14

Hardinge, General Sir Henry 127, 130, 152–3
Hardwicke, Lord 51–2
Harrison, William xix
Hawarden, John 310
Hodgshon, Francis 204
Hodgson, Allan 352
Hodgson, Anthony 158
Hodgson, Francis 274
Hodgson, Ralph 285
Hodgson, Revd Francis 313–14
Hogarth, Bishop William 189, 196–7, 203, 250–1, 253, 273, 291, 302, 307, 313-317
Holderness. Dom John 345
Holland, Mr 127
Holme, Francis 211, 368
Horrabin, Richard 139
Houghton, William 331
Howard, Francis 367
Howard, Philip 53, 60
Howe, Joseph 200, 207, 210, 285, 353, 386–7
Howick, Viscount Henry 133–9, 141–2, 143, 144, 145, 147
Hull, William 283
Humble family 268
Humble, Richard 79
Hurst, William 377
Hutchinson, Bonaventure 330–1, 347
Hutton, Dom Placid 268

Ingleton, John 181
Irving, Revd T.S. 308

Jackson, Constantine 328–9
Jackson, Robert 310
Jakes, Francis 36–7

James II 3, 178, 180
James III 178–9, 181
Jefferson, Thomas 339
Jenison, Augustine 264, 374
Jenison family (Hurworth) 55
Jenison family (Walworth) 55
Jenison, Francis 18
Jenison, James 199
Jenison, John (Hurworth) 9
Jenison, John (Walworth) 9, 18
Jenison, Ralph 13
Jenks, Silvester 180
Johnson, James 393
Johnson, Mr 205
Joy, Matthew 209
Joy, Mr 374

Kearney, Francis 162
Kearney, Philip 161, 277–8, 369
Kelly, John 162
Kennedy, Revd J. 383
Kennet family 13
Kennet, Nicholas 13
Kirby, Thomas 37
Kitchen, Edward 317
Knight, William 306, 307

Lambton, George 108, 127, 128, 129, 130, 136, 142
Lambton, Lord, Earl of Durham 149, 155
Langdale, Catherine 88
Larkin, Charles 157–61, 162–3, 164–5, 253
Lawson, Catherine 219
Lawson, Sir Henry 95, 279, 356, 366, 367

Lawson, Sir John 203, 222, 235, 236, 237, 240–1, 300–1, 356, 371, 393
Leadbitter, Jasper 340, 342
Leadbitter, Margaret 329
Leadbitter, Nicholas 332, 340
Leckonby, Thomas 200, 207–8, 286
Leigh, Anne 78
Leyburn, Bishop John xx, 6, 334, 338, 352, 358, 360, 363, 386
Liddell, Henry Thomas 133, 134–6, 137, 139–41, 143–5, 147, 148
Liddell, Thomas 317
Lingard, John 108, 192, 196, 197, 227, 228–9, 287, 389
 character and approach 115, 246
 dispute with Barrington 114–20, 166n
 on election, 1807 121
 at Ushaw College 119–20
Londonderry, Marquis of 148
Longstaffe, Owen 319
Losh, James 137, 150–1, 152, 155, 196, 391
Lowe, Dom George Augustine 357
Lumley family 267
Lumley, Lord Richard 3

Macartney, Revd Andrew 365–6
Macaulay, Thomas B. xiv–xv
MacDonald, Thomas 279–80
Macquet, Charles 383
Maddox, Mr 375–6
Maire family 55
Maire, Francis 22, 303
Maire, Henry 241, 242, 313, 317
Maire, John 366
Maire, Mary 234, 275
Maire, Sir Thomas 9

Index of Persons

Maire, Thomas 317
Maire, William 183, 266
Maltby, Bishop Edward 163, 252, 307
Manning, Cardinal Henry xiii–xiv, xv
Markham, Mary 90
Marsh, Jerome 353
Mayes, John 312
Mayes, Lawrence 178–9, 312
Mayes, Nicholas 311
McAnulty, Bernard 162
McClelland, V. Alan xxi
McDermott, Anthony 161, 272
McEvoy, James 280
Meaburne, Anthony 9, 285
Meaburne, Anthony (II) 285
Menard, Monsieur 378
Metham, Revd Anthony 309
Meynell, Edward 312
Meynell, Mary 312
Meynell, Mr 129
Meynell, Thomas 83, 312
Meynell, William, S.J. 209–10, 374
Mickleton, James 10–13, 185
Midford, Roger 204
Milburn, David xxi
Milner, Bishop 127, 139, 191, 216, 244
Minto, Lord 252
Mitford, Roger 334, 360
Monck, Sir Charles 127, 131–2
Moody, Luke 371
More, Hannah 63, 116
Morris, Michael xviii
Mostyn, Bishop Francis 250, 278, 311, 373
Mountney, Ursula 327–8
Murphy, Richard 207, 282
Musgrave, General 67

Nandyke, Thomas 312
Naylor, Dom Ambrose 362
Naylor, Dom John 231
Needham, Daniel 374
Needham, John Turberville 60
Newman, Cardinal John xiv, xv, 408
Newton, Elizabeth 302
Newton, William 200, 350
Newton, William, S.J. 361
Nixon, Thomas 210, 211
Norman, Edward xviii
Northumberland, Duke of 122

O'Connell, Daniel 161
Oliver, William 342
Ord, Clare 360
Ord, W.H. 151, 366
Orrell, Revd Joseph 380
Owen, Robert 161–2

Paine, James 282
Paoluci, Cardinal 14
Parker, John 367
Parker, Thomas 379
Peacock, Thomas 302
Pearson, Thomas 264
Peat, Lady 278, 296
Peel, Robert 132
Pemberton, William 373–4
Penswick, Bishop Thomas 233, 248–9
Pepper, William 379
Perceval, Spencer 114
Percy, Hugh, 3rd Duke of Northumberland 153
Percy, Lord 122
Peters, James 365
Petre, Benjamin 335, 336

Petre, Bishop Francis 182–4, 266
Petre, Lord 240
Phillips, Ambrose Lisle 162–3
Phillpotts, Revd Henry 107, 128–9
Pickering, Lancelot 317
Pippard, George 386
Pitt, William 189
Pius IX 252
Pius VI 62
Pius VII 212
Platt, Ralph 162
Pleasington, Joseph 209, 363–4
Pope, Dom James 344
Potts, Luke 360
Powlett, William 152
Poynter, Bishop 112, 129, 212
Prince Charles 179
Prince Henry 179
Pugin, Augustus Welby 192–3, 311, 392
Pyatt, Ann 275

Radcliffe, Arthur 337
Radcliffe, Col. Thomas 336
Radcliffe, Edward, 2nd Earl Derwentwater 5
Radcliffe family 333, 335–6, 385, 386
Radcliffe, Francis, 1st Earl Derwentwater 3, 5, 335, 405
Radcliffe fund 333–4
Radcliffe, James, 3rd Earl Derwentwater 7
Radcliffe, John 336
Radcliffe, Lady Elizabeth 333
Radcliffe, Lady Mary 264, 336
Radcliffe, Sir Edward 203–4, 333
Radcliffe, Sir Edward (II), bequests 334

Radcliffe, Sir Francis 333, 386
Raffa, Dom Anthony 23, 268, 269–70
Rayment, Benedict 301, 317
Rice, Edmund 278
Richardson, John 209
Richardson, Mr 385
Riddell, Bishop William 191, 223, 373
Riddell, Edward 8, 17–18
Riddell, Edward Horsley 64
Riddell, Mr 233
Riddell, Mrs 354
Riddell, Ralph 340, 347–8
Riddell, Revd W. 156
Riddell, Robert 334–5, 385
Riddell, Thomas 56, 339, 352, 354–5, 356
Riddell, Thomas Horsley 64
Riddell, Thomas (II) 352
Riddell, William 271, 355
Riddell, William, Vicar Apostolic 156, 161, 162–3, 201, 233, 250
Ridley, M.W. 127
Ridley, Sir Matthew 213
Ridsdale family 314
Rivers, Richard 204
Roby, James 301
Rogerson, John 383
Rose, Christopher 209
Russell, Lord John 163, 252
Russell, Matthew 120
Rutter, Henry 69, 196, 199, 203, 207, 208, 213, 214, 233, 282–3, 313, 364, 388, 392–3
  advice from Banister 222–5
  correspondence with Banister 216–29, 235, 237–9
  dress 219–20
  duties 222

Index of Persons

finances 220–1
house move 228
leaves Minsteracres 228–9
at Minsteracres 218–29
opinion of gentry 222
publications 228
social life 220–2
surveillance of M. Gibson 234–5
as tutor 217–18
views on Douai 243, 245
wish to move 225
Rutter, John 382
Ryding, Dom Andrew Bernard 346

Salvin, Bryan (II) 81, 82
Salvin, Catherine (née Thornton) 358
Salvin, Edward John 83
Salvin family 55, 65, 68, 80–6, 95, 296–7
Salvin, Gerard (V) 81
Salvin, Gerard (VII) 86
Salvin, Marmaduke 86
Salvin, Ralph 9, 16
Salvin, Ralph (II) 81
Salvin-Thornton dispute 358
Salvin, William 81, 236, 358
Salvin, William (II) 81
Salvin, William Thomas 82, 83–5, 126, 155
Sanderson, Nicholas 210, 211
Sanderson, William (Hodgson) 349
Savile, Sir George 65–6
Sayer family 309
Scott, John 209
Scott, William 127, 276
Seaforth, William, 5th Earl 13
Selby, Thomas 68, 361, 362

Selby, Walter 122, 362
Selby, William 8
Sewell, Nicholas 209, 266
Shaftoe, James 9
Shaftoe, John 340
Sharp, Matthew 341
Sharples, Henry 380
Sharrock, Bishop 247
Sharrock, Dom Dunstan 354
Sharrock, Dom John 349
Sheldon, Edward 95
Sheldon, Thomas 66
Sheridan, Dom James 271
Shippersden, Mr 124
Shirley, Mrs 35
Sidmouth, Viscount 148
Sidney, Marlow John 139, 394–5
Silvertop, Albert 72, 381
Silvertop, Bridget 387
Silvertop, Charles 243
Silvertop, Elizabeth 387
Silvertop family 72–7, 95, 218–29, 283, 381–2
Silvertop, George 67–8, 72–6, 123, 126, 129, 138–9, 141, 155, 291, 304, 381–2
Silvertop, George (I) 218
Silvertop, George (II) 242–3
Silvertop, Henry 243
Silvertop, Jane 371, 383
Silvertop, John 67, 74–5, 218–19, 228, 234–5, 242, 287
Silvertop-Maire, Catherine 303–4
Silvertop, Mary 387
Silvertop, William 72
Simpson, Dom Richard 344
Simpson, John 293
Singleton, Michael 341–2

Skelton, Dom John Elphege 352
Skelton, Dom John Gregory 343
Slater, Dom Bernard 270
Slater, Thomas 304–5, 306
Smeaton, John 79
Smith, Bishop 112, 139
Smith, Bishop James xx, 309, 328, 334
Smith, Bishop Richard xix
Smith, Bishop Thomas xiv–xv, 124, 198, 203, 204–5, 228–9, 241, 246–8, 266, 267, 315, 362, 394
Smith, James 179–80
Smith, John 42–3, 156, 288–90, 353
Smith, Revd Robert 373
Smith, Thomas 299
Smythe family 55, 292, 295
Smythe, George 292
Smythe, Sir Edward 9, 65, 292, 294
Smythe, William 292
Spain, Dom Leo 270–1
Standish, Edward 201
Stanley, John Massey 373
Stanley, Lady Mary 372–3
Stanley, Sir Thomas Massey 372
Stapleton, Miles 60
Stephenson, George 83–5
Stephenson, George (curate) 149
Stephenson, Robert 85
Sterne, Laurence 64
Stewart, Lord Charles 152, 153
Stonor, Bishop 216
Stonor, Christopher 239
Stonor, Revd Christopher 179
Storey, Thomas 83, 298–9, 310–11, 314, 364
Stout, Thomas 360, 365
Strathmore, 10th Earl 120
Strickland, William 206, 211, 367, 368

Sutton family 13
Sutton, Robert 334
Swift, Roger xxi
Swinburne, Algernon 69
Swinburne, Edward 61, 64
Swinburne family 345, 381
Swinburne, Henry 61–4, 69, 74, 287, 344
Swinburne, John Edward 64
Swinburne, Lady 69–70, 135
Swinburne, Martha (née Baker) 62, 63–4, 287
Swinburne, Sir Edward, sons 64
Swinburne, Sir Edward (V) 346
Swinburne, Sir John 8, 27, 268–70, 345
Swinburne, Sir John Edward (VI) 346
Swinburne, Sir John (III), travel 61
Swinburne, Sir John (IV) 61
Swinburne, Sir John (VI) 69
Swinburne, Thomas 285–6
Swinburne, Thomas Anthony 286

Talbot, Bishop James 237
Talbot, Bishop Thomas 237–9
Talbot, Thomas 297
Tassou, Pierre 314
Taylor, John 75
Taylor, M.A. 127, 130
Taylor, Nicholas 275
Tempest family 281
Tempest, Jane 72, 281
Tempest, Sir Francis 8, 281
Tempest, Stephen 54–5
Tempest, William 3, 267
Thompson, Elizabeth 79
Thompson, Peter 329–30, 331, 338–9

Index of Persons

Thompson, William 352
Thornton family 358–60
Thornton, Isabella 358
Thornton, James 358
Thornton, John 8, 223, 229–31, 358
Thornton, John, S.J. 369
Thornton, Margaret 358
Thornton, Mary 358
Thornton, Thomas 358
Thorp, Charles 160
Tidyman, Michael 211, 213–14, 215, 370, 371, 372, 376–7, 378
Tocketts, Alexius 264
Todd, John 332
Towneley, Charles 156
Towneley family 282, 283
Towneley, Richard 70–1
Trevelyan, Walter 358
Trollope, Robert 345–7
Tudor, Lady Mary 333
Tunstall, Cuthbert 66–7, 87
Tunstall family 86–94
Tunstall, Francis 86
Tunstall, Marmaduke 60, 66, 86–7, 236, 239, 240, 241, 274
Tunstall, Marmaduke (b 1743) 88–94
Turner, Dom Thomas 356
Turner, Mr 198

van Mildert, Bishop William 149, 153–4, 155, 160, 296
Vane, Lord Harry 76
Vane Powlett, Hon W.J.F. 128, 130
Vane, William Henry, Marquess of Cleveland 152, 168–9n
Vergy, Monsieur 211
Vergy, Peter 367

Wailes, William 316
Walker, Augustine 285, 343
Walmesley, Bishop 233
Walsh, Edward 208–9, 212, 266
Walsh, John 206, 366, 367, 386–7
Walton, Bishop William 183–4, 196, 202, 208, 313, 364
Warham, Mr 205
Warrilow, William 196, 206–7, 211, 367, 388–9, 392
Waterton, Mr 198
Waterton, Thomas 265, 300
Weedall, Henry 249
Weldon, James 210
Wellesley, G.V. 149
Wellington, Duke of 152, 153, 154–5
Wells, John 306
Wesley, John 30, 109–10
West, Revd F.A. 151
Whalley, Richard 383–4
Wharton, Richard 120, 124, 127, 128
Wheeler, James 266
Whytehead, Francis 274, 275
Widdrington, Anne 328
Widdrington, Edward 3
Widdrington, Edward Horsley 8, 18, 352, 353
Widdrington, Elizabeth 353
Widdrington family 5
Widdrington, Henry 347
Widdrington, Henry Francis 73, 281–2
Widdrington, Henry, S.J. 363
Widdrington, Lady Jane 281
Widdrington, Lord 405
Widdrington, Lord William 327
Widdrington, Lord William (III) 352

Widdrington, Ralph 3, 19, 347
Widdrington, Robert 355, 361
Widdrington, Roger 360
Widdrington, William 8
Wilkinson, John 273–4
Wilkinson, Thomas 42
William III, supporters 3–4
Williams, Bishop Thomas 264–5, 337
Williams, Thomas (Dominic) 181–2
Wilson, Dom John 281
Wilson, Thomas 36
Wiseman, Nicholas xiv–xv, 125, 163, 193, 248–9, 252, 307
Witham family 55, 313, 318
Witham, George 318
Witham, Henry Thomas 125, 129, 155, 250–1, 303–4, 313, 318
Witham, Marmaduke 9
Witham, Revd George 178–9, 180–1
Witham, Robert 184, 205
Witham, Thomas 197, 359
Witham, Thomas Edward 284, 318, 380–1
Witham, William 309
Worswick, John 286, 317
Worswick, Revd James 158, 162, 164, 196, 211, 365, 388, 389–92, 393
Wright, William 83

Yates, John 293–4
Yaxlee, John 13

INDEX OF PLACES AND SUBJECTS

A History of Ushaw College (Milburn) xxi
abstinence laws 40
age, of Catholic population 33
agriculture 32, 53–4
Alnwick 211, 366–9
Alnwick Abbey 77
Amerston Hall 305
Ancroft 366
Anglican bishops, press criticism 24
Anglican clergy, reports of Catholics 27
Anglican livings, in Catholic gift 7
Anglican parishes 20–1
Anglicanism, Larkin's attack 160
annuities 52
anti-Catholicism
    Barrington-Lingard dispute 114–20
    campaigning 107, 108–11
    following restoration of hierarchy 163
    incitement 149, 150–1
    legislation 14, 51, 52
    and national identity 111
    Newcastle and Gateshead 386
    petitions 148
    in response to French riots 126
apostasy 68–9, 80
archdeacons xix
archpriests xix
armed forces, Catholic relief 114
baptisms, Newcastle 388

Bar Convent (York) 58, 300
Barnaby Rudge (Dickens) xiv
Barnard Castle 317–18, 319
Battle Hill, Hexham 338–9, 340
Beaufront 333
Beaufront Castle 343–4
Beaufront Woodhead 343
Bellingham 349, 350–1
bench-rents 276, 322n
Benedictines 210
    Beaufront 343–4
    Birtley 268–71
    Chester le Street 267
    Ellingham 374
    Gateshead House 272
    Hesleyside 348, 350
    Longhorsley Tower 354
    Newcastle upon Tyne 386
    nuns 364–5
    Ryton 281
    Swinburne Castle 352
Benediction 197
benefactors 340
bequests
    Basil Forcer 356
    Bridget Silvertop 393
    Dilston 334–5, 336
    Hexham 339, 340
    Isabella Thornton 358
    Jane Silvertop 384
    Lady Haggerston 356, 369, 376
    Lady Radcliffe 343
    Lord Derwentwater 335

Margaret Clavering 381
Mary Butler 366–7
Mountney 332
Ralph Errington 343
Sir Thomas Haggerston 356
Berrington Hall 31, 210, 372, 381
Berwick 28, 203, 376–81
Bible Societies 139
Biddlestone 231, 361, 361–2
Billingham 310
Birtley 268–71
Bishop Auckland 42–3, 300–2
bishops in ordinary
   petitioning for return xix–xx
   powers xix
Blackhill 292
Blyth 394–5
Board of British Catholics 126
books, publication of 227
Bothal 29
Brief of Suppression 207
British Roman Catholic Tests Regulation Bill, 1823 132
Brough Hall 300
building funds 394
buildings, remote locations 23–4
Burn Hall 86
Burton Constable 87
Butterby, estate and paper mill 82

Callaly Castle 17, 19, 209, 328, 363–6
Callaly, Catholic population 365, 366
Capheaton, Catholic population 345, 347
Capheaton Hall 345
Carmelites 279, 300–1, 316, 363
Cartington Castle 360
catechetical instruction 225

Catholic Committee 177–8, 234, 235–7, 242
Catholic Defence Association 253
Catholic Defence Societies 160
Catholic Directory 159
Catholic laity, attitude to anti-Catholics 111
Catholic population 248, 381
   age 33
   Alnwick 367, 368, 369
   Barnard Castle 319
   Biddlestone 361, 362
   Birtley 268
   Bishop Auckland 300
   Callaly 365, 366
   Capheaton 345, 347
   Chester le Street 268, 270
   Chollerton 352, 353
   concentrations 30
   Croxdale 298
   Darlington 314, 316, 317
   Dilston 337–8
   distribution 29–30
   Durham city 264–5, 266
   Ellingham 373, 374–5
   Esh 293, 295
   Felling 271
   Felton 354
   Gateshead 268, 272, 386
   Haggerston 370, 372
   Hartlepool 305, 307
   Hesleyside 348, 350
   Hexhamshire 339
   Houghton le Spring 279
   Kyloe 372
   Longhorsley Tower 353
   Minsteracres 382–3
   Morpeth 355

Index of Places and Subjects

Netherwitton 358, 359–60
Newcastle 386, 388, 391
nominal 43–4
North Shields 392
as proportion of whole 407
reasons for decline 28–9
relative size 112–13
Ryton 281, 282
Simondburn 350
size of 5–6, 7, 20–1, 24
South Shields 273
Stamfordham 347–8
Stockton 310, 311
Sunderland 273, 274, 275, 276–7
Thropton 360–1
Tudhoe 298
Tynemouth 392, 394
Wooler 385
Yarm 311–12
Catholic Question
   Barrington-Lingard dispute 114–20
   context and overview 107–8
   Durham by-election, 1813 124–6
   election, 1820 127–9
   election, 1826 129–31, 135–47
   election, 1841 16
   as election issue 1807 120–3
   enactment of emancipation 154–5
   Northumberland by-election 1826 133–5
   opposition to emancipation 152
   parliamentary voting 154
   petitions 147–50
   pro- and anti campaigning 108–13
   support for emancipation 152–3
   see also emancipation
Catholic Relief Act, 1778 25, 188
Catholic Relief Act, 1791 188–9, 404, 407–8
Catholic Relief Acts, negotiations 234
Catholic Relief Bill, 1825 132–3
Catholicism, anti-Catholic view of 108–10
Catholics
   Durham 9
   exclusion 407–8
   loyalty 118
   Northumberland 8
   position in society 406–7
   power and influence 7
   property and wealth 8–9
   records of xv–xvii
Census, 1705 6–10, 24
Census, 1767 24–5
Census, 1780 25
Census of Religious Worship, 1851 xvii, 41–4
chapel attendance 31
chapels and churches
   Alnwick 367–9
   appearance 186–7
   architects 192–3
   arson 22
   attacks on 386
   Barnard Castle 319
   Birtley 270–1
   building 189–90
   Darlington 315–16
   dedications 193
   Esh Laude 294–5, 296
   Felling 271–2
   financing 190–2
   Gateshead 272–3
   Hartlepool 306
   Hexham 339–42

Houghton le Spring 281
Hutton Henry 305
licensing 188–9
list of buildings 194
location 232
Minsteracres 382
near Bishop of Durham's palace 10–13
Newcastle 389–91
Newhouse 292
oversight of building 192
plain appearance 197–8
Ryton 284
Stella House 283–4
Stonecroft Farm 330
Sunderland 275–8
Tynemouth 394
see also individual churches
chaplaincies
   advantages of 226–7
   Chandler's list 20
   changes 184
   problems of 327–32
   re-institution 185
chaplains
   accommodation 232
   dress 219–20
   pastoral responsibilities 219, 231
   relations with gentry 216–17, 232–3
   status 231–2
   as status symbols 203
   see also priests
Cheeseburn Grange 19, 347–8
Chester le Street 267–71
cholera epidemic 159
Chollerton 352–3
Christian Brothers 278

Church
   hierarchical structure xix–xx
   invisibility 185–6
civic responsibility, Catholic involvement 156
clergy, age 215
clerical Agents 178
Cliffe Hall 6, 309, 312–13
coal industry, protection of interests 16
coal-mining 32, 54, 55, 302
   Croxdale 85
   Durham 301
   Felling 77–8
   Salvin family 85
   Stella mines 72–3, 74, 76
   transport 79, 84–5
Cocken Hall 279, 301
Cockerton Field House 279, 316
Cockshaw 339–40, 341
collecting, art and artefacts 60
commerce 32, 53
Commission for Forfeited Estates 15
Committee of the Three Denominations 110
confirmations
   Callaly 363, 364
   Dilston 334, 337
   Ellingham 374
   Hexham 338
   during Leyburn's visit 6
   Netherwitton 358
   Newcastle 386
   Swinburne Castle 352
   Thropton 360
Congress of Vienna 126
Consett 383
conversions 29

Index of Places and Subjects

convert cardinals, ignorance of Catholic history xiii–xv
converts 386–7
Cowpen 43, 214
Cowpen Hall 394–5
Crook Hall 189, 243, 285, 286, 287, 299, 383
Croxdale 34, 85–6, 296–300
Croxdale Hall 80, 82, 86, 296–7
Croxdale Paper Mill 81–2
cultural education 58–65

Darlington 28, 309, 310, 313–17
data, reliability and sources of xv-xvii, xxi, 30
  sources xxi
Declaration and Protestation of Catholic principles 236–7
demographic change, effects on religious practice 33
Dilston Castle 332–8
Dilston, Catholic population 337–8
Dilston Hall, chapel closure 19
Diocesan Missionary Establishment, Wooler 385
diocese, name of 253
dissension, as treason 108–9
Dockendale Hall 381
Doctor Syntax 56
Dominicans 327–8, 331, 340–1, 347, 363
door-pence 162
Douai 58, 88–9, 286, 287, 383
  French Revolution 242–3
  Gibson at 238–9
  re-establishment 243–4
  replacement for 234
  Smith at 247

Douai's Day: The English College at Douai 1568-1793 (Ushaw) xxi
double taxation 14
dowries 52, 54
dress 219–20
Durham
  1851 Census 42
  Catholic population 9
  by-election, 1813 124–6
  Episcopal Visitations 25, 26–7
  High Sherriff 156
  Jesuit mission 266
  Leyburn's visit 6
  petitions 149
  revision of town charter 3
  University 160–1
Durham Advertiser 130
Durham and Sunderland Railway company 85
Durham Chronicle 108
Durham city
  1688 attack 263
  Catholic population 264–5, 266
  church building 267
  confirmations 264
  mission stations 263
  schools 265, 266
Durham County Advertiser 108

Ecclesiastical Titles Act 1851 163, 253
education 57–65, see also schools
election, 1807 120–3
election, 1820 127–9
election, 1826 129–31, 135–47
  adoption meeting 142
  Catholic voters 131–2, 145–7
  polling 143
  results 145

subscription dinners 137–40, 141–2
election, 1841 163
Ellingham 34, 35–6, 373, 374–5
Ellingham Hall 209–10, 373–6
emancipation 68, 408–9
  calls for repeal 163
  campaign for 76, 113–14, 123–4
  enactment 154–5
  favourable environment 113
  Northumberland by-election 1826 134–5
  opposition to 152
  support for 110, 152–3
  see also Catholic Question
enfranchisement 131–2, 134
English College, Lisbon 334
English, use in worship 196
Episcopal Visitations 25, 26–7, 30, 48n
  1801 299
Esh 292–6
Esh Laude 288, 290–1, 294–5
Eshott House 370
Eslington Hall, mission 19
estates, fragmentation 52
evangelism, risks of 28–9
ex-Jesuits 207–11
Ex Porta Flaminia 163
expatriate colleges 57–8
expatriate seminaries, closure 177
expatriates 55

famine, Ireland 44–5
Farewell Hall 82, 86
Fauconburg, Viscount (III) 55
Felling 271–2
Felling colliery 77–8, 79–80

Felling Hall 23, 77, 268–70, 386
Felton 352, 354
Felton Park 353
Fenwick 372
field sports 56
financial arrangements
  geographical development 190–2
  of missions 187–8
  secular clergy 202–3
first Synod of Westminster xiv
Flaminian Gate 173n
Flass Hall 296
forty-shilling Irish freeholders 154
France 126, 177, 300–1
Franciscans 327–31, 347
freedom of movement 14
Freemasons 343
French priests 212–15, 287, 298, 314, 376, 383
French Revolution
  as arising from Catholic corruption 115–17
  Douai 242–3
  effects of 113
  exile of priests 212–13
Friendly Societies 158–9
Friends of Religious Liberty 124

Gainford 36–7, 318–19
gaming 93
Gateshead 268, 272–3, 376, 386
Gateshead House 22, 23, 272, 386
Gentleman's Magazine 57–8
gentry
  bankruptcy 55
  conflicts with priests 404
  context and overview 51
  education 57–65

Index of Places and Subjects

exclusion from military commissions 66-8
financial status 406
Grand Tour 59-65
as intellectuals 70-1
lifestyles 56
living abroad 55
observation of Lent 223-4
politics 65-70
power and influence 404-5
priests' dependence on 200-2
property and wealth 52-5
quality of life 56
relations with chaplains 216-17, 232-3
risk of decline 55
sale of estates 55
scholarship 70-1
in society 56-7
summary and conclusions 95-6
gentry houses, and population density 31
geographical development 184-95
building programme 189-90
chaplaincies 184
consolidation 186
financing 190-2
ideological factors 190
Gilesgate, Durham 263, 266
Gordon Riots 25, 29, 388
Gothicism 192-3
Grand Tour 59-65, 229, 369
Greatham 310

Haggerston Castle 18, 31, 210, 229-31, 369-73
Haggerston estates, dairy farming 95
Hamsterley Hall 61, 62, 285
Harbourhouse 13
Hardwick Hall 22, 23, 303-5
Hartburn, population density 31
Hartlepool 305-8
Hartlepool Dock and Railway Company 84
Hencotes 340
Hesleyside 27, 348, 350, 355
Hexham 253, 338-43
Hexhamshire, Catholic population 339
hierarchy, restoration of 163, 235-6, 251-3
High Mass 195, 197
High Sheriff, Durham 156, 318
History of England (Lingard) 227
Holy Communion 198
Holy See, diplomatic relations under James II 178
holydays, reduction 40
Houghton le Spring 279-81
House of Lords, northern peers 152
Huguenots, support for 126
Hutton Henry 303, 305
Hylton Castle 321n

ideology, and church building 190
incomes 53, 199-201
industrial development 28, 32, 53, 54, 184, 302, 383
inflammatory speeches 149
informal toleration 28-9, 51
inheritance, ensuring 52-3
intellectuals, gentry as 70-1
Ireland
famine 44-5
as risk to national security 112-13
Irish Catholics

attracted by industry 302
enfranchisement 132
Larkin's popularity with 161
militancy 161–2
as priests 162
suspicion of 161–2
Irish migration xxi, 44–5, 407
Irish people 44–5
Irish priests 215–16
Irish Question 215
ironworks 302
isolation 29, 187
Italy, Grand Tour 60–5

Jacobite Rising, 1715 14, 18–20, 185, 329, 386, 405
Jacobite Rising, 1745 22–4, 185, 265, 274, 405
Jacobites, continued loyalty 4–5
Jacobitism xxi, 333, 405
Jesuits
    Alnwick 366–7, 368
    Berwick 376
    Biddlestone 361–2
    Callaly Castle 363, 364
    Cheeseburn Grange 347
    Ellingham Hall 373, 375
    former 207–11
    Gateshead House 272
    Haggerston Castle 369, 370–1
    Hardwick Hall 303
    incomes 200, 201
    Longhorsley Tower 353
    Newcastle 385, 386, 388
    restoration of 212
    suppression 206–12, 388–9
    wealth 12
    at Yarm 312

Jubilee 198, 265–6, 386

Kirkwhelpington 27, 345, 346
Knights of St. Patrick 161
Kyloe 27, 31, 372

Lanchester 28, 35
landowners, church building 192
landscape gardening 74
Lartington 41–2
Lartington Hall 303, 317–19, 381
law 71
laxity, in regulation of Catholics 13–14
lay-clerical relations 242
lay control, of missions 188
lay patrons, conflicts with priests 404
Layton, Sedgefield 13
lead-mining 54
leadership, discontinuity 177–8
legislation, anti-Catholic 14
Lent 223–4
Liege Academy 211
Life of Christ (Rutter) 228
lime kilns 53–4
Lintz Hall 285
Longhorsley 34, 360
Longhorsley Tower 353–5
Longhoughton, mixed marriages 35
Low Mass 195
Lowick 27, 31
loyalty 112, 118

marital status, Catholic population 33–4
marriages
    mixed 34–7, 79, 407

Index of Places and Subjects 457

property and wealth 54
  suitable 54–5
Mass, attendance 41–3
May Devotions 197
medicine 71
Metham fund 309–10
Methodism 28, 30, 109–10, 150–1
middle class 191, 340, 404
Middlesbrough 311
Middleton colliery 78
Middleton estate 79
migration xxi, 33, 44–5, 407
military commissions, exclusion from 66–8
militias 3
ministry, extent of 21
Ministry of All the Talents 114
Minsteracres 73, 74, 75, 218–29, 381–3
mission
  context and overview 177–8
  control of 21–2
  County Durham 10–13
  discretion 29
  disruptions 27
  effects of lay control 188
  facilities 248
  financial arrangements 187–8
  French priests 212–15
  gentry-chaplain relations 216–17
  geographical development 184–95
  increased visibility 198
  Irish priests 215–16
  jurisdiction 232, 235
  lay-clerical relations 242
  meeting growing demand 198
  preaching 196

priests' incomes 199
  regular clergy 206
  resilience 405
  resistance to change 187
  restoration of hierarchy 252–3
  safety of 187
  secular clergy 203–6
  suppression of Jesuits 206–12
  transfers to secular clergy 210–11
  vicars apostolic 180–4, 234–52
  worship 195–8
mission buildings, remote locations 23–4
mission stations 21–2, 263, 411–14
  autonomy 157
  loss of 188
  range 30
  see also named locations
mixed marriages 34–7, 79, 407
mob attacks 22, 23, 263, 272, 386, 388
Morpeth 3, 355–8
mortgages 52
Mountney bequest 332

Netherwitton 27, 31, 34, 358, 359–60
Netherwitton Hall 19, 358–60
New Testament, Sidney's edition 139
Newcastle 385–96
  1851 Census 42
  building funds 389, 392
  Catholic population 386, 388, 391
  marriages 34
  missions 185
  petitions 150–1
  plunder and destruction 4
  public meeting 150–1
  revision of town charter 3
  Sheriff 156

St Mary's Cathedral 193
Newcastle Declaration 126
Newcastle Hibernian Benevolent Society 159
Newcastle Standard 160
Newcastle Upon Tyne Friendly Society 158–9
Newhouse 292–3
newspapers, criticism of Anglican bishops 24
North of England Protestant Alliance 162
North Shields 28, 392–4
north-west Durham, mission stations 281–4
Northern Brethren's Fund 203–6
Northern District, extent xx–xxi
Northern Political Union 158, 160
Northumberland 8, 122, 133–5
Norton 35

Oath of Supremacy 132, 236
official protection 22–3
Old Elvet, Durham 3, 22, 263–4, 265, 336
ordinations 216
Orthodox Journal 127
Oxford Movement xiv

Papal Aggression 252–3
papal infallibility 118
parishes, population density 30–1
parliamentary constituencies 120
parliamentary petitions 123, 126, 147–50, 242, 253
parliamentary reform, campaign for 157
patrons, conflicts with priests 404

penal laws, operation of 14
personal piety 196–7
petitions 147–9, 242, 253, 338, 378–9
pew-rents 162
pilgrimage, Grand Tour as 60–1
political exclusion 407–8
political liberty, resistance to 29
politics 65–70, 76
Pontoise 376
Pontoise nuns 364–5
Pontop Hall 207, 284–7, 383
Poor Clares 117–18, 316, 370–1
Pope
  allegiance to 108–9
  ridicule of 125
Popish Chapells within 7 miles of ye Bpp. of Durham Palace 10–12
power and influence, of gentry 404
preaching 196
Presentation Brothers 278
Preston upon Tees 309
priest holes 21, 185
priests
  autonomy 404, 408
  conflicts with lay patrons 404
  dependence on gentry 200–2
  freedom 14
  French 212–15, 287, 298, 310, 314, 376, 383
  incomes 199–201
  Irish 215–16
  mobility 225–6
  ordinations 216
  recruitment 215
  scholarship 226–7
  shortage 214–15, 216, 290–1
  workload 29
  see also chaplains

Primitive Methodists, anti-Catholicism 110
private chapels 186
pro-Catholic campaigning 108, 112
processions 196
professions 71
proofs of loyalty 112
Propaganda, lack of contact with 111–12
property and wealth 37, 95
  anti-Catholic legislation 14
  capital 52
  factors affecting 54
  marriages 54
  overview 16–18
  protection of 15–18
  supplementary incomes 53
  windfalls 54
proscription 406
proselytism 232
protection, official 22–3
Protestant Alliance 253
Protestant Dissenters, anti-Catholicism 110, 252–3
Protestant trusteeships 56
Protestants, reactions to Relief Act 25
Protesting Catholic Dissenters 111, 237
public meetings 150–1
public office 156
public schools, standards 57
publication, of books 227

Quakers, railways 83
quality of life 56

radicalism 409
Radicals 110, 124, 136, 147, 156–7

railways 79, 83, 84–6, 311
Reformation Society 160
regional approach, advantages of xviii
Registration Act 15–16
regular clergy, relations with vicars apostolic 206–7
Relatio (Smith) 248
Relief Act 1778 202
Relief Act 1791 113
Relief Act 1817 68, 132
Relief Bill 1825 130
religious conformity, as legal requirement 108–9
religious freedom 407–8
religious practice, effects of demographic change 33
residency, length of 32
residential ties 404
Return of Papists 1705 345–7, 386
Revolution 1688 3–4, 185, 386
risk 23–4
Roman Catholic Bible Society 139
Roman Catholic Elective Franchise Bill 132
Romanos Pontifices 206
Rome 59, 111–12
Rosary 197
Royal Society 70
Ryton 28, 73, 281, 282, 284

Sandhoe 349, 350, 351, 374
scholarship 70–1, 86–94, 226–7
schools 25
  Alnwick 368
  Barnard Castle 319
  Berwick 378–9
  Blyth 395
  Darlington 317

Esh 295, 296
Fenwick 372
Haggerston 373
Haggerston Castle 371
Hartlepool 307
Hexham 342
Houghton le Spring 280
Morpeth 356–7
Netherwitton 358
Newcastle 390
Scorton Hall 371
Stockton 310–11
Sunderland 278–9
Thornley 308
Tudhoe Academy 298–9
see also education
science education 58
Scorton Hall 371
secular clergy
 administration of funds 202–3
 increased employment of 210–11
 Northern Brethren's Fund 203–6
Sedgefield 308
seminary education xxi
sermons 196
servants, discipline 225
Simonburn 27
Simondburn, Catholic population 350
Sisters of Mercy 278
Sledwich Hall 308–9
social exclusion 407–8
social hierarchy 37
social integration, gentry 57
social mobility 77
Society of Jesus *see* Jesuits
socio-economic structure 37–9
socio-political features, of laity 405

south Durham 308–9
South Shields 273
speeches, inflammatory 149
Ss Mary and Cuthbert, Berwick 379
Ss Mary and Thomas Aquinas, Ryton 284
St Andrew's, Newcastle 390–1
St Augustine's, Darlington 267
St Bede's, Morpeth 356, 357
St Cuthbert's, Blyth 395
St Cuthbert's, Durham 267
St Cuthbert's, Tynemouth 394
St Godric's, Thornley 308
St Helen Auckland Hall 301
St Helen's Hall 279
St Joseph's, Gateshead 273
St Joseph's, Sedgefield 308
St Mary's, Alnwick 368
St Mary's, Blackhill 292
St Mary's Cathedral, Newcastle 193
St Mary's, Hartlepool 307–8
St Mary's, Hexham 342
St Mary's, Newcastle 392
St Mary's, Stockton 311
St Mary's, Sunderland 277–8
St Mary's, Swinburne 353
St Michael and All Angels, Houghton le Spring 280
St Michael's, Esh Laude 294–5
St Michael's, Houghton le Spring 281
St Ninian's, Wooler 383–4, 385
St Omer 363
St Osmund's, Gainford 319
St Roberts, Morpeth 357–8
St Thomas of Canterbury, Longhorsley 355
St Wilfrid's, Bishop Auckland 302

Index of Places and Subjects 461

Stamfordham, Catholic population 347–8
Stanhope 29–30
Stanley Hall 285–6
Stations of the Cross 196
Status Animarum 1830–1930 44
Stella Hall 19, 201, 207, 281, 282, 283
Stella House 283–4, 371
Stella mines 72–3, 74
Stockton 309–11
Stockton and Darlington Railway 83, 301–2
Stonecroft Farm 19, 327–32
Stonyhurst College 211
strict settlement 52
Stuarts, claim to throne 109
Sturton Grange 366
subscription dinners 137–40, 141–2
Sunderland 23, 273–9
supplementary incomes 53
suppression of Jesuits 206–12, 388–9
surveys xv–xvii, 45
Swinburne Castle 334, 352–3

Tees Valley Railway 318
tenancies, Catholic-owned properties 9
Tenter Hill House 384
The Brooms 284, 287–92, 295
The Courts of Europe at the Close of the Last Century, By the Late Henry Swinburne 64
The Desperate Faction?/ The Jacobites of North-east England 1688–1745 (Gooch) xxi
The Divine Office for the Use of the Laity (Cordell) 227
The Garden of the Soul 197

'The Second Spring' (Newman) xiv
Thornley 308
Thropton 360–1
Thropton Old Hall 360
toleration 28–9, 51, 117, 406
Tone Hall 349
town charters 3
Towneley Group 70–1
trade unionism 158
Travels in Spain (Swinburne) 62
Travels in the Two Sicilies in the years 1777, 1778, 1789 and 1780 (Swinburne) 63
treason 108–9
Tudhoe 297, 298
Tudhoe Academy 298–9
tutoring 57
Tweedmouth 366
Tynemouth 392–4
Tynemouth Castle 3, 393

universities, standards 57
University of Durham 160–1
urbanization 184, 188, 383, 404
Ushaw College 117, 119–20, 189, 299, 305, 383
Ushaw Magazine xxi

Vespers 196
vicars apostolic
    appointment of xix, xx
    Briggs, Bishop John 249–50
    clerical Agents 178
    Dicconson, William 182
    Gibson, Bishop Matthew 234–7
    Gibson, Bishop William 237–46
    Hogarth, Bishop William 250–1
    jurisdiction 408

Maire, William 183–4
  Mostyn, Bishop Francis 250
  overview 251
  Penswick, Bishop Thomas 248–9
  Petre, Francis 182–3
  postholders 178–84
  relations with regular clergy 206–7
  Riddell, Bishop William 250
  Smith, Bishop Thomas 246–8
  Williams, Thomas (Dominic) 181–2
  Witham, Bishop George 180–1
  York meeting 1838 249
voting, on Catholic Question 154
  see also enfranchisement

war, effects on population 28
Warkworth, mixed marriages 36
Whenby 334
Whigs, Catholic support 123–4
Whittingham, population density 31
Widdrington Castle, forfeiture 19
Widdrington fund 200
windfalls 54
Witton Shields 354, 359–60
Wolsingham 35, 42, 295
Wooler 383–5
workers, safety of 4
working class 404
worship 195–8
Wycliffe Hall 309

Yarm 310, 311–12